Destination Branding:
Creating the Unique Destination
Proposition

Destination Branding: Creating the Unique Destination Proposition

Nigel Morgan and Annette Pritchard
University of Wales Institute, Cardiff

Roger Pride
Welsh Assembley Government

Revised Second edition

ELSEVIER

AMSTERDAM • BOSTON • HEIDELBERG • LONDON • NEW YORK • OXFORD
PARIS • SAN DIEGO • SAN FRANCISCO • SINGAPORE • SYDNEY • TOKYO

Butterworth-Heinemann is an inprint of Elsevier

the director of Master in Tourism Management (www.mtm.iulm.it) at IULM and she is in charge of the Territorial and Tourism Sector of the IULM University Foundation in Milano. She is focusing her research on destination management, competitive strategies, innovation and performance of tourism firms. She has conducted training programs and has provided tourism management and destinations development advice for many public and private organisation of the tourism industry.

Lisa T. Fall Ph.D. is an associate professor in the School of Advertising & Public Relations at the University of Tennessee. She is a former public relations manager and newspaper/magazine freelance writer. She holds an Accreditation in Public Relations (APR) from the Public Relations Society of America and is on the editorial board of the *Journal of Promotion Management*. Her research centres on public relations in the travel, tourism, and hospitality leisure markets.

David Gertner Ph.D. is currently Associate Professor at Pace University, New York, with past appointments as professor and program chair at universities in Brazil and the USA. During his career, he has been active in various professional associations, consulted for companies and corporations, worked in executive education, and served on the board of several organizations. A book, and numerous articles, book chapters and essays of his have been published and presented in international periodicals and at conferences worldwide.

Fiona Gilmore is an independent communications strategy consultant. Over the last 20 years, she has advised on communications and brand strategy for global leaders, including Vodafone, Unilever and Giorgio Armani, and given counsel on positioning strategies for Britain, Northern Ireland, Wales, England and Hong Kong.

Derek Hall is a partner of Seabank Associates and a Visiting Professor at HAMK University of Applied Sciences, Finland. He lives in Scotland and has longstanding research and publication interests in tourism and gender issues, tourism and regional development in socialist and post-socialist societies, and in transport policy.

Leo Jago is a Professor of Tourism and Director of the Centre for Tourism and Services Research at Victoria University and a Visiting Professor at Bournemouth University. His key research interest relates to event management and evaluation and he has published a wide range of articles in this and related fields. He is on a range of Editorial Boards and was appointed as an inaugural Fellow of CAUTHE. He has had extensive operational experience having owned and operated tourism facilities for over 18 years.

Philip Kotler is the S.C. Johnson Distinguished Professor of International Marketing at the Kellogg School of Management, Northwestern University, Evanston, Illinois. His *Marketing Management* is one of the world's leading textbooks on marketing, and he has published 25 other books and over 100 papers in leading journals. His research spans strategic marketing, consumer marketing, business marketing, services marketing, and e-marketing. He has been a consultant to IBM, Bank of America, Merck, General Electric, Honeywell and many other companies. He has received honorary doctorate degrees from 10 major universities in the USA and other countries.

Cindia Ching-Chi Lam is Senior Lecturer with the Institute For Tourism Studies (IFT), Macau. Her research interests range from tourist behaviour, customer choice, and quality of life to investor behaviour and accounting. Cindia has been the editor of the research notes for *Tourism and Hospitality e-Review* (Macau, China). Additionally, she is a certified accountant and also dedicates to the research of management accounting, accounting education and accounting history.

Charles Lubbers Ph.D. is a Professor and Chair of the Department of Contemporary Media and Journalism at the University of South Dakota, USA. He has over 50 publications, is the past chair of the Public Relations Division of the National Communication Association and past head of the Public Relations Division of AEJMC, is the editor of Teaching Public Relations and has been active in the Association for Education in Journalism and Mass Communication (AEJMC), National Communication Association (NCA), Public Relations Society of America (PRSA) and the International Academy of Business Disciplines (IABD).

Nigel Morgan is Professor of Tourism Studies in the Cardiff School of Management, at the University of Wales Institute, Cardiff. He has published extensively on destination marketing and development and tourism advertising and branding and sits on a number of editorial boards, including the *Annals of Tourism Research, Journal of Vacation Marketing* and the *Journal of Place Branding and Public Diplomacy*.

Trevor Mules is Professor of Tourism and Head of the Department of Tourism, Leisure, Hotel and Sport Management at Griffith University, Queensland

Australia. He has been involved in research on the impacts of special events for almost 20 years and has published widely on event economics and management.

Wally Olins is a co-founder of Wolf Olins – a leading branding and identity consultancy. He has advised many of the world's foremost public and private sector organisations on identity, branding and communication. He has written several books on the subject, including the seminal work *Corporate Identity*, which was first published in 1989 and has been reprinted many times in many languages. He is visiting professor at Lancaster University, Duxx University in Mexico and Copenhagen Business School. He was awarded a CBE in 1999 and received the Bicentenary Medal from the Royal Society of Arts in 2000.

Can Seng Ooi is Associate Professor at Copenhagen Business School. He has been doing tourism research since 1996 and has published extensively, including in the *Annals of Tourism Research, Tourism* and the *Scandinavian Journal of Hospitality and Tourism*. With the support of the Danish Strategic Research Council, he is heading a comparative research project on Place Branding, the Arts and Culture.

Adrian Palmer is Professor of Marketing at Swansea University, Wales. Before joining academia he held management positions in the travel and transport sector and has authored 5 books and over 50 refereed journal papers (listed at http://www.apalmer.com). He is a member of the editorial advisory board for *European Journal of Marketing, Journal of Marketing Management* and *Journal of Vacation Marketing*. He is a Fellow of the Chartered Institute of Marketing and was Foundation Chair in Marketing at University of Ulster.

Rachel Piggott has worked in marketing for Air New Zealand, RCI Europe Ltd, O'Neill and Sanyo and headed up the advertising and communications department responsible for the creation and media implementation of the 100% Pure New Zealand Campaign.

Roger Pride began his career in the travel/tourism industry and worked in sales management and advertising, before joining the Wales Tourist Board in 1985. Since then, Roger has undertaken several roles within WTB and is now Marketing Director at the Welsh Assembly Government (including VisitWales). He has a particular interest in destination branding and developed a branding strategy for Wales Tourist Board that led to the award winning 'Wales Two Hours and a Million Miles Away' campaign.

Annette Pritchard is Professor of Critical Tourism Studies and Director of the Welsh Centre for Tourism Research in the Cardiff School of Management at the University of Wales Institute, Cardiff. She has written extensively, including over a dozen books, on critical tourism studies, destination marketing, tourism advertising and branding and is Visiting Professor at IULM University, Milan. She currently sits on the editorial boards of several journals, including the *Annals of Tourism Research* and *Tourism and Cultural Change,* and was previously convenor of the editorial board of *Leisure Studies.*

Chris Ryan is Professor of Tourism at the University of Waikato, editor of *Tourism Management* and for several years a member of Tourism Waikato's Advisory Board. He is also a member of the New Zealand's Ministry of Tourism Special Projects Committee. He is the author of over 100 papers and book chapters and several books.

Jan Slater Ph.D. is Professor and Head of the Department of Advertising at the University of Illinois – Urbana/Champaign, USA. She publishes on brands and brand relationships. Her experience includes 20 years in the advertising industry, having worked in both private industry and advertising agencies. Until 1990, she owned her own agency in Omaha, Nebraska.

Weng Si (Clara) Lei is a lecturer in the Institute for Tourism Studies (IFT), Macau. She received her Ph.D. from University of Leeds in the United Kingdom. Her research interest falls in the area of hospitality with a specific focus on foreign direct investment.

Michael F. Smith Ph.D. is Associate Professor at La Salle University, Philadelphia, and is Chair of the National Communication Association's Public Relations Division. His research interests include place promotion, activism, and public relations in warfare, and he has published in the *Handbook of Public Relations*, the *Encyclopedia of Public Relations*, and elsewhere.

Leiza J. Wood is the former Brand Western Australia Manager of the Western Australian Tourism Commission. She has managed a range of strategic development and innovation initiatives and has worked with Singapore Airlines and as a travel consultant.

Anne Zahra Ph.D. lectures in tourism finance and law at the University of Waikato. She has a background in financial control and administration in education and tourism and joined the Department of Tourism Management at Waikato in 2001.

List of Figures

List of Tables

List of Case Studies

The Case Studies and Further Reading can be found at URL:
www.elsevierdirect.com/9781856178204

Acknowledgements

There are many people and organisations to whom the editors are indebted for their help and support in producing the revised second edition of this book. We would particularly like to thank all our contributors. The chapters written by Wally Olins and Philip Kotler and David Gertner are based on papers which appeared in *The Journal of Brand Management* April 2002, volume 9, numbers 4/5 and we are grateful to Henry Stewart Publications for allowing us to include revised versions here. We would also like to express our gratitude to all the staff at Elservier, particularly our editor Eleanor Blow.

Nigel and Annette would like to thank colleagues, researchers, students and friends at UWIC and beyond for exchanging ideas and opinions on destination branding and Roger would like to thank all his colleagues at the Welsh Assembly Government and VisitWales. Finally, our thanks are due to all those readers of the various editions of this book who, through their encouragement and feedback led us to produce this revised second edition. *Diolch yn fawr*.

Nigel Morgan & Annette Pritchard
Cardiff School of Management, UWIC

Roger Pride
Welsh Assembly Government

1st May 2009

Abbreviations

ACM	Asian Civilization Museum
ASEAN	Association of South-East Asian Nations
ASP	application service provider
ATC	Australian Tourist Commission
BDI	brand development indexing
BSE	bovine spongiform encephalopathy
CEE	Central and Eastern Europe
CEO	chief executive officer
CINDE	Coalicíon Costarricense de Iniciativas para el Desarrolo
CIS	Commonwealth of Independent States
CRC Tourism	Australian Co-operative Research Centre for Sustainable Tourism
CTA	Carmarthenshire Tourist Association
DCRT	Department of Culture, Recreation and Tourism
DMO	Destination Marketing Organization
DMS	destination management system
DTO	district tourism organization
EU	European Union
FY	fiscal year
GDN	global distribution network
GDP	gross domestic product
GDS	global distribution system
GPTMC	Greater Philadelphia Tourism and Marketing Committee
IDA	Irish Development Agency
INCAE	Insituto Centroamericano de Administración de Emprasas
IOC	International Olympic Committee
ITCR	Insituto Tecnológico de Costa Rica
LOTR	*The Lord of the Rings*
MICE	meetings, incentive, corporate and exhibitions
MMP	mixed member proportional
MPAF	market potential assessment formula
NAFTA	North American Free Trade Agreement
NTO	national tourism organization
NTPC	National Tourism Plan Committee

NZTB	New Zealand Tourism Board
NZTIA	New Zealand Tourism Industry Association
NZTIF	New Zealand Tourism Industry Federation
NZTPD	New Zealand Tourism and Publicity Department
OLRS	online reservation system
PATA	Pacific Area Travel Association
PDA	personal digital assistant
RLO	regional liaison officer
RNC	Republican National Convention
ROI	return on investment
RTO	regional tourism organization
SAM	Singapore Art Museum
SARS	severe acute respiratory syndrome
SME	small or medium-sized enterprise
STB	Singapore Tourism Board
SWOT	strengths, weaknesses, opportunities and threats
SWOTC	strengths, weaknesses, opportunities, threats and constraints
TCA	Tourism Council Australia
TDAS	Tourism Development Assistance Scheme
TIA	Travel Industry Association of America
TIS	tourist information system
TNZ	Tourism New Zealand
TT&H	travel, tourism and hospitality
VJP	Visiting Journalists Program
WA	Western Australia
WATC	Western Australia Tourism Commission
WTB	Wales Tourist Board
WTO	World Tourism Organization

Introduction

Nigel Morgan, Annette Pritchard and Roger Pride

It is widely acknowledged that branding has the potential to play a crucial role in destination development but the relationship between branding and places is not always straightforward and it is certainly not well understood. Branding has been applied to consumer products for well over a century, but the idea of destinations pursuing formalised brand strategies as we understand them today only originated in the 1990s. Whereas earlier 'image-building' marketing activities in the 1980s by cities such as New York and Glasgow (encapsulated by the slogans 'I love New York' and 'Glasgow's miles better') foreshadowed such strategies, a strategic approach to destination branding was first introduced at a national level in countries such as Spain, Hong Kong and Australia (Baker 2007). Then major US cities like Seattle, Las Vegas and Pittsburgh embraced it, responding to a need to compete more effectively, to create a strategic decision-making framework and to increase accountability to their stakeholders. Many destinations now see place branding (which is broader than simply tourism and may encompass aspects of investment, exports, culture, sports, events, education and immigration) as a major part of their armoury. Indeed, the Destination Marketing Association International, the world's largest official destination marketing organisation designates the development of a brand strategy as one of the critical items needed for accreditation in its Destination Marketing Association Accreditation Program (Baker 2007).

Since the second edition of this book appeared in 2004 the landscape of destination branding studies has changed radically. Then, there were only one or two textbooks which addressed the topic of destination branding; now there are several books which address the broader field of place branding (including Anholt 2005 and 2007; Jaffe and Nebenzahl 2006, Baker 2007 and Dinnie 2008) and a journal of Place Branding and Public Diplomacy (established in 2004), whilst each year there are a number of conferences and events where academics, branding consultants and destination management organisation professionals gather to discuss good practice. This revised second edition of our destination branding book gathers together an international mix of marketing professionals, branding consultants and leading academics to discuss a branding offers marketers an opportunity to counter the substitutability problem, they remind us that destinations face a number of particular challenges – each of which has the potential to derail the best branding strategy. As their discussion of destinations such as Nepal and Oregon suggest, political pressures, external environmental changes and stakeholder concerns all have to be addressed if a destination brand is to prosper and grow. That said, they argue that successful branding brings significant rewards and the reminder of their chapter discusses how strong destination brands can be built around 'wish you were here' value, emotional appeal and celebrity and conversational capital, focusing on examples, including Australia, Cuba, New Zealand and Spain.

In chapter 6, Chris Ryan and Anne Zahra spotlight the challenge of politics in branding cities and regions. Readers of this collection will by this stage be fully aware of the significance of politics in the branding process and Ryan and Zahra remind us that the branding of places must be examined in its wider context. Any collection on destination branding would be incomplete without such a discussion of the contentious arena in which such place branding activities exist. Complimenting Olins' historical perspective on nation branding, this chapter reinforces that contemporary place branding is not simply a rational marketing activity: it is also a political act. Using New Zealand as their case study, Ryan and Zahra explore the changing nature of the public–private sector relationship, noting that changes in government policy and personnel cannot but impact on tourism promotion and practice. The place marketing challenges identified in this chapter (professionalism versus enthusiasm; short-term versus long-term perspectives; competition versus cooperation; and the political significance of tourism) will resonate heavily with marketers currently grappling with the problems of branding places.

The political theme continues in Derek Hall's chapter on Central and Eastern Europe (CEE), which shifts the focus from the local and regional to the national and international. The chapter explores issues of provenance in CEE where nation branding has been influenced by the need to portray an 'EU-style identity'. Hall takes the reader on a tour of the region, highlighting how destination branders in CEE face many of the challenges articulated in the previous chapters, including inadequate finance, lack of expertise, short-term, and a lack of partnership approaches and networks. These emerge as major obstacles to the effective branding of the CEE nations – the importance of which cannot be underestimated in a marketing environment dominated by confused, contradictory and ill-developed destination identities. Having said this, branding offers such states the opportunity to create newly shaped national identities, drawing a distinct line between past and present – although Hall leaves us in no doubt that these nations face considerable problems in their efforts to appeal to western tourism markets and position themselves in an enlarged and evolving Europe.

Shifting the focus somewhat – but not totally – away from the political challenges of place branding, Adrian Palmer then examines the challenges and opportunities that online marketing offers destination branders. Such is the importance of the Web that most of the case studies in part 3 also discuss its role since many of the featured destinations have a significant online presence. In chapter 8, Adrian thus focuses on the wider impacts the Web, e-commerce and m-commerce will have on destination branding. He shows that destinations can benefit from the internet by developing a coherent position in the marketplace, by increasing their market-share by getting closer to customers, and subsequently by ensuring delivery of high levels of customer satisfaction. A central feature of the chapter is an examination of Destination Management Systems (DMS) – which allows the resources of a destination to be linked so that a potential visitor sees a coherent visit experience, rather than a series of disjointed resources. Of course, there are many challenges in making DMS work effectively, and these are also discussed in this chapter. In particular, Adrian underlines that, whilst new technology offers exciting challenges and opportunities, we should not lose sight of the basic principles of cooperation which are a prerequisite for destination marketing success. Clearly, it is likely that if the stakeholders in a destination do not trust each other with a conventional marketing programme, then merely adding new technology is in itself unlikely to bring about success. Palmer's contribution reminds us that trust and leadership will remain key issues in electronic destination marketing.

This part of the book is aptly concluded by an examination of the financial costs of destination branding. There are very few published financial evaluations of destination marketing and the study here by Lisa Fall and Charles Lubbers is a welcome contribution in this area. Taking the USA as their case study, Fall and Lubbers argue that the tourism industry needs to demonstrate fiscal accountability and justify promotion expenditures, just as any other. DMOs spend a significant amount of money promoting their products and services and in the aftermath of 9/11, the travel industry engaged in tremendous efforts to encourage US residents to continue travelling. But when it comes to *measuring* the effectiveness of such promotional techniques, the industry is not as assertive in its efforts. Hence, Fall and Lubbers examine the relationship between state tourism budgets and state tourism expenditures, investigate the relationship between state populations and size of promotional budgets and determine what states have the best return-on-investment. Their study demonstrates that spending money does, indeed, make money. As a result they suggest that, by incorporating evaluation measures into their planning, managers can better determine just which tactics they should retain and which they should eliminate from their communication strategy.

Destination branding in practice

Building on these discussions of context and challenge, part 3 of the book presents eight detailed case studies of destination brands. Firstly, Roger Pride develops his various contributions on Wales to examine how the Wales Tourist Board (now Visit Wales) adopted the mentality of a challenger brand. He briefly highlights the principles of challenger branding and then demonstrates how they are being used to create a positioning and branding strategy to establish Wales as a world class golf destination. A challenger brand is largely idea-centred and Roger discusses how Visit Wales' idea is to represent the destination as the antidote to the clear positioning of its competitors – positioning golf in Wales as the opposite to the serious, corporate-dominated experience in England, Scotland and Ireland. The chapter is an intriguing study of a challenger idea, which is attempting to re-write the rules, to represent thought leadership, and to provoke re-evaluation of Wales and of what a golf holiday should be.

Following this discussion of challenger branding, Fiona Gilmore's chapter also emphasises the value of harnessing powerful ideas. In her contribution, however, she argues that in the information age the challenge for cities seeking to market themselves is to nourish the imagination of their citizens – the inner force. In her thoughtful case study of Shanghai, Fiona argues that economic prosperity and competitiveness depend not only upon a city's location and infrastructure but also upon its capacity to build new business and exploit innovation. At the same time, she says, the arts and cultural scene of a city must be nurtured for it stimulates the imagination, and creates for the city an image and a reputation that will help attract investment and talented individuals. In the case of Shanghai, in the last two decades it has moved from the post-industrial to the information era and achieved a skyline that took 50 years to create in New York and 30 in Hong Kong. The city is beginning to acknowledge that its greatest assets are its citizens and their creativity. But Gilmore suggests that this inner force must be further harnessed if the city is to achieve its aspirations following its successful bid to host the 2010 World Expo.

Chapter 12 presents Shane Crockett and Leiza Wood's detailed analysis of the Western Australian Tourism Commission's (WATC) branding approach from the first edition. Whilst the brand has since developed, we have retained it as an excellent case study of how, based on intensive consumer research, government–industry partnerships and infrastructural developments, the state went beyond tourism to create a state brand. Although now a historical study, this chapter provides a rich source of good practice for place branders everywhere through its discussion of the state's repositioning task, the development of Brand Western Australia (BWA) and the measures adopted to evaluate its marketing and partnership strategies. As Crockett and Wood demonstrate, successful destination branding must embrace a host of activities, including infrastructural development, product enhancement, protection against environmental degradation, changes in organisational culture, and promotional partnerships – all based on intensive market research to identify consumer desires. This case study of BWA demonstrates that when combined with the development of a distinctive, broad visual language and strong creative promotional executions, these activities can provide the platform for a successful destination brand.

Continuing the theme of developing a place brand beyond tourism, Rachel Piggott, Nigel Morgan and Annette Pritchard examine the brand of New Zealand in chapter 13. In this contribution, the authors particularly spotlight the value of targeted and integrated public and media relations' activities in destination brand building and coordination. The current initiatives driven by Tourism New Zealand represent the first ever global branding strategy for the destination and the chapter examines how PR is being used to support New Zealand's overall branding strategy by tapping into the power of the international media in order to showcase its landscapes, peoples, cultures and tourism activities. The chapter concludes that PR, linked to the opportunities presented by special events and movies (notably *The Lord of the Rings* trilogy during 2001–2003) and the Web can be a cost-effective tool in the drive to create strong destination brand relationships.

In chapter 14, Jan Slater discusses how Louisiana developed its powerful travel destination brand. Such success is no mean task in the USA where annual state government tourism promotional spending exceeds half a billion dollars and the domestic audience accounts for over a billion tourism trips. As Slater explains, Louisiana wholeheartedly embraced branding to communicate and emphasise the 'feel' and 'personality' of the place. Whilst it has many attractions, it is its brand identity, which has positioned the state as one of the fastest growing tourism destinations in the USA. Significantly, the process has been underpinned by the development of a strong advertising agency–DMO partnership. The former, through their insightful 'mining' of existing consumer research, were able to develop a strong, differentiating, brand proposition and identity for the state which remained largely unchanged in the decade since its conception in 1993. As Slater highlights, however, the key to success here is the power behind the Louisiana brand (built around food, culture, music, scenery, architecture, and history) – a substantial advertising budget, well-targeted media placements and an effective integrated campaign with advertising as its cornerstone.

In chapter 15, Can Seng Ooi discusses the Singapore Tourism Board's (STB) vision for Singapore as the capital and hub of the New Asia – the gateway through which visitors should visit or pass through when they are in the region. Thus, its 'New Asia – Singapore' brand embraces this regional brand and strategy, as well as providing a focused marketing direction for the place as a stand-alone destination. The city state has also positioned itself as the arts and cultural capital of the region, and, at the same time, draws on the 'exoticism' of its neighbouring destinations – a quality which it is itself trying to re-establish. Can Seng's chapter thus examines the branding of Singapore holistically, encompassing the particular challenges and opportunities the STB has faced since the new positioning was launched in 1996 – from the 'Millennium Mania' promotions in 2000 to the 'Singapore Roars' initiative in 2003, following the end of the SARS outbreak. He also reminds us of the importance of materialising the brand expectations, discussing how the STB is making 'New Asia – Singapore' live by directing tourists' attention to the Asia in the largely modern city that is Singapore – by rejuvenating Chinatown and re-introducing street markets and Chinese language road signs.

In the penultimate chapter of the collection, Mike Smith underlines that potential tourists' perceptions of places are crucially important, but notoriously difficult to influence. Such perceptions are strongly shaped by the media and whilst media relations' efforts have always been considered part of the destination branding marketing mix, news media placements often are uncontrolled. His chapter on Philadelphia's hosting of the 2000 Republican National Convention offers an interesting case study of how places can use 'spotlight events' as an opportunity to garner valuable media exposure, to lure potential corporate and association decision makers, and to reinvigorate community development efforts – if they are managed well and have a little luck. Using a combination of participant observation, analysis of official documents, and a review of media coverage, Smith offers a fascinating insight into how Philadelphia 2000, the non-partisan, non-profit organisation responsible for all details of the event, managed the media relations efforts, positively influenced the 15,000 media representatives in the city for the event, and used this national event to reinforce and extend the city's branding messages for both national and regional audiences.

In our final chapter, written by Graham Brown, Laurence Chalip, Leo Jago and Trevor Mules, the focus on the relationship between destination branding, events and the media continues – this time in Australia. After discussing the growing importance of event tourism, the authors examine the nature of destination image in the context of conceptual and applied frameworks before evaluating the status of the relationship between event management and tourism by discussing several research projects in Australia. The chapter then considers the implications of the Sydney Olympic Games on Brand Australia. Brown, Chalip, Jago and Mules provide a richly researched insight into how Australia's destination marketers shrewdly harnessed the global reach of the Games to promote not only Sydney's, but the whole of Australia's tourism image to the world. The case study clearly demonstrates how the 'best ever games' was used to strategically advance Brand Australia. Whilst the authors point out that much of the momentum was lost in the changed international climate following 9/11, SARS and the war in Iraq, they leave the reader in no doubt as to the long-term value of hosting the global event.

Concluding thoughts

The success of many of the branding initiatives discussed in part 3 shows that destinations can indeed have reputations which have celebrity value and emotional appeal. That does not mean, however, that it is easy to build a strong destination travel brand. Managers have to overcome both the politics and the paucity challenges – outsmarting rather than outspending their competitors. The examples from this book show that it takes patience to establish positive reputations and building a powerful destination reputation is a long-term effort – exemplified here by Spain and Singapore. Of course, there are destination brands that have seemingly emerged from obscurity to achieve instant fashion – notably here in the case of New Zealand. Such rapid elevation to celebrity status, however, often owes much to a culmination of long-term economic, political, social and cultural factors. Often such instant stardom also belies long-term marketing activity and investment built on detailed marketing research, planning and consistent positioning.

Certainly, the collection demonstrates that those destinations that have emerged as reputation winners do have a number of common features. They are brands based on a vision which is founded on intensive stakeholder, consumer and competitor research and which is expressed with care and discipline in everything that communicates the brand's personality. Once the brand personality has been identified, marketers must have the courage to stay with the brand's essence – whilst refinements may be made to how the values are expressed in the brand architecture, the essentials of the brand personality should remain consistent. The secret is to continually evolve and enrich the original brand personality, building on the initial strengths to strengthen their appeal and to broaden the market. Take the examples discussed here of Singapore, Spain, Oregon and Australia, which have all woven 'new' attributes (such as culture, heritage and modern architecture) into their original brand personalities.

Whilst many of the chapters in this collection focus on branding *per se*, most have also sought to reinforce that place branding is not merely a rational marketing activity but a political act. Tourism offers communities the potential to build both identities and viable economies. In many countries, however, the tourism industry itself is often politically weak, lacks visibility and is extremely fragmented. The real sources of power in such a vacuum are often the DMOs and a handful of major companies, particularly the airlines. In these cases the DMOs must rise to the task of being the primary front-line promoter for any destination. However, as government financing continues to be squeezed as a result of the global financial crisis, it is critical that the DMO maintains its role as coordinator of promotional resources. Unless it takes command of both branding and product development, in a changing and confused stakeholder market, the large operators and transportation companies in a destination will simply take to the market what they believe is the most appealing product. This will be both at the expense of small players within the industry and the dilution of any broader brand identity. In a world where a handful of major countries attract almost three-quarters of international tourist arrivals, most destinations will at best be niche players competing on the margins. They will be reliant on effective, targeted branding strategies that have the potential to squeeze maximum value from their small budgets. This is a difficult but by no means an impossible task – particularly if the power of industry partners and the Web can be harnessed.

Clearly, DMOs need to work with bodies on a collaborative and integrative basis outside traditional advertising. This is particularly true of niche destinations with a small share of voice. Such destinations must be alive to alternatives to advertising and focus on the branding opportunities offered by sports, cultural and political activities. Examples include the Beijing Olympics in 2008, the release of the movie *Australia* in 2008 and the Ryder Cup in 2010.

All have or will provide worldwide interest and platforms for public relations and promotional campaigns. DMOs must look to the future to consider the opportunities offered through interactive media, digital television (video on demand, interactive booking) and the Web (itinerary planning and 'look and book'). In the long-term, mobile communication may become more important than conventional PC-based communication and destinations should already be offering SMS, podcasts and mobile website services and product listings to satnav service providers. These media cannot be ignored as, not only do they interactively engage visitors pre-trip, they also provide direct marketing opportunities for relationship building, which can be resurrected and sustained post-trip. The web is an ideal platform for developing and projecting a destination brand in order to provide the industry with the best selling environment. In the past, the internet could not contribute much to brand-building, but that is no longer true. Broadband can convey rich imagery, and personal time spent on web pages has increased hugely and it is its seamless combination of information, contact, transaction, entertainment and relationship services that distinguishes the internet from the off-line world. It is what makes it so successful.

In addition, online social networks are a new and powerful arena for destination marketers as these networks, and the user-generated content, which they stimulate, may become central to those holiday decisions that are based on recommendation, as they are excellent sources of word of mouth feedback about destination experiences. Destinations can and should actively encourage the creation of user-generated content about the destination, wherever it is published, equally, they should use it in their own communication channels and integrate it with their own content. Blogs (a contraction of the term weblog) are particularly important for destination marketers because so many people include travel experiences and travel diaries in their blogs. A blog is usually maintained by an individual with regular entries of commentary, descriptions of events, or other material such as graphics, video or music. Thus, blogs are ideal channels of conversations about places and blogging has grown exponentially in recent years – at the start of 2008 there were over 115 million blogs, twice as many as there were in April 2007 and more than triple the number in 2006.

The potential of such communication opportunities in destination reputation management deserves more attention from both academics and practitioners, as does the role of joint destination marketing partnerships. Place branding is an extremely complex and highly political activity that can enhance a nation's economy, national self-image and identity. Many organisations and groups thus have vested interests in the promotion of particular identities (many of which may be in direct conflict with the interests of others) and we need much more work on how these interests intersect. In particular, there is a pressing need for study of the processes underpinning the support in the public and private sectors for place branding. National brands can encompass several regional sub-brands that require accommodation in the overall brand and, more complex still, supra-brands may involve cooperation across several regions and countries as smaller, less well-known places attempt to gain a foothold in the international marketplace. Whilst there is a rapidly expanding body of work on the process of destination branding, we still do not understand the extent to which these brands impact on the populations of these countries. We also have little understanding of the extent to which place brand management is a collective activity embraced by residents and smaller trade operators. Research also needs to explore the relationship between culture and branding, given that it is their cultural differences that imbue most places with a sense of place. Why do destination marketers so often ignore a place's unique cultural attributes in the rush to promote sun, surf and sand or lake, land and mountain? Above all, perhaps, as indicated by Fall and Lubber's chapter here, there is a pressing need for more study of the wider effectiveness of tourism marketing and promotional activity – which remains wide-open for examination.

It is common practice for books to conclude with such calls for further work. In the field of place branding, however, these opportunities are particularly significant, as more bridges need to be built between those who practice and those who comment on destination reputation management. Such bridges would enrich the field of destination branding, strength its research base and enhance both theory and praxis. We hope that this book will be one such bridge. Whilst it has a coherent structure, we are well aware that not everyone will read it from start to finish; some will simply want to dip into its individual parts or chapters. Whichever way you choose to use the book, we hope you find it an enjoyable read and a useful resource. It is not all-inclusive. The subject has now become too large and too important to make such a claim but we hope that students and scholars of destination marketing will find enough of interest here to provoke further critical study and debate.

References

Anholt, S. (2007) *Competitive Identity* (London: Palgrave).

Anholt, S. (2005) *Brand New Justice – The Upside of Global Branding* (Oxford: Elsevier).

Baker, B. (2007) *Destination Branding for Small Cities by Bill Baker* (Creative Leap Books) Portland, Oregon.

Chiesa, T. (2009) Navigating yet another perfect storm: The promise of sustainable travel & tourism, 97–105 in *The Travel & Tourism Competitiveness Report,* World Economic Forum.

Dinnie, K. (2008) *Nation Branding: Concepts, Issues, Practice* (Oxford: Butterworth-Heinemann).

Jaffe, E. and Nebenzahl, I. (2006) *National Image & Competitive Advantage* (Copenhagen: Copenhagen Business School Press).

Pride, R. (2008) The Welsh Brand – Connecting Image with Reality? Presentation at the Institute of Welsh Affairs Wales in the World Conference, Cardiff.

Part 1

Destination Branding in Context

1

Introduction

Nigel Morgan, Annette Pritchard and Roger Pride

Introduction

Since the first edition of this book appeared in 2002, work on destination branding has gathered momentum. It was stated in the introduction to the first edition that the topic was no mere academic bandwagon but a significant development in the marketing of destinations, and beyond this, in the marketing of places. So it has proved. Today, destination branding is one of the hottest topics amongst place marketing professionals and politicians, from Switzerland and Slovenia to New Zealand and New York and a multitude of places in between. Indeed, so rapidly has the area developed that this collection of essays has been revisited after only two years, bringing together a new group of destination branding experts from the worlds of industry and academe.

In expanding this second edition to seventeen chapters, the editors asked their original collaborators to re-examine their contributions in the light of developments in the intervening period and invited nine further writers to add six new chapters. As a result, the collection has been extended in both scope and scale, enabling the reader to explore more issues in greater depth, to compare place branding activities across a wider range of international case studies and to benchmark the progress of destination branding. Thus, this book goes further than simply providing more case studies than the first edition. Then, the editors felt that part of the purpose of the book was to state the case for destination branding: to raise its profile amongst a range of audiences, including practitioners, politicians, destination stakeholders, academics and students. Now, they feel that the challenge is to assemble a collection that enables the reader to place destination branding in a wider context, to recognize more clearly the complex challenges facing marketers and to explore how a variety of places has met those challenges.

Destination branding

Perhaps the key argument of the book is the notion that places currently offer the greatest untapped branding opportunities. Choice of holiday destination is a significant lifestyle indicator for today's aspirational consumers and the places where they choose to spend their squeezed vacation time and hard-earned income increasingly have to have emotional appeal, high conversational capital and even celebrity value. The World Tourism Organization endorses this view, suggesting that the twenty-first century will see the emergence of tourism destinations as fashion accessories. Indeed, as style symbols, destinations can offer similar consumer benefits to highly branded lifestyle items. These are used to communicate statements and group memberships, just as vacation trips are expressive devices communicating messages about identity, lifestyle and status. Travel for leisure is increasingly permeating the discourse of everyday life, but remains a highly involving experience, extensively planned, excitedly anticipated and fondly remembered. Souvenirs and mementos evoke and materialize those experiences, photographs and 'wish you were here' postcards are shared with friends and relatives, and logo-emblazoned merchandise and luggage labels proclaim 'been there, done that' to any observers who care to notice (Clarke, 2000; Westwood, 2000; Doorne *et al.*, 2003).

At the same time as they are tapping into the emotional power of travel as 'experience', destination brands are also beginning to reach beyond the tourism industry. Many of those brands at the leading edge of destination marketing, such as the examples of Singapore and New Zealand discussed in this book, are seeking to position themselves as holistic place brands; indeed, many countries, states and regions are embarking on brand-building initiatives that are inclusive of tourism and economic development. Take New Zealand. Beginning as a tourism-led development, following a redesign in 2003, the website www. newzealand.com now takes the web consumer to a general 'splash' about the country and then offers a choice of clicking through to travel or business opportunities. Although this 'total' branding task is by no means easy, the rewards are enormous and, drawing on many case studies from the cutting edge of destination marketing practice, the chapters in this collection evidence this view. Written by an international mixture of marketing professionals, branding consultants and leading academics, the subsequent chapters address a varied range of destinations, many at different stages of development and all grappling with the challenges presented by destination branding. What is striking, however, is the commonality of their approaches to the process and the recurring themes that emerge as key to successful destination brand building.

The reader should not, therefore, be surprised that several of the chapters reiterate similar themes. This simply reflects the fact that there are certain key issues facing contemporary destination marketers, whether their activities are at national, regional, state or city level. The ways in which each destination seeks to tackle such issues will depend on local circumstances, finances and resources; there will always be local solutions to global challenges. However, the contributions included here suggest that there are common elements to these solutions: key issues and activities that every marketer seeking to achieve successful destination branding must address. These include: the often destructive role of politics in crafting brands; the essential role of inclusive, comprehensive and ongoing market research in identifying and creating the brand values; the need to build alliances and partnerships across all the stakeholder groups; and the value of 'brand champions' who have the vision, commitment and staying power to drive the brand development.

Even the most successful brands have to evolve, however, and in revisiting some of these case studies after even a couple of years, it can be seen how the marketers of destinations such as Australia, Louisiana, New Zealand and Wales are developing, enriching and advancing the brand personalities of these places. Certainly, market conditions have been extremely challenging since the first edition was written and it is interesting to examine the responses of a number of worldwide destinations to the recent global crises. Several of the chapters here deal with the legacy of 11 September 2001 (e.g. Fall and Lubbers), the severe acute respiratory syndrome (SARS) crisis (e.g. Ooi) and the recent international security threats of terrorism and war (e.g. Morgan and Pritchard). In this context, a new theme has emerged from this second edition: the importance of public and media relations, including both crisis communications and public relations (PR) designed to lever the marketing impacts of special events. Those discussed in detail include the 2000 Republican Convention, the 2000 Sydney Olympics, the Rugby World Cup 2003, the 2010 World Expo and the PR opportunities associated with the filming of the *Lord of the Rings* movies in New Zealand. To achieve effective destination branding, marketers must be in the business of delivering impactful experiences, not merely co-ordinating media relations and constructing clever brand identities. The world's most successful destination brands have achieved this and those who seek to emulate them must follow the same principles, many of which are articulated and evidenced in the following chapters.

Destination branding in context

The book is organized in three parts: the first places destination branding in its wider context, the second explores destination branding challenges and the third comprises eight case studies of successful destination branding initiatives. Following this introduction, in Chapter 2 Wally Olins takes a historical perspective on the nation as brand. Confronting those who, despite the weight of historical evidence, suggest that nation branding is both unfeasible and objectionable, he concludes that it is not the concept that they detest so much as the word 'brand'. Taking France as his case study, Olins demonstrates how every nation throughout history has (re)invented itself as regimes and circumstances have changed. In a thought-provoking piece, which sets the tone for the collection, he convincingly argues that there are many analogies between the management of nation and corporate brands, and that it is a combination of snobbery, ignorance and semantics which prevents many from recognizing that.

Next comes Simon Anholt's wide ranging exploration of 'provenance' in branding which illustrates how successful 'nation' brands provide trust, quality and lifestyle connotations that consumers can associate with themselves. In an eclectic discussion, Anholt demonstrates how such brand images are by no means superficial, neither are they restricted to the realm of economic exchange. Instead, a nation's brand image can profoundly shape its economic, cultural and political destiny. His suggestion here (and elsewhere) that global brands could be the ultimate (re)distributor of global wealth is an intriguing thought which should stimulate wider debate (see Anholt, 2003). Simon also reminds us that changing nation reputations and building brands are difficult, complex and long-term challenges which require honesty, objectivity and, above all, an empathetic understanding of the consumers' mindspace. It is only then that nation branders will be able effectively to utilize and capitalize on people's perceptions of places.

The first part of the book is concluded by Philip Kotler and David Gertner's exploration of the country as brand, product and beyond. A perfect complement to Simon Anholt's essay, this chapter examines how widely held country images affect consumer (and other stakeholder) attitudes towards a country's products and services, profoundly influencing abilities to attract investment, businesses and tourists. Having reviewed the extensive empirical research underpinning the 'country-of-origin effect', Kotler and Gertner then examine the ways in which nations adopt strategic marketing management tools in order to manage their reputations. In particular, they discuss image management, the attraction of tourists and inward investment, and the manipulation of new market opportunities. They conclude their chapter (and the first part of the book) by outlining a strategic management framework for nation branding. This sets the stage for the following five chapters, each of which addresses destination branding challenges.

Destination branding challenges

This part of the book opens with Nigel Morgan and Annette Pritchard's overview of the key challenges facing place marketers. While they suggest that branding offers marketers an opportunity to counter the substitutability problem, they remind us that destinations face a number of particular challenges, each of which has the potential to derail the best branding strategy. As their discussion of destinations such as Nepal and Oregon suggests, political pressures, external environmental changes and stakeholder concerns all have to be addressed if a destination brand is to prosper and grow. That said, they argue that successful branding brings significant rewards and the remainder of their chapter discusses how strong destination brands can be built around 'wish you were here' value, emotional appeal and celebrity and conversational capital, focusing on examples including Australia, Cuba, New Zealand and Spain.

In Chapter 6, Chris Ryan and Anne Zahra spotlight the challenge of politics in branding cities and regions. Readers of this collection will by this stage be fully aware of the significance of politics in the branding process, and Ryan and Zahra remind us that the branding of places must be examined in its wider context. Any collection on destination branding would be incomplete without such a discussion of the contentious arena in which such place branding activities exist. Complimenting Olins's historical perspective on nation branding, this chapter reinforces that contemporary place branding is not simply a rational marketing activity: it is also a political act. Using New Zealand as their case study, Ryan and Zahra explore the changing nature of the public–private sector relationship, noting that changes in government policy and personnel cannot but impact on tourism promotion and practice. The place marketing challenges identified in this chapter (professionalism versus enthusiasm, short-termism versus long-term perspectives, competition versus co-operation, and the political significance of tourism) will resonate heavily with marketers currently grappling with the problems of branding places.

The political theme continues in Derek Hall's chapter on Central and Eastern Europe (CEE), which shifts the focus from the local and regional to the national and international. The chapter explores issues of provenance in CEE where nation branding has been influenced by the need to portray an 'EU-style identity'. Hall takes the reader on a tour of the region, highlighting how destination branders in CEE face many of the challenges articulated in the previous chapters, including inadequate finance, lack of expertise, short-termism, and a lack of partnership approaches and networks. These emerge as major obstacles to the effective branding of the CEE nations, the importance of which cannot be underestimated in a marketing environment dominated by confused, contradictory and ill-developed destination identities. Having said this, branding offers such states the opportunity to create newly shaped national identities, drawing a distinct line between past and present, although Hall leaves us in no doubt that these nations face considerable problems in their efforts to appeal to Western tourism markets and position themselves in an enlarged and evolving Europe.

Shifting the focus somewhat, but not totally, away from the political challenges of place branding, Adrian Palmer then examines the challenges and opportunities that electronic marketing offers destination branders. Such is the importance of the world wide web that most of the case studies in Part Three also discuss the role of the web, since many of the featured destinations have a significant online presence. In Chapter 8, Adrian thus focuses on the wider impacts the web, e-commerce and m-commerce will have on destination branding. He shows that destinations can benefit from the internet by developing a coherent position in the marketplace, by increasing their market share by getting closer to customers, and subsequently by ensuring delivery of high levels of customer satisfaction. A central feature of the chapter is an examination of destination management systems (DMS), which allow the resources of a destination to be linked so that a potential visitor sees a coherent visit experience, rather than a series of disjointed resources. There are many challenges in making DMS work effectively, and these are also discussed in this chapter. In particular,

Adrian underlines that, while new technology offers exciting challenges and opportunities, we should not lose sight of the basic principles of co-operation which are a prerequisite for destination marketing success. It is likely that if the stakeholders in a destination do not trust each other with a conventional marketing programme, then merely adding new technology is in itself unlikely to bring about success. Palmer's contribution reminds us that trust and leadership will remain key issues in electronic destination marketing.

This part of the book is aptly concluded by an examination of the financial costs of destination branding. There are very few published financial evaluations of destination marketing and the study here by Lisa Fall and Charles Lubbers is a welcome contribution in this area. Taking the USA as their case study, Fall and Lubbers argue that the tourism industry needs to demonstrate fiscal accountability and justify promotion expenditures, just as any other. Destination Marketing Organizations (DMOs) spend a significant amount of money promoting their products and services, and since the September 11th terrorist attacks the travel industry has engaged in tremendous efforts to encourage US residents to continue travelling. But when it comes to measuring the effectiveness of these promotional techniques, the industry is not as assertive in its efforts. Hence, Fall and Lubbers examine the relationship between state tourism budgets and state tourism expenditures, investigate the relationship between state populations and size of promotional budgets, and determine what states have the best return on investment. Their study demonstrates that spending money does, indeed, make money. As a result they suggest that, by incorporating evaluation measures into their planning, managers can better determine just which tactics they should retain and which they should eliminate from their communication strategy.

Destination branding in practice

Building on these discussions of context and challenge, Part Three of the book presents eight detailed case studies of destination brands. First, Roger Pride develops his original contribution on Wales to examine how the Wales Tourist Board (WTB) has adopted the mentality of a challenger brand. He briefly highlights the principles of challenger branding and then demonstrates how they are being used to create a new positioning and branding strategy to establish Wales as a world-class golf destination. A challenger brand is largely idea centred and Roger discusses how the WTB's idea is to represent the destination as the antidote to the clear positioning of its competitors, by positioning golf in Wales as the opposite to the serious, corporate-dominated experience in England, Scotland and Ireland. The chapter is an intriguing study of a challenger idea which is attempting to rewrite the rules, to represent thought leadership, and to provoke re-evaluation of Wales and of what a golf holiday should be.

Following this discussion of challenger branding, Fiona Gilmore's chapter also emphasizes the value of harnessing powerful ideas. In her contribution, however, she argues that in the information age the challenge for cities seeking to market themselves is to nourish the imagination of their citizens: the inner force. In her thoughtful case study of Shanghai, Fiona argues that economic prosperity and competitiveness depend not only upon a city's location and infrastructure but also upon its capacity to build new business and exploit innovation. At the same time, she says, the arts and cultural scene of a city must be nurtured for it stimulates the imagination, and creates for the city an image and a reputation that will help to attract investment and talented individuals. In the case of Shanghai, in the past two decades it has moved from the postindustrial to the information era and achieved a skyline that took fifty years to create in New York and thirty years in Hong Kong. The city is beginning to acknowledge that its greatest assets are its citizens and their creativity. But Gilmore suggests that this inner force must be further harnessed if the city is to achieve its aspirations following its successful bid to host the 2010 World Expo.

Chapter 12 presents Shane Crockett and Leiza Wood's detailed analysis of the Western Australian Tourism Commission's (WATC) branding approach from the first edition. Although the brand has since developed, it has been retained as an excellent case study of how, based on intensive consumer research, government–industry partnerships and infrastructural developments, the state went beyond tourism to create a state brand. Although now a historical study, this chapter provides a rich source of good practice for place branders everywhere through its discussion of the state's repositioning task, the development of Brand Western Australia (Brand WA) and the measures adopted to evaluate its marketing and partnership strategies. As Crockett and Wood demonstrate, successful destination branding must embrace a host of activities, including infrastructural development, product enhancement, protection against environmental degradation, changes in organizational culture and promotional partnerships, all based on intensive market research to identify consumer desires. This case study of Brand WA demonstrates that, when combined with the development of a distinctive, broad visual language and strong creative promotional executions, these activities can provide the platform for a successful destination brand.

Continuing the theme of developing a place brand beyond tourism, Rachel Piggott, Nigel Morgan and Annette Pritchard examine the brand of New Zealand in Chapter 13. In this contribution, the authors particularly spotlight the value of targeted and integrated public and media relations activities in destination brand building and co-ordination. The current initiatives driven by Tourism New Zealand represent the first ever global branding strategy for the destination, and the chapter examines how PR is being used to support New Zealand's overall branding strategy by tapping into the power of the international media in order to showcase its landscapes, peoples, cultures and tourism activities. The chapter concludes that PR, linked to the opportunities presented by special events and movies (notably *The Lord of the Rings*) and the world wide web can be a cost-effective tool in the drive to create strong destination brand relationships.

Jan Slater returns to her original contribution in Chapter 14 to discuss how Louisiana continues to develop its powerful travel destination brand. Such success is no mean task in the USA, where annual state government tourism promotional spending exceeds half a billion dollars and the domestic audience accounts for over a billion tourism trips. As Slater explains, Louisiana has wholeheartedly embraced branding to communicate and emphasize the 'feel' and 'personality' of the place. Although it has many attractions, it is its brand identity that has positioned the state as one of the fastest growing tourism destinations in the USA. Significantly, the process has been underpinned by the development of a strong advertising agency–DMO partnership. The former, through its insightful mining of existing consumer research, was able to develop a strong, differentiating, brand proposition and identity for the state which has remained largely unchanged in the decade since its conception in 1993. As Slater highlights, however, the key to success here is the power behind the Louisiana brand (built around food, culture, music, scenery, architecture and history), a substantial advertising budget, well-targeted media placements and an effective integrated campaign with advertising as its cornerstone.

In Chapter 15, Can Seng Ooi discusses the Singapore Tourism Board's (STB) vision for Singapore as the capital and hub of the New Asia; the gateway which visitors should visit or pass through when they are in the region. Thus, its 'New Asia–Singapore' brand embraces this regional brand and strategy, as well as providing a focused marketing direction for the place as a stand-alone destination. The city state is also positioning itself as the arts and cultural capital of the region and, at the same time, drawing on the 'exoticism' of its neighbouring destinations: a quality which it is itself trying to re-establish. Can Seng's chapter thus examines the branding of Singapore holistically, encompassing the particular challenges and opportunities the STB has faced since the new positioning was launched in 1996, from the 'Millennium mania' promotions in 2000 to the 'Singapore roars' initiative in 2003, following the end of the SARS outbreak. He also reminds us of the importance of materializing the brand expectations, discussing how the STB is making 'New Asia–Singapore' live by directing tourists' attention to the Asia in the largely modern city that is Singapore, by rejuvenating Chinatown and reintroducing street markets and Chinese language road signs.

In the penultimate chapter of the collection, Mike Smith underlines that potential tourists' perceptions of places are crucially important, but notoriously difficult to influence. Such perceptions are strongly shaped by the media, and although media relations efforts have always been considered part of the destination branding marketing mix, news media placements often are uncontrolled. His chapter on Philadelphia's hosting of the 2000 Republican National Convention offers an interesting case study of how places can use spotlight events as an opportunity to garner valuable media exposure, to lure potential corporate and association decision makers, and to reinvigorate community development efforts, if they are managed well and have a little luck. Using a combination of participant observation, analysis of official documents and a review of media coverage, Smith offers a fascinating insight into how Philadelphia 2000, the non-partisan, non-profit organization responsible for all details of the event, managed the media relations efforts, positively influenced the 15 000 media representatives in the city for the event, and used this national event to reinforce and extend the city's branding messages for both national and regional audiences.

In the final chapter, written by Graham Brown, Laurence Chalip, Leo Jago and Trevor Mules, the focus on the relationship between destination branding, events and the media continues, this time in Australia. After discussing the growing importance of event tourism, the authors examine the nature of destination image in the context of conceptual and applied frameworks before evaluating the status of the relationship between event management and tourism by discussing recent research projects in Australia. The chapter then considers the implications of the Sydney Olympic Games on Brand Australia. Brown, Chalip, Jago and Mules provide a richly researched insight into how Australia's destination marketers shrewdly harnessed the global reach of the Games to promote not only Sydney's, but the whole of Australia's tourism image to the world. The case study clearly demonstrates how the 'best ever games' was used to advance Brand Australia strategically. Although the authors point out that much of the momentum was lost in the changed international climate following 11 September, SARS and the war in Iraq, they leave the reader in no doubt as to the long-term value of hosting *the* global event.

Concluding thoughts

The success of many of the branding initiatives discussed in Part Three shows that destinations can indeed become brands that have celebrity value and emotional appeal. That does not mean, however, that it is easy to build a strong destination travel brand. Managers have to overcome both the politics and the paucity challenges; outsmarting rather than outspending their competitors. The examples from this book show that it takes patience to establish brand reputations and building a powerful destination brand is a long-term effort, exemplified here by Spain and Singapore. There are destination brands that have seemingly emerged from obscurity to achieve instant fashion, notably here in the case of New Zealand. Such rapid elevation to celebrity status, however, often owes much to a culmination of long-term economic, political, social and cultural factors. Often such instant stardom also belies long-term marketing activity and investment built on detailed marketing research, planning and consistent positioning.

Certainly, the collection demonstrates that those destinations that have emerged as brand winners do have a number of common features. They are based on a vision that is founded on intensive stakeholder, consumer and competitor research, and expressed with care and discipline in everything that communicates the brand's personality. Once the brand personality has been identified, marketers must have the courage to stay with the brand's essence; refinements may be made to how the values are expressed in the brand architecture, but the essentials of the brand personality should remain consistent. The secret is continually to evolve and enrich the original brand personality, building on the initial strengths to strengthen their appeal and to broaden the market. Take the examples discussed here of Singapore, Spain, Oregon and Australia, which have all woven 'new' attributes (such as culture, heritage and modern architecture) into their original brand personalities.

Although many of the chapters in this collection focus on branding *per se*, most have also sought to reinforce that place branding is not merely a rational marketing activity but a political act. Tourism offers communities the potential to build both identities and viable economies. In many countries, however, the tourism industry itself is often politically weak, lacks visibility and is extremely fragmented. The real sources of power in such a vacuum are often the DMOs and a handful of major companies, particularly the airlines. In these cases the DMOs must rise to the task of being the primary front-line promoter for any destination. However, as government financing continues to be squeezed, it is critical that the DMO maintains its role as co-ordinator of promotional resources.

Unless it takes command of both branding and product development, in a changing and confused stakeholder market, the large operators and transportation companies in a destination will simply take to the market what they believe is the most appealing product. This will be at the expense of both small players within the industry and the dilution of any broader brand identity. In a world where a handful of major countries attracts almost three-quarters of international tourist arrivals, most destinations will at best be niche players competing on the margins (Piggott, 2001). They will be reliant on effective, targeted branding strategies that have the potential to squeeze maximum value from their small budgets. This is a difficult but by no means an impossible task, particularly if the power of industry partners and emerging media such as the world wide web can be harnessed.

Clearly, DMOs need to work with bodies on a collaborative and integrative basis outside traditional advertising. This is particularly true of niche destinations with a small share of voice. Such destinations must be alive to alternatives to advertising and focus on the branding opportunities offered by sports, cultural and political activities. In this collection, examples include the Sydney Olympics in 2000, the Americas Cup in 2003, the Ryder Cup in 2010 and the release of *The Lord of The Rings* trilogy during 2001–2003. All have or will provide worldwide interest and platforms for public relations and promotional campaigns. DMOs must look to the future to consider the opportunities offered through interactive media, digital television (video on demand, interactive booking) and the world wide web (itinerary planning and 'look and book'). These media cannot be ignored, as not only do they interactively engage visitors pre-trip, but they also provide direct marketing opportunities for relationship building, which can be resurrected and sustained post-trip. The potential of such opportunities deserves more attention from both academics and practitioners, as does the role of joint destination marketing partnerships.

Place branding is an extremely complex and highly political activity that can enhance a nation's economy, national self-image and identity. Many organizations and groups thus have vested interests in the promotion of particular identities (many of which may be in direct conflict with the interests of others) and much more work is needed on how these interests intersect. In particular, there is a pressing need for study of the processes underpinning the support in the public and private sectors for place branding. National brands can encompass several regional sub-brands that require accommodation in the overall brand and, more complex still, suprabrands may involve co-operation across several regions and countries as smaller, less well-known places attempt to gain a foothold in the international marketplace. Although there is a growing body of work on the process of destination branding, there are no studies that investigate the extent to which these brands impact on the populations of these countries. We still have little understanding of the extent to which place brand management is a collective activity embraced by residents and smaller trade operators. Research also needs to explore the relationship between culture and branding, given that it is their cultural differences that imbue most places with a sense of distinctiveness. Why do destination marketers so often ignore a place's unique cultural attributes in the rush to promote sun, surf and sand, or lake, land and mountain? Above all, perhaps, as indicated by Fall and Lubber's chapter here, there is a pressing need for more study of the wider effectiveness of tourism marketing and promotional activity, which remains wide open for examination.

It is common practice for books to conclude with such calls for further work. In the field of place branding, however, these opportunities are particularly significant. Papadopoulos and Heslop (2002) have noted how marketing journals are dominated by small numbers of authors, and thus academic journals (and conferences) perhaps reflect too narrow a range of views and opinions. More bridges certainly need to be built between those who practise and those who comment on destination brand management. Such bridges would enrich the field of destination branding, strengthen its research base, and enhance both theory and praxis. It is hoped that this book will be one such bridge. It has a coherent structure, but the editors are well aware that not everyone will read it from start to finish; some will simply want to dip into its individual parts or chapters. Whichever way you choose to use the book, we hope you find it an enjoyable read and a useful resource. It is not all inclusive. The subject has already become too large and too important to make such a claim. Many examples of good practice have been left out and at best it is hoped that students and scholars of destination marketing will find enough of interest here to provoke further critical study and debate.

References

Anholt, S. (2003) *Brand New Justice – The Upside of Global Branding*. Oxford: Butterworth-Heinemann.

Clarke, J. (2000) Tourism brands: an exploratory study of the brands box model. *Journal of Vacation Marketing* 6: 329–345.

Doorne, S., Ateljevic, I. and Bai, Z. (2003) Representing identities through tourism: encounters of ethnic minorities in Dali, Yunnan Province, People's Republic of China. *International Journal of Tourism Research* 5: 1–11.

Papadopoulos, N. and Heslop, L. (2002) Country equity and country branding: problems and prospects. *Journal of Brand Management* 9: 294–314.

Piggott, R (2001) Building a brand for a country. Can commercial marketing practices achieve this in a government-funded environment? Unpublished MBA dissertation, University of Hull.

Westwood, S. (2000) The Holiday Brand, what does it mean? An exploratory study of brand equity in the context of the package holiday experience. In Robinson, M., Evans, N., Long, P., Sharpley, R. and Swarbrooke, J. (eds) *Management, Marketing and the Political Economy of Travel and Tourism, Reflections on International Tourism*. Sunderland: Business Education Publishers, pp. 517–536.

2

Branding the nation: the historical context

Wally Olins

Introduction

Why do they get so excited? I never cease to be amazed at the violent reactions that the concept of branding the nation provokes. There is clearly something about it that sets some people's teeth on edge. A visceral antagonism brings the most unlikely individuals and groups, at least temporarily, into the same camp. Commentators from every part of the political and social spectrum have at different times in very different publications expressed their loathing and contempt for the idea as repellent and superficial; that is when they do not regard it as entirely risible. In almost every country I have visited where the notion has been discussed, a few individuals have expressed their revulsion to it in the strongest terms. Michel Girard (1999), a French academic, encapsulates this view:

> *In France the idea of re-branding the country would be widely unacceptable because the popular feeling is that France is something that has a nature and a substance other than that of a corporation. A corporation can be re-branded, not a state. One can take a product, a washing powder for instance, and then change the name which is actually done very regularly. Regular re-branding is normal, particularly in the life of consumer products, but can this actually be the case for countries? ... A country carries specific dignity unlike a marketed product ... In France it is unimaginable for Chirac to attempt to re-brand France.*

Girard carries on in this vein, telling us about 'the superior dignity of statehood', and so on. So rebranding is OK for a corporation but not for a nation. In other words corporations change, merge, divest, invest and rebrand and reinvent themselves but nations do not change, they are immutable. Their verities are eternal. How do you relate this view to the historical reality that almost every nation has reinvented itself as its regimes and circumstances have changed?

Since Michel Girard claims that it is unimaginable for President Chirac to rebrand France, let us take a cursory look to see whether any other leaders in French history have found the same difficulty. France is a nation that has had five republics, two empires and at least four kingdoms. France has been Royalist, Republican and Imperial. It has been Egalitarian and Absolutist in turns and occasionally, even at the same time, always with the same vigour, sense of destiny and intellectual conviction that distinguishes the French political and cultural scene. Even within my lifetime France has lived with three Republics, a dictatorship called Vichy, and contemporaneously a dissident alternative calling itself France Libre. Just a few glimpses at certain points in French history underline the point.

As a kingdom under the Bourbons nobody was more glorious an autocrat in the tradition of Divine Right than le Roi Soleil, Louis XIV. Versailles was erected as the physical embodiment of absolute power. Then came the First and most significant Revolution in 1789. The France of the Revolution was a completely different entity from the France of the Bourbons. Not only was the traditional nobility exiled and dispersed, the Royal Family executed, a Republic proclaimed, religion excoriated, and an entire social and cultural system turned on its head, but every little detail changed too. The Tricolour replaced the Fleur de Lys, the

Marseillaise became the new anthem, the traditional weights and measures were replaced by the metric system, a new calendar was introduced, God was replaced by the Supreme Being and the whole lot was exported through military triumphs all over Europe. In other words the entire French package was changed. You may not like the term, you may prefer to talk about a new or reinvented nation or state, but if revolutionary France was not a new brand I do not know what is.

Only a very few years later another rebranding operation took place. General Bonaparte made himself Emperor. Empire was a concept entirely new and hitherto entirely alien to France. France had been a kingdom and then briefly a republic, but France had never had an Emperor before. Napoleon crowned himself Emperor at his own coronation although he brought the Pope from Rome just to be on hand. He introduced new titles, rituals, uniforms, honours and decorations, not to speak of a new legal and educational system. *Le Moniteur*, the Napoleonic newspaper, was managed by skilful spin doctors using all the most sophisticated techniques of the day. In his rapidly assembled Empire he gave new names to a number of extremely short-lived new countries, some of which, such as Illyria and the Parthenopean Republic, sounded very pretty. He wished a number of his closest relatives and marshals as rulers on various parts of Europe; the current Swedish royal family descends directly from Napoleon's Marshal Bernadotte. Under Napoleon, France was not big enough: the whole of Europe was rebranded. All this effort was commemorated and memorialized by a number of artists and writers, of whom Jacques-Louis David was perhaps the most gifted.

The rebranding of France has proceeded sporadically and often violently ever since. Napoleon's Empire gave way to the restored Bourbons, who were overthrown and replaced by a bourgeois Monarchy, which was followed by a Second Republic which turned itself into a Second Napoleonic Empire. In an attempt to re-create the glory of his uncle, the first and incomparably greater figure, Napoleon III and the Second Empire went down to humiliating defeat by Prussia in 1870. By the time the Third Republic emerged from the ashes of the Second Empire, French politicians had become the world's specialists at branding and rebranding the nation. The Third Republic, as Professor Eric Hobsbawm (1992) makes clear, wanted to make Republicanism respectable, hence for example, the Bastille Day celebrations initiated in 1880, nearly 100 years after the Bastille fell.

The Third Republic collapsed in the defeat of 1940 and was replaced by Petain's Vichy. Under Vichy, France was rebranded yet again; the Republican slogan, or as branding people would put it strapline, 'liberté, egalité, fraternité' was replaced with 'travail, famille, patrie'. Although the Vichy regime is now regarded as a humiliating and shameful period in French history, there is no doubt that it was, one might say, a new brand with a powerful and for some time popular, political, cultural and social ideology. After Vichy came the Fourth Republic and then the Fifth, which is France's current political and cultural incarnation. Each time the reality has been modulated the symbolism has changed with it, and each time France has presented a new version of itself both internally and to the outside world. Of course it is true that there is continuity underneath the change. The French people and France itself continue to demonstrate many traditional characteristics. Vichy, for example, presented a face of France that had existed as a powerful minority point of view throughout the life of the Third Republic, and still, unhappily, exists today. Nevertheless, the changes are not superficial or cosmetic or meaningless, they are real and profound. The reason why nations continue both explicitly and sometimes implicitly to shape and reshape their identities or, if you prefer, explicitly and implicitly to rebrand themselves is that their reality changes and they need to project this real change symbolically to all the audiences, internal and external, with whom they relate.

I cite the example of France in detail both because so distinguished a commentator as Michel Girard insists that France has never been rebranded, and because at least in my judgement, of all the countries in the world, France is probably the one that has been most influential in the branding and rebranding of other nations. But you can make similar observations about almost but not quite every nation. Dominic Lieven, in his magnificent book *Empire* (2000), puts it superbly. 'The revolutionary nationalist doctrine of 1789 was both absolute and abstract. It demanded a far higher level of commitment to the state than was the case in a traditional monarchy … .' In other words the new French republican state was much more self-consciously a nation, much more self-aware, more aggressive and more determined to create homogeneity – to create consistency and coherence – than any nation ever had before. As all of us in the branding business know, consistency and coherence are what branding is all about. Lieven goes on to talk about nascent German nationalism in these terms:

More important in the long run were the nationalist doctrines developed at this time above all by German Romantics. This put a heavy stress on ethnicity, and above all language, as the essential defining elements in community identity … ethnic nationalism was inherently populist: the true bearer of authentic national culture was a peasantry that had retained its customs, folk music and languages.

This romantic, peasant nationalism harking back to a mythical golden age is the second and equally significant strain in national identity and national branding.

The combination of French revolutionary nationalism and folksy German romanticism, Jacques-Louis David meets Caspar David Friedrich so to speak, was the starting point for the self-conscious, self-aware nation which emerged throughout the nineteenth and twentieth centuries. These new nations or brands, usually carved out of old multilingual, multinational empires, or patched together from a variety of fragments ruled by minor princelings, used all the powers at their disposal to create a unitary state, with a single or dominant language and a single or dominant religion. Sometimes they invented or reconstructed national myths, for instance Finland's Kalevalla, sometimes they even invented a new language, such as Israel's modern Hebrew. They used universal male military conscription and universal primary education to create a feeling for national identity that could be shared by all those living inside the nation and respected, admired, feared or at the very least acknowledged by its neighbours. Whether they were very big and powerful like Bismarck's Germany or very small and quite insignificant like Montenegro they went through a recognizable process that we could very easily compare and contrast with current commercial branding techniques.

Bismarck's newly unified Germany, created out of the French collapse of 1870, had an Emperor, a Kaiser. The word Kaiser was deliberately chosen because it appeared to hark back to Charlemagne, the Holy Roman Empire and the Caesars of Roman antiquity. William I, the old, proud Hohenzollern King of Prussia who became under Bismarck's pressure the first Kaiser of the Second Reich, hated the title. He thought it pretentious, bombastic and bogus. It was all of those things, but it was certainly symbolic of the new German brand. His grandson William II, the one who went to war in 1914, loved being a Kaiser. The newly invented country celebrated a range of newly reinvented myths, folklore and traditions. Wagner's celebration of Teutonic myths and legends in his operas, supported by a panoply of other artists and writers, reinforced Germany's industrial, economic and military power with a massive cultural presence and helped to make Germany the most admired and by some the most feared new brand of the nineteenth century. Germany was emulated by Italy and eventually by all the new nations in Central and Eastern Europe that emerged from the ashes of the multinational, multilingual Habsburg and Ottoman empires that collapsed in 1918. Ataturk's branding operations in the defeated Ottoman Empire after World War I rivalled those of the first French Revolution in scope and scale; they involved a new alphabet, new clothing, (all men had to wear smart western headgear or at least a Turkish version of it), ethnic cleansing, a new name for the nation and new names for all its inhabitants, and perhaps most importantly in view of recent developments, a secular rather than a religious state.

The influences of the late eighteenth and early nineteenth century nationalists can be felt right through to today. After 1945, the collapse of the great European colonial empires created a new wave of nations. Many of these gave themselves new names: Ceylon became Sri Lanka, Gold Coast became Ghana, Southern Rhodesia became Zimbabwe and its capital Salisbury, Harare. The Dutch East Indies became Indonesia. Its capital Batavia was renamed Jakarta and its multiplicity of languages was replaced by the newly coined Bahasa Indonesian. The former Belgian Congo became plain Congo, then Zaire, then Congo again. Entirely new countries such as Pakistan and Bangladesh emerged from what had been the British Indian Empire. Bangladesh has had three names in just over half a century; first it was part of India as East Bengal, then it became East Pakistan and then Bangladesh. How about that for rebranding the nation?

All of these new countries attempted to break away from their immediate colonial past. In doing this many of them, like their predecessors in nineteenth century Europe, uncovered, discovered or invented a precolonial heritage; Zimbabwe was a semimythical African empire located more or less where present-day Zimbabwe lies. The historical relationship between ancient Zimbabwe and contemporary Zimbabwe is negligible; the emotional relationship, however, is close. All this is an orthodoxy. All the historians and political scientists who have studied the subject, Hobsbawm, Geller, Kedourie, Benedict Anderson, Dominic Lieven and many others, share more or less similar views. As nations emerge they create self-sustaining myths to build coherent identities. When political upheavals take place, colonial masters are overthrown or a new regime emerges, as in Eastern Europe in the 1990s, the nation reinvents itself.

We have to presume that Michel Girard and similar harsh critics of rebranding would agree that nationalism and national identity have been the fundamental ideas that fuelled the creation of nation states over the past two centuries. It seems then that it is not the ideas that they argue about, so much as the words. Image and national identity are fine, but 'brand' sticks in the gullet. If instead of using the word 'brand' and other corporate expressions such as straplines in this chapter I had used words such as identity, national image and national identity, no well-educated person with any historical knowledge would have raised an eyebrow. So why is it perfectly OK to talk or write about the rise of nationalism and growth of new nation states; the need for postcolonial societies to invent a mythical past through names of semihistorical empires, or for nations such as Indonesia even to invent a new language, but it suddenly becomes all wrong if these concepts are associated with those that have been used by clever corporations and their brands for many years?

Is it because the techniques used in corporations and nations seem to be converging? Over the past few decades, some nations such as Spain and Australia whose realities have changed, have very carefully and deliberately adapted the techniques used by corporations in marketing themselves and their products and services in order to help them to project a new, revised or in some way modified view of themselves. Spain under Franco was an isolated, backward, poverty-stricken dictatorship. Today Spain is a democracy, an active and lively member of the European Union, with a decent standard of living and some pretty good companies by world standards, and above all perhaps, Spain makes a significant global cultural contribution. Should Spain have made a coherent effort to project the new reality – to rebrand itself – or should it have allowed old and entirely inappropriate prejudices to linger on? Spain chose to rebrand itself. So have a number of other countries, whose reality has been out of line with the perceptions. Only a few people would seriously argue that Spain should not have done this, or even that it has not worked.

Following the example of Spain, Ireland and elsewhere, many other nations whose reality has dramatically changed (because, for example, of the collapse of communism) are looking for ways of demonstrating their tourist potential, attracting inward investment or developing brands both for home consumption and for export. These newly reinvented nations are competing both with each other and with older established entities in a very harsh and turbulent commercial environment. The nation that makes itself the most attractive wins the prizes, and others suffer. Scotland is OK: although it is a small country, it has been around for a long time; it has tartans, kilts, Scotch whisky, the Highlands, *Braveheart* and the Edinburgh Festival. Other countries of a similar size, say Slovakia or Slovenia, are not so fortunate. How many people know where they are or the significant differences between them? In order to compete effectively on a world stage they need all the resources that contemporary branding techniques can offer.

There is nothing new in all this. The problem seems to be not so much with what goes on but with the words used to describe it. It appears that it is the word 'brand' that raises the blood pressure. It seems to me that there are three reasons why the word 'brand' acts like a red rag to a bull to some people: snobbery, ignorance and semantics. Snobbery because some so-called intellectuals seem to think that business is a contemptible and boring activity with no intellectual, cultural or social content, which is solely dedicated to making profits and has no relevance to society as a whole. So nations should not seem to be associated with any activities in which commerce is engaged. Well, there is no doubt that business is about making money. But to make money business people have to exploit and attempt to manipulate human emotions just like political leaders. Businesses have to create loyalties; loyalties of the workforce, loyalties of suppliers, loyalties of the communities in which they operate, loyalties of investors and loyalties of customers. In creating these loyalties they use very similar techniques to those of nation builders. They create myths, special languages, environments that reinforce loyalties, colours, symbols, and quasi-historical myths. They even have heroes: Richard Branson and his famous informality, his heroic ballooning trips and his other self-aggrandizing activities, Jack Welch, the firm, tough, legendary hero of GE, and Anita Roddick, the staunch defender of sustainable environments, to mention just three.

Many business leaders would like to be as ruthless as political leaders. Their problem is that they do not command the same resources. Unlike Robespierre, Kemal Ataturk or Saddam Hussein, they cannot actually control what people wear, what they call the days of the week or what the corporate alphabet looks like, and they cannot execute people either; I can think of plenty of business leaders who would do all of these things if they could. They can fire people, though: 'downsizing' is the jargon. I suppose you could say that Pol Pot downsized Cambodia. When you look hard some of the analogies are pretty close. It is silly snobbery to assume that they have nothing to do with each other.

The second factor is ignorance. Most business people do not know anything about the history of the nation in which they were born and in which they live. Many are even shockingly ignorant about the history of the organization for which they work. Unfortunately, it is also true that most academics know nothing about how business works, so each side assumes that the other lives in another and entirely foreign world and that there is no overlap or relationship between them. It is this combination of snobbery and ignorance that is lethal. I am not suggesting that branding the nation is the same as branding a company, only that many of the techniques are similar; that people are people whether they work in a company or live in a nation and that means that they can be motivated and inspired and manipulated in the same way, using the same techniques. In fact, although it is dangerous to take the analogies too far, branding businesses and branding nations do have a lot in common. This will become especially true as service brands, with their focus on staff and internal communications, become more significant. I have written at more length on this topic elsewhere (see Olins 1999).

However, the underlying problem may be semantics: words and what they seem to mean. For so many commentators, of whom Girard is typical, a brand means a label on washing powder; it means Finish, or maybe Body Shop or Virgin. It means cheap, transient, crass, commercial trivia that are both superficial and insignificant, whereas the nation is permanent and deeply significant and has huge emotional, even spiritual connotations. Well, all of us who work with corporations and their brands understand that fizzy drinks, trainers, mobile phones and other apparently insignificant and entirely unmemorable trivia give real emotional and spiritual value to some lives. Many brands help to create a sense of identity, of belonging: just like the nation. Michel Girard and other commentators may not like it, but that does not make it any less true. Anyway, whether they like it or not, they had better get used to it because, so far as I can judge, interest in branding the nation is rising very rapidly. Within the next decade or so it will become, I believe, quite normal national practice; and then all the discussions will be focused around which countries do it well and which badly.

Acknowledgement

An earlier version of this chapter first appeared in *The Journal of Brand Management*, April 2002; 9(4/5): 249–261.

References

Girard, M. (1999) States, diplomacy and image making: what is new? Reflections on current British and French experiences. Paper presented at a conference on Image, State and International Relations, London School of Economics, 24 June 1999.

Hobsbawm, E. (1992) Mass-producing traditions: Europe 1870–1914. In Hobsbawm, E. and Ranger, T. (eds) *The Invention of Tradition*. Cambridge: Cambridge University Press, Pages 263–308.

Lieven, D. (2000) *Empire*. John Murray, London.

Olins, W. (1999) *Trading Identities – Why Companies and Countries are Taking on Each Others' Roles*. The Foreign Policy Centre, London.

3

Nation-brands and the value of provenance

Simon Anholt

Introduction

Take a look at the really successful global brands around you, and you may notice that they all have something in common. Every one of them comes from a place that has a brand image of its own, and the product is quite often strongly linked with that image. It is an Italian car, associated with the Italian qualities of style, speed and innovative design. It is French perfume, sold on French chic, classiness and wealth. It is a Japanese TV, majoring on the Japanese virtues of high-tech expertise, miniaturization and value for money. It is American fashion, bursting with street credibility and youthful rebellion. Just like manufacturers' brands, place brands evoke certain values, qualifications and emotional triggers in the consumer's mind about the likely values of any product that comes from that place. A place brand can behave just like a manufacturer's brand, providing an umbrella of trust, a guarantee of quality, which kick-starts the entry of its new 'sub-brands' on the marketplace.

It is not surprising that most of the world's successful commercial brands come from the top ten place brands: America, Britain, France, Italy, Spain, Scandinavia, Japan, Switzerland, Germany and South Korea. America is undoubtedly the world's leading place brand, partly because it has been so thoroughly and expensively marketed to the rest of the world over the past century. Having Hollywood as your advertising agency certainly helps, and hiring NASA as your sales promotion agency, which periodically sends a rocket into orbit to demonstrate the superiority of American technology to a gawping planet, is a stroke of genius. (And what a place brand Hollywood is, by the way, just in case anybody doubted that smaller places than nations can have potent brand equities all of their own.)

For a brand's home town or home country to add this helpful dose of free additional equity, the only requirement is that the product should 'chime' with its place of origin in the consumer's mind, and that some kind of logic links the two. This logic may be simple or creative: in the case of manufactured brands, it could be the straightforward logic that links Benckiser, a manufacturer of household cleaning products, with a new household cleaning product; or it could be the more lateral sort of logic that links Caterpillar, a manufacturer of bulldozers, with rugged footwear. In exactly the same way, brands from countries can range from simple national produce – pizza from Italy or soft drinks from America – to more unexpected but equally attractive pairings, such as skis from Slovenia (Elan), clothing from Australia (RM Williams) or phones from Finland (Nokia).

When you try to match provenance with product, there are some pairings that clearly make brand sense, and others that just do not. People might well buy Indian accountancy software (the success of firms such as Infosys and WIPRO, two of the very few technology firms to outlast the IT bubble, have certainly helped this association) or perhaps even a stylish Lithuanian raincoat, and although I am tempted to say that they probably would not buy Peruvian modems or Zimbabwean perfume, attitudes can and do change quickly. Fifteen years ago, who would have believed that we Europeans could be happily consuming Chinese Tsingtao beer or Malaysian Proton cars? or that one of the hottest selling perfumes in Paris is Urvâshi, manufactured in India by a company that previously specialized in hydraulic brake fluid? Or, indeed, who would have believed that one of the world's most successful and fastest growing manufacturers of jet aircraft would be a Brazilian company, Embraer?

The importance of nation-brands beyond branding

The idea that countries behave rather like brands is by now fairly familiar to most marketers, and to many economists and politicians too. Originally a recondite academic curiosity, the notion is gaining broader acceptance, and its value as a metaphor for how countries can position themselves in the global marketplace in order to boost exports, inward investment, tourism and much more besides, is pretty well understood. International marketers, too, are at last beginning to understand just how much equity can be added to their brands through the judicious leveraging of their real or perceived country of origin. John Pantzalis and Carl A. Rodrigues (1999) have even proposed that the movement of international capital is influenced by perceptions of countries as brands by investors. Thus, they claim, brand positioning and brand management (where the brand is the country) become critical in attracting global capital, and they also affect how and when capital may flee a country in situations such as the 1997 financial crisis. It is certainly a striking thought: that apparently hard-headed investors may form their view of a country's economic prospects as a result of the way in which that country's brand image has been presented to them in the media, or that they may class several countries together because of superficial brand associations (the 'Asian tigers', for example), rather than anything more scientific.

Clearly, there is far more to a powerful place brand image than simply boosting branded exports around the world: if we pursue the thought to its logical conclusion, a country's brand image can profoundly shape its economic, cultural and political destiny. What ultimately makes the European Commission decide which countries will be considered for membership of their élite club, and in which order? Their brand image, of course, and what it might or might not ultimately contribute to the brand image of the European Union itself. When complex wars erupt between countries, and even experts are hard-pressed to say which is truly the victim and which the aggressor, it is surely the brand image of each country that sways world opinion towards its customary black-and-white view. And when suspects are tried by international courts for acts of terrorism or espionage, how sure can we be that the jury is not swayed by their brand of origin? One can even make a case for place branding encouraging more moderate foreign policy: after all, there is nothing like a proper sense of the value of a nation's good name to make its leaders think twice before acting aggressively or irresponsibly towards their neighbours.

A positive place brand encourages inward investment, and tourism is a magnet for talent (both new immigrants and returning members of the diaspora), and if properly managed can create a renewed sense of purpose and identity for the inhabitants of the country, region or city. After all, one of the best known functions of brand is to act as convenient, everyday shorthand for what a product or company stands for: why not for a city or country too? Both are handy reductions for far more complex and contradictory realities, and thus play a precious role in our busy modern lives. The importance of the issue is certainly not lost on the world's governments, and although the vocabulary and the methodology differ widely, many are currently looking to buff up their brand images. A few shining examples of countries that have successfully 'rebranded' themselves, or at least demonstrated competent management of the way their attributes are perceived abroad, have also helped the trend to accelerate. Japan, Ireland, Spain, Germany and Scotland are often-quoted cases of countries whose public perception has dramatically altered over a relatively short period, to the enormous benefit of the country's economic health and self-respect. Many others continue to work hard on the problem: New Zealand, Australia, India, Wales, Taiwan, Croatia, Slovenia, South Korea and Britain.

Then there is a handful of megabrand countries, such as America, Japan, Italy and France, whose public image seems so powerful, positive and all-pervasive that one may think they hardly need to bother managing it. These are the countries that appear effortlessly synonymous with certain valuable attributes (France for chic and quality of living, Italy for style and sexiness, America for technology, wealth, power, youth appeal, and much more besides), and each time a new brand emerges from one of these countries, it seems to have a head start over all its competitors in the global marketplace. More than anything else, it is the example of such powerful nation-brands that continues to stimulate other countries to follow suit, and carve out their perceptual niche on the commercial and cultural map of the world.

Emerging nations and the importance of brand image

One of the great advantages of brands over commodities is that they are an infinitely sustainable resource; that is, as long as their value is maintained through careful marketing. Their value resides primarily in the mind of the consumer, not the factory of the producer, and once created, that makes them surprisingly difficult to destroy. Clearly, the notion of exporting branded rather than unbranded products is a compelling one for many countries. Developing countries could especially benefit from a movement towards global brand export: it is part of a sustainable wealth-creation behaviour that could ultimately help them to escape from the poverty cycle. As it stands, though, most developing countries are enmeshed in a pattern of economic behaviour that keeps them poor: selling unprocessed goods to richer nations at extremely low margins and allowing their buyers to add massive 'value' by finishing, packaging, branding and retailing to the end user. This process often helps to deplete the source country's resources while keeping its foreign revenues at a break-even level at best.

Creating and selling international brands is the classic trick of industrialized nations. It is one born of necessity, perhaps, since some of the world's richest nations have precious few commodities to export, but it is one that many poorer nations would do well to emulate. For it is conceivable that if consumers in developing countries are faced with the choice between yet more brands from the industrialized nations, and new brands from 'colleague countries' in the developing world with no shady colonial past, they might just feel more comfortable with the latter. Global brands as the ultimate distributor of wealth? It is certainly an intriguing thought (see Anholt, 2003).

The stage appears to be set for the emergence of many poorer countries as respected, even privileged places of origin for successful commercial brands. Still, many barriers must be overcome. Brazil, one of the most strongly branded countries in the world, produces almost no international commercial brands. This is surprising, because 'Brand Brazil' has so much going for it – the merriment of samba dancing at carnival time; awesome rainforests as endangered as they are exotic; sex, beaches, sport, adventure – and all of these attributes could contribute to the brand print of almost any successful youth product on the market today, especially in the food, cosmetics, fashion, music, and even automotive and industrial fields. Certainly, these are clichés that may be depressing, even insulting, to the average Brazilian, but they are undeniably a fine platform on which to build a believable global brand. It is one of the tasks of advertising and marketing to manipulate these clichés into something more creative, more substantial, fairer and truer.

The fact that there are negative associations (pollution, overpopulation, poverty, crime, corruption) within the brand print of Brazil is not necessarily a cause for great concern, at least from the branding point of view. After all, a strong brand is a rich brand, and richness implies a complex and satisfying mix of many different elements. The brand equity of the USA also contains a significant proportion of negative elements, but this does little to diminish its attraction, especially when the audience you are dealing with is composed of younger consumers, whose prickly, contradictory nature means that they demand to challenge and be challenged. Brand value is not an excuse to do nothing about these problems, of course, but it is a reason not to despair.

At first glance, the emergence of poorer countries such as Brazil as exporters of global brands and as brands in their own right may seem like a very distant prospect, yet the oddest things do happen. The mighty Tata Corporation of India, for example, recently acquired the Tetley Tea Company of England, the world's second largest teabag manufacturer: a spectacular reversal of the traditional arrangement, where the tea is grown in a poor country and sold at a low price to a brand-owner in a rich country, who sells it on to rich consumers at a vastly higher price. And China has proved full of nasty surprises for many Western manufacturers: more than $270 billion has been invested in Chinese ventures, by thousands of foreign firms, since 1992, yet few Western companies have succeeded in making any money in China. Whirlpool, for example, launched enthusiastically in China in 1994, building factories to manufacture the domestic appliances it confidently expected to sell to the Chinese, only to find that it could not compete against domestic brands. (Indeed, one of these rival firms, Haier, now markets products under its own brand name in North America, and has become the world's number two manufacturer of refrigerators). After losing more than $100 million and shutting down most of its factories, Whirlpool now manufactures washing machines for Guangdong Kelon, another of its Chinese competitors, which are sold to Chinese consumers under the Kelon brand. So perhaps the next great nation-brand association in the making is China, soon to be recognized by consumers worldwide as a byword for quality domestic appliances.

What it takes

Naturally, launching a global brand requires flair, confidence and chutzpah, especially if you do not come from a top ten country. It requires objectivity to an unusual degree: the ability to see yourself as others do, and to accept that this is, at least in commercial terms, more important than the way you see yourself. It requires government support. And it requires constant investment in the place brand itself, which in turn requires commitment, collaboration and effective synergy among the main communicators of the country's image in the global media: usually the tourist board, the airline and the major food producers, because these are the routes by which the national brand is most commonly created and exported.

Indeed, a very common problem for smaller places is the fact that place branding is an international exercise by default, yet because they are not big consumer corporations, they do not have the funds to compete with these companies in global advertising clout. Few destinations or small countries have the advertising dollars of the big marketers – the major airlines, car hire companies, hotel chains and tour operators – or, indeed, of the world's heaviest advertisers, the packaged goods companies and automobile manufacturers. For make no mistake: in competing for precious moments of the mindshare of today's message-fatigued consumer, every advertised brand is a threat, and soap powder and cars are as much a competitor to the small nation or region as other, directly competing countries.

Yet there is hope even for the smallest niche players in nation-branding. Until a few years ago, building a global brand invariably required lots of cash to buy advertising media: before the internet arrived, this was the sine qua non of global marketing. You just could not think of building a worldwide brand for less than $50 or 100 million a year: quite simply, as in all extremely mature and heavily exploited markets, every media vehicle had its own value calculated to the nth degree, and there were no bargains. But with the arrival of the internet, there are still bargains for anyone who knows how to recognize them: although most of the online commercial media space is priced in line with offline media, the barriers to entry are still very low and, unlike any other global medium, there are still huge opportunities for smaller players to outsmart rather than outspend their richer competitors. Anything that is truly news, or which genuinely gives value to the reader, can usually be sure of a free online ride around the planet.

Until recently, it was also true to say that the biggest hurdle that emerging country manufacturers had to overcome before launching their brands onto the international market was the common consumer perception of poor manufacturing quality: the feeling that unless it comes from Europe, Japan or North America, it cannot be properly made; but, again, circumstances are conspiring to change people's minds. For this, we have the rich country producers to thank: over the past few decades, consumers have become very familiar with those humble little stickers on the underside of their American or European-branded goods ('Made in Taiwan', 'Made in Vietnam', 'Made in Thailand', 'Made in Mexico', and many more besides), and they have quietly absorbed the fact that a great many of the products they buy are manufactured (to the high standards required by those American and European brand-owners, naturally) in poor countries. The American and European brand-owners could hardly have done their supplier nations a better favour. The perception only has to be enhanced a little further, and brought repeatedly to the consumer's attention, and yet another barrier preventing the development of global brands from emerging markets is removed.

What is the last obstacle standing in the way of emerging countries as producers of global brands? It may be purely psychological: a simple lack of self-confidence. After years of acting as mere suppliers to more commercially successful nations, many 'third world' countries suffer from what you might call Groucho Marx syndrome ('I'd never belong to a club that would have someone like me as a member'): the idea that nobody in a rich country could possibly be interested or attracted by brands coming from a country so poor and unimportant as theirs. Well, that perception is probably less true now than it has ever been before. For the past decade or so, there has been a pronounced shift in Western tastes and fashions, towards 'asianization', a yearning for the values of older, wiser, more contemplative civilizations than our own. Never before has there been such a vogue for the 'ethnic', the organic, the exotic. There is World Music (currently the fastest growing part of the big record labels' catalogues, and fast overtaking the hitherto unquestioned dominance of the big American popular entertainers); World Cinema (occasionally rivalling the success of Hollywood blockbusters); World Cuisine; the phenomenal surge of interest in alternative, Eastern and pseudo-Eastern remedies (acupuncture, shiatsu, aromatherapy); and much more besides.

The Western consumer is attracted as never before by the cultures and the products of distant lands. Now, surely, is the time for the rightful owners of the truly exotic place brands to leverage the power they hold over the imagination of the world's richest consumers. Now is the time for them to start making back some of the money that they have paid rich countries for their products over the past century, to begin to reverse the relentless flow of wealth from poor to rich, and to redress some of the imbalance between the lucky and the unlucky places of the Earth. This is one kind of aid that emerging countries could find truly valuable: the international branding expertise that can create unexpected and inspiring connections between countries and consumers, and that will enable countries to launch their products onto the global marketplace with confidence, with a big noise and, above all, with pride in their origins. Simplistic, maybe, but undeniably attractive: just add the right branding expertise to a country living on sweatshop labour and breakeven trading, and you have the beginning of a fast-growth manufacturer economy instead of a submerging service state. After all, marketing has done much to increase the unequal distribution of wealth during the past century, so why shouldn't marketing be used to reverse the trend, and balance things out a little better during the next?

Changing a country's brand image

It certainly looks as though a healthy brand is the remedy for at least some of the economic and political ills of most places. But, as I have said, very few places are lucky enough to possess a powerful, distinctive international brand, and perhaps only two or three of those brands are truly positive in the areas that will most benefit the country's future development. The rest will have to work out how to manage and enhance their brand images. Changing the world's perceptions of a place is neither easy nor quick; after all, its brand image has often evolved over many centuries, shaped by wars, religion, diplomacy (or the lack of it), international sporting triumphs or disasters, famous and infamous sons and daughters, and latterly by the brands it exports, as long as the brand is prepared to be explicit about its country of origin.

A place brand is like the proverbial supertanker, which takes five miles to slow down and ten miles to change course. All the 'place brand manager' can realistically hope to do is identify and isolate the positive existing perceptions of the country and calculate how to enhance whatever contributes to these in the country's external communications, while downplaying anything that does not. The logic behind this approach is standard marketing practice: each place is competing for consumer attention alongside a million other phenomena in the media, and unless its every appearance in the public domain continually and accurately reinforces a few simple, basic, coherent truths, it is highly unlikely that a homogeneous image will ever form itself in the consumer's mind. In this respect, all brands are rather like those children's games where you have to join up the dots to draw the outline of an animal: unless the game is made pretty easy for the consumers (i.e. the dots are numbered), they are unlikely ever to make out the tiger or the bunny.

Perceptions of places can also change far more quickly and more completely than might be expected. Perhaps the most dramatic example of how a new place brand can be dreamed up, communicated and established across much of the world is the case of Walter Scott and Brand Scotland: Scott almost single-handedly 'invented' the image of modern Scotland, portraying a land so attractive, picturesque and compelling, it has remained rooted into the consciousness of Europe, and beyond, for centuries. It is a heartening example of how people can, if they are passionate and determined and talented enough, sway the world's view of a nation.

The best example of brand turnaround from our own times is undoubtedly that of modern Japan: thirty years ago, 'Made in Japan' was a decidedly negative concept, as most Western consumers had based their perception of 'brand Japan' on their experience of shoddy, second rate products flooding the marketplace. The products were cheap, certainly, but they were basically worthless. In many respects, the perception of Japan was much as China's is today. Yet

Japan has now become enviably synonymous with advanced technology, manufacturing quality, competitive pricing, even style and status. Japan, indeed, passes the best branding test of all: whether consumers are prepared to pay more money for functionally identical products, simply because of where they come from. It is fair to say that in the 1950s and 1960s, most Europeans and Americans would only buy Japanese products because they were significantly cheaper than a Western alternative; now, in certain very valuable market segments, such as consumer electronics, musical instruments and motor vehicles, Western consumers will consistently pay more for products manufactured by previously unknown brands, purely on the basis that they are perceived to be Japanese. Little wonder that the UK consumer electronics retailer Dixons, when they launched their own hi-fi brand, gave it a mock-Japanese name, Matsui, in order to borrow – or steal – a little of the brand equity of Japan.

In an age where countries are beginning to invest huge sums in shaping and promoting their brand equities, one cannot help wondering how long such pilfering will be tolerated. Perhaps the Italian region of Tuscany's recent announcement that it would take steps to protect its 'natural imagery' from copyright theft (it seems that two-thirds of all car adverts, for example, are shot in Tuscany, no matter in which country the car is made), will prove to be the first of many.

What it takes to build a place brand

Of all the qualities needed by those who are responsible for nurturing the image of a place, objectivity is one of the most valuable, and one of the hardest to achieve. After all, marketing directors who are responsible for marketing a product are generally salaried employees, seldom the inventor or manufacturer of the product, and so do not find it too difficult to take a cool, objective view of the brand they are building: indeed, good ones are prized partly because of their ability to see the brand in the same way as the consumer. But when the product does not come out of a factory, but is the homeland of the people trying to market it – where they and their parents and grandparents were born, raised, schooled and trained – when they are public servants rather than marketing professionals, and when branding easily becomes confused with foreign policy, tourism or trade promotion, objectivity becomes an extremely elusive quality.

A lack of objectivity can be fatal to the proper branding of a place, no matter how good the intentions at the start. Typically, I find that a country branding programme will start with communications ministries and public affairs departments producing lists of their country's achievements and natural advantages: the nation's most distinguished sons and daughters, the role it has played in world events, its own major historical moments, gems of architecture and natural beauty, regional cuisine, language and folklore, all served up with pages of indigestible demographics and statistics about GDP and income per capita. The idea is that this mass of data is then distilled into a pithy slogan and a raft of quasi-tourism collateral, and thus the country is marketed to a waiting world.

From the point of view of a busy consumer halfway across the world, of course, the historical achievements and natural advantages of most countries are of little interest, and seldom add up to anything that could be described as a coherent or powerful brand. Indeed, since branding programmes are most urgently needed by the smaller, poorer and newer countries, it is all the more likely that such facts will make pretty unimpressive reading to the detached observer. On more than one occasion, I have been faced with the tricky task of gently explaining to a very proud and very patriotic minister that the world will not be enthralled by the fact that the world's first all-metal suspension bridge was invented by a man whose grandfather came from his country, or that over sixty different species of wild grass grow along his eastern coastline.

I know of no better metaphor for any marketing task than trying to chat up someone in a crowded bar. In effect, you walk up to somebody whom you have never met, and have a few seconds in which to convince them that you are worth getting to know better. Sometimes, a joke will do the trick, but unless you know something about the person you are talking to, the right approach is always partly guesswork. (Fortunately, place marketers can use research to reduce the uncertainty.) Either way, few people will fall in love with a stranger who kicks off the conversation with a long list of his natural advantages, impressive family tree and key historical achievements.

No, the place to start working out how to brand a country is often not with the country itself, but with the consumer and the marketplace. In the very limited amount of mindspace that each consumer has available to store perceptions of distant places, one must identify where there are gaps and where there are opportunities. Is there room for a country that is the ultimate youth brand? Which country could most credibly seize this opportunity? Which country is best suited to become the ultimate downshifter's paradise? Which country could position itself as the next technological minipower? Which could be the most natural source country in the world for alternative dietary and medicinal brands? Where might the best service businesses in the world be built? Another good starting point is by looking at the resource which, for most places, is their most valuable asset: the people who live there. Building a place brand strategy around the skills, aspirations and culture of its population is far more likely to result in credible, sustainable and effective results than something cooked up by a team of ministers or PR consultants in closed meeting rooms.

It is also important to remember that branding a country is not the same thing as promoting tourism. The promotion of tourism obviously occupies more common ground with nation-branding than any other aspect of a country's external affairs, but it is merely a part of the whole. Although the economies of more and more places do depend on tourism, other factors may be equally important, such as stimulating inward investment and aid, encouraging both skilled and unskilled workers to immigrate, promoting the country's branded and unbranded exports internationally, increasing the international business of the national airline, facilitating the process of integration into political and commercial organizations such as the European Union or the World Tourism Organization, and a wide range of other interests.

It is the sum total of these interests that compels a place to think hard about the overall image that it presents to the rest of the world, and it is often the case that the image presented by the tourist industry is irrelevant, unhelpful or even damaging to the country's other international initiatives. A fairly typical example of this dissonance between tourist branding and national branding was faced by both Scotland and Ireland: both countries enjoyed an extremely valuable tourist image based around wild, empty countryside, quaint old-world charm, and a populace widely perceived as warm-hearted, uncomplicated, old-fashioned, rustic and utterly unsophisticated – hardly a useful image to have lodged in the minds of American or Japanese corporations deciding where to build their newest semiconductor plant. And yet such contrasts and even contradictions, for the very reason that they exist in the real world, can be resolved, harmonized and believably communicated in a country's branding programme. It takes creativity, objectivity, branding sense and a deep understanding of the way in which consumer logic works, or can be encouraged to work, in each target country and each target audience.

Conclusion

It is no paradox to predict that in today's global marketplace, where brands and products can come from almost literally anywhere, their 'rootedness' will surely become more and more important to consumers in their constant search for brands with trustworthiness, character and distinctiveness. For some time now, the ultimate ambition of many companies has been to turn themselves into 'global brands', and as part of the process that leads to this vague nirvana, they have attempted systematically to remove every clue as to their country of origin. British Airways' decision several years ago to graduate from mere national carrier to global travel brand, drop the explicit reference to its country of origin, and bear images from many different nations on its tailplanes, was one of several instances of this type. But the crucial point that they and many other large corporations often overlook in their rush to appear global, is that a global brand is not the same thing as a brand that comes from nowhere: indeed, in many of the most successful cases, it is a brand that may be sold everywhere, but comes from somewhere quite definite. Coca-Cola, Pepsi, McDonald's, Nike, Levi's, Timberland and Marlboro, for example, would be half the brands they are today if they were not most decidedly from America. British Airways would never have become the world's favourite airline if it had not been, first and foremost, British airways: the existing perception of 'brand Britain' in the minds of much of the world's population (methodical, punctual, predictable, efficient, traditional, heritage-obsessed, class-ridden, status-driven, ceremonious, boring), makes Britain the perfect, the ultimate, the supremely logical provenance for any brand in the business of air travel, hospitality and tourism. It is easy to be wise after the event, but by cutting off its connection with its provenance, British Airways simply pulled the plug on its principal brand equity.

It is the very rootedness of many global brands that gives them their power: a strength of identity, a character, that is entirely absent from many of the corporate constructs that today aspire to become the new generation of global brands. It is human nature, the first time you meet someone, to ask them where they come from. And as the likelihood of that person coming from the same place as you do becomes smaller with every year that passes, the question becomes increasingly relevant. Place of origin is hard equity, which does not need to be built from scratch, because it already exists in the consumer's mind, and has a definite shape and form. Too many brands these days, and perhaps especially 'global' brands, because of their tendency to be large and diffuse in their activities, are rather soft in outline (typically the large international conglomerates: Vivendi, Corus, Thales, etc.). This already means that it is very hard for them to occupy a meaningful and memorable position in the mind of the consumer (I don't know what they do, I don't know where they come from) and the situation is often worsened by their attempts to rebrand themselves as 'global citizens'.

The company names generated to this brief, often with the precise intention of appearing stateless, are therefore entirely culture free and entirely uninteresting: it is a classic reaction to the terrifying prospect of having to communicate with millions of people in hundreds of countries. In reality, of course, people are not really offended at all by people (or companies) from other countries having foreign names, even hard-to-pronounce ones. If you think about it, nothing could be more normal, and it tends to make the person (or company) more interesting. The point is that people do not actually mind products coming from abroad; in fact, they quite like it. There appears to be a natural tendency in most product sectors for consumers gradually to turn away from their familiar national brands, and seek the newness and stimulation of the exotic – this has already occurred in Britain with beer, cars, clothing and, more recently, even financial services.

The consequence of this is that many brands may ultimately stand a better chance of survival abroad than at home. Samsung, a Korean company selling mobile phones in Sweden, the home country of mobile phones, may find this more of an opportunity than a predicament, as Swedes turn away from the almost official, state-run image of Ericsson, their national and global brand leader, towards something a little different, which helps them to stand out from the crowd. And who knows, Ericsson may ultimately find that they can do better business in Seoul than in Stockholm.

So, one way or another, the branding of products and services from places, and the branding of those places themselves, will increasingly be seen as a key focus of marketing, as well as a crucial component of foreign and domestic policy, international relations, economic and cultural development, trade and tourism. For the first time, the art and science of branding has an opportunity to prove its value beyond the tired old litany of 'improving shareholder value', and become recognized as one of the most valuable and relevant disciplines of postindustrial society.

References

Anholt, S. (2003) *Brand New Justice – The Upside of Global Branding.* Oxford: Butterworth-Heinemann.

Pantzalis, J. and Rodrigues, C. A. (1999) *Country Names as Brands – Symbolic Meaning and Capital Flows*, available from http://www.sba.muohio.edu/abas/1999/pantzajo.pdf (accessed December 2003).

4

Country as brand, product and beyond: a place marketing and brand management perspective

Philip Kotler and David Gertner

Introduction

This chapter examines how widely held country images affect attitudes towards a country's products and services and ability to attract investment, businesses and tourists. It assesses the role of strategic marketing management in promoting the country's image, attractiveness and products. Because product features are easily copied, brands have been considered a marketer's major tool for creating product differentiation. Even when differentiation based on product characteristics is possible, often consumers do not feel motivated or able to analyse them in adequate depth. Therefore, the combination of brand name and brand significance has become a core competitive asset in an ever-growing number of contexts (Aaker, 1991).

The American Marketing Association defines a brand as a 'name, term, sign, symbol, or design, or a combination of them intended to identify the goods and services of one seller or group of sellers and to differentiate them from those of competition.' Brands differentiate products and represent a promise of value. Brands incite beliefs, evoke emotions and prompt behaviours. Marketers often extend successful brand names to new product launches, lending existing associations to them. As a result, they speed up consumers' information processing and consumers' learning. Brands have social and emotional value to users. They have personality and speak for the user. They enhance the perceived utility and desirability of a product. Brands have the ability to add or subtract the perceived value of a product. Consumers expect to pay lower prices for unbranded products or for those with low brand equities, whereas they pay premiums for their treasured or socially valued brands. Brands have equity for both customers and investors. Brand equity translates into customer preference, loyalty and financial gains. Brands are appraised and traded in the marketplace. Brand equity has been pointed out to include many dimensions, such as performance, social image, value, trustworthiness and identification (Lassar *et al.*, 1995).

The question of concern to us here is: can a country be a brand? Is there such thing as country brand equity? Shimp and Saeed (1993) applied the term 'country equity', referring to the emotional value resulting from consumers' association of a brand with a country. Country names amount to brands and help consumers to evaluate products and make purchasing decisions. They are responsible for associations that may add to or subtract from the perceived value of a product. Research has supported that consumers are more willing to buy products from industrialized nations as a result of country equity (Wang and Lamb, 1983; Cordell, 1993; Agbonifoh and Elimimiam, 1999). Products bearing a 'Made in Germany', 'Made in Switzerland' or 'Made in Japan' label are commonly regarded as high quality, owing to the reputation of these countries as top world manufacturers and exporters. At the same time, 'Made in Suriname' or 'Made in Myanmar' labels may raise doubts about the quality of the products owing to the low country brand equity.

In some instances a country may deliberately use its name to promote its products. For almost two decades now, American consumers have regarded Café de Colombia (Colombian coffee) as a top-quality coffee. The character of Juan Valdez has helped to designate the country name 'Colombia' as a stamp of a high-quality coffee brand. This 'quintessential cafetero' and his mule are portrayed in a logo created in 1981 to be used as a seal of guarantee issued by the National Federation of Coffee Growers of Colombia (FNC, 2003). The Café de Colombia logo has been extensively used in advertising, promotional materials and coffee packages, providing a good example of integrated marketing communications as well as of consistency. Efforts to promote Colombia as a brand of coffee included the sponsorship of the two-week-long US Open tennis tournament in Flushing Meadows in 1995 (*Chicago Tribune*, 1995). Consumer advertising featuring the logo has paid off. Colombia is the leading exporter of coffee to the USA and Café de Colombia holds over 40 per cent of the speciality coffee market in the USA. A 1995 survey found that 83 per cent of Americans interviewed associated the logo with coffee and 53 per cent properly identified it with Colombian coffee (*Chicago Tribune*, 1995).

Even when a country does not consciously manage its name as a brand, people still have images of countries that can be activated by simply voicing the name. Country images are likely to influence people's decisions related to purchasing, investing, changing residence or travelling. Country image can be understood as:

> *the sum of beliefs and impressions people hold about places. Images represent a simplification of a large number of associations and pieces of information connected with a place. They are a product of the mind trying to process and pick out essential information from huge amounts of data about a place* (Kotler *et al.*, 1993).

A country's image results from its geography, history, proclamations, art and music, famous citizens and other features. The entertainment industry and the media play a particularly important role in shaping people's perceptions of places, especially those viewed negatively. Not only are product categories such as perfumes, electronics, precision instruments, wines, cars and software strongly identified with certain places, but so also are societal ills such as AIDS epidemics, political riots, civil rights violations, attacks on the environment, racial conflict, economic turmoil, poverty and violent crime. All of these have been repeatedly and strongly associated with certain locales. Of course, different people and groups are likely to hold different stereotypes of nations since the mental phenomenon is inherently subjective. However, sometimes they are widespread and pervasive across elements of the same group; they are social cognitions, mental representations shared by members of a given society.

Most country images are stereotypes, extreme simplifications of the reality that are not necessarily accurate. They might be dated, based on exceptions rather than on patterns, on impressions rather than on facts, but nonetheless pervasive. The simple pronunciation or spelling of a brand name in a foreign language may impact product perceptions and attitudes. Leclerc *et al.* (1994) found in one experiment that the French pronunciation of a brand name affects the perceived hedonism of the products and attitudes towards the brand. They also found that the French branding influence persisted even in a product taste test, that is, with a direct sensory experience with the product.

Country images, or knowledge structures related to places, or place schemata, are commonly used as shortcuts for information processing and consumer decision heuristics. People, especially in low-involvement situations, are sloppy cognitive processors. They resist changing or adjusting their cognitive structures or prior knowledge. They prefer to adjust what they see to fit what they know. They may fill in information that is not presented or distort the reality to fit their mental representations. People are also more likely to attend information that confirms their expectations. They disregard information that challenges their knowledge structures, in a process known as confirmation bias. They avoid the effort necessary to reconstruct their cognitions, unless misrepresentations have a cost for them or they find utility in the revision of their schemata. Therefore, images can be long lasting and difficult to change. They can be assessed and measured, and they may be managed and influenced by place marketers as well.

The impact of country names on attitudes towards products

In many countries, mandatory product labelling requires marketers to disclose a product's place of origin. This legal requisite has raised the interest of marketing researchers and practitioners in understanding consumers' attitudes towards foreign products. For over three decades, the so-called country-of-origin effect has been the object of extensive investigation. In 1993, a book edited by Papadopoulos and Heslop presenting only original research on the topic was published. In 1994, Peterson and Jolibert identified 184 articles published in academic journals dealing with country image effects. Country of origin has become an integral part of the repertory of extrinsic cues to product evaluations along with price, brand name, packaging and seller, as opposed to the study of the role of intrinsic qualities of the product such as materials, design, style, workmanship, colour and smell. Country-of-origin studies have been developed for a variety of durable and non-durable consumer products, including cars, electronics, apparel, smoke detectors and pickles. Findings consistently support that consumers pervasively use country-of-origin information as an indicator of quality. The simple manipulation of the country-of-origin or 'Made in' label has been observed to influence people's attitudes, even when subjects are given a chance to see, touch, feel or taste the very same physical product (Nagashima, 1970; Terpstra, 1988; Chao, 1989; Hong and Wyer, 1990; Wall *et al.*, 1991; Johansson *et al.*, 1994; Jaffe and Martinez, 1995; Liefeld *et al.*, 1996; Li *et al.*, 1997; Papadopoulos and Heslop, 2000). Research has also evidenced that national stereotypes affect relationships between manufacturers and foreign clients (Khanna, 1986).

The effect of country of origin has been observed through research using different methods such as survey, experiments and conjoint analysis. In most studies country of origin is used as an independent variable, while attitudes towards a product or a country's product serve as the dependent measure. Perceived quality has also been used as a dependent measure, operationalized in many ways. Some authors contend that relevant quality dimensions are different for different products, and that a given country of origin can be highly regarded in one dimension, such as Volvo's reputation for safety, while it may score low in another, for example serviceability (Garvin, 1987). Questions have also been raised about whether country image would really be a summary construct or should be decompounded in different dimensions (Min Han, 1989) such as country of design and country of assembly (Ahmed and D'Astou, 1999), country of brand (Hulland, 1999), country of product design, country of parts manufacture and country of product assembly (Insch and McBride, 1998).

Another line of investigation concerns the impact of the country of origin on highly valued global brands, such as Sony, Honda and Daimler–Mercedes. The topic has practical implications given the fact that, for cost or logistical reasons, global marketers constantly relocate manufacturing facilities or create new ones to better serve local, regional or global markets. Some studies report that country-of-origin information can be less important when other indicators of quality exist (Heslop and Liefeld, 1988; Chao, 1989; D'Astou and Ahmed, 1992). For example, a global brand such as Sony could counteract a negative effect of country of origin (Tse and Lee, 1993), but the opposite can also happen, namely people think less of Sony when it is produced in a country of low esteem.

Some investigators suggest that country-of-origin effects can only be understood with respect to ethnocentrism (Brodowsky, 1998). Most studies using the construct ethnocentrism apply the CETSCALE developed by Shimp and Sharma (1987). One example of this is the Malinchismo effect (Bailey *et al.*, 1997). In Mexico the term Malinchista designates betrayers of Mexico, those who purchase foreign products and devaluate the Mexican identity. The name comes from a Mexican woman known as La Malinche who served as interpreter to

Cortez during the Spanish invasion in 1519. La Malinche became Cortez's confidant and mistress and helped him to defeat the Aztec King Montezuma II. Extending the understanding of the ethnocentrism effect, Klein *et al.* (1998) researched how animosity towards a foreign nation would affect negatively the purchase of products. To this end they investigated the attitudes of Chinese consumers towards Japan and Japanese products. The authors argue that ethnocentrism and animosity have different implications for perceptions of product quality. Animosity is a country-specific construct, whereas ethnocentrism is described as people viewing their own in-group as central and rejecting what is alien, unfamiliar. Examples of animosity would include Jewish consumers avoiding German products, discussed by Hirschman (1981), and Australian and New Zealand consumers boycotting French products in protest against nuclear tests in the South Pacific.

Other studies have investigated a number of possible mediators of the country-of-origin effect. Motivation has been studied as a possible one and research supports that country-of-origin effect is more likely to occur when consumers are under low motivation (Gurhan-Canli and Maheswaran, 2000a). Researchers have also investigated the role of cultural dimensions in the country-of-origin effect. For example, individualism and collectivism have been used to explain why consumers prefer home country products over imported ones even when provided with information that the foreign product is superior (Gurhan-Canli and Maheswaran, 2000b). In conclusion, extensive research has supported the impact of country of origin on attitudes towards foreign products. Export promotion authorities in many countries recognize that their country's reputation constitutes an important asset to be managed.

Marketing countries and managing their brands

In a world of over six billion people living in nearly 191 independent states (and in many others still fighting for their sovereignty) the challenge of building a nation's wealth has become a critical business arena. Approximately 80 per cent of the world's population lives in the third world, most of them in poverty. Problems such as low living standards, population growth, job shortage and infrastructure are plaguing nations worldwide (Kotler *et al.*, 1997). The challenge of national economic development has gone beyond the limits of public policy. The new economic order has transformed economic development into a market challenge as well. Nations compete with other nations and strive to devise sources of competitive advantage (Porter, 1989). Thus, today there are more reasons why nations must manage and control their branding.

The need to attract tourists, factories, companies and talented people, and to find markets for their exports requires that countries adopt strategic marketing management tools and conscious branding.

Strategic place marketing concerns the enhancement of a country's position in the global marketplace. It requires understanding the environmental forces that may affect marketability, that is, the strengths and weaknesses of the country to compete with others, such as the size of domestic market, access to regional trade areas, education of the population, tax incentives, skilled labour, cost of labour, security and others. It also entails monitoring the external environment, that is, a dynamic understanding of opportunities and threats, as well as the competitive forces in the environment. The process must involve government, citizens and businesses, all with a shared vision. It requires setting and delivering the incentives and managing the factors that may affect place buyers' decisions, including image, attractions, infrastructure and people. The following subsections will deal with different tasks of country brand management, namely, managing the image, attracting tourists, attracting factories and companies, and seeking new market opportunities.

Managing the image

Why do many more tourists visit Greece than Turkey? The Turkish claim that they have longer coasts, less polluted waters and as many superb archaeological sites. Still, an overwhelmingly larger number of vacationers seeking sun and antiquities pick Greece instead of the neighbouring Mediterranean country. Turkey has tried to reposition the country and manage its troubled image. It has hired a public relations firm to promote the country worldwide as a major democracy, quite different from the image of a human rights violator spread many years ago by the film *Midnight Express*. Tourism is a pivotal industry to Turkey's economy and a large-scale international campaign has been implemented to make tourists perceive the 'Turkey' brand as closer to Greece's position (Kotler *et al.*, 1999).

Assessing a brand's image and how it compares to its competitors' images is a necessary step to design the country's marketing strategy. Today there are many reasons why nations must manage and control their branding. The need for attracting tourists and factories and companies requires conscious branding strategies for the different target groups. However, some of the branding may be in conflict; for example, when Ireland wants to attract tourists (beautiful country image) and software experts (high-tech image). 'Strategic image management (SIM) is the ongoing process of researching a place's image among its audiences, segmenting and targeting its specific image and its demographic audiences, positioning the place's benefits to support an existing image or create a new image, and communicating those benefits to the target audiences' (Kotler *et al.*, 1993, pp. 142–3). To be effective, the desired image must be close to reality, believable, simple, appealing and distinctive (there are already too many 'friendly places' out there). In this task, there are several tools available to brand managers. One is a catchy slogan such as 'Spain – everything under the sun', 'Flanders – Europe's best business location', 'Miami – financial capital of South America' and 'Scotland – silicon glen'. Visual images or symbols also play a role, such as the Eiffel Tower (Paris/France), Big Ben (London/ England), Red Square (Moscow/Russia), the Statue of Liberty (New York/ USA) and the Corcovado-Christ Statue (Rio de Janeiro/Brazil). Events and deeds are also strongly connected to places and used to promote a country's image, such as the Oktoberfest (Germany), Carnival (Brazil) and Wimbledon Tournament (England).

Confronting a negative image can be an arduous challenge. The brand manager has no control over environmental factors that may keep tourists and investors away, such as natural disasters, political turmoil and economic downturns. Even more difficult can be controlling how the media and the press disseminate a country's problem, often creating or perpetuating stereotypes. A Turkish spokesperson once said that Turkey receives much worse press than it deserves. In some instances, managers mistakenly try to fix the country's image without fixing the problems that gave rise to it. No amount of advertising or public relations will make an unsafe place safer, for example. Attracting tourists to the place without fixing the problem will lead visitors to badmouth the country and worsen its image. To improve a country's image, it may be easier to create new positive associations than trying to refute old ones. When many people hear the name Chicago, the Bulls and Michael Jordan come more often to mind than Al Capone.

Attracting tourists

In the 1990s, according to the World Tourism Organization (WTO), international tourism arrivals grew at an average rate of 4.3 per cent a year. In 2002, international tourism grew by 3.1 per cent, the number of international tourism arrivals reaching a total of 715 million (WTO, 2003). Furthermore, travel and tourism generate directly and indirectly 11.7 per cent of global gross domestic product (GDP) and nearly 200 million jobs (WTO, 2001). By 2020, the number of people travelling internationally is forecast to increase to 1.56 billion (WTO, 2000) and the revenue from international tourism should gross more than $2 trillion (ECPAT, 1999). Tourism creates direct and indirect jobs in hotels, restaurants, consulting, transportation and training; it increases tax revenues; and it helps in the exporting of local products. These benefits do not come without a price, however. Tourism has been criticized for the destruction of the natural environment and threats to local cultures (Kotler *et al.*, 1997). Country brand managers must understand that different places attract different tourists. The tourism market can be segmented by the attractions that tourists seek, such as natural beauty, sun, adventure, gaming, events/sports or culture/history. The market can also be segmented by areas, regions or locations, by seasons, by customer's characteristics or by benefits (Kotler *et al.*, 1993, 1999). To be successful in the tourism industry a country must be very specific about what it wants to market and to whom.

Countries with natural beauty, archaeological sites or a strong culture and history will attract natural tourists, those drawn to the existing features of the place. If too few natural attractions exist, the country needs to undertake investment marketing to build attractions or to promote events that will attract tourists. Money also has to be spent to build an adequate infrastructure, safety and services. Tourist managers must undertake research to understand the values that tourists seek as users (performance, social and emotional values), as buyers (convenience and personalization) and as payers (price and credit). The competitive environment must also be meticulously analysed. Consumers have literally thousands of destination choices. They will be drawn to destinations that they perceive to offer the best value either because the destinations offer the most benefits or because they are inexpensive or more accessible.

Tourism requires image making and branding grounded in the place's reality. The tourist manager can use different tools. France ran a campaign to persuade French people to display a warmer attitude towards tourists. Moreover, effective promotional campaigns do not necessarily require huge budgets. For example, in 1998, Foote, Cone & Belding developed an inexpensive and effective campaign for the Jamaica Tourist Board. On its way to the 1998 World Cup in France, to promote Jamaica as a friendly place, the Jamaican soccer team – called the Reggae Boys – took the largest soccer ball ever, about five storeys high, from Jamaica's capital, Kingston, to public spaces in different cities, such as New York, London and lastly Paris. In each place, people were asked to sign the ball and wish good luck to the Reggae Boys. With a modest investment of $886 000, the campaign received media space valued at over $5 million. In 1999, Mediaweek (see Consoli, J. (1999)) granted it the 'Best campaign spending $1 million or less award'. Jamaica received 33 600 more visitors than in the previous year and had an increase in tourist revenues of $50 million (Consoli, 1999). Famous residents, events and new attractions can also help to build or revamp a destination's image. The ultramodern Guggenheim Museum in Bilbao, Spain, has given a strong facelift to the city of Bilbao and has helped to attract visitors and new investors. Hosting sports events such as the Olympics can give another lift to a country's image. In spite of tourism's importance, a country cannot expect the income generated by tourism to solve all of its problems. On the contrary, the country may first need to solve its problems to be able to generate the wanted tourism income.

Attracting factories and companies

In 1996, Intel Corporation's worldwide site location team was asked to make a recommendation about where the company should place its first plant in Latin America. Numerous countries fiercely competed to be the recipient of the $300–500 million investment, money that would bring in new jobs, taxes, complementary industries and new exports (100 per cent of the production would be exported to the USA). It could also leverage the confidence of other global investors in the country. The analysis took several months of hard work by a number of highly ranked Intel executives. It included several field trips before the team was ready to recommend a shortlist of four countries: Brazil, Chile, Mexico and Costa Rica. The final choice was not Brazil, then the largest Latin American economy and market. Nor did Mexico, a member of the North American Free Trade Agreement (NAFTA) and the most accessible location to Intel's headquarters, become the choice. Chile, the fastest growing and most stable economy of the continent with one of the best and least expensive telecommunication services in the world, also lost out. Surprisingly, Costa Rica won the prize (Nelson, 1999).

Costa Rica, the smallest of the four finalists, a country with only 3.5 million people, ended up winning the Intel plant. The country was not even on the original shortlist. Costa Rica won because it used many of the principles of place marketing. It also counted on the great job of the officials of Coalición Costarricense de Iniciativas para el Desarrolo (CINDE, Costa Rica's Investment Promotion Agency). CINDE followed the recommendation of the World Bank to target the electronics industry. A consultant from the Irish Development Agency (IDA), that country's successful investment promotion agency, also assisted in Costa Rica's effort. Instead of waiting for Intel's questions, CINDE's officials anticipated them and provided the information that Intel may need. The pursuit for Intel's investment involved the active participation of many people, including business professors at the Instituto Centroamericano de Administración de Empresas (INCAE), state ministers and the dean of the Instituto Tecnológico de Costa Rica (ITCR). Even the country's former President

Table 4.1   Basic information sought by a business searching for a location

Local labour market
Access to customer and supplier markets
Availability of development sites facilities and infrastructure
Transportation
Education and training opportunities
Quality of life
Business climate
Access to R&D facilities
Capital availability
Taxes and regulations

Source: Kotler *et al*. (1993, p. 232).

José Maria Figueres became involved and personally discussed the business with Intel's executives. President Figueres, who was educated at West Point and pursued graduate studies at Harvard, had been committed to attracting high-technology investments to Costa Rica, rather than investments based on cheap labour or the exploitation of national resources (Nelson, 1999).

One of the most interesting facets of place marketing deals with countries' efforts to attract new factories and business investments. These are expected to create new jobs and economic growth, with an overall benefit to the country's economy. Because of the dramatic improvements in telecommunication and transportation services worldwide, global companies are now searching for new locations that may bring down their costs. This has transformed supply chain management, logistics and site selection in core competencies within global companies. Country marketers must understand how companies make their site selection. Usually they begin the process by choosing a region in which to invest (e.g. Latin America) and collecting information about the potential country candidates (Table 4.1). In this phase, each country must be able to provide accurate and reliable information. Better, it should anticipate informational needs, as CINDE did in the case of Intel's site selection. The country should understand the locational characteristics that companies are seeking as they relate to labour, tax climate, amenities, higher education, schools, regulation, energy, communication and business (Table 4.2).

Today countless countries and cities are trying to attract high-tech industries. One of the reasons that Costa Rica could attract Intel investments was the high level of technical education in the country and the number of electronics firms already located there (Nelson, 1999). As Harvard Professor Michael Porter (1998) argues, competing or complementary industries tend to form clusters of excellence that build productivity. The rivalry and competitive pressures among

Table 4.2   Locational characteristics: old and new

Characteristics	Old	New
Labour	Low cost, unskilled	Quality, highly skilled
Tax climate	Low taxes, low service	Modest taxes, high services
Incentives	Least cost production, cheap land and labour	Value-added adaptable labour force, professionals
Amenities	Housing and transportation	Culture, recreation, museums, shopping, airport
Schools	Availability	Quality schools
Higher education	Not key	Quality schools and research facilities
Regulation	Minimum	Compatible quality of life and business flexibility
Energy	Cost/availability	Dependability/reliability
Communication	Assumed	Technology access
Business	Aggressive chamber of commerce, etc.	Partnerships

Source: Kotler *et al.* (1999, p. 227).

companies located in these clusters force them to innovate. That would explain concentrations of similar businesses in places such as the Silicon Valley (IT and software) and New Jersey (pharmaceuticals). Countries must define the industries that they wish to build and plan sites to appeal to these specific industries from the very beginning.

To compete, countries must be prepared to offer strong financial incentives to lure prospects. These incentives include tax exemption, work training, infrastructure investments, interest subsidies and even stakeholder participation. Attracted by the potential proceeds of new factories and businesses, some nations fail to analyse the true cost of successfully attracting a company or plant. Incentive wars have led to a situation in which each created job costs tens of thousands of dollars that may never return to the community. The inducements can far exceed the benefits that the country might receive. For example, in the late 1990s a new governor of the southern Brazilian state of Rio Grande do Sul questioned the incentives offered by his predecessor to an automobile manufacturer. Withdrawing from the deal, Ford decided to build the new facility in the state of Bahia, which offered Ford even more inducements to attract the business. It is important to remember, however, that studies have shown that although government inducements play an important role in the site decision process, they rarely determine the final result. Proximity to consumer or supplier markets, qualified labour and confidence in the administration are likely to be more crucial aspects in the development of the decision. Numerous cases also show that the decision is also highly influenced by the market performance of the promotion agency and the commitment of local authorities.

Seeking new market opportunities

An infinite number of out-of-the-box ideas exists that places can use to take advantage of further market opportunities. In 2003, for example, New York's mayor announced the nomination of the first city chief marketing officer (Kleinfield, 2003). His job was described as being 'to offer the city and its contents and inimitable mystique as a brand available for corporate purchase.' Business opportunities envisioned by New York included having city agencies endorsing products, having corporate names associated or exposed in landmarks, franchising names of neighbourhoods to all sorts of products, sponsoring credit cards that allow holders to redeem points to be used in the city's attractions, and charging fees for people and companies willing to name public places. New York's example shows how with creativity places can move beyond the traditional 'marketing place' arena and replicate the market success of brands such as NBA and NASCAR.

Conclusion

A great deal of empirical research has attested that country images are important extrinsic clues in product evaluations. They are familiar, they elicit associations and they can influence product evaluations and purchase decisions. Country images can lend a positive reputation to a whole category such as French wines or perfumes, or even brand it, as in the case of Café de Colombia. Beyond serving as brand names, countries can be products as well. They compete in the market for tourists, factories, businesses and talented people. Thus countries must embark on more conscious country branding. This requires the following strategic management approach:

1. The country needs to carry out a SWOT analysis to determine its chief strengths, weaknesses, opportunities and threats.
2. The country then chooses some industries, personalities, natural landmarks and historical events that could provide a basis for strong branding and story telling.
3. The country should then develop an umbrella concept that would cover and be consistent with all of its separate branding activities. Among the possible

concepts would be a country of pleasure, quality, security, honesty or progress, or other concepts.

4. The country then allocates sufficient national funds to each branding activity deemed to have a potentially large impact.
5. The country creates export controls to make sure that every exported product is reliable and delivers the promised level of performance.

Acknowledgement

An earlier version of this chapter first appeared in *The Journal of Brand Management*, April 2002; 9(4/5): 249–261.

References

Aaker, D. A. (1991) *Managing Brand Equity: Capitalizing on the Value of a Brand Name*. Simon & Schuster Trade.

Agbonifoh, B. A. and Elimimiam, J. U. (1999) Attitudes of developing countries towards country-of-origin products in a era of multiple brands. *Journal of International Consumer Marketing* 11(4): 97–116.

Ahmed, S. A. and D'Astou, A. (1999) Product-country images in Canada and in People's Republic of China. *Journal of International Consumer Marketing* 11(1): 5–22.

Bailey, W., Pineres, G. and Amin, S. (1997) Country of origin attitudes in Mexico: the Malinchismo effect. *Journal of International Consumer Marketing* 9(3): 25–41.

Brodowsky, G. H. (1998) The effects of country of origin and country of assembly on evaluations about automobiles and attitudes toward buying them: a comparison between low and high ethnocentric consumers. *Journal of International Consumer Marketing* 10(3): 85–113.

Chao, P. (1989) The impact of country affiliation on the credibility of product attribute claims. *Journal of Advertising Research* 29(2): 35–41.

Chicago Tribune (1995) In love with Juan Valdez at U.S. Open. *Chicago Tribune* 3, 4, 12 September.

Consoli, J. (1999) Best campaign spending $1 million or less: Foote, Cone & Belding. *Mediaweek and Brandweek* (24 May), 40(21): P22.

Cordell, V. (1993) Interaction effects of country-of-origin with branding, price, and perceived performance risk. *Journal of International Consumer Marketing* 5(2): 5–16.

D'Astou, A. and Ahmed, S. A. (1992) Multi-cue evaluation of made-in concept: a conjoint analysis study in Belgium. *Journal of Euromarketing* 2(1), pages 9–29.

ECPAT (1999) *ECPAT International Newsletter*: Issue No. 28, ECPAT, 1 August, based on WTO projections. http://www.ecpat.net/eng/Ecpat_inter/IRC/ articles.asp?articleID=134&NewsID=20 (viewed on 14 January 2001).

FNC (2003) *History of the Logo: Juan Valdez*. The National Federation of Coffee Growers., http://juanvaldez.com/menu/logo.html (viewed on 18 August 2003).

Garvin, D. A. (1987) Competing on the eight dimensions of quality. *Harvard Business Review* 65 (November/December): 101–109.

Gurhan-Canli, Z. and Maheswaran, D. (2000a) Determinants of country-of-origin evaluations. *Journal of Consumer Research* 27: 96–108.

Gurhan-Canli, Z. and Maheswaran, D. (2000b) Cultural variations in country of origin effects. *Journal of Marketing Research* 37: 309–317.

Heslop, L. and Liefeld, J. P. (1988) Impact of country-of-origin on consumer judgments in multi-cue situations: a co-variance analysis. Working Paper No. 88-101, Carleton University.

Hirschman, E. C. (1981) American Jewish ethnicity: its relationship to some selected aspects of consumer behavior. *Journal of Marketing* 45: 102–110.

Hong, S. and Wyer, R. S. (1990) Country of origin, attributes and product evaluations: the effects of time delay between information and judgements, *Journal of Consumer Research* 17: 277–288.

Hulland, J. S. (1999) The effects of country-of-brand and brand name on product evaluations and consideration: a cross-country comparison. *Journal of International Consumer Marketing* 11(1): 23–40.

Insch, G. S. and McBride, B. (1998) Decomposing the country-of-origin construct: an empirical test of country of design, country of parts and country of assembly. *Journal of International Consumer Marketing* 10(4): 69–91.

Jaffe, E. D. and Martinez, C. R. (1995) Mexican consumers' attitudes towards domestic and foreign products. *Journal of International Consumer Marketing* 7(3): 7–27.

Johansson, J. K., Ronkainen, I. and Czinkota, M. I. R. (1994) Negative country-of-origin effects: the case of the new Russia. *Journal of International Business Studies* 25: 157–177.

Khanna, S. R. (1986) Asian companies and the country stereotype paradox: an empirical study. *Columbia Journal of World Business* 21(2): 29–38.

Klein, G., Ettenson, R. and Morris, M. D. (1998) The animosity model of foreign product purchase: an empirical test in the People's Republic of China. *Journal of Marketing* 62: 89–100.

Kleinfield, N. R. (2003) Battery park, get ready for the bunny; branding in New York is just the beginning. *New York Times* (6 April): A29.

Kotler, P., Haider, D. H. and Rein, I. (1993) *Marketing Places: Attracting Investment, Industry, and Tourism to Cities, States and Nations.* Free Press.

Kotler, P., Jatusripitak, S. and Maesincee, S. (1997) *The Marketing of Nations.* New York: Simon & Schuster Trade.

Kotler, P., Asplund, C., Rein, I. and Haider, D. H. (1999) *Marketing Places Europe: Attracting Investment, Industry, and Tourism To European Cities, Communities, States and Nations.* Financial Times/Prentice Hall.

Lassar, W., Mittal, B. and Sharma, A. (1995) Measuring customer-based brand equity. *Journal of Consumer Marketing* 12(4): 11–19.

Leclerc, F., Schmitt, B. H. and Dube, L. (1994) Foreign branding and its effects on product perceptions and attitudes. *Journal of Marketing Research* 31: 263–270.

Li, Z. G., Fu, S. and Murray, L. W. (1997) Country and product images: the perceptions of consumers of People's Republic of China. *Journal of International Consumer Marketing* 10(1/2): 115–139.

Liefeld, J. P., Heslop, L. A., Papadopoulos, N. and Walls, M. (1996) Dutch consumers use of intrinsic, country-of-origin, and price cues in product evaluation and choice. *Journal of Consumer Marketing* 1(9): 57–81.

Min Han, C. (1989) Country image: halo or summary construct? *Journal of Marketing Research* 26: 222–229.

Nagashima, A. (1970) A comparison of Japanese and US attitudes toward foreign products. *Journal of Marketing* 34: 68–74.

Nelson, R. (1999) Intel's site selection decision in Latin America. *Thunderbird Case Series*, A06-99-0016.

Papadopoulos, N. and Heslop, L. A. (eds) (1993) *Product and Country Images: Impact and Role in International Marketing.* Haworth Press.

Papadopoulos, N. and Heslop, L. A. (2000) Countries as brands. *Ivey Business Journal* 65(2): 30–36.

Peterson, R. and Jolibert, A. (1994) A quantitative analysis of country-of-origin effects. Working Paper. Austin, TX: University of Texas.

Porter, M. (1989) *The Competitive Advantage of Nations.* New York: Simon & Schuster Trade.

Porter, M. (1998) Clusters and the new economics of competition. *Harvard Business Review* (November/December): 77–90.

Shimp, T. and Sharma, S. (1987) Consumer ethnocentrism: construction and validation of the CETSCALE. *Journal of Marketing Research* 24: 280–289.

Shimp, T. A. and Saeed, S. (1993) Countries and their products: a cognitive structure perspective. *Journal of the Academy of Marketing Science* 21: 323–330.

Terpstra, V. (1988) Country-of-origin effects for uni-national and bi-national products. *Journal of International Business Studies* 19: 235–255.

Tse, D. K. and Lee, W. (1993) Removing negative country images: effects of deposition, branding, and product experience. *Journal of International Marketing* 1(4): 25–48.

Wall, M., Liefeld, J. and Heslop, L. A. (1991) Impact of country-of-origin cues on consumer judgments in multi-cue situations: a covariance analysis. *Academy of Marketing Science* 19: 105–113.

Wang, C. K. and Lamb, C. W. (1983) The impact of selected environmental forces upon consumers' willingness to buy foreign products. *Journal of the Academy of Marketing Science* 11: 71–85.

WTO (2000) Tourism market trends 2000: long-term prospects. http://www.worldtourism.org/market_research/facts&figures/market_trends/long-t_prospects.htm (viewed on 18 August 2003).

WTO (2001) Special Report Number 18. 14 January 2002. http://www.world-tourism.org/newsroom/Releases/more_releases/December2001/WTO_TT RC_Summ.pdf (viewed on 15 July 2001).

WTO (2003) World tourism in 2002: better than expected. http://www.world-tourism.org/newsroom/Releases/2003/jan/numbers2002.htm (viewed on 18 August 2003).

Part 2

Destination Branding Challenges

5

Meeting the destination branding challenge

Nigel Morgan and Annette Pritchard

Introduction

A destination brand can be developed in a variety of ways, most obviously in advertising, through direct marketing, personal selling, on websites and in brochures, but also through public and media relations, and through the co-operation of destination marketing organizations (DMOs) with journalists, event organizers and film-makers. Moreover, place promotion, defined as 'the conscious use of publicity and marketing to communicate selective images of specific geographic localities or areas to a target audience' (Gold and Ward, 1994, p. 2), not only involves advertising and publicity, but also encompasses 'flagship' developments and 'spotlight' events in the arts, media, leisure, heritage, retailing or sports industries (Ward, 1998).

There is now a sizeable industry-focused literature covering destination marketing issues from stakeholder involvement (e.g. Morgan *et al.*, 2003) to marketing management (e.g. Kotler *et al.*, 1993; Ritchie and Crouch, 2000) and destination branding (e.g. Morgan *et al.*, 2002). It is well established that a destination is not a product (see Buhalis, 2000; Morgan and Pritchard, 2000) and, while there are significant opportunities in the imaginative and responsible application of classical marketing approaches to places, destinations cannot (and should not) be promoted as if they were soap powder. Simon Anholt (1998) argues that a more useful metaphor than 'country as product brand' is 'country as corporate brand'. Moreover, he further suggests that some of the misconceptions surrounding the possibilities of destination or country branding spring from the notion that today's marketers can actually 'brand' or 'rebrand' a place. More accurately, what they are attempting to do is to co-ordinate an existing brand relationship, to work with and often gradually to change existing perceptions (and misconceptions) of places. In this task, however, they face a number of key challenges, many of which are beyond their control.

Destination branding

Branding is perhaps the most powerful marketing weapon available to contemporary destination marketers confronted by tourists who are increasingly seeking lifestyle fulfilment and experience rather than recognizing differentiation in the more tangible elements of the destination product such as accommodation and attractions. Most destinations have superb five-star resorts and attractions, every country claims a unique culture, landscape and heritage, each place describes itself as having the friendliest people, and high standards of customer service and facilities are now expected. As a result, the need for destinations to create a unique identity – to differentiate themselves from their competitors – is more critical than ever. Indeed, it has become the basis for survival within a globally competitive marketplace dominated by a handful of leading destinations which attract over two-thirds of the worldwide tourism market (Piggott, 2001).

All successful brands have social, emotional and identity value to users: they have personalities and enhance the perceived utility, desirability and quality of a product (Kotler and Gertner, 2002). When consumers make choices about products, including destinations, they are making lifestyle statements since they are buying into an emotional relationship (Urdde, 1999; Sheth *et al.*, 1999). Choice of vacation destination has become a significant lifestyle indicator for today's consumers and the places where they choose to spend their increasingly squeezed vacation time and hard-earned income have to be emotionally appealing, with high conversational and celebrity value. The battle for consumers in tomorrow's destination marketplace will be fought not over price but over hearts and minds, and this is how places have moved into territories previously reserved for consumer brands.

Brands have been conceptualized in four key ways, as communication devices (e.g. de Chernatony and Riley, 1998), perceptual entities (e.g. Louro and Cunha, 2001), value enhancers (e.g. Wood, 2000) and relationships (e.g. de Chernatony and Segal-Horn, 2001). Broadly speaking, in marketing terms a brand represents a unique combination of product characteristics and added values, both functional and non-functional, which have taken on a relevant meaning that is inextricably linked to that brand, awareness of which may be conscious or intuitive (Macrae *et al.*, 1995). Brand advantage is secured through communication that highlights the specific benefits of a product, culminating in an overall impression of a superior brand. The image the product creates in the consumer's mind, how it is positioned, is crucial to its ultimate success.

Brand managers position their brands so that they are perceived by the consumer to occupy a niche in the marketplace occupied by no other brand; thus for marketers, the value of a successful brand lies in its potential to reduce substitutability. Brand managers differentiate their product by stressing attributes that they claim will match their target markets' needs more closely than other brands and then they create a product image consistent with the perceived self-image of the targeted consumer segment (Shiffman and Kanuk, 2000). Consumers have their own 'brand wardrobes' from which they make selections to communicate, reflect and reinforce associations, statements and memberships; in effect, 'consumers enrobe themselves with brands, partly for what they do, but more for what they help express about their emotions, personalities and roles' (de Chernatony, 1993, p. 178).

Given the nature of this brand–consumer connection, there is increased focus among marketers on differentiation through relationships and emotional appeals, rather than through discernible, tangible benefits (Westwood *et al.*, 1999). Thus, 'it is our perceptions – our beliefs and our feelings about a brand that are most important' (Lury, 1998, p. 4). However, mere emotion is not enough, the key is to develop a strong brand that holds unique associations for the consumer which can be articulated as a clear point of difference (Hallberg, 1995). Such is the importance of this product positioning that it has been described as the essence of marketing, and different consumer meanings can be assigned to the same product via different positioning strategies, depending on the audience and stage in the brand life cycle.

The challenges of destination branding

No matter where destinations are in the life cycle, by comparison to branded products and services, managers in destination organizations face peculiar branding
challenges. In particular, they have small budgets, exert little management control
and are vulnerable to both external and internal political pressures, with many
stakeholders to consider. Most DMOs have very limited budgets and yet they have
to market globally, competing not just with other destinations, but also with other
global brands. Proctor and Gamble, the world's biggest advertiser, spends millions
each year promoting its various brands, and countries such as Croatia, Vietnam
and Egypt still have to vie with them for consumer mindshare in a crowded environment characterized by spiralling media costs. One corporate giant such as Sony
probably spends as much on its annual global advertising budget as the combined
totals of most of the world's national destination organizations.

In addition to their limited resources, DMOs all operate in a very volatile
external environment. While every product is affected by external change,
tourism is particularly vulnerable to political strife, economic downswings, terrorism and environmental disasters. In today's world this seems more apparent
than ever, with the Iraq conflict and terrorist attacks in Turkey, Saudi Arabia,
Bali, Kenya and Madrid, severe acute respiratory syndrome (SARS), September
11, the UK foot and mouth and bovine spongiform encephalopathy (BSE) outbreaks, volcanic eruptions and hurricanes in the Caribbean, political instability
in Fiji, oil spills off the Galapagos Islands and the Asian economic collapse of
the late 1990s. The list of recent crises that have damaged international travel
to particular destinations seems never ending. Moreover, when it is a small
country with a limited share of voice in the global media that is affected, the
results can be devastating. Although tourists may resume 'normal' travel habits
after a single terrorist event, it is becoming clear that investors may take longer
to return to what they perceive as unreliable business climates. In addition, sustained terrorism, war or political instability and the consequent negative media
coverage can cause long-term damage to a destination's image.

Take the example of Nepal in southern Asia. A remote, landlocked country
only slightly larger than Arkansas, Nepal is among the poorest and least developed
countries in the world, with over 40 per cent of its population living below
the poverty line. However, as home to eight of the world's ten highest peaks
(including Mount Everest), tourism has become a significant foreign currency
earner for Nepal and during the 1990s its tourism sector enjoyed an unpreced-
ented period of growth, with international arrivals peaking at 492 000 in 1999.
During 2001–2002, however, the country's tourism industry collapsed. Arrivals

fell by over 20 per cent in the wake of a highly publicized airline hijacking, the subsequent five-month suspension of key flights to Nepal's international airport and a series of internal political crises culminating in a declaration of a state of emergency in 2001. Combined with the legacy of 11 September 2001, these incidents of terrorism, constitutional crisis and violence between the government and Maoist insurgents all contributed to a major downturn in international tourism under the spotlight of the global media. Only in 2003 did international tourism to the country begin to recover, partly as a result of Nepal's successful staging of celebrations of the 50th anniversary of the 1953 conquest of Everest (Baral *et al.*, 2004).

Such external pressures on marketing activities not only highlight tourism's vulnerability to a hostile environment, but also remind us that destinations are a composite of a bundle of different components, including accommodation and catering establishments; tourist attractions; arts, entertainment and cultural venues; and the natural environment (Buhalis, 2000; Ritchie and Crouch, 2000). Destination marketers have almost no control over these different aspects and a diverse range of agencies and companies are stakeholders in the marketing of a place. Public sector destination marketers have to reconcile an array of local and regional interests, and craft promotional appeals acceptable to a range of constituencies. These vary from local and national government agencies, through environmental groups and trade bodies, to tour operators and airlines (see Morgan *et al.*, 2003).

Some of the reasons why Brand Oregon, designed to be inclusive of tourism and economic development, began to fall apart in the late 1980s, included: the tourism sector's resistance to direction from the top; the failure by some economic development organizations to see the connections between Oregon's lifestyle and business opportunities; and the tourism regions' reluctance to produce advertising and publications consistent with the state's branded campaign (Curtis, 2001). In addition to such compromising of the creative process of marketing destinations, destination brand building is frequently undermined by the short-termism of the tourism organizations' political masters. A destination brand's lifespan is a longer term proposition than the careers of most politicians and Julie Curtis of the Oregon Tourism Commission urges destination marketers to 'stay the course' and resist making changes too quickly, since 'it takes many years to establish a brand image, establish name recognition and develop strong awareness of a destination or product' (Curtis, 2001, p. 81).

Nowhere is the paradox of public policy and market forces more sharply defined than in destination branding. Political considerations have compromised many a creative execution; as Bob Garfield, editor of Advertising Age and long-time advertising critic, has said of destination advertising:

> *When you look at the ads … you can see transcripts of the arguments at the tourist boards … the membership of which all wanted their own interests served … you can see the destruction of the advertising message as a result of the politics* (Garfield, 1998).

In this sense, successful destination branding is about achieving a balance between applying cutting-edge solutions to a marketing problem and the real politick of managing local, regional and national politics. The real success stories reflect destination brands that have been able to resist the political dynamic (which is exerted at all levels of the political scene). These are brands that have strong marketing heritages and are consistent, but at the same time evolve and appear continually contemporary and fresh. This is easy to write but difficult to achieve and that is why the same destinations are constantly cited as classic examples of cohesive, long-term branding, because they are a rare breed and they succeed against the odds. Thus, Ireland has been running the same basic brand proposition in its various campaigns for some decades and while marketing directors and executives change the brand values remain constant.

Branding destination: making it happen

As we have seen, limited budgets, the lack of management control, and internal and external pressures pose unique challenges for destination marketers. Yet the creation of brand saliency – the development of an emotional relationship with the consumer – can hold the key to destination differentiation. In the 1980s there were several highly successful marketing campaigns that centred on a consistent communications proposition. New York's 'I love NY' and the 'Glasgow's miles better' campaigns are two of the best known. In these, and in many other instances, the campaigns focused on logos and slogans, but they were less branding initiatives and could be more accurately termed 'sloganeering'. In building a meaningful destination brand, the essence is to create an emotional relationship between the destination and potential visitors, as in the current 'Being at one' New Zealand brand position. Here, the branding activities concentrate on conveying the essence or the spirit of the destination (Morgan and Pritchard, 1999).

Countries often showcase their history, their culture and their beautiful scenery in their marketing, but many destinations have these attributes and it is critical to build a brand on something that uniquely connects a destination to the consumer now or has the potential to do so in the future. It must also be a proposition that the competition wants and may be able to copy, but that they cannot surpass or usurp. For example, other world cities can claim to be romantic or spiritual, but only Rome (or more strictly, the Vatican) is The Eternal City: it has that epithet, it had it first and no other place can now claim it. Virginia in the USA has had phenomenal success with its Virginia is for Lovers campaign, but no destination can surpass Paris's associations with romance. Whatever proposition is used it must also have the potential to evolve in a long-term branding campaign, so it is essential to get it right. However, the point of differentiation must also reflect a promise that can be delivered and that matches expectations. Good destination branding is therefore original and different, but its originality and difference need to be sustainable, believable and relevant. For instance, one destination that has transcended the commodity nature of the product and promised a unique (yet credible) experience is India. There are many exotic countries that a tourist could visit and most have breath-taking scenery and fascinating heritage, yet such is the emotional power of the subcontinent with its poignant history and diverse cultures that its promise to the consumer (seen powerfully in its 1998 campaign) – that a visit to India can actually change you – is sustainable.

If successful, such activities have an impact not only on how the rest of the world regards a place, but also on how that place views itself. This has very much been the case recently in Australia. Here, the achievements of the Sydney 2000 Olympics (in sporting, marketing, operations management and facility design terms), coupled with the ongoing aggressive branding of the country as a whole, has created a new view of Australia as a cosmopolitan, outward-looking country, and many of the country's politicians saw Sydney 2000 as symbolizing the modernization of the Australian economy. It has been estimated that the exposure gained through hosting the Games accelerated Australia's marketing by a decade, as well as generating billions in additional foreign exchange earnings and opening up the country to a new group of visitors (Morse, 2001; Tibbott, 2001; Brown *et al.*, 2002).

Achieving celebrity

Image is all important and how a place is represented can inspire people to visit and revisit it (Coshall, 2000; Tapachai and Waryszak, 2000). Never was the saying 'accentuate the positive and eliminate the negative' more true than in destination branding. Destination branding can help to bridge any gaps between a destination's strengths and potential visitors' perceptions. Place reputations are not made in a vacuum and neither are tourist choices, so place marketers must

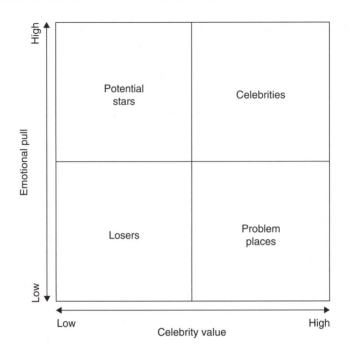

Figure 5.1 The destination celebrity matrix

establish how their destination's image compares with those of its key competitors. How the destination rates according to 'wish you were here?' appeal and celebrity value is critical: do tourists regard it as a fashion accessory, a must-see place on every aspirational traveller's shopping list, or as a fashion faux pas, somewhere with no conversational value and even less status (Figure 5.1)? Figure 5.2 takes this celebrity matrix and illustrates a range of destination brands measured on the axes of emotional appeal and celebrity value. How people relate to any destination brand depends on their own individual interests, opinions and experiences and such positioning maps must be used in conjunction with psychographic analyses of key market segments.

On any positioning map, however, brand winners are those places that are rich in emotional meaning, have great conversation value and hold high anticipation for potential tourists. By comparison, brand losers have little meaning, even less status, virtually no conversation value and zero anticipation for tourists. Problem places are those destinations that are talked about for all the wrong reasons and, far from holding an emotional appeal, actively repel potential tourists. Places that currently offer little emotional pull face an uphill task if they are ever to become destination winners. Other destinations that do have high emotional pull but currently have limited (although growing) celebrity value hold huge untapped

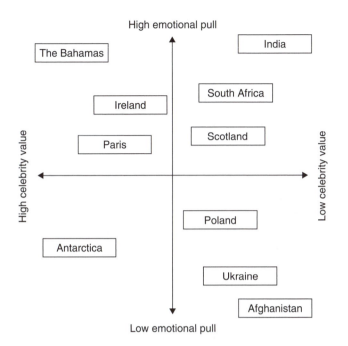

Figure 5.2   The destination brand positioning map

potential and could be tomorrow's winner destination brands (Figure 5.2). Take
the destination of Cuba, officially closed to US tourists since 1960, but still associated with glamour and fashion and fast becoming a popular destination for
European tourists. A number of airlines, cruise and ferry companies are already
anticipating an end to the US travel ban and experts predict that several million
tourists will travel to the island in the first year, many via the new international
airport at Cayo Coco, an island off Cuba's north coast, which was opened in
2003 at a cost of $300 million. The challenge for the marketers of such emer-
ging destinations is to craft identities that convey and build on their emotional
appeal and that will (re)turn them into places with high celebrity value.

The destination brand fashion curve

Recognizing that branding is a two-way process done with and not to the consumer, Weinreich (1999, pp. 25–26) has suggested that instead of thinking in
terms of the traditional product or brand life cycle, brand managers should be
thinking of the S-curve, which charts a brand's life and development through
birth, growth, maturity, decay and death (although of course, the time frames are
elastic and could encompass anything from weeks to centuries). Instead of seeing the S-curve as tracking sales volume over time, managers should consider

it as a series of stages in the brand's relationship with its consumers, revealing useful insights into a brand's communications requirements.

Developing this concept and translating it to tourism destination brands, we can see that at first the market is small and many places become chic in spite of (or owing to) their lack of advertising activities because the destination is exclusive. Here the destination brand is at the beginning of its fashionable phase and its visitors are trendsetters who, although few in numbers, are influential opinion formers. Yet, as the destination becomes famous and loses its cutting-edge appeal, these tourists move onto the next new place since they do not want to be seen somewhere that has become popular and rather passé. In the famous phase, a destination brand's consumers are loyal and affluent, but at any time the destination's brand values may become irrelevant to them, hence the ongoing need to remain fresh and appealing. If the place fails to remain contemporary, it will drift into the familiar zone where everyone knows about the destination, but it has lost its appeal; it has become 'overwarm, cuddly and sentimental, the antithesis of ... cool' (Weinreich, 1999, p. 28). Becoming familiar can ultimately lead a destination to fatigue, to find it difficult to attract lucrative market segments. If it becomes very badly damaged, a destination brand's core values will need to be reassessed and its relevance to target markets redefined and revitalized.

For every success story such as Ireland and Spain, there are numerous destinations that have become fatally fatigued, having failed to maintain long-term marketing and advertising effort, or that have been affected by external change. All brands can show signs of age, needing refreshment in the face of modern competition, and even the most classic of brands need to remain contemporary. Such is the speed of change in today's market, destination brands that fail to evolve are brands that will fail to compete. No destination brand can ever remain static, and marketers need to recognize when a place has reached a point when the brand requires refreshment. Failure to advance and develop the brand will eventually lead to stagnation and ultimately to brand decay (Figure 5.3).

Brand building

The first stage in the process of building or refreshing any destination brand is to establish the core values of the destination and its brand; these should be durable, relevant, communicable and hold saliency for potential tourists (Table 5.1). This should consider just how contemporary or relevant the brand is to today's tourism consumer and how it compares with its key competitors. For instance, when the Oregon Economic Development Department began its revival of

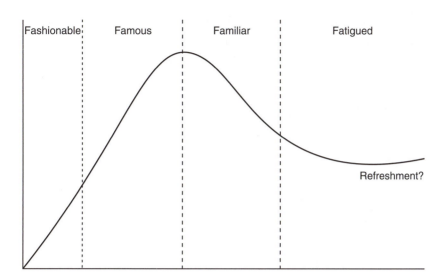

Figure 5.3 The destination brand fashion curve

Table 5.1 The five phases in destination brand building

Phase one	Market investigation, analysis and strategic recommendations
Phase two	Brand identity development
Phase three	Brand launch and introduction: communicating the vision
Phase four	Brand implementation
Phase five	Monitoring, evaluation and review

Brand Oregon in the mid-1990s, it initiated a series of research projects that surveyed local businesses, regional economists, other US states with similar programmes and previous visitors, as well as visitors who had never actually been to the state (Curtis, 2001). This process (similar to recent exercises conducted by the brand developers of, among other places, Switzerland, Hawaii, Wales, Western Australia and New Zealand) assisted Oregon's brand managers to build brand value and salience with existing and potential consumers.

Once this market investigation is complete, the next phase is to develop the brand identity. Of primary importance to this phase are the concepts of the brand benefit pyramid and brand architecture (more of which below). Once the brand's core values have been established, they should underpin and imbue every component of the brand identity, from photography, colour, typography and tone of voice to the brand marque, so that the brand values are cohesively communicated. A brand design style guide, which ensures consistency of message and approach, should also reinforce the brand values. The vision (which must be shared and 'bought into' by all its stakeholders and potential consumers) should be clearly expressed in the brand's core values, which are consistently reinforced through the product and in all marketing communications, both above and below the line, every execution in all media contributes to maintaining brand presence. To be successful in creating an emotional attachment a destination brand has to be:

- credible
- deliverable
- differentiating
- conveying powerful ideas
- enthusing for stakeholders and partners
- resonating with the consumer.

Brand personality and the benefit pyramid

Critical to the success of any destination brand is the extent to which the destination's brand personality interacts with the target markets. Just like people, all brands should be complex and rich. In fact, the most powerful brands are those with the richest personalities, yet complex personalities are quite rare in a world where brand attributes are often arbitrarily and superficially constructed. Traits such as 'friendly', 'natural' and 'contemporary' are popular hoped-for descriptors but they hardly help to build an engaging or aspirational brand. Destination brand building is all about developing a rich, relevant brand personality. 'Developing' is the key word here; successful brands never atrophy, instead they reflect and respond to changes in consumers' lives, and while the brand's core values remain the same, its personality will continue to evolve.

A brand's personality has both a head and a heart: its head refers to the logical brand features, while its heart refers to its emotional benefits and associations. Brand propositions and communications can be based around either a brand's head or its heart: head communications convey a brand's rational values, while heart communications reveal its emotional values and associations. Brand benefit pyramids sum up consumers' relationships with a brand and are frequently established during the consumer research process where consumers are usually asked to describe what features a destination offers and what the place means to them. Using the research, it should then be relatively straightforward to ascertain what particular benefit pyramids consumers associate with the destination in question (Figure 5.4).

The benefit pyramid can be instrumental in helping to distil the essence of a destination brand's advertising proposition. This refers to the point at which

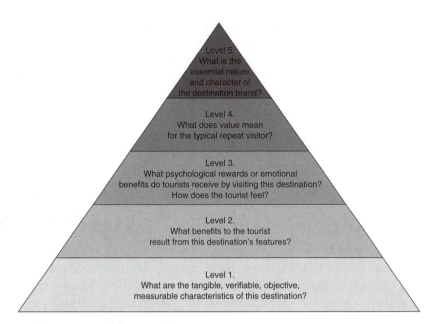

Figure 5.4 The destination brand benefit pyramid

consumer's wants and the destination's benefits and features intersect; any communication (through advertising or public relations) should then encapsulate the spirit of the brand. Many ideas may be initially suggested, but the challenge is to develop a proposition that makes the destination brand relevant, contemporary and appealing, and establishing the brand's architecture can be critical to this process.

Establishing brand architecture

A brand architecture should reflect all the key components of a destination brand, including its positioning, its rational (head) and emotional (heart) benefits and associations, together with its brand personality. A brand's architecture is in essence the blueprint that should guide brand building, development and marketing, and is a device that can be used by all destination brand managers. More and more tourism destinations are looking to establish their brand architecture in order to put themselves ahead of their competitors. When they are whole countries, destinations are often composite brands (being composed of many different places). Yet consumer research that reveals and establishes a destination's brand architecture should enable marketers to see clearly the elements and contributions of these various composite brands. It is a device that is critical to the development of destination suprabrands and sub-brands. Take Britain: it is a destination suprabrand and the sub-brands (Scotland, Wales, London and the

English regions) are both part of, and at the same time, distinct from it. Thus when VisitBritain began the reappraisal of the Britain tourism brand in 2002 in the wake of falling international visitor numbers (fuelled by the high value of sterling, the BSE and foot and mouth outbreaks, and September 11), the realigned positioning had to create a 'whole' that was informed by and yet enriched the constituent parts (Hall, 2004).

One of the most successful destination suprabrands must surely be that of Spain. Once a destination with an image for poor-quality service and facilities, in the early 1980s the Spanish government began what was to become one of the most consistent and successful brand-building exercises in destination marketing, supported by a significant financial commitment, which is ongoing today. The suprabrand of Spain attracts over 50 million visitors a year and has the world's third largest promotional budget for tourism. While Espana is the main brand, its cities (such as Barcelona, Madrid, Valencia and Seville) and regions (such as Andalusia and Galicia) are the second-level brands. At the country level Spain has remained remarkably constant in its advertising, with each campaign promoting the diversity and variety of the country, focusing on its heritage and culture, as well as the staple sun and sand product. At the heart of the brand for over twenty years has been Joan Miro's logo, designed in 1983 (the year he died) by mixing elements from his own pictures and his own alphabet. As a piece of modern art, this logo both symbolizes Spain's past and looks to the future, and incorporates representations of the sun (yellow and red), the stars, and the bullring (black) to portray Spain. The shifts in the campaigns from 'Everything under the sun' (first used in 1984) to 'Passion for life' (1992–95) to 'Bravo Spain' (introduced in 1997) and into the current 'Spain marks' have been gradual and well thought out, and have never compromised the brand values.

The Bravo Spain campaign, which replaced the unpopular 'Spain by ...' campaign of 1996, was tested in the key markets of the UK, Germany and France, where it was seen positively: the word Bravo conjured up images of approval, allaying fears in Spain of any negative connotations of its association with bullfighting. Intended to communicate a different, modern Spain, this campaign used strong, visually impactful images in its television, press and poster executions. In the print adverts (which were the backbone of the campaign) the consistent image was of a blurred photograph with a larger, perfectly focused close-up window showing some detail of the photo. Every region of Spain featured in the adverts, which mixed well-known attractions (such as the new Bilbao museum) with lesser known sites (such as Valencia's new concert hall) and included interesting copy and a small map indicating the location of the scene in the poster. This campaign has since been superseded by 'Spain marks', which uses strong black and white main images with smaller colour images echoing some aspect of the main picture. Thus, one execution portrays the ripped seat of a man's jeans with a smaller colour photograph of the Pamplona bull-running festival and the small ad copy suggests that you should 'Mix with the people and share their passion for life until you forget where you're from. Be marked by www.Spain.info'.

Conclusion

The success of countries such as Spain shows that destinations can become brands that are contemporary and yet timeless, and that can remain in the famous phase of their brand fashion curve over a prolonged period. That does not mean, however, that it is easy to build a strong place brand. It takes patience to establish brand reputations and building a powerful destination brand is a long-term effort, which more often than not yields incremental and not exponential results. For a brand to be genuinely successful, the vision also has to be reflected in the product and service experience. In the case of Spain, this meant creating a public–private partnership to reposition the country on the world stage. In 1992 the Olympics was attracted to Barcelona and the World Expo to Seville, five years later the iconic steel-framed and titanium-sheathed Guggenheim Museum was opened in Bilbao, and dilapidated beachfronts have been refurbished in key seaside resorts from Benidorm to Majorca.

There are those destination brands that have seemingly emerged from obscurity to achieve instant stardom. Such rapid elevation to celebrity status, however, often owes much to a culmination of long-term economic, political, social and cultural factors. The apparently effortless appearance of Ireland as a cool, fashionable destination, for instance, is the result of over twenty years of economic turnaround, coupled with the breakthrough of Irish culture (especially the performing arts) onto the world stage. Often such instant stardom also belies long-term marketing activity and investment built on detailed marketing research, planning and consistent positioning. Ireland has continuously invested heavily in product development and in its marketing activities, and has consistently outspent all of its competitor destinations in the British Isles.

Those destinations that have emerged as brand winners have a number of common features, in addition to being well-funded. They have all been based on a vision that is founded on intensive stakeholder, consumer and competitor research, and that is expressed with care and discipline in everything that communicates the brand's personality. Many have set out to be inclusive brands, forged through partnership and alliance, and many are spearheaded by forward-looking, innovative and committed managers. The commitment and energy of such 'brand champions' is a vital but often overlooked ingredient in any successful destination branding strategy. Such people could be influential politicians or they could be brand envisioners drawn from the destination's marketing organization. This is not to say, however, that the branding should be exclusively directed from the 'top down' and we have seen how this can be counterproductive, as in the case of Oregon in the mid-1980s. The best brands are those that are flexible and inclusive, with a broad base of support. Indeed, the development of such partnerships is often a beneficial spin-off from destination brand-building activities, creating greater cohesion between tourism marketers and economic development agencies (Crockett and Wood, 1999; Curtis, 2001).

In addition to being well supported by internal stakeholders, those destination brands that have the greatest celebrity value also tend to be those that embrace creativity. The choice of branding and advertising agencies is crucial here, since they must produce work that advances the brand and reinforces its values and personality. Successful destination brands usually have consistent, relevant, appealing advertising, characterized by high production values: advertising that is often cutting-edge and extremely creative. This is not to suggest, however, that destination brand managers must not be prepared to adjust misdirected communications. Spain showed that swift action to correct an unpopular expression of the brand's personality (the 1996 'Spain by …' campaign) can prevent long-term damage to the brand. Continuous monitoring and evaluation of the communications is the key here, as is open-mindedness and a willingness to embrace change on the part of the brand managers.

Any change must be managed within the overall consistency of the brand. Once the brand personality has been identified, marketers must have the courage to stay with the brand's essence: while refinements may be made to how the values are expressed in the brand architecture, the essentials of the brand personality should remain consistent. The secret is continually to evolve and enrichen the original brand personality, building on the initial strengths to strengthen their appeal and to broaden the market. Oregon, for instance, took its established reputation as a pristine natural environment and enriched the brand's personality through including a focus on the destination's built environment and its cultural attractions (Curtis, 2001) (Figures 5.5 and 5.6). This is similar to the strategy adopted by Spain, which wove culture, heritage and an emerging reputation for modern architecture into its original brand personality based around sun and sand. Likewise, Ireland has added culture, 'coolness' and quality to its established

Figure 5.5   Reviving Brand Oregon around the 'capturing the moment' theme

Figure 5.6   Reviving Brand Oregon: communicating the diversity of activities

identity as a laid-back, friendly destination, and Australia has added sophistication and a cosmopolitan dimension to its youthful, fun, nature-orientated personality.

There are significant and unique challenges facing destination marketers, but these should not prevent them from persevering in their aims, as successful branding brings enormous rewards. Destinations cannot afford to ignore branding as it offers an innovative and effective tool with which mangers can establish emotional links with the consumer, particularly if a multiagency-driven suprabrand is constructed. Just as in the marketing of consumer goods, branding has the potential to engender consumer loyalty and position destinations to appeal to consumers' self-images and lifestyles. Moreover, while tourism is just one element of any destination's economy it should be integral to place marketing since it supports and leads the development of a place brand. The creation of celebrity and emotional appeal through a destination brand opens the way for other economic development-orientated agencies to communicate to would-be investors and residents.

References

Anholt, S. (1998) Nation-brands of the twenty-first century. *Journal of Brand Management* 5: 395–404.

Baral, A., Baral, S. and Morgan, N. J. (2004) Marketing Nepal in an uncertain climate: confronting perceptions of risk and uncertainty. *Journal of Vacation Marketing* 10(2): 186–192.

Brown, G., Chalip, L., Jago, L. and Mules, T. (2002) The Sydney Olympics and Brand Australia. In Morgan, N. J., Pritchard, A. and Pride, R. (eds) *Destination Branding: Creating the Unique Destination Proposition.* Oxford: Butterworth-Heinemann, pp. 163–185.

Buhalis, D. (2000) Marketing the competitive destination of the future. *Tourism Management* 21: 97–116.

Coshall, J. T. (2000) Measurement of tourists images: the repertory grid approach. *Journal of Travel Research* 39: 85–89.

Crockett, S. R. and Wood, L. J. (1999) Brand Western Australia. A totally integrated approach to destination branding. *Journal of Vacation Marketing* 5: 276–289.

Curtis, J. (2001) Branding a state: the evolution of Brand Oregon. *Journal of Vacation Marketing* 7: 75–82.

de Chernatony, L. (1993) Categorising brands: evolutionary processes underpinned by two key dimensions. *Journal of Marketing Management* 9(2), April, pp. 173–188.

de Chernatony, L. and Riley, D. F. (1998) Defining a 'brand': beyond the literature with expert interpretations. *Journal of Marketing Management* 14: 417–443.

de Chernatony, L. and Segal-Horn, S. (2001) Building on services. Characteristics to develop successful services brands. *Journal of Marketing Management* 17: 645–670.

Garfield, R. (1998) Personal interview.

Gold, R. and Ward, S. V. (eds) (1994) *Place Promotion. The Use of Publicity and Marketing to Sell Towns and Regions.* Chichester: Wiley.

Hall, J. (2004) Branding Britain. *Journal of Vacation Marketing* 10(2): 171–185.

Hallberg, G. (1995) *All Consumers Are Not Created Equal.* New York: Wiley.

Kotler, P., Haider, D. H. and Rein, I. (1993) *Marketing Places*, New York: The Free Press.

Kotler, P. and Gertner, D. (2002) Country as brand, product, and beyond: A place marketing and brand management perspective, *Journal of Brand Management*, 9(4–5): 249–261.

Louro, M. and Cunha, P. (2001) Brand management paradigms. *Journal of Marketing Management*, 17(7–8): 849–876.

Lury, G. (1998) *Brandwatching.* Dublin: Blackhall.

Macrae, C., Parkinson, S. and Sheerman, J. (1995) Managing marketing's DNA: the role of branding. *Irish Marketing Review* 18: 13–20.

Morgan, N. J. and Pritchard, A. (1999) Building destination brands. The cases of Wales and Australia. *Journal of Brand Management* 7: 102–119.

Morgan, N. J. and Pritchard, A. (2000) *Advertising in Tourism & Leisure*, Oxford: Butterworth-Heinemann.

Morgan, N. J. and Pritchard, A. (2004) (PR)omoting place: the role of PR in building New Zealand's destination brand relationships. *Journal of Hospitality and Leisure Marketing* in press. Volume 11, 2004.

Morgan, N. J., Pritchard, A. and Piggott, R. (2002) New Zealand, 100% Pure. The creation of a powerful destination niche brand. *Journal of Brand Management* 9: 335–354.

Morgan, N. J., Pritchard, A. and Piggott, R. (2003) Destination branding and the role of the stakeholders: the case of New Zealand. *Journal of Vacation Marketing* 9: 285–299.

Morse, J. (2001) The Sydney 2000 Olympic Games: how the Australian Tourist Commission leveraged The Games for tourism. *Journal of Vacation Marketing* 7: 101–109.

Piggott, R. (2001) Building a brand for a country. Can commercial marketing practices achieve this in a government-funded environment? Unpublished MBA dissertation, University of Hull.

Ritchie, B. J. R. and Crouch, G. I. (2000) The competitive destination – a sustainable perspective. *Tourism Management* 21: 1–7.

Schiffman, L. G. and Kanuk, L. L. (2000) *Consumer Behavior*, 7th edn. New Jersey: Prentice Hall International.

Sheth, J. N., Mittal, B. and Newman, B. I. (1999) *Customer Behaviour. Consumer Behavior and Beyond.* Orlando, FL: Dryden Press.

Tapachai, N. and Waryszak, R. (2000) An examination of the role of beneficial image in tourist destination selection. *Journal of Travel Research* 39: 37–44.

Tibbott, R. (2001) Olympic economies. Sydney and the destination economy. *Locum Destination Review* 3: 33–34.

Urdde, M. (1999) Brand orientation: a mindset for building brands into strategic resources. *Journal of Marketing Management* 15: 117–133.

Ward, S. V. (1998) *Selling Places: The Marketing and Promotion of Towns and Cities, 1850–2000.* London: E. and F. N. Spon.

Weinreich, L. (1999) *11 Steps to Brand Heaven. The Ultimate Guide to Buying an Advertising Campaign.* London: Kogan Page.

Westwood, S., Morgan, N. J., Pritchard, A. and Ineson, E. (1999) Branding the package holiday – the role and significance of brands for UK air tour operators. *Journal of Vacation Marketing* 5: 238–252.

Wood, L. (2000) Brands and brand equity: Definition and management, *Management Decision* 38(9): 662–669.

6

The political challenge: the case of New Zealand's tourism organizations

Chris Ryan and Anne Zahra

Introduction

'Absolutely positively Wellington', 'Auckland – city of sails', 'Manaakitanga – feel the spirit – Rotorua', 'Rangitikei – the best kept secret', 'Christchurch – the garden city', 'Palmerston North – knowledge city' – are all examples of destination branding undertaken by local and regional tourism organizations in New Zealand. For its part, '100% Pure New Zealand' is a branding and positioning campaign of the national tourist organization, Tourism New Zealand (TNZ). This chapter does not, however, seek the rationale behind such branding slogans, but rather tries to explain the national and local political scenarios that contextualize such exercises of national and regional tourism organizations (NTOs and RTOs).

Why? The authors do not perceive the issue of 'branding' to be solely an issue of promotion or that RTOs and NTOs only exist to promote a destination. In its fullest sense marketing is about product design and service delivery beside simple promotion, and thus to divorce branding and the promotion that NTOs and RTOs undertake from the wider context is believed to be self-defeating if one wishes to understand the nature of these marketing exercises, why they have been initiated and what they purport to do. To understand the marketing activities undertaken by Tourism Organizations, it needs to be appreciated that for the most part they are quasi-public sector bodies, primarily funded by local and national government, and often have elected politicians present upon their executive and/or advisory boards. In addition, in some instances, the funding authorities will effectively delegate to the NTO or RTO a number of responsibilities that de facto places the NTO or RTO in the position of possessing that authority's main source of tourism expertise. Thereby, the tourism organization becomes an important source of advice and indirectly influences policy in matters beyond promotion. Product development thus shades into a consideration of social and environmental issues. The discourse of this chapter is to describe, at least partially, the politics that contribute to and emerge from this situation.

This chapter will examine the role of both New Zealand's NTO and its RTOs within a context of political change at the level of both national and local governmental policy. The chapter is informed by the first author's past and continuing membership of RTO committees and research undertaken for RTOs, and by the second author's doctoral research into New Zealand's RTOs and her participation in various discussions at the level of RTONZ, a group of RTOs meeting at a national level under the auspices of the Tourism Strategy 2010 (Tourism Strategy Group, 2001) that is currently the determining document of action for the New Zealand Ministry of Tourism, the Tourism Research Council and other major parties in New Zealand Tourism. This chapter therefore differs from that in the first edition by presenting a more detailed analysis of changes at the national level during a period since approximately 1980, and a description of how local policies have been very much influenced by governmental policies at a central level.

The chapter will first examine the reasons for public sector involvement in tourism and document what has happened in New Zealand in the last two decades of the twentieth century and the first years of the new millennium, thereby providing a context from which it may be possible to make generalizations that have some applicability to at least the English-speaking world. Among the conclusions reached are, first, at least in New Zealand, that the policies of central government have been significantly important in determining the structures of what may be seen as primarily promotional bodies. It may be that New Zealand is particularly sensitive to this, possessing but one House of Representatives, elected for a period of but three years, and possessing little countervailing power at a regional or local level of politics. Consequently, New Zealand's governments, in spite of an adoption of a mixed member proportional (MMP) style of voting like Germany's, has experienced a swing from the neoclassical economics to a more directive style of economic intervention in little more than a decade. A second conclusion is that the NTO and RTOs are often forced to justify their existence on the premise that they are an effective investment of national and local government funds in that they generate an economic return. Third, for all their shortcomings, RTOs represent a forum where the parochialism of local politics (and personalities) engages in a dialectic with regional and national debate in a manner not always found in local politics. RTOs are thus contributors not only to tourism, but also to civic action. It needs to be stated that the authors believe that there exists in tourism a need for a proactive public sector in developing and implementing plans in tourism. Tourism, as an industry and as a series of market transactions, consumes places and both publicly and privately owned resources. The private development of place creates public costs in terms of infrastructure, for example, road and medical facilities, and to argue, as some political parties and politicians in New Zealand have in the past, that neither local or national government has a role to play in such considerations is not a view shared by the authors. Inasmuch as that role, sometimes by default, falls within the jurisdiction of RTOs, the result is a continuing tension between, on the one hand, their status as promoters of their regions and as representatives of their industry members and, on the other, their role in, at the very least, raising awareness of the social and environmental issues associated with tourism.

The role of the public sector in the New Zealand context since the 1980s

NTOs and RTOs are quasi-sector public bodies and their conception, existence, disappearance (in some cases) and re-emergence have depended directly on, or at least been influenced by, the actions of the government and national bodies. Wanhill (2000) argued that in the latter part of the twentieth century, faced with the increased globalization of market power, governments responded by retreating to 'core tasks'. Among these Wanhill (2000, p. 224) included:

> *protection of the environment to preserve public heath and well-being; the guardianship of future generations through sustainable development …*

correcting for market failure ... In this respect, industrial policy should not be about 'picking winners', but rather about providing institutional arrangements to support private entrepreneurial success ...

New Zealand was no different to other developed economies, and it could be claimed that, in the 1980s, New Zealand went further down the path of deregulation and privatization than many other economies. Prior to 1984 New Zealand's National Tourism Organization, the New Zealand Tourism and Publicity Department (NZTPD), was not only a promoter of tourism but also a major tourism operator. The department's commercial operations included the Government Tourist Bureau, which had 215 staff in April 1984, Tikki Tours and the administration of tourist reserves such as Whakarewarewa and Wairakei tourist parks in Rotorua (NZTPD Brief to the Minister July 1984, AAAC 7923 W5158/138 ADM 070 Part 2, Archives New Zealand, Wellington). These commercial and administrative functions were subsequently divested from the NTO in the late 1980s under the neoclassical economic policies associated with the then finance minister, Roger Douglas, and which in New Zealand were termed 'Rogernomics'.

Private enterprise did have a role in the direction and functions of the NTO before these reforms in the late 1980s. The Tourism Council, established in 1983, and its predecessor the Tourism Advisory Council, established in 1978, were 'appointed by the Minister to assess and advise upon the major developments and trends affecting the growth of the tourism industry in New Zealand and to consider and advise upon the activities and policies required to achieve the most beneficial expansion of the industry' (NZTPD Brief to the Minister July 1984, AAAC 7923 W5158/138 ADM 070 Part 2, Archives New Zealand, Wellington). One example was the publication, in 1984, of the document 'New Zealand Tourism: Issues and Policies', which was to influence the direction of the tourism industry over the next five years. However, composed of successful businessmen and the senior players of the tourism sector, towards the end of the 1980s the membership of the Tourism Council was becoming frustrated as they were asked for advice on policy and direction, especially marketing, but they had no authority (Burt, pers. comm., 2003)[1]. However, with forthcoming elections in 1990, and the fact that some of the key tourism industry players had strong political connections with the National Party (who were in opposition

---

[1] David Burt joined the New Zealand Tourist and Publicity Department in 1984 as a planner, when the New Zealand Tourism Board (NZTB) separated from the Ministry of Tourism in 1991 David moved with the NZTB. He has worked for the New Zealand's NTO for nearly 20 years and is now Events Manager for TNZ.

at the time), a window of opportunity appeared for a change of policy (Burt, pers. comm., 2003). The subsequent success of the National Party led to the establishment of the New Zealand Tourism Board (NZTB), a crown entity, with the purpose of marketing and developing New Zealand as a visitor destination (New Zealand Tourism Department Newsletter, April/May 1991) in which the industry had executive authority over direction. This allowed industry to formulate policy and direction, in so far as it applied to marketing, which was a fundamental shift in thinking (Burt, pers. comm., 2003).

Wanhill (2000) argues that industry policy should not be about 'picking winners' but rather about providing institutional arrangements to support private enterprise. From this perspective it is interesting to examine what happened in the first half of the 1990s in New Zealand. Norman Geary, who was chairman of the NZTB from its creation in 1991 to 1995 and a private sector operator, spoke unashamedly about picking winners (Winder, pers. comm., 2003; Burt, pers. comm., 2003). The joint venture marketing activities undertaken by the board led to some of the private sector being substantial beneficiaries of marketing monies. The fact that there were particular winners and others that were precluded led to questions of equity and fairness in the way the NZTB worked (Winder, pers. comm., 2003)[2] and indeed a Parliamentary Commission of Inquiry was established in 1994. However, the NZTB emerged from this comparatively little changed.

Wanhill claims that there are four reasons for government intervention in tourism, these being 'the complexity of the tourist product, its institutional structure, guardianship of the resource base and market failure' (Wanhill, 2000, p. 225). Already in 1984 the language gaining currency was that the government should become involved in the business sector only if there was a clear case of market failure (Plimmer, pers. comm., 2003a)[3]. Neil Plimmer, general

---

[2] Peter Winder worked for the New Zealand Tourism Board from 1995 and 2000 as part of the Management Team. His responsibilities included: responsibility for the Board's Purchase and Accountability relationship with Government, tourism policy, business planning and strategy, industry development, regional tourism strategies, market research and the Board's interests in VIN, Qualmark and the New Zealand Way Ltd. Peter then became CEO of Local Government New Zealand and was instrumental in the Local Government's response to the New Zealand Tourism Strategy 2010. Peter is now with Auckland Regional Council, as Director of Transport.

[3] Neil Plimmer was General Manager of the Tourist and Publicity Department 1980–1991, Executive Director of the Ministry of Tourism 1991–1994, and Acting Director of the Office of Tourism and Sport 2000.

manager of the New Zealand Tourist and Publicity Department, has the following reflections on the debate of market failure during this period:

It became apparent that the NZTP needed more sophisticated arguments for its marketing budget than simply that tourism was of high potential as a job creator and foreign exchange earner, if it was to withstand Treasury pressure. I invited the Director of the Institute of Economic Research (Allan Bollard) to a long lunch to work over this concept (of market failure). I recalled him saying that if tourism really worked the way I was describing it, it was as much a case of public good as market failure. The Department achieved a reasonable mastery of both these concepts and wrote Ministerial briefings and cabinet papers on them as required, generally holding the fort on that front.

Later the secretary of the Treasury, Graeme Scott, warned me that the Department should not rest easy about its funding, based on market failure or public good arguments. Where market failure occurred in terms of the separate activities of the companies, then they should club together, and only if 'clubbing' was shown to be impossible should the government perhaps intervene. Related to this was the notion of 'free riders'. Well, it was just as easy to show that the tourist industry because of its huge diversity was most unlikely to 'club' effectively to fund overseas marketing and that free riding was easy as it was to show market failure (Plimmer, pers. comm., 2003a).

Elliot (1997) argues that any rationalization of public sector management is based upon five general principles, public interest, public service, effectiveness, efficiency and accountability. However, 'public interest' is in itself a difficult area to define, and there may well be a shifting consensus or interpretation over time. Following Hall's (1994) categorization of the role of the public sector in tourism it is possible to note briefly the changing nature of the public sector–private sector relationship in the tourism industry that occurred in New Zealand in the final decades of the twentieth century.

Government as a source of planning

The NZTPD during the 1980s undertook a real leadership role in planning, having a section of the organization dedicated to planning, development and research:

We had reached a half million visitors to the country and the pressure was on to get tourism recognised as a legitimate use of demand on the environment and a natural use of resources. There was pressure on more development and tourism was not taken seriously in a policy sense. When we started to address planning issues it became obvious that there was very little at the regional or local government level to handle this beast called tourism. Whilst we were commenting on district and regional plans as they came up we realised there was not the framework to follow through on it' (Burt, pers. comm., 2003).

Some of the larger projects during this period were providing input for Rotorua's geothermal field, future development and planning options for Rotorua, hydro development options for the Kawarau River and their impact on the Queenstown tourism industry and managing the growing pains of Queenstown (AAAC 7923 W5158/212 PDR 0951 Part 5, Archives New Zealand, Wellington).

During much of the period of the 1990s in New Zealand, conservative governments retreated from this planning function in the belief that the market was a better regulator of needs than central direction. This effectively left issues of resource management to regional and local authorities, but the remit of the Resource Management Act 1991 meant that such authorities were not to develop prescriptive methods of control but had to assess potential outcomes of proposals and to respond accordingly by either granting or refusing a resource consent.

The New Zealand Tourism Strategy 2010, released in August 2001, put planning back on the agenda. This strategy and its forty-three recommendations could have simply remained an industry 'wish list', but the Labour government adopted a leadership role and committed monies to study the recommendations and implement them. Recommendation 11 proposed the adoption of a whole sector model to reduce complexity and improve efficiency in tourism planning and development by 2004. Recommendation 27 proposed that by mid-2002, territorial local authorities and central government confirm their long-term commitment to the tourism sector and confirm infrastructure. Recommendation 40 stated that central and local government and the private sector develop a model and agree on roles and responsibilities in relation to tourism infrastructure needs. The new Ministry of Tourism, established in 2001, funded a four-step programme initiated by Local Government New Zealand which culminated in 'Postcards from Home: The Local Government Tourism Strategy' of May 2003. The Ministry continues to support planning by providing further funding to Local Government New Zealand to investigate the Resources Management Act and Tourism and produce a best practice guide. It has also funded research into the impact of tourism on locales with small populations and hence a low ratepayer base in order to assess the ways in which such communities absorb the costs associated with significant tourism flows and impacts. Consequently, New Zealand is seeing a complete turn of the policy cycle, with government again taking a leadership, albeit in a different guise to the 1980s.

Government as a source of legislation and regulation

As is evident from the above, governments at a local and national level became increasingly reactive rather than proactive through the legislative framework adopted in New Zealand in the 1990s. The main focus of the 1980s was deregulation, 'although the tourism industry in New Zealand and globally had been lightly regulated in economic terms (I am here not talking about health and safety or quality standards type of regulation). That is compared with agriculture, manufacturing and service sectors such as banking' (Plimmer, 2003b). The little regulation that existed was slowly eroded away with some examples being the removal of price controls on room rates, the liberalization of liquor licensing laws, deregulation of bus transport and taxis, liberalization of shop trading hours and aviation, and the removal of prescriptive planning approaches to land use.

Therefore, the 1990s saw tourism being assessed through a policy framed by the Resource Management Act of 1991, various amendments to the 1989 Local Government Act and similar legislation. The policy direction was to free the market from constraints. Thus, the Resource Management Act, while concerned about a need to protect and sustain environments, also permitted economic benefits to be weighed in the balance, and one consequence of this, as will be argued below, was to politicize at local level the whole issue of development in a way that had not previously existed. This is not to ignore the fact that development is itself a political and social action, but the legislation of the 1990s arguably led to inconsistent policies between different territorial authorities.

In 2002 the tide is changed yet again. The government, in its revisions of the Resources Management Act and environmental protection policies in 2003, and its continual advocacy for sustainable tourism, is placing legislation and regulation back on the agenda. Mark Burton, as Minister of Tourism, addressed the 2000 New Zealand Tourism Industry Association (NZTIA) conference with reference to the emergent tourism strategy by asking 'What can we learn from structures and processes adopted in other countries?' (Coventry 2000a). He also wanted to know the costs involved and what legislation or regulations might be required to implement the plan, and it was this desire that prompted the commission of research projects by the Tourism Research Council, funded by the Ministry, into issues as diverse as licensing arrangements for commercial operations in the Conservation Estate and the aforementioned work on financing local infrastructure.

Government as a co-ordinating body

Tourism is a diffuse industry or sector, and co-ordination is arguably required both vertically (i.e. between local, regional and national institutions) and horizontally (i.e. between agencies at the same level of activity. The NZTPD in the 1980s placed significant emphasis on this co-ordinating role. The Tourism Advisory Service was established in 1983, with the objective of assisting regional and local authorities and tourist operators to develop and promote tourism within their regions. Regional liaison officers (RLOs) were funded by the department and located in the regions. The role of the RLOs was threefold: marketing liaison, development and information provision – namely to provide detailed information on tourism-related subjects, including information on government assistance and marketing and research data, and to aid organizations and individuals in decision making (AAAC 7923 W5158/138 ADM 070 Part 2, Archives New Zealand, Wellington). Some of these RLOs played significant roles in helping to establish and guide the RTOs in their embryonic stages. The RLOs were some of the few survivors of 'leave it to the market' and lasted into the early 1990s under the NZTB.

In the 1980s the NZTPD also undertook a co-ordinating function with:

- international tourism organizations such as the World Tourism Organization (WTO) and Pacific Area Travel Association (PATA), and also developed close links with Australian tourism bodies
- national organizations: it provided co-ordinating and secretarial services to the Tourism Council and the general manager was the deputy chairman; the general manager of the NZTPD was on the executive of the New Zealand Tourist Industry Federation (NZTIF), the Peak Industry Association; the general manager was on the board of the Tourist Hotel Corporation and the Maori Arts and Crafts Institute in Rotorua; the NZTPD was represented on the Council of the New Zealand Institute of Travel; there was representation on the External Aviation Policy Committee; a department officer sat on governing body of the Aviation and Travel Industry Training Board (AAAC 7923 W5158/138 ADM 070 Part 2, Archives New Zealand, Wellington).

The co-ordinating function the government provided allowed the industry to address complex problems in a unified way and facilitated the industry to make rapid progress in meeting the demands of increasing number of international and domestic visitors. The increase in international visitor numbers was 6.3 per cent in 1983, 15.2 per cent in 1984 and 16.5 per cent in 1985. The percentage growth in foreign exchange earnings in 1985 was 45.3 per cent (primarily due to the significant increase in Japanese and US markets compared with Australia and the UK, which traditionally spend less money) (AAAC 7923 W5158/212 PDR 0951 Part 5, Archives New Zealand, Wellington). Through the NZTPD's co-ordinating role, RTOs were better supported through the dissemination of information of what was going on at higher levels through seminars in the regions and the RLOs.

As national government retreated from this co-ordinating function in the 1990s, the need for co-ordination meant that local authorities and their proxies such as RTOs became the site of discourse as to the need, nature and direction of co-ordination. Pavlovich's (2000) case study of tourism entrepreneurs in the Waitomo, and her application of network theory to this location, indicates just how transient the nature of these relationships can be at the local level where personalities can become an important determinant of action. In New Zealand the paradox therefore emerged where, as a Conservative government preached the ideology of free markets, its proxy, the NZTB, started to promote marketing networks among regions which of necessity involved planning implications as to resultant flows of tourists. Even more ironic was that networks were being promulgated at a time when there were few data available as to the flows of those tourists, whether international or domestic. This situation of 'informational loss' was itself due to a 'reform' of the 1989 national government that replaced the NZTPD with the NZTB, which had as its prime purpose the overseas marketing of New Zealand, not a data collection process of flows of tourists within New Zealand.

The pendulum is again swinging back: senior members of the Ministry of Tourism are interacting, facilitating and sitting on many bodies, for example the policy manager of the Ministry of Tourism was a member of the Local Government New Zealand Tourism Project Team and TNZ, and ministry staff conduct seminars in the regions, again disseminating information and supporting the RTOs and regional operators.

Government as entrepreneur

Historically, in New Zealand, the government had been a leading industrial player as the owner and operator of airlines, hotel chains and attractions. Over the latter half of the twentieth century this function had been supplanted by the private sector, with the final stage being one of privatization of a number of assets, including that of Air New Zealand in 1989. Nonetheless, citing issues of national importance and a need to ensure access to New Zealand by overseas tourists, in 2002 the government injected NZ$850 million into the ailing Air New Zealand in return for shares following the collapse of that company's subsidiary, Ansett Australia. Technically, through the Ministry of Tourism, the government still has ownership of some assets, notably the Maori Arts and Crafts Institute, but in all cases the government plays no direct role in either daily management or setting strategic directions.

Government as a stimulator of tourism development

Government can act as a stimulator in at least three ways: by operating systems of grants and tax benefits, seeking to promote place through marketing initiatives and sponsoring research.

Grants and tax benefits

Government can operate systems of grants and tax benefits, or provide a source of low-interest loans, as was done by the UK under the 1969 Tourism Development Act. In the 1980s New Zealand, along with many other countries, had the following incentives available for tourism operators: tax depreciation allowances for large new accommodation projects, Export Programme Grants Scheme, Export Performance Incentive – tax rebate on foreign exchange earnings, Export Market Development Incentive – tax rebate on marketing and promotion expenditure overseas, Regional Promotion Assistance Scheme and the Tourist Facilities Grants Scheme (AAAC 7923 W5158/138 ADM 070 Part 2, Archives New Zealand, Wellington). None of these grants and tax benefits survived the Rogernomic reforms, except for the Tourist Facilities Grants Scheme, and the 1990s was a desert wasteland for grants and tax relief for RTOs and tourism operators in New Zealand.

It could be said that New Zealand is now moving into a semi-arid zone when it comes to grants to stimulate economic development. The Ministry of Tourism administers a Tourism Facilities Grants programme of NZ$300 000 and special business advisory programmes for Maori tourism operators, and has secured funding for specific programmes as indicated above in the example of assessing funding of infrastructure in Rotorua, Queenstown, Kaikoura and Stewart Island.

Promoting place through marketing initiatives

Many countries possess national tourist boards as a means of promotion and marketing, and New Zealand is no different. Tourism New Zealand, in 2003, received about NZ$70 million for the marketing and promotion of the brand 'New Zealand'.

Out of all the roles of the public sector in tourism (Hall, 1994) it is the promotion of place through marketing that assumes the forefront, but even so this promotional budget has not always grown. For example, in 1991, the newly established NZTB had an annual budget of $55 million (AAAC 7924 W5158/2 0806 Part 2, Archives New Zealand, Wellington), a figure that remained more or less constant for much of the 1990s.

Sponsoring research

Tourism research was very high on the NZTPD agenda in the 1980s. In December 1981 the Department convened a seminar on the Co-ordination and Planning of Tourism Research. The general manager, Neil Plimmer, explained the purpose of the seminar:

> *There is clearly a very rapid growing interest in research into tourism throughout New Zealand. We see it in government departments and agencies, in the universities, in private companies, and in the institutions of tourism.*

> *It is worth asking why all this is happening? I am sure that it relates to the increasing sophistication and complexity of tourism. Our competitors are spending more money in analysing consumer wants and in developing the most advanced marketing strategies. The gains of tourism are becoming more widely appreciated and more countries, airlines and companies are fighting for a share of the global tourism market. They are doing it from the basis of improved research and we must do the same.*

> *An important reason for the surge in research in New Zealand is the growing competition for scarce resources between different sectors of the economy within New Zealand. Forestry, fishing, agriculture, manufacturing are all involved in research designed to improve the performance of their sector and to stress its importance and tourism must do the same.*

> *A further reason why research is being undertaken more widely must be simply a matter of costs. Building costs, production costs, media costs for advertising and travel costs of all sorts are escalating rapidly, in many cases in real terms. It obviously follows that investment decisions involving large outlays of money have to be made on the best information available. The sums are too great to be left to 'seat of the pants' judgements.*

Clearly if we want to compete for tourism in the world market and if we want to compete for resources for tourism within New Zealand, we are going to have to move towards more professionalism (Plimmer, 1982).

The research undertaken by the NZTPD was quite sophisticated and state of the art for its day. In 1980 research was orientated towards a better understanding of the economic impact of tourism, with early estimates being produced in 1982 (Plimmer, pers. comm., 2003a). In marketing, psychographics and the values, attitudes, lifestyle approach to segmentation was used as early as 1982/83 (Plimmer, pers. comm., 2003a). Another research demand in the 1980s was for data relating to each region as planners and promoters in each region found it difficult to deduce much relevance from nationally aggregated statistics. Over time, the International Visitor Survey and the Domestic Tourism Survey were regionally segmented and regional profiles prepared. By 1989 the tourist activity model was able to generate historical, current and forecast data by regions or major tourist towns (Plimmer, pers. comm., 2003a). This is not the forum to discuss all the research undertaken by the NTO in the 1980s, but significant emphasis and investment were placed on research, as evidenced by the quarterly newsletter *New Zealand Tourism Research* which existed throughout the decade and the money that went into research increasing from $50 000 in 1980 to $1 million in 1990/91 (Plimmer, pers. comm., 2003a).

Research continued into the 1990s, but it was split between the NZTB, which focused solely on marketing, and the ministry, but with the ministry's diminishing personnel and budgets very little could be achieved and the view predominated that if the tourism industry wanted research they should fund it. This led to a debate about the need for a national tourism research strategy and Ryan and Simmons (1999) argued that such a strategy, and then the proposed modes of its funding, were defensible upon grounds of market failure.

Once again the public sector involvement in tourism has turned 360 degrees and research as a high priority is back on the agenda. The Tourism Research Council, established in 2001, seeks to co-ordinate the work of projects funded through the Foundation of Research, Science and Technology (the means by which the government directs public sector research funding), TNZ and the Ministry of Tourism, and at regional and local level through various initiatives of local authorities, RTOs and district tourism organizations (DTOs). One outward sign of this has been the establishment of the Tourism Research Council website and the full disclosure of statistical data and a research bibliography. Whereas previous thinking was that the market placed value on the data through a willingness to pay, in 2003 the thinking is that data only possess value if they are freely disseminated for others to use, and it is that use in informing better decision taking that provides value for such datasets.

Government as a facilitator of economic activity

In the 1980s the NZTPD took the view that the management of tourism involved taking an informed and integrated approach to both marketing and development, instead of just focusing on marketing as many other NTOs did. In turn, development required a holistic view of what central and local governments and the private sector could do (Plimmer, pers. comm., 2003a). Grants and subsidies as forms of facilitators of economic activity have already been discussed, but others included the Tourist Facilities Development Scheme, and projects funded under this scheme included Napier's Marineland, Rotorua's Agridome and Taupo's Huka Village. The NZTPD built its development arm, especially after 1984, to increase its input into regional, district and maritime planning schemes, with the RLOs having a large role to play here. All these schemes created a better environment for tourism investment to proceed and for regions, cities and towns to gain stronger benefits from tourism (Plimmer, pers. comm., 2003a).

In the 1990s New Zealand's new-right governments sought to facilitate growth through the removal of what were perceived as restraints upon the market. As noted, this included changing environmental legislation by removing prohibitions per se through the enforcement of policies such as zoning, and replacing them by one of awarding consents where it could be shown that overall the balance between economic, social and environmental impacts resulting from a development were beneficial. Similarly, changes in employment contract law effectively replaced collective bargaining with individual employee–employer contracts.

In 1998, however, a Labour (centrist–left party)–Alliance (representing a range of socialist tendencies) government was elected. In consequence, the government has a predisposition towards proactive planning, but does so from the perspective of facilitating entrepreneurial activity to address social problems while retaining profitability, rather than seeking specifically to direct industry. In 1999, the Finance Minister, Dr Michael Cullen, said that the budget was about 'a new start for a new century. While government says it doesn't want to pick winners, regulate, subsidise or compel', he added, it does want to help businesses find new markets 'and become winners … At times it means getting the regulatory framework right so that short term optimism does not damage the wider public commercial good. At times it means ensuring the right financing options are available. At times it means taking a direct leadership role' (cited by

Coventry, 2000a). As described above, the Ministry of Tourism has been pro-active, and in some instances works with the Department of Economic Development with reference to projects that involve regional development. For example, one research project in 2003 included the Ministries of Economic Development and Tourism working with the Department of Conservation on policies pertaining to concession licensing.

Government as a protector of the public interest

It can be argued that the government is fulfilling the role of custodian of the 'public interest' when seeking to be a facilitator of business, while also considering the social implications of such entrepreneurial activity. As is evident, however, the interpretation of public interest and means of implementing that role have been the subject of debate and changing policies in New Zealand as elsewhere.

Public interest issues such as environmental protection, the social impact of tourism, roads and energy were addressed in the 1980s by the Tourism Council and NZTPD in documents such as 'Growing pains' and 'New Zealand tourism: issues and policy' (AAAC 7923 W5158/212 PDR 0951 Part 5). Maori, heritage and cultural tourism and Maori representation were all dealt with by the NZTPD (Plimmer, 2003b) yet were put on the back burner from a public policy perspective until late in the 1990s, and the subsequent 2010 Tourism Strategy tabled these issues for discussion and policy implementation.

Such policies are recognized as existing within a widely based domain. Mark Burton, Minister of Tourism, in discussing the then proposed tourism strategy at the 2000 New Zealand Tourism Industry Conference, stated the following.

How do we ensure the New Zealand public is behind the strategy? ... The strategy will only succeed if it has wide backing. We must quickly reach out to the wider business community, to local government, to important interest groups like Forest and Bird and the Fish and Game Council, and to iwi (Maori tribal groups). To realise our tourism potential, we must enlist as broad a spectrum of support for tourism as possible ... But, perhaps most importantly: How do we ensure that tourism growth is sustainable? For New Zealand to benefit from tourism growth we must ensure it is sustainable – not just economically but also culturally, socially and environmentally ... Tourism growth must not come at a cost to our natural heritage and our way of life ... When presented with the strategy, I will be very pleased if it has managed to answer these questions! I want us to have a clear direction forward and a clear identification of roles and buy into responsibilities (cited by Coventry, 2000b).

It is evident from this quote that the New Zealand government in 2000 had a wider perspective of a tourism strategy beyond issues of promotion, and also an extended view of who are the stakeholders within tourism.

Politics and politicking

It can be discerned from the above discussion of the role of the public sector that change has taken place and is an outcome of political action and the personalities present. Labour Ministers such as Mike Moore and Fran Wilde left their mark on the tourism industry. Moore was very supportive of the industry and was able to obtain continued government funding for NZTP and tourism in the Rogernomics regime. Fran Wilde, in the short time she was Tourism Minister, abolished the Tourism Council, and set up the Tourism Strategy Marketing Group under Jim Scott and the Tourism Forum as another industry body for her to deal with instead of the NZTIF.

Personalities and politics continued under the national government ministers: 'John Banks had a simple philosophy. His view was that the best government was the one that let the industry dictate the future and he did not interfere, when he picked his man, in this case Norman Geary, he put total trust in him and he left him (to it). So Norman had the ability to really drive foreword his vision for the marketing of New Zealand and you cannot underestimate that, the man was immensely powerful he was the el supremo' (Burt, pers. comm., 2003).

The next period was even more political and has been dubbed the 'Murray McCully affair'. A minister arguably went beyond ministerial powers by intervening in the marketing policies of the then NZTB on the grounds that, in his view, it was insufficiently promoting New Zealand as the first country to see the new millennium, and was failing to grasp opportunities presented by hosting the 2000 America's Cup. As a result of his intervention, the chief executive officer (CEO) and a number of directors resigned in protest about what was seen as both an undeserved criticism of the Tourism Board and an intervention in the daily functions of the board, thereby overstepping the functions of a minister.

Politicization of both the industry and its issues continued after the McCully affair. The NZTIA, as a significant pressure group, was able to secure more public sector support (and funding) for the industry and its organizations, including the Office of Tourism and Sport and TNZ, and arguably less directly for RTOs by making local politicians more aware of the importance of tourism as a contributor to the New Zealand economy, if only through the amount of attention the news media paid to the industry and its politics. This was symbolized by the 2000 annual conference of the NZTIA, having as its keynote speaker the Prime Minister, Helen Clark. Its then CEO, Glenys Coughlan, was effective in ensuring that the industry association retained sufficient political presence to refute initiatives such as a tourist tax and to sustain current public funding of border controls while voicing criticisms relating to other legislation such as the Employment Contracts Act and Resource Management Act. In addition, by publicly supporting the Office of Tourism and Sport, it successfully helped to secure monies for research initiatives that were currently not funded by the industry itself, but which were nonetheless orientated towards market research needs. One example was the re-establishment of a domestic visitors' monitor. Here there was a congruence of interest between the wider industry, the NZTIA, the Office of Tourism and Sport and the predisposition of a Labour government to a more interventionist form of government compared with that of its predecessor.

Thus far, since 1999, the Labour government has adopted a hands-off approach as far as the promotion of New Zealand by TNZ has been concerned, apart from one minor criticism by the Prime Minister that there is more to the country than scenery and a green image (Hendery, 2000). Incidentally, this illustrates either the ironies or pragmatism of politics, whereby a left-of-centre government this decade has rejected direct intervention in overseas marketing, while a conservative, market-led government of 1998 sought to interfere directly.

While events in Wellington may be thought peripheral to the marketing of tourism at a regional level, given the small community that is New Zealand's decision makers in tourism at both regional and national level, the linkages are such that changes at the top cannot but affect the regional promotion and tourism policies being undertaken.

The regional tourism organizations

Such national events and considerations have impacted upon RTOs both directly and indirectly, albeit to differing extents depending on the nature of the region and the historical antecedents of the RTO concerned. RTOs are not uniform within New Zealand. In the 1980s local authorities were reorganized and regional councils, representing a third tier of government between the national and local levels, were established. 'The NZTPD and the Tourism Industry Federation (a precursor of the NZTIA) tried to consolidate these "bits and pieces" tourist promotion bodies across the country into thirteen regional tourist organizations (RTOs). This was the first time the term RTOs was used' (Staniford, pers. comm., 2002)[4]. The Industry Federation took a firm stand that there should be only thirteen RTOs, based on the regional councils' geographical distribution, but this was beset with problems (Staniford, pers. comm., 2002). The NZTPD also took the same view (Plimmer, pers. comm., 2002). However in the late 1980s, it became apparent that at the local level individuals and groups had different agendas and it was impossible to secure collaboration. One example was that Wanaka, Queenstown and Dunedin councils were initially to work together, but in the end the reality of local politics meant that Queenstown went its separate way (Staniford, pers. comm., 2002).

At the time of writing, in 2003, there are twenty-six RTOs, but their administrative boundaries differ from those of the twelve regional councils that exist. Most RTOs are funded by local authorities but some are also funded by regional councils. Regional councils are funded both by local authorities and through the ability to levy their own rate, and under Section 593(b) of the Local Government Amendment Act, can become involved with tourism promotion if all local authorities within a regional council's jurisdiction unanimously agree. Hence, in the example of the Manawatu-Whanganui Regional Council, that council stepped in to establish an RTO given differences of opinion that existed between Whanganui and Palmerston North City Councils and Manawatu District Council as to the promotion of tourism. However, inasmuch as the resultant River Region RTO has a limited budget and was staffed by a part-time consultant, its ability to provide direction for better funded and arguably more energetic (and competing) District Tourism Councils was limited. A further factor that limited the ability of River Region RTO was that the administrative boundaries of the Manawatu-Whanganui Regional Council were and remain inconsistent with patterns of tourism flows or nodal points of tourism attractions. For example, the region covers both the east and west sides of the Tararua Ranges, and roads and resultant traffic flows differ as to the approaches to Wellington.

The regional council Environment Waikato covers a large part of central North Island New Zealand, stretching from the west coast from Raglan and Kawhia, to the east coast and the Coromandel Peninsular. In this instance there

---

[4]Tony Staniford was the Chief Executive of the New Zealand Tourist Industry Federation, the peak tourism industry body in New Zealand, from 1972 to 1993.

exist two RTOs, those of Tourism Waikato and Tourism Coromandel, but both of these have linked with the RTOs of Rotorua, Auckland and Taupo to establish a Central North Island Marketing Network. Yet this network also illustrates the variations that exist within RTOs. Tourism Waikato, while covering a large region that includes the tourist hotspot of Waitomo with its cluster of adventure operations and the glow-worm caves, is dominated in its funding by Hamilton City Council, both in absolute terms and in funding per head of population. Hamilton City Council provides 75 per cent of the total funding (Tourism Waikato, 2001) yet, because some councillors do not perceive Hamilton as being a 'tourist attraction', while others adhere to the ideological view that the industry should pay for its own organizations, the RTO has had difficulty in sustaining its own revenues. The nature of the debate was clearly shown by the webpage sustained by local member of parliament, Bob Simcock (http://www. bobsimcock.co.nz/press/main9.htm). On 22 October 1999 he wrote:

The City Vision members oppose any expenditure on tourism promotion. They argue that the council doesn't promote plumbers, so why should it promote the tourism sector. But this is the sort of purist nonsense that gives them a bad name. The benefits from tourism are spread widely … The Mayor and others appear to be more interested in scoring some point over surrounding Waikato councils who they believe are not paying their fair share of the costs of Tourism Waikato … But the idea of promoting Hamilton in separation from the rest of the Waikato is silly (Simcock, 1999).

This debate was not unique. Exactly the same issues arose in the case of Palmerston North City Council and the surrounding Manawatu District Council, albeit in a different format, in 1994. At that time the City Council established Tourism Manawatu, funded entirely by the city council, it being aware that promotion of the city without reference to the surrounding attractions made little sense. However, some within the district council saw this as an attempt by the city to 'take over' the promotion of 'their' area and 'their' attractions, and in consequence a rival tourism promotional body was established with district council support. It was not until there was a meeting of all mayors under the auspices of the Manawatu-Whanganui Regional Council that the issue was solved. Parochialism bedevils tourism policies in New Zealand. Examples can be found where personalities and differences have led to intensely held views, but nonsensical outcomes. For example, both of the small communities of Foxton and Waihi (each of which has a population of under 10 000), in the 1990s had, for some time, not one but two competing tourism promotional bodies. Colleagues at other universities in New Zealand could probably provide other examples of local politics inhibiting sensible actions.

Even the more successful RTOs have not been without their political battles. Tourism Rotorua is one of the larger RTOs in New Zealand in that it employs about seven people (by comparison, Tourism Waikato employs a CEO and two staff, as does Tourism Coromandel). Rotorua has a history of being a tourist location since the 1850s, and tourism accounts for about 20 per cent of the city's gross domestic product (GDP) (Butcher *et al.*, 2000). Yet in the mid-1990s its then CEO resigned on a matter of what to him was an issue of principle in that he argued that the RTO's mandate was to serve all tourism businesses and organizations and not simply the interests of the largest commercial members with the largest promotional budgets. Today, Tourism Rotorua has been able to initiate policies based upon Agenda 21 and cautiously advance concepts of environmental good practice, and in 2003 was grappling with the implications of local government reform that required councils to consider wider social impacts of change.

Local government and regional tourism organizations

The relationship between RTOs, their industry memberships and their local authorities has been ambiguous, to say the least. The RTOs generally have a membership derived from the commercial stakeholders of the tourism industry, membership of which will often include the accommodation and attractions sectors, among others. Yet the membership fees are generally nominal, as size of membership acts as one of the validating criteria when an RTO purports to represent 'the local industry'. Hence, in many instances the major funding of an RTO is derived from local government. The same model is true for many of the DTOs. Consequently, the size of budget between RTOs varies considerably. Tourism Auckland thus has a budget of about NZ$5.5 million, while Tourism Waikato has a budget of less than NZ$500 000. The contributions made by local authorities to RTOs vary considerably, both in absolute terms and in terms of rate support per head of population. Thus, in the case of Tourism Waikato, one authority, Hamilton City Council, provides 75 per cent of the total funding (about NZ$3 per head of population), while support from one other member local council is assessed at 75 cents per head of population. For the DTOs, the funding can be even more disparate. Horowhenua District Council funds its DTO to a figure of over NZ$100 000, while Rangitikei District Council provides no direct funding at all to Rangitikei Tourism, which is otherwise an entirely operator-funded body. Indirect support is provided by Rangitikei Tourism holding a contract to run two visitor information centres from the district council, a role that it was re-examining in early 2001. In other cases local authorities directly fund visitor information services (e.g. Palmerston North City Council).

It should not be thought that these funds are the sole revenues available to DTOs and RTOs. In many instances the RTOs co-ordinate specific marketing promotions, which are then funded by those stakeholders and members who have a specific interest in the promotion. For example, attraction and site operators in Northland and other regions adjacent to Auckland partook in, and financed, promotional activities aimed at those attending the defence of the America's Cup in 1999/2000 and again in 2002 through initiatives made by the RTOs.

Probably the most successful RTO in attracting industry support has been that of Wellington. There the value of industry support in 1999/2000 was estimated as being about NZ$3.1 million (Coventry, 2000c). This is partly funded by the accommodation sector imposing a small fee on its bed rates, and then passing this to its RTO. The first author was involved in an attempt to follow this model in another New Zealand city. First, the local motel association was reluctant to support the initiative on the grounds that the RTO did little for them. Second, when the manager of the largest hotel promised to provide several thousand dollars to the fund, local moteliers grumbled that it 'was alright for him, it is not his own money!' Finally, the local motel association agreed to the concept, but on the proviso that as the main beneficiary of tourism was the local retail and restaurant sector, they would participate if the local retailers and restaurants did so. As there was no one retail organization that could represent all of the town's retailers (as the moteliers well knew) the initiative failed. As Rob McIntyre, CEO of Wellington's RTO in 2000 stated, 'Another factor in Wellington City Council's strong investment is the significant pressure on Totally Wellington to leverage from the private sector. Last year we achieved about $2 million industry support in cash, contra and collective buying-benefit for the city' (cited by Coventry, 2000d).

The attitude of local authorities is also shown by the statements made about tourism within their local annual plans which, under the amended Local Government Act, they are required to produce. In their survey of local authorities in New Zealand and their attitudes towards tourism planning, Page and Thorn (1998, p. 183) concluded that 'This study however, is perhaps more disturbing because of the implication the findings have at the national level. Only the local and regional councils have any role at all in terms of managing tourism growth in New Zealand, and it is apparent that even there, involvement is limited.' Again, differences can be found. Whereas many city councils are practically silent on tourism issues, others make more specific mention. For example, in its Annual Plan, Dunedin City states that:

> *Tourism, along with education, is a key sector in the Dunedin economy. The role of this function is to promote Dunedin, locally and overseas, as*

an attractive venue for leisure, conferences and educational tourism. The main objective is to get more tourists to Dunedin and to keep them here longer and this achieved through funding provided to Tourism Dunedin (Dunedin City Council, 2000, p. 45).

In 2002 Page and Thorn replicated their earlier study. They concluded that little had changed over the intervening five years. They refer to a lack of communication and co-ordination in matters pertaining to sustainability, of low levels of funding and the low political importance possessed by tourism. It should be noted that the survey was undertaken in August 2000, and hence at a period when many of the recent initiatives mentioned above had not yet started, or were at best embryonic. Nonetheless, one of their major findings was a need for a clear vision and direction for tourism, and the issue is whether the Tourism Strategy 2010 is sufficient to address those needs.

This brief review indicates that the levels of funding of RTOs and DTOs and the level of concern about tourism being expressed by local authorities vary quite considerably. Why is this? A number of reasons can be suggested. First, as Page and Thorn (1998) found, there is a widespread lack of understanding of the impact being made by tourism at a regional and local level. This is in part due to past deficiencies in statistical series, but the issue is now being addressed by RTOs themselves as they seek to substantiate their existence. Certainly, as is evidenced by the case of Tourism Taranaki, which in 2000 ceased to exist for a time [see various issues of *Inside Tourism* (Coventry) for coverage of this debate], RTOs have no privileged right of existence. Consequently, a number of RTOs commissioned research from various bodies as to the economic impact that tourism made upon their local regions. For example, Butcher *et al.* (2000) estimated that tourism in Rotorua was worth NZ$463 million and employed 3500 full-time employees, thereby making it the third most important source of employment in the city. Dudding and Ryan (2000) estimated that tourism was worth NZ$87 million to the Coromandel, while Hughes and Ryan (2001) estimated that tourism was contributing about 4.3 per cent to local GDP in the case of the region served by Tourism Waikato. The objective of commissioning such studies is that RTOs often use the findings to persuade councillors that tourism is an activity that is worth supporting from the public purse.

Second, attitudes will vary as to how local authorities perceive their region's standing in the national portfolio of tourist attractions, and how the regions are perceived by other key players in the industry. In this respect one cannot overlook the importance of the national carrier, Air New Zealand. It might be said that Air New Zealand has an interest in the promotion of New Zealand by TNZ and the

RTOs on the premise that if New Zealand is perceived as an attractive place to visit, then demand for its services will increase. Equally, as a domestic as well as an international operator, Air New Zealand would wish to serve those places that possess the ability to sustain profitable flows of visitors and that have the necessary infrastructure in place. Local authorities are very aware of that issue. For example, Queenstown sought, and gained, improvements to its airport which included extending the runway and building new terminal facilities not only to permit direct international flights, but also to enable Air New Zealand to fly its new, larger jets on domestic flights direct into the town, thereby bypassing Dunedin. Equally, Rotorua councillors were dismayed by the news that Air New Zealand was withdrawing jet services from their city as the runway was too short, although arguably, in international terms, given that Hamilton is but an hour away and possesses a full-length runway and existing flights to Australia, opportunities exist for joint marketing initiatives between the two locations. Nonetheless, parochial pride and perceived economic necessity meant that Rotorua District Council, in 2002, bought out the private-sector interest in the airport and committed themselves to capital expenditures of, it is estimated, about NZ$20 million in extending the runway and upgrading terminal facilities.

The importance of such scenarios was amply demonstrated when Geoff Burns, then manager of International Markets for Air New Zealand, expressed the view at the 2000 New Zealand National Tourism and Hospitality Research Conference, that Air New Zealand wishes to co-operate with about only five RTOs who had the marketing clout to attract international visitors. Indeed, the then managing director of Air New Zealand, Jim McCrea (2000), argued that it was Air New Zealand's policy to 'leverage off major events'; such events tend to be within a limited number of locations owing to the infrastructure needs required. This has been seen as preserving the status quo of airborne passengers to reconfirm what has been known as the golden triangle of tourism in New Zealand, centred upon Auckland, Rotorua, Christchurch and Queenstown. This has meant that other RTOs have to compete with that perception, while the domestic market also becomes extremely important to them. Local authorities that perceive themselves as being of national importance tend to fund their RTOs better.

But herein lies another issue for the relationship between the RTO/DTO and the local authority. As Page and Thorn (1998, 2002) found, rarely in local authority planning departments can there be found tourism 'specialists', and thus the expertise is more likely to be found within the RTOs. As 'tourism experts', RTOs are staffed by those who also express concerns about environmental and social aspects of tourism. Thus, the example has been given of Tourism Rotorua seeking to encourage environmentally good practices, while NZTIA, to its credit, has also undertaken Agenda 21 initiatives. However, the paradox has arisen that the RTO has sometimes been less enthused by pro-development policies than have some local councillors, who therefore become critical of their RTO for not full-heartedly proclaiming a short-term promotional policy. While it is not possible here to go into all the details, the instance of Queenstown Lakes District Council and its pro-development mayor's attitudes towards issues of zoning is an interesting case study. This dispute terminated in the Queenstown Lake Landscape Decision whereby the Environmental Court effectively renounced the piecemeal approach of the council and reinforced the protection of the environment by upholding then existing zoning regulations, which have had implications for property and tourism development in the town (Schöllmann, 2000; Miller, 2001). Certainly the RTO and the tourism industry were not at one on these issues, some placing environmental protection before development, some arguing that the economic case must have precedence, and some seeking a middle way.

Finally, issues between RTOs and local authorities are sometimes made difficult because of intercouncil rivalry and distrust, as evidenced above. RTOs have to stand independently of their funders, even while they seek to encourage a better understanding of tourism and the needs for funding. However, Dymond (1997) found congruence between local authorities and RTOs as to their priorities with reference to tourism. The leading three priorities for both groups were 'tourism's contribution to the economy', 'consumer satisfaction' and 'local satisfaction'. Yet the first author has found examples where local councillors and operators have expressed views that seem to imply a competitive rather than a strategic stance. For example, dissatisfaction has been expressed by some Waitomo operators with Tourism Waikato, arguing that it is too orientated towards Hamilton City to the detriment of the Waitomo. At another RTO's board meeting that the author attended, a councillor stated that he knew nothing about tourism other than the fact he enjoyed going on holiday. In his defence it must be stated that he was an advocate of many initiatives. On another occasion, a special meeting was convened (to which the author was invited) by a councillor who had previously shown no interest in tourism. This councillor had attended a conference where James Strong, the then CEO of Qantas, had been the keynote speaker. After playing a thirty-minute tape of Mr Strong's talk, the councillor demanded to know what 'his area' was doing about tourism. The remaining two hours were then taken up with an explanation of what was being done with the limited funding being made available. More seriously, some regions still feel a loss of independent political direction following the reforms of local government in 1989 that reduced the number of local authorities in New Zealand, and for example, in the past the relationship between Queenstown and it's surrounding region has not always been harmonious.

The political complexities between RTOs and local government are currently being addressed as a consequence of the 2010 tourism strategy and the response of RTONZ and Local Government New Zealand. The Tourism Strategy 2010 made reference to NewRTOs and currently the Ministry of Tourism has funded research relating to the way in which RTOs work. For example, at the time of writing, current research is being conducted on their use of research and statistics, while the underlying question remains of their funding, functions and relationship in economic planning in the new structures of local government, given recent amendments to the Local Government Act and changes being introduced in the Resource Management Act.

Conclusion

Thus far, much of what has been written seemingly has little to do with destination marketing, but from this brief discussion of political scenarios in New Zealand as they affect tourism at national and local levels, a number of dimensions can be identified. They include those of professionalism versus enthusiasm, short-termism versus long-term perspectives, competition versus co-operation, and tourism being considered not at all versus tourism being perceived as an important economic and social factor. These factors, and others, may be represented in a diagram as shown in Figure 6.1. One side of the diagram may be thought to represent the positive dimensions, the other the more chaotic, if not negative.

Politics is generally assumed to be about the use of power, and the role of power structures. For an industry that is so economically significant, tourism is politically weak. It is weak because its base is comprised of many, small concerns, not all of which are strongly economically motivated. At a local level, except for some rural areas and the urban areas of Rotorua, Queenstown and to a lesser extent Christchurch and Dunedin where tourism is well established and highly visible, the industry lacks real political clout. It has been argued that this could be addressed if more of those involved in tourism stood for local political positions. Given such a vacuum, the real sources of power in New Zealand tourism politics, prior to 2001, might be said to have been Air New Zealand, a few large companies such as Tourism Holdings, and public-sector or quasi-public-sector organizations such as TNZ and then the existing Office of Tourism and Sport. Much of the industry is represented by pressure groups such as the Tourism Industry Association and its various member bodies, and thereby almost by default the NZTIA has assumed some political influence. Within this scenario it becomes possible for individuals to achieve significant levels of influence, at least within certain spheres. Among these players are the

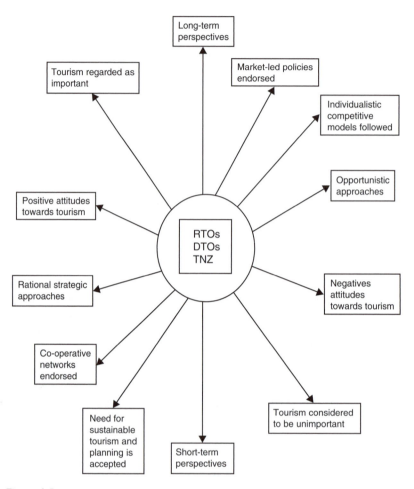

Figure 6.1 Dimensions of political perspectives

CEOs of a number of the RTOs, and to a lesser extent DTOs. Certainly at a regional level and district level, such CEOs can possess an important ability to influence policies within the domain of tourism and those things that impinge upon it. Given the small world of New Zealand (which has a population of only 4.1 million but is larger than the UK in land area), personality and a proven record of successful ventures can go far in generating a political influence, as personal networks are important (although this may be true of many societies).

Because of the high level of public funding of TNZ, RTOs and DTOs, these organizations exist within a political framework with varying degrees of ease. As was demonstrated by the McCully affair and at least at the anecdotal level, by the interventions of councillors at the level of RTOs and DTOs, political interference can sometimes be direct. That the intervention does not happen more regularly or more often is due to the constitutional rules, understood if not written, that generally prohibit politicians from direct interference in the day-to-day running of organizations such as RTOs. However, such organizations occupy an uncertain legal ground. Although heavily funded by the public purse, they are not part of the 'civil service'. They possess industry members, and may engage in direct commercial activities themselves if they run visitor information centres that sell products on a commission basis. While many would perceive their essential function as being that of the promotion of a region, and as offering advisory services to their industry membership, because of their expertise they are often asked to go beyond this. They may, for example, become involved in product development through the encouragement of event and conference promotion. Although regionally based, their awareness of actual tourism flows has made the RTOs (at least in the Central North Island region) one of the biggest supporters of network marketing initiatives whereby resources are combined. Owing to their awareness of social and environmental issues pertaining to tourism, they may at times be seen as inhibiting entrepreneurial activity if it is felt that such activity is dominated by short-term needs with possible negative longer term consequences.

As stated previously, the very ambiguity of the nature of an RTO or a DTO is in part its strength. These organizations create a forum where the public and private sector meet, and where the needs of local authorities to create a planning regime interface with the need of operators to sustain themselves financially. By reason of their position, and the linkages that CEOs of RTOs and DTOs have with national organizations, the local interfaces with the national, and flows of information proceed in both directions. To be effective networks require density of points, communication flows, discerned directions, information and a willingness to participate. Within their own communities RTOs and DTOs provide a key component in such networks, and thereby play an important role in information dissemination and opinion formation.

Do all of these considerations impact upon regional and destination marketing? In a direct sense the answer has to be generally 'no', in spite of the occasional example of elected politicians attempting to frame the content of marketing direction. But indirectly the answer has to be in the affirmative, for it is the political scenario that influences the level of budgets being made available to TNZ, RTOs and DTOs. In most cases budgets are tied to the annual cycle of public-sector budgeting and what elected politicians feel they can allocate from revenues derived from taxes and rates, and over which spending departmental heads engage in sometimes bitter disputes. In these considerations tourism is possibly still perceived as a frivolous source of expenditure compared with sewage disposal, roads, medicine and health. From this arises two concerns: first, the continuing emphasis on economic performance, sometimes embodied by expressed concern about social and environmental matters, and second, by a search for the type of 'catch-all' slogans that were illustrated at the start of this chapter. In a world where conventional marketing wisdom dictates that relationship marketing is the way to progress, such broadband marketing approaches as 'sloganeering' has little to recommend itself. Until recently this was a practical issue for cash-strapped tourism organizations, but seemingly an answer has been provided by the internet. Thus, TNZ's strategy is, to a large extent, web based, with its theme of '100% Pure New Zealand' acting as a portal to various types of 'kiwi experiences'. At the same time, though, businesses themselves are increasingly bypassing promotional organizations for direct selling, but recognize that for marketing based around special events and trade shows, where a 'public face' to a region or destination is required, the RTOs and DTOs still have an important function.

In reviewing this chapter for the second edition of this book, almost all of the above conclusions still stand. But events have not stood still in the intervening years. The position of Air New Zealand has been very much weakened in the period since the collapse of Ansett Australia in spite of an almost overwhelming share of the domestic market. In early 2004 not only did it and Qantas fly trans-Tasman routes, but so did a number of other airlines, including Emirates, Thai, Royal Brunei and Virgin Blue. The tourism industry itself was severely adversely affected by the severe acute respiratory syndrome (SARS) epidemic in early 2003, although far less seriously in New Zealand than in other parts of the world. But perhaps the major change domestically has been the emergence of a new and far more proactive Ministry of Tourism under the current Labour government. Arising almost phoenix like from the former Office of Tourism and Sport, it has emerged and taken a strongly proactive line, albeit at times veiled by working through the Tourism Research Council. The ministry is seeking to implement many of the recommendations of the Tourism Strategy 2010, and it is significant that the current government has provided a major part of the additional funding that the strategy identified as being needed for purposes of implementation. A significant part of the strategy related is to NewRTOs and their rationalization and creation of shared resources. It is the view of the authors that given current funding regimes the reduction in the number of RTOs is not likely to occur, but what is emerging is an embryonic secretariat through RTONZ which is potentially permitting not only closer co-operation in promotional activities, but also a greater awareness of regional economic impacts within a commitment to sustainability. Already moves are afoot to establish a parallel framework of Maori Regional Tourism Organizations, while a Maori mark of authenticity in the arts has been established and new initiatives in the Visitor Information Network and the establishment of the 'I-sites' branding have been undertaken.

In short, the earlier chapter wrote of a vacuum in creating a sense of direction. In the last days of the old National government and the early days of the current government a momentum had been established that produced the Tourism Strategy 2010. Past such strategies have subsequently collected dust while lying on shelves, but in this case under current government policies and aided through major private sector bodies such as those represented through the NZTIA and the Tourism Research Council, monies and time are being provided. In addition, the major RTOs are increasingly liaising with TNZ and hosting update days continually to inform, learn from and enthuse their commercial memberships. The Tourism Strategy identifies as enablers technology, people, research and development, infrastructure, investment and quality, and the current ministry is working in partnerships across these groupings in a wider framework of social and environmental legislative enactments. Indeed, while the period of Rogernomics unleashed a torrent of change across the New Zealand landscape, the current changes, although more quiet, are in many ways just as significant. By drawing people into a network of liaisons current policy seems to be harnessing the energies of people that previously were directed towards the protection of regional or district interests.

What conclusions can be reached from this review? It certainly appears that central government policy is important in determining the environment within which action takes place. A second conclusion is that a pendulum has swung and that the early 2000s are in many ways a revisiting of the policies of the 1980s, but within a context of a more mature industry and a greater appreciation of the economic contribution that tourism makes to the New Zealand economy. Third, people do make a difference, and the government has sought to be inclusive and engage important decision makers and influencers in their policies. Fourth, at the local level, there is still a parochial interest, as is evident from the time that RTO CEOs have to spend with local councils, especially those that derive funding from more than one council. Fifth, promotional activities that are the apparent rationale of the NTO and RTOs are determined to a surprisingly large extent by the political and social environment within which the NTO and RTOs operate. While day-to-day operations are those of brochure production, trade fairs, and so on, CEOs spend a considerable proportion of their time engaged in a wider political scene. Perhaps this is a sign of industry maturation. The past has been characterized by the leitmotiv that for all its economic importance the industry possessed remarkably little political power. Such power comes from participation in political processes, and that too is another conclusion that emerges from this review. Effective promotion and marketing require investment and resources, and in the quasi-public sector occupied by the NTO and RTOs, such resources emerge not from conventional sources of profit taking, but from effective lobbying and engagement with elected representatives. Finally, there is an undercurrent that is gaining strength within New Zealand, that tourism promotion without reference to wider environmental and social implications is potentially short-sighted. Currently there is an emphasis on Green Globe 21 as both a marketing and sustainability planning mechanism, although whether this is viable in the longer remains to be tested. In short, currently New Zealand is passing through an interesting phase of potential change. It is too early to assess the extent to which it is durable, and the possible outcomes, but the change over the two years since the first edition of this book is indeed palpable.

References

Archives New Zealand/Te Whare Tohu Tuhituhinga O Aotearoa, Head Office, Wellington: AAAC 7923 W5158/183 ADM 070 Part 2; AAAC 7923 W5158/212 PDR 0951 Part 5; AAAC 7924 W5158/2 0806 Part 2.

Burt, D. (2003) Interview on 22 May 2003.

Butcher, G., Fairweather, J. R. and Simmons, D. (2000) *The Economic Impact of Tourism on Rotorua.* Tourism Research and Education Centre, Lincoln University, Report No. 17/2000.

Coventry, N. (2000a) Tourism strategy may benefit from increased resources. *Inside Tourism,* No. 310 (15 June). Paraparaumu Beach: South Pacific Media Services.

Coventry, N. (2000b) Minister ponders strategy. *Inside Tourism,* No. 319 (17 August). Paraparaumu Beach: South Pacific Media Services.

Coventry, N. (2000c) Retaining council support isn't easy. *Inside Tourism,* No. 318-2 (11 August). Paraparaumu Beach: South Pacific Media Services.

Conventry, N. (2000d) New Chief Eyes Slowdown. Inside Tourism. September 21, Number 234. Paraparaumu Beach: South Pacific Media Services.

Dudding, V. and Ryan, C. (2000) The impacts of tourism on a rural retail sector: a New Zealand case study. *Tourism Economics* 6: 301–319.

Dunedin City Council (2000) *Annual Plan, 2000/1.* Dunedin, New Zealand.

Dymond, S. (1997) Indicators of sustainable tourism in New Zealand: a local government perspective. *Journal of Sustainable Tourism* 5: 279–293.

Hall, C. M. (1994) *Tourism and Politics: Policy, Power and Place.* Chichester: Wiley.

Hendery, S. (2000) Pure NZ message paying off for tourism. *New Zealand Herald* (27 December): C1.

Hughes, W. and Ryan, C. (2001) Estimates of the value of tourism for Tourism Waikato. Unpublished document. Hamilton: Waikato Management School, University of Waikato.

Local Government New Zealand (2003) *'Postcards from Home': The Local Government Tourism Strategy, May 2003.* Wellington: Local Government New Zealand.

McCrea, J. (2000) ANZ's industry contribution is sometimes under-appreciated. *Inside Tourism*, No. 296 (9 March). Paraparaumu Beach: South Pacific Media Services.

Miller, M. (2001) Court sets rules for Wakatipu. *Southland Times* (2 January).

New Zealand Tourism Department (1991) *Newsletter* (April/May).

Office of Tourism and Sport, New Zealand Tourism Industry Association, New Zealand Tourism Board, Department of Conservation and Air New Zealand (1998) *Tourism Research and Development Strategy*. New Zealand: Office of Tourism and Sport.

Page, S. J. and Thorn, K. (1998) Sustainable tourism development and planning in New Zealand: local government responses. In Hall, C. M. and Lew, A. A. (eds) *Sustainable Tourism.* Harlow: Longmans, pp. 173–184.

Page, S. J. and Thorn, K. (2002) Towards sustainable tourism development and planning in New Zealand: the public sector response revisited. *Journal of Sustainable Tourism* 10: 222–238.

Pavlovich, K. (2000) The organisation of supply in a tourism destination: an analysis of a networked community – the Waitomo Caves Village. Unpublished PhD thesis. Hamilton: Waikato Management School, Waikato University.

Plimmer, N. (2002) Interview on 17 December 2002.

Plimmer, N. (2003a) Interview on 12 June 2003.

Plimmer, N. (2003b) Personal communication 12 June 2003.

Ryan, C. and Simmons, D. (1999) Towards a tourism research strategy for New Zealand. *Tourism Management* 20: 305–312.

Schöllmann, A. (2000) Local authority regulation and promotion of tourism – the management of conflict in Queenstown. Paper presented at the 4th New Zealand Tourism and Hospitality Research Conference, AUT, Auckland, New Zealand.

Simcock, B. (1999) Tourism Waikato – a victim of a visionless council. http://www.bobsimcock.co.nz (22 October).

Staniford, T. (2002) Interview on 17 August 2002.

Tourism Strategy Group (2001) *New Zealand Tourism Strategy 2010.* Wellington: Tourism Strategy Group.

Tourism Waikato (2001) *Waikato Regional Tourism Strategy: 2000–2010: A Strategy for Sustainable Growth and Development.* Hamilton: Tourism Waikato.

Wanhill, S. (2000) Issues in public sector involvement. In Faulkner, B., Moscardo, G. and Laws, E. (eds) *Tourism in the 21st Century: Lessons from Experience.* London: Continuum Books, pp. 222–242.

Winder, P. (2003) Interview on 8 May 2003.

7

Branding and national identity: the case of Central and Eastern Europe

Derek Hall

Introduction

At national and local levels, postcommunist reimaging in Central and Eastern Europe (CEE) has been informed by a requirement to portray a Europeanness which conforms to requirements for European Union (EU) accession, and the projection of a safe, stable and welcoming environment to encourage foreign direct investment and international tourism. Branding of CEE destinations is taking place alongside the development and marketing of niche tourism products which represent a response to changing global tourism demand and the need to raise per capita levels of tourist receipts. Recruited in the processes of national identity projection and representation, niche development has proceeded rapidly, notably in the areas of heritage and culture, nature and ideals of sustainability.

Within a context of change, diversity and differentiation, this chapter attempts to:

- examine ways in which national identity is employed in tourism branding and promotion in CEE
- evaluate relationships between processes of restructuring, the emergence and re-emergence of national identities and tourism marketing.

Tourism holds a significant position in the substantial political, economic and social restructuring processes that have taken place in CEE since the early 1990s. By the end of the twentieth century, the impact of travel and tourism in CEE was estimated to have a gross domestic product (GDP) equivalent of €95 billion. The sector was reckoned to employ 21.3 million people, representing 11.7 per cent of the region's workforce (WTTC/WEFA, 1999).

International tourism was important in the region under communism, and in many cases long before that (Hall, 1991). Until the late 1980s (except in Yugoslavia) it was usually directly managed through monopolistic state organizations: travel and tourism bureaux, hotel chains, transport companies and guide services. 'Social' domestic tourism, entailing the provision of subsidized transport and accommodation for prescribed periods, was usually available for urban workers and their families. Inbound international tourism was intended to assist the generation of convertible currency and to help provide a positive image for the country and region. Pursuit of the latter was often counterproductive because of poor levels of service and infrastructure, bureaucratic restrictions and inflexibility. With the exception of Yugoslavia, most international tourism was generated from other state socialist countries, whose tourists were largely inured to, and thereby unwittingly helped to perpetuate, such poor service levels. The 'brand' was ideology, and the foreign language marketing used was often grammatically fractured and semantically ambivalent. The resulting ambience was parodied by Malcolm Bradbury (1983, 1984) and captured in the reportage of James Cameron (1967) and Eric Newby (1984), amongst others.

In the late 1980s and early 1990s tourism development became embedded within processes of economic, political and social restructuring. Such relationships and processes both embraced and reflected price liberalization, privatization, deregulation, institution capacity building, changing personal mobility, infrastructural upgrading, enhanced and reoriented foreign trade and investment, and currency convertibility (Jaakson, 1996). Those countries of post-communist Central Europe (Hungary, Czech and Slovak republics, Poland and Slovenia), spatially and structurally best placed for EU integration and amongst those states acceding in 2004, have revealed mixed tourism fortunes in recent years (Table 7.1). This followed notable growth in international tourism activity during the 1990s, which itself had roots in developments under way before 1989. The Baltic states have shown significant growth in receipts in recent years since being in line for EU accession. By contrast, tourism and its economic

Table 7.1 Central and Eastern Europe: international tourist arrivals and receipts, 1990–2000

Country	International tourist arrivals (millions)			International tourism receipts (US$ million)			Receipts per capita (US$)
	1990	*1995*	*2000*	*1990*	*1995*	*2000*	*2000*
EU entrants							
Czech Republic	7.28	3.38	5.70	419	2875	2869	503
Estonia	na	0.53	1.10	na	353	505	459
Hungary	20.51	19.62	15.57	824	2640	3424	220
Latvia	na	0.52	na	na	20	131	241[a]
Lithuania	na	0.65	1.23	na	77	391	318
Poland	3.40	19.22	17.40	358	6614	6100	351
Slovakia	0.82	0.90	1.05	70	620	432	411
Slovenia	0.65	0.73	1.09	721	1084	957	878
Other CEE							
Albania	0.03	0.04	na	4	65	na	1929[b]
Belarus	na	0.16	na	na	23	17	62[b]
Bosnia-Herzegovina	na	0.04	0.11	na	7	17	155
Bulgaria	1.59	3.47	2.79	320	473	1074	385
Croatia	7.05	1.49	5.83	1704	1349	2758	473
Georgia	na	0.09	na	na	na	na	1042[a]
Macedonia, FYR	0.56	0.15	0.22	45	19	37	168
Moldova	na	0.03	0.02	na	4	4	235
Romania	3.01	2.76	3.27	106	590	364	111
Russia	na	10.29	21.17	na	4312	na	406[a]
Serbia/Montenegro	1.19	0.23	na	419	42	na	112[a]
Ukraine	na	3.72	na	na	3865	na	502[a]
Other CIS							
Armenia	na	0.01	0.03	na	5	45	1500
Azerbaijan	na	0.09	0.68	na	70	na	135[a]
Kazakhstan	na	na	na	na	122	na	na
Kyrgyzstan	na	0.04	na	na	5	na	136[b]
Tajikistan	na	na	na	na	na	na	na
Turkmenistan	na	0.22	na	na	na	na	640[b]
Uzbekistan	na	0.09	na	na	na	na	77[b]
USSR	7.20	–	–	2752	–	–	–

Sources: World Trade Organization (WTO, 2002a, b); author's additional calculations.
[a] 1999 figure, [b] 1998 figure, na: data not available.

impact in relatively unstable South-eastern Europe and the Commonwealth of Independent States (CIS) tended to stagnate or even decline within often fluctuating annual trends (Hall, 2000; Light and Dumbrāveanu, 1999). In these countries, where private sector underfunding is often a problem, a low level of infrastructure support has often persisted (Bachvarov, 1999). Further, in some, particularly former Soviet states, data accuracy remains questionable.

Tourism branding in Central and Eastern Europe?

Destination branding, with its core objective of producing a consistent, focused communication strategy (Morgan and Pritchard, 1998, p. 147), confronts at least three major constraints in CEE. First, a lack of adequate finance to support appropriate marketing campaigns – a common trait – has been exacerbated by limited experience of global markets and a lack of appropriate expertise. Second, tourism destination marketers may be pressured to return short-term results when long-term investment is required to build a consistent brand. Such a dilemma may be reflected in message inconsistency. Third, whereas centralized, relatively authoritarian regimes can impose some control and coherence over the component parts of a destination image, it is more difficult within market economies to develop a coherent brand for destinations that are composed of myriad products and environments.

At a general level, branding approaches in CEE have been faced with at least three sets of constraints. First, the immediate postcommunist period of 1989–1992 imposed new and relatively distinct images of countries and regions suddenly being open, inviting and embarking on a process of substantial transformation. Within five years, however, much of this factor had been dissipated, such that, except for the cities of Prague and Budapest, which have sustained strong identities through urban-cultural imagery, little apparent long-term competitive advantage appeared to have been gained, with often confused, contradictory or absent destination images portrayed.

Second, CEE has tended to be associated with an image of indifferent quality and limited product ranges. Some mass marketing alludes to this in an optimistic manner, for example: 'Moscow is now a cosmopolitan city and shoppers may be surprised at the variety' (Premier Holidays, 2000, p. 92). Cheapness in some aspects (food, transport, attractions, shopping) is still extolled in certain mass-market brochures (e.g. Balkan Holidays, 2003, pp. 7, 9). There is perpetuated a sense of undifferentiated destinations, with often expensive but poor-quality hotel accommodation. Although the particular way of relating to the customer under state socialism – studied indifference – has largely passed from Central Europe, elements remain in areas to the east and south-east.

Third has been the need for those countries seeking EU accession to align their legislative, political and economic institutions and practices with those of Western Europe and to ensure consonance with requirements of the *acquis communautaire*. While acceptance for membership of Euro-Atlantic institutions has been the goal of several countries' transition processes, it has not been an easy or straightforward pathway, even for relatively advanced states such as the Czech Republic (Hall, 2004).

A requirement for brand development is clearly evident at a number of levels. Indeed, although both tourism activity and per capita levels of tourism income have significantly increased across the postcommunist world, CEE still lags behind much of the rest of Europe (Table 7.2).

European economic and political convergence, and the leisure search for new experiences and products, provide a potentially wide range of opportunities for the branding, segmentation and marketing of CEE tourism (e.g. Roberts and Hall, 2001). At a national level, a number of promotion 'straplines' have been adopted to encapsulate desired brand images: uniqueness, accessibility, security, ecological friendliness. At a destination level, most notable branding has been pursued for urban 'cultural' destinations, with attempts to embed them within explicitly 'European' heritage and progress themes, as exemplified by *Krakow 2000: European City of Culture* (Blonski, 1998).

Although the conditions for destination branding across CEE differ considerably, several common factors suggest the importance of projecting strong

Table 7.2 Central and Eastern Europe: international tourist arrivals and receipts as a proportion of the European total

Central and Eastern Europe	1985	1995	1999	2000
% of European international tourist arrivals	19.0	23.7	22.6	20.9
% of European international tourist receipts	4.6	11.0	12.8	12.9

Sources: WTO (1998, pp. 164–165; 2000, pp. 19–20, 26–27; 2002a, b); author's additional calculations.
Central and Eastern Europe (CEE) includes all those countries falling within the WTO's 'Central/East Europe' region, together with Albania and the states of (former) Yugoslavia which are subsumed under the WTO's 'Southern Europe' region.

brand images either sectorally or geographically based. These include the requirement to:

- emphasize a 'Europeanness'
- generate customer loyalty through repeat visits
- raise per capita tourism income levels.

More specifically, although the relative importance of factors varies from country to country, branding is required to respond to:

- new and changing market demands, including the impacts of EU enlargement
- increasing market differentiation
- the need to disassociate from the recent past
- the desire to (re-)create a (new) national image, which may, paradoxically, emphasize heritage factors drawing on the distant past
- the need to disassociate from regional instability.

Although better knowledge of markets is required, as relatively little market survey work on international tourists to CEE appears to have been undertaken, marketing does have a long pedigree in the region, and its resurgence is strongly evident (e.g. Meler, 1997; Martin and Grbac, 1998) with the presence of internationally linked groups such as S Team Bates Saatchi & Saatchi Advertising Balkans, as well as Western organizations such as Millennium PR of London, both involved in marketing tourism for Serbia (Popesku, 2003). Much effort is being put into producing lively and imaginative websites, with marketing messages and logos that are emerging as branding tools in their own right (e.g. Slovenian Tourist Board, 2003).

Changing market demands

The growth of cultural and heritage tourism has coincided with a postcommunist reinvigoration of a sense of historical perspective and a heightened awareness of nationality to accompany the (re-)creation of new state systems. Images of heritage are often used, somewhat paradoxically, as a vehicle of restructuring and modernization, particularly in rural regions (e.g. Light, 2000). The 1990s saw increasing diversification of niche marketing. Some segmentation, such as gastronomy (e.g. Csapo et al., 2000; Kraus, 2000; National Authority for Tourism, 2000), has been based on local economic back-linkages, particularly with restructuring rural economies. Other segments, such as health and spa resorts (e.g. Popesku, 2000) and heritage trails (e.g. Kornecki, 2000), draw on a fund of local cultural tradition that can be traced to classical times.

By contrast, the rapidly growing activity holiday segments (e.g. Wieczorek, 1999; Stifanic, 2000) represent direct responses to perceived demand, although appropriate infrastructure and quality levels may not yet be in place.

Ironically, urban cultural tourism, notably in Prague and Budapest, was transformed in the 1990s into a mass activity, exacerbating congestion and infrastructural problems (e.g. Simpson, 1999). Nonetheless, the image projection of Prague ('City of a hundred spires') in particular as 'cool', signifies the potential of CEE destinations to be marketed as fashion accessories. For example, cities such as Kraków, the former national capital in southern Poland which was largely untouched by wartime damage but harmed by postwar industrial pollution, and Dubrovnik, the ancient walled city of Ragusa on Croatia's Dalmatian coast targeted in the conflict with Serbia, bestowed with Unesco World Heritage Site status, are consolidating or reviving their heritage-related brand images.

While numerically, international tourism in postcommunist CEE has increased substantially, in South-eastern Europe and much of the former Soviet Union, destinations have not been able to take advantage of the potentially wide range of tourist markets opened to them. This is partly due to lingering images of regional instability, poor service, infrastructure and facility quality, and possibly, more recently, the shadow effect of the EU's 2004 enlargement.

Destination branding and image construction: escaping from South-eastern Europe

Positioned on the western edge of the Islamic world, the Balkans, a term loosely coterminous with South-eastern Europe, is a region that has been subject in recent history to largely pejorative image constructions in the West. Dictionary definitions of 'balkanize' tend to emphasize diversity, conflict and fractionalization (Todorova, 1994; Hall and Danta, 1996), and the recent history of South-eastern Europe has done little to persuade potential tourist markets that this subregion should be perceived otherwise. It has therefore been one role of tourism marketing for destination countries on the fringe of South-eastern Europe to distance themselves from 'Balkanness' and to employ branding to this end. The examples of Slovenia and Croatia can illustrate some of the issues raised. In both cases, as recently emergent independent states formerly of the Yugoslav federation, their use of branding has positively attempted to assist the creation of a new national image, and negatively, to distance themselves from the Yugoslav past.

Yet the two are very different. Embracing a short length of coast, a diversity of inland products and sharing borders with two EU member states, Slovenia views itself firmly within a Central Europe of mainstream European culture and economy. Croatia also sees itself as Central European, yet its long coastline was the essential ingredient of the pre-1991 Yugoslavia tourism product, and as such may be many Westerners' only experience of 'Yugoslavia', an image not easy to dispel.

Slovenia

As one of the favoured CEE states for early EU accession, Slovenia has used tourism as a key ingredient in its postindependence economic and political strategy and national image projection. With just 47 kilometres of Adriatic coastline, even when part of Yugoslavia, emphasis in Slovenia was placed upon interior attractions, the development of which in many cases dates from Austro-Hungarian times: Lake Bled and the Julian Alps, Postojna and other extensive karstic cave systems, and the Lipica stud farm, famous for supplying Lippizaner horses to the Spanish Riding School in Vienna (since 1580). As such, there has been a long continuity in the image promotion of these destinations and their products, although markets have varied and changed. More recent Slovenian promotion has emphasized niche segmentation within an environmentally friendly framework. For example, the integration of gastronomy and tourism has been pursued, reinforcing a rural–cultural emphasis and efforts to increase added value to many of Slovenia's products, as encapsulated in promotions for 'wine journeys' (e.g. Fujs and Krasovec, 1996).

Needing to establish both an individual national identity and a suitable vehicle for (re-)attracting both established and new Western markets, 'The sunny side of the Alps' was initially adopted as a national tourism promotion strapline, embodying positive attractions of climate, topography and contiguity with Western Europe. Following Italian objections, this was replaced in the mid-1990s with 'The green piece of Europe', symbolizing a philosophical shift in terms of emphasizing, or at least suggesting, a nature-based, environmentally aware tourism product.

In both cases, product differentiation and quality association can be seen in the way in which the country has gone to some lengths to reinforce the mental geographical imagery of Slovenia being firmly part of ('Western' or 'civilized') Europe, by:

- emphasizing its Central European credentials (Habsburg heritage, Alpine associations, contiguity with Austria and Italy)

■ distancing itself from any 'Balkan' association, a desire underscored by the political requirement to put the country's Yugoslav past firmly behind it.

For example, Slovenia's appearance ('Lakes and mountains of Slovenia') in a mass tourism brochure largely devoted to Croatia, talks of 'delightful villages and warm and hospitable people, whose lives are still steeped in the traditions of centuries of Austrian rule' (Transun, 1998), thereby emphasizing a Central/Western European heritage, untainted by more recent (Communist, Yugoslav war) years, and the break-up of the Austro-Hungarian empire with the outcome of World War I. Indeed, for the purposes of the world's media, the Slovenia Tourist Board (1999, p. 1) considered it necessary to state bluntly: 'Slovenia is actually situated in Central Europe not in Eastern Europe at all!'

Although the country won its independence after a short skirmish with the Yugoslav army in 1991, a Slovenia Tourist Board was not established until 1996, with the mission:

> to promote Slovenia as a country with a clear and distinctive identity and clearly defined comparative and competitive advantages and thereby assist the Slovene economy by marketing Slovene tourism in a concrete manner (Slovenia Tourist Board, 1998b, p. 1).

In its 1997 marketing plan the Tourist Board began to promote the country's tourism resources in terms of five sector 'clusters': coast and karst, mountains and lakes, health resorts, cities and towns, and the countryside. A new logo was developed which incorporated four flower heads (green, yellow, red and white) breaking out of a blue square base adjacent to the name *Slovenija* (Slovenia Tourist Board, 1998a). This has been adopted comprehensively on promotional material, including stylized brochures for each of the five sector clusters, although compared with those used previously it is an arguably less clear and articulate brand in conveying the country's distinctive positioning.

Slovenia has found it difficult to generate the tourist numbers comparable to those before the disintegration of the Yugoslav federation, yet as a consequence of diversification, niche orientation and season extension, by the mid-1990s the country was enjoying the highest level of receipts per international tourist arrival in CEE. In 1997, at $1219, this was almost twice the level of next highest Croatia, with $661, and more than six times higher than the levels of Hungary ($199) and Bulgaria ($166). By 2000, the gaps had narrowed somewhat, with average per capita receipts of $878 for Slovenia, $473 for Croatia,

$386 for Bulgaria and just $220 for Hungary (Table 7.1). With near neighbours Italy, Austria and Germany providing almost 60 per cent of the country's tourist arrivals, as well as generating high-spending cross-border excursionists, Slovenia's branding emphasis on natural and cultural attractions has benefited from an environmental diversity located within a relatively compact country appealing to affluent, hard-currency neighbours.

Croatia

Like Slovenia, Croatia was a former Austro-Hungarian, and thus Roman Catholic, constituent member of Yugoslavia. Constituting the bulk of the former Yugoslavia's coastline and thus much of its tourism industry, it has not been one of the favoured countries for early EU accession. Unlike Slovenia, Croatia was enmeshed during the first half of the 1990s in continuing hostilities both on its own soil and in Bosnia, with a consequent collapse of the country's tourism industry and an undermining of much of its credible image as a postcommunist democracy. Perhaps the most notable erstwhile brand image of the Yugoslav coast, the medieval walled city of Dubrovnik, was deliberately shelled by Serbs and Montenegrins during the hostilities as a means of undermining Croatia's economy.

Under these circumstances, it was vital, following the cessation of conflict, that Croatia should establish a national tourism marketing policy which, closely allied to national image rebuilding, would, as a brand, convey a distinct image:

- to differentiate clearly the country from its neighbours
- to reassure former markets that quality and value had been restored
- which, through the country's major tourism attributes, could secure long-term competitive advantage.

Involving an appeal to previous mass tourism markets on a destination basis while seeking to develop sector-based niche specialisms within a national framework, Croatia's attempt at destination branding was complemented by the adoption in the mid-1990s of a tourism marketing logo: a half-circle of multicoloured balls radiating from a half-orange, half-red sun-like ball, with the word CROATIA below, symbolizing the conjunction of sun and sea as well as a new dawn for Croatian tourism. But name apart, this visual cliché was little different from those adopted by several other tourism destinations. Indicating this weakness, some marketing material subsequently adopted a supplementary slogan below the CROATIA: *Small country for a great holiday.*

From 1997, more concerted efforts were made to (re-)establish a national destination brand:

- a new national brand logo was launched: the word CROATIA with the horizontal line through the two 'A's made wavy to symbolize the sea. The first 'A' is placed in a blue square (dark blue above the wave, light blue below) which is complemented by another, red, square immediately above the preceding O: 'the logotype is interwoven with the symbol ... (which) ... is actually the visual code of the Republic of Croatia' (Ljubicic, 1997, p. 27). This is the chequerboard coat of arms as adopted for the national flag with strong historical associations. This visual code is also to function as a brand on crockery, food items and souvenirs;
- three international tourism-related conferences were hosted in Dubrovnik in September 1997. These were intended to help relaunch both Croatia and Dubrovnik onto the West European tourism agenda, following the physical and symbolic assaults of the Yugoslav wars. Their purpose was to project a strong renewed brand image of Dubrovnik as a cherished World Heritage Site symbolizing not just the phoenix-like restoration of the city, but also of (eastern) Adriatic tourism and of Croatia itself. Through the platform provided by the conferences, particular groups of opinion formers and representatives of upper income niche markets were specifically targeted for the projection of this message.

Complementing the country's reappearance in mass tourism brochures during the later 1990s, marketing copy reinforced the need for Croatia to recapture previous markets:

> *If you have been to Croatia before – and many hundreds of thousands of British holidaymakers have – you will know already the delights that await you there in 1999* (Transun, 1998, p. i).

Indeed, during 1998 national newspaper advertising (in the UK at least), saw the CROATIA logo promoted alongside the slogan 'A new welcome. An old friend'. This mirrored glossier mass-market promotion material:

> *Croatia – welcome back old friend ... An old friend with a new name ... The population is 90% Roman Catholic. So many aspects of Croatia will remind you of Italy, Spain and France, where strong family values remain and churches are always full on Sundays* (Holiday Options, 1998, p. 4).

The message was clear: Croatia as a destination brand was familiar, 'like us', safe, pious, trustworthy: comfortably European and a natural component part of the successful Mediterranean tourism product. Whether this is the appropriate brand image for the markets being targeted – in some of which at least, churches are unlikely to be full on Sundays – is contestable.

But at much the same time, Meler and Ruzic (1999, p. 643) were arguing that the Republic of Croatia did not have a clear image because there was not a recognizable economic and marketing identity from which to develop it. Despite the country's relative success in attaining 1990 levels of international arrivals and receipts, such an image is still unclear. For example, Balkan Holidays (2003, p. 99) describes the country for the 2004 mass market as:

> *situated on the crossroads between central Europe and the Mediterranean, this enchanting corner of Europe … the 'Land of a thousand islands' … a unique country of fascinating culture, unrivalled natural beauty and rich history and tradition. It basks in almost constant (sic) sunshine.*

As a 'new' destination for 2004, Thomas Cook's (2003, p. 302) depiction is of:

> *a relatively hidden gem on the tourist trail, Croatia combines a wealth of history, culture and unrivalled natural beauty … it enjoys a typically Mediterranean way of life …*

Thus history, culture and natural beauty are emphasized, as they are for most other destinations featured in such brochures. A 2003 newspaper campaign emphasizes a retrospection: 'Croatia … the original spirit of the Mediterranean', featured over an Adriatic island twilight photograph with its very explicit Venetian architecture. In the absence of a positive national image, Meler and Ruzic (1999) suggested that the establishment of a tourism identity must be part of a trinity of vehicles – the other two being exports and inward investment – which need to be appropriately positioned in relation to key markets in order to help establish a positive and coherent image for the country. But surely in the case of Croatia, with its diverse coastline and interior, substantial north–south extent and unusual horseshoe configuration, the relatively negative image that 'Croatia' received in the early 1990s coupled with the strong brand identity of such icons as Dubrovnik suggests that more emphasis should be placed on specific destination rather than country imagery, alongside the promotion of specific segments to act as an interface between coast and interior, such as cultural tourism and ecotourism (e.g. Jordan, 2000).

Russia's constrained branding

The marketing of Russian destinations is at best constrained and fragmentary, and only partially attempts to overcome images of instability and lack of security.

For example, at a recent World Travel Market in London, the most prominent Russian representation was expressed along two dimensions:

- organization-based, notably Intourist, with its corporate branding (e.g. Intourist, 2000) but offering a limited range of 'products' (Moscow, St Petersburg, Golden Ring, Cruise of the Tsars, Trans-Siberian Railway, Silk Road)
- geographically focused, with the representation of Daghestan and Kamchatka, located at the south-western and eastern extremities of the Russian Federation, being particularly notable.

Daghestan is a Muslim republic the size of Scotland with a population of 2.1 million, within the Russian Federation (e.g. Gammer, 2002). The promotion of tourism is represented exclusively through material produced by the Daghestan Tourism Ministry (1996). While adopting a motif and consistent presentational style, this is written in neo-Soviet/Malcolm Bradbury style. Although representing substantial evidence of cultural and natural heritage, Daghestan's tourism promotional material also extols the presence of manufacturing industry (e.g. Tsapieva, 2001), and in its English language version, retains a map wholly in the Cyrillic script. Thus, although distinctiveness and national identity (Silvertseva, 1999) are expressed, they are done so in an uncompromising manner and with little regard to specific market characteristics. Allusion is also made to the propinquity of Chechnya, whose conflict spilled over the border into Daghestan in 1999, bringing with it a major refugee problem and a very explicit constraint in tourism promotion and development.

By contrast, the isolated Kamchatka peninsula, on Siberia's Pacific rim, is being promoted by small, private companies offering activity holiday products (e.g. Lena and Friends, 1999; Sampo-Tour, 1999; Kamchatintour, 2000) within a land of snow, volcanoes and pure nature. Although organizationally fragmented, there is a strong sense of identity and purpose conveyed by the Kamchatka promotional material, which is written in mostly good, direct English, employing strong illustrations, emphasizing safety and security, and providing website location follow-up. Closed to the outside world for seventy-four years, this identifiable geographical unit has rapidly become one of the more effectively branded destination areas of Russia, albeit primarily targeting Japanese and US markets rather than Europe. There is also strong evidence of collaboration and partnership (e.g. Wild Russia, 2003), both among indigenous firms, and between them and incoming operators, such as the UK Muir's Tours (2003).

Clearly, the enormous extent and diversity of Russia lends itself to differentiation and a fragmentation of image projection. The branding of both 'traditional' (e.g. Moscow, St Petersburg, Silk Road) and 'new' (e.g. Kamchatka) destinations should be balanced with the need for product branding and more discerning market segmentation. Retention of the Intourist administrative brand may not endear, for example, Western adventure tourists looking for destinations and activities that would have been antithetical to the philosophy of the Soviet-period Intourist. This may suggest that the combination of small, private companies pursuing branded niche activities is the most likely way forward to market the myriad products and regions yet to be developed for tourism within the Russian Federation. An overarching need, however, will be the continued assurance of safety and security within what is still a potentially unstable country embracing significantly volatile regional components.

Conclusion

Integration into the global economy and preparation for accession to the EU have been prime foreign policy driving forces, especially of the more advanced economies of Central Europe (Hall and Danta, 2000). National identity and image formation have been consciously moulded towards these ends in a number of cases. International tourism has been recruited to play a significant role in this process, both in terms of image reinforcement and as an international binding agent. However, destination branding and positioning strategy are generally still poorly developed in much of the region's tourism industry, owing to a combination of lack of finance, experience and expertise.

A change in emphasis from a destination to a product focus is taking place in the more advanced countries pursuing niche segmentation and in those states of South-eastern Europe wishing to shake off Balkan connotations. The value of an established brand lies not least in the perceptions of consistency and quality that it represents. Within and between the countries and regions of CEE, quality is not consistent and the marketing message, from individual destinations and countries and collectively at a regional level, may be equally unclear. Indeed, it is questionable whether 'Eastern Europe' and 'Central and Eastern Europe' are meaningful or helpful labels with which to be associated in image-formation terms.

If CEE tourism is to improve further its level of per capita income, co-ordination between government action and tourism industry promotion would appear vital to project clear, positive national, regional and destination images that can contextualize and emphasize quality and differentiation. Across the region there is limited evidence of co-ordination of local, regional and national tourism interests. This is perhaps understandable given that over much of the region there has been a desire to reduce any form of centralized planning as a reaction to the previous half-century of state socialist impositions and the association of co-operation with collective action and thus collectivization. Yet collaboration, networks and partnerships are essential in assisting the generation of appropriate brand images if the various components of the region wish to position themselves in relation to key international tourism markets.

References

Bachvarov, M. (1999) Troubled sustainability: Bulgarian seaside resorts. *Tourism Geographies* 1: 192–203.

Balkan Holidays (2003) *Summer. Bulgaria Croatia Slovenia Montenegro Romania.* London: Balkan Holidays.

Blonski, K. (1998) *Krakow 2000: European City of Culture.* Krakow: City and Voivodship of Krakow.

Bradbury, M. (1983) *Rates of Exchange.* London: Secker and Warburg.

Bradbury, M. (1984) *Welcome to Slaka.* London: Secker and Warburg.

Cameron, J. (1967) *Point of Departure.* London: Arthur Barker.

Csapo, K., Nagyvathy, E. and Pakozdi, J. (2000) *Hungary: Flavours of a Country.* Budapest: VIVA Media Holding.

Daghestan Tourism Ministry (1996) *Discover Daghestan.* Makhachkala: Daghestan Tourism Ministry.

Fujs, V. and Krasovec, M. (1996) *Wine Journeys in Slovenia.* Ljubljana: Vas Travel Agency and Republic of Slovenia Ministry of Agriculture, Forestry and Food.

Gammer, M. (2002) Walking the tightrope between nationalism(s) and Islàm(s): the case of Daghestan. *Central Asian Survey* 21: 133–142.

Hall, D. (ed.) (1991) *Tourism and Economic Development in Eastern Europe and the Soviet Union.* London: Belhaven.

Hall, D. (2000) Evaluating the tourism–environment relationship: Central and Eastern European experiences. *Environment and Planning B: Planning and Design* 27: 411–421.

Hall, D. (ed.) (2004) *Tourism and Transition: Governance, Transformation and Development.* Wallingford: CAB International.

Hall, D. and Danta, D. (eds) (1996) *Reconstructing the Balkans.* Chichester: Wiley.

Hall, D. and Danta, D. (eds) (2000) *Europe Goes East: EU Enlargement, Diversity and Uncertainty.* London: The Stationery Office.

Holiday Options (1998) *Dalmatian Riviera & Islands.* Burgess Hill: Holiday Options.

Jaakson, R. (1996) Tourism in transition in post-Soviet Estonia. *Annals of Tourism Research* 23: 617–634.

Jordan, P. (2000) Restructuring Croatia's coastal resorts: change, sustainable development and the incorporation of rural hinterlands. *Journal of Sustainable Tourism* 8: 525–539.

Kamchatintour (2000) *The Kamchatka Peninsula: Hidden Pearl at the Treasury of the Earth.* Petropavlovsk: Kamchatintour.

Kornecki, M. (2000) *The Trail of Wooden Architecture.* Krakow: Krakowska Agencja Rozwoju Turystyki SA.

Kraus, V. (2000) *South Moravian Vineyards and Wine Cellars.* Valtice: Vinarskou Akademii Valtice.

Lena and Friends (1999) *Heli-skiing/Snowboarding: Kamchatka, Russia.* Petropavlovsk: Lena and Friends.

Light, D. (2000) Gazing on communism: heritage tourism and post-communist identities in Germany, Hungary and Romania. *Tourism Geographies* 2: 157–176.

Light, D. and Dumbrāveanu, D. (1999) Romanian tourism in the post-communist period. *Annals of Tourism Research* 26: 898–927.

Ljubicic, B. (1997) New look Croatia. *Croatia* (Summer): 27–29.

Martin, J. H. and Grbac, B. (1998) Smaller and larger firms' marketing activities as a response to economic privatization: marketing is alive and well in Croatia. *Journal of Small Business Management* 36: 95–99.

Meler, M. (1997) Marketing in transition conditions: example of the Republic of Croatia. *Eastern European Economics* 35: 66–74.

Meler, M. and Ruzic, D. (1999) Marketing identity of the tourist product of the Republic of Croatia. *Tourism Management* 20: 635–643.

Morgan, N. and Pritchard, A. (1998) *Tourism Promotion and Power: Creating Images, Creating Identities.* Chichester: Wiley.

Muir's Tours (2003) *Muir's Tours – Siberia – Kamchatka.* Reading: Muir's Tours. http://www.nkf-mt.org.uk/Siberia_Kamchatka_Trek.htm

National Authority for Tourism (2000) *Romanian Gastronom.* Bucharest: National Authority for Tourism.

Newby, E. (1984) *On the Shores of the Mediterranean.* London: Harvill Press.

Popesku, J. (2000) *Spas and Health Resorts in Serbia.* Belgrade: National Tourism Organization of Serbia.

Popesku, J. (2003) Personal communication. President, Centre for Responsible and Sustainable Tourism Development, Belgrade, 8 August.

Premier Holidays (2000) *Short Breaks.* Cambridge: Premier Holidays.

Roberts, L. and Hall, D. (2001) *Rural Tourism and Recreation: Principles to Practice.* Wallingford: CAB International.

Sampo-Tour (1999) *Amazing Kamchatka: Peninsula on the Edge of the World.* Petropavlovsk: Sampo-Tour.

Simpson, F. R. (1999) Tourist impacts in the historic centre of Prague. Resident and visitor perceptions of the historic built environment. *Geographical Journal* 165: 192–200.

Sivertseva, T. (1999) Daghestan: the quest for national identity. *Central Asian Survey* 18: 359–372.

Slovenia Tourist Board (1998a) *Marketing of Slovenia's Tourism: Corporate Image.* Ljubljana: Slovenia Tourist Board. http://www.tourist-board.si/podoba-eng.html

Slovenia Tourist Board (1998b) *Slovenian Tourist Board: The Role of STB.* Ljubljana: Slovenia Tourist Board. http://www.tourist-board.si/vloga-eng.html

Slovenia Tourist Board (1999) *Slovenia at a Glance: Some Brief Notes for Press Visitors.* Ljubljana: Slovenia Tourist Board. http://www.slovenia-tourism.si/enews/article-01.html

Slovenian Tourist Board (2003) *Welcome to Slovenia.* Ljubljana: Slovenian Tourist Board. http://www.slovenia-tourism.si/

Stifanic, D. (2000) *Vrsar: Bike Eco Ride.* Vrsar: Tourist Association of Vrsar.

Thomas Cook (2003) *Summer Sun. April to October 2004*, 2nd edn. Peterborough: Thomas Cook.

Todorova, M. (1994) The Balkans: from discovery to invention. *Slavic Review* 53: 453–482.

Transun (1998) *Transun's Croatia.* Oxford: Transun.

Tsapieva, O. (2001) Post-Soviet socio-economic development in Daghestan. *Central Asia and the Caucasus* 2: 168–176.

Wieczorek, E. (1999) *The Silesian Voivodship Invites: Active Tourism.* Katowice: Silesian Voivodship Tourist and Promotion Office.

Wild Russia (2003) *Wild Russia.* Saint Petersburg: Wild Russia. http://www.wildrussia.co.uk

WTO (1998) *Tourism Market Trends: Europe.* Madrid: World Tourism Organization.

WTO (2000) *Tourism Highlights 2000*, 2nd edn. Madrid: World Tourism Organization.

WTO (2002a) *Compendium of Tourism Statistics 1996–2000.* Madrid: World Tourism Organization.

WTO (2002b) *Tourism Highlights 2002.* Madrid: World Tourism Organization. http://www.world-tourism.org

WTTC/WEFA (Wharton Econometric Forecasting Associates) (1999) *Travel and Tourism – Jobs for the Millennium.* London: World Travel and Tourism Council.

8

The internet challenge for destination marketing organizations

Adrian Palmer

Introduction

Tourism destinations are probably one of the most difficult 'products' to market, involving large numbers of stakeholders and a brand image over which a destination marketing manager typically has very little control. The diversity and complexity of tourism destinations is well documented (e.g. Heath and Wall, 1991; Palmer and Bejou 1995; Leiper, 1996), and this makes brand development very difficult for national, regional and local tourism organizations. Destination branding necessarily involves the focused attention of all tourism-related organizations in a destination, and this can create major challenges in getting all stakeholders to develop a coherent theme for the destination brand. There have been many notable successes in developing strong tourist destination brands (e.g. the brand development pro-grammes for New York and Spain), but equally many efforts at co-operative mar-keting have failed to gain momentum. This chapter reviews the challenges and opportunities arising from the technologies of high-speed data transmission (comprising, among others, the world wide web, the internet, e-commerce and m-commerce) for the marketing of tourism destinations.

Co-operative promotion of tourism destinations has conventionally focused on the production of joint publicity brochures, often distributed through shared stands at exhibitions (although many organizations have done much more, such as operating booking services). The development of electronic commerce now offers opportunities for collaboratively marketing tourism destinations. There is the potential to create 'virtual co-operation', whereby potential tourists can browse through websites of individual facilities at a destination and develop a coherent picture of the destination experience on offer. The development of sophisticated destination management systems (DMS) allows the resources of a destination to be linked so that a potential visitor sees a coherent visit experi-ence, rather than a series of disjointed resources. There are many challenges in making DMS work effectively, and these are discussed later in this chapter.

There is a strong consensus that 'image' is a pivotal aspect of a marketing strategy for a destination and numerous authors have investigated the use of image in brand formation for destinations (Heath and Wall, 1991; Chon, 1991). It is argued that despite a multiplicity of products and services under the one brand umbrella, the formation of a brand identity can be achieved to give the destination a common marketing purpose and direction. Examples are the Brand Australia initiative to gain partnerships between all state tourism bodies within Australia, Queensland's 'Destination Queensland: Beautiful One Day, Perfect the Next!' campaign and the Brand Ireland campaign to promote south-ern and Northern Ireland as a single tourism destination. The development of a central brand for a destination faces new challenges and opportunities from evolving electronic distribution channels. While the internet can allow suppliers in a destination to come together to create a strong centralized site, the internet can also facilitate a stronger presence for individual tourism suppliers in the marketplace, who are now able to reach their potential markets more directly. In the context of tourism destination brands, it is quite possible that individual companies who make up a tourist destination may seek to open up direct chan-nels with their existing and prospective customers, rather than channelling more effort into the development of a central brand for the destination. This may be a real possibility where an operator offers a unique facility such as a theme park, the appeal of which is not directly related to the area in which it is located.

Search engines are increasingly allowing internet users to search out types of activity rather than destinations per se.

Electronic marketing of tourism destinations

The potential of the internet is already quite apparent, and the scale of its impact will grow rapidly. Increasingly the internet will be accessed from different types of equipment: television, handheld personal digital assistant (PDA) devices, kiosks, computer games consoles, etc. Worldwide, the number of people buying online is forecast to increase from 143 million in 2001 to 446 million in 2005, with expenditure increasing from US$634 billion to more than US$5 trillion over the same period (*Computer Industry Almanac*, 2002). Tourism-related services have emerged as a leading product category to be promoted and distributed to consumer markets through the internet and are expected to account for an increasing share of this rapidly growing market, rising from less than 10 per cent of online commerce in 1998 to 35 per cent or more in 2003 and beyond. The nature of consumers' search activity, involving multiple choice of suppliers and comparison of facilities, prices and availability, is facilitated by the search capabilities of the internet. Increasingly, tourism suppliers are able to profile consumers and provide a selection that is based on their needs. Electronic commerce offers great flexibility for tourism suppliers operating in volatile markets. The promotional message can be changed much more quickly than is the case where the requirement to print brochures leads to long lead times between a policy decision being made and the implementation of that decision. Electronic commerce is very good at handling clearance of perishable capacity close to the time of use and managing yields effectively. Customers benefit from such channels by gaining immediate gratification of their requests, greater choice, accurate and up-to-date information, and an easy-to-use interface. Similarly, the costs of obtaining information are reduced for customers and the wide diversity of information can be represented on one terminal. Many tourism destination marketing organizations have developed websites with varying levels of interactivity. An interactive website provides a good opportunity for the multiple suppliers involved in a tourism destination to fashion together uniquely the specific components of a destination offer, which are sought by individual visitors.

Faced with a rapid increase in information availability through the internet, a crucial role is played by the methods used to guide individuals through the enormous range of destination options available. In this sense internet-based marketing is no different to traditional marketing in that consumers seek to

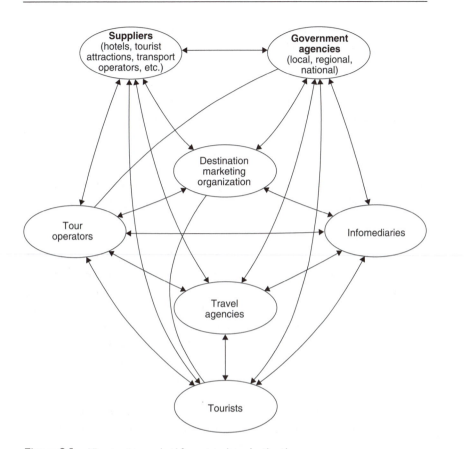

Figure 8.1 'Routes to market' for a tourism destination

simplify their choice by using a combination of intermediaries, trusted brand names and established business relationships. Within the tourism sector, the role of tour operators has simplified the purchase process of tourism buyers by prepackaging the elements of a vacation that might otherwise be difficult to assemble individually. The use of trusted brand name tour operators and the emergence of branded virtual intermediaries has helped to reduce the perceived riskiness of tourism purchases. The complexity of a tourist destination's 'routes to market' in an electronic environment is illustrated in Figure 8.1.

The fundamental distribution channel in the travel industry is made up of three important players: principals, intermediaries and customers. Principals provide travel services to end-users. Intermediaries pass information about these services onto potential customers and try to influence targeted customers to use their channel. They also facilitate in customizing the principal's services to the end-user's needs and handling paperwork and after-sales enquiries. An early move to create an electronic distribution channel was provided by global distribution systems (GDS), which represented a closed, dedicated connection of terminals displaying travel information about airlines, hotels, car rentals, cruises and other travel products. Used almost exclusively by travel agents, the GDS created a linear distribution chain. With advances in communication and software, GDS, such as those operated by Sabre, Galileo, Amadeus and Worldspan, have been reduced to just one component of a much larger system of networked travel information. Increasingly, internet-based travel companies, online access providers and other virtual communities appeal directly to consumers and travel agents, thereby circumventing the traditional GDS. The world wide web has made this possible and GDS are being transformed into global distribution networks (GDN). This is the larger 'ecosystem' in which the constituents of a distribution system unite, and has dramatically affected how travel products are distributed in the travel industry. This emerging distribution channel facilitates the multidimensional flow of information and transactions, with any organization in the channel able to distribute travel information and complete a transaction directly with customers. However, direct booking of travel services is not always a feasible option for service principals owing to the complexity and sensitivity of channel partners, in addition to the extra costs incurred by maintaining their own dedicated fulfilment centres.

Tourist destinations can benefit from the internet by developing a coherent position in the marketplace, increasing their market share by getting closer to customers (actual and potential), and subsequently by ensuring delivery of high levels of customer satisfaction. The role of information integration and brokerage is especially applicable to destination marketing organizations (state tourism departments, national tourism offices, and city convention and visitor bureaux) as they rarely have a product of their own to sell. Instead, their role is to match buyers with sellers, demand with supply and producers with consumers by positioning and promoting a place as a tourism destination brand.

Destination marketing organizations can embrace internet technology at a number of levels. At its simplest, a world wide web page is essentially an electronic document which allows multiple users (consumers) to access and download information from the page to their own computers. Each webpage can be stored on numerous computer servers all connected to the internet, which in effect broadens the distribution of the webpage to a larger number of potential users around the world. The flexibility to update and then distribute a webpage electronically has created exciting marketing possibilities for tourism suppliers. The world wide web can be compared to a product brochure that is constantly up to date, graphical and colourful, capable of text, audio and video images, cheap and easy to copy, and accessible by millions of readers around the world.

Many destination marketing organizations, especially small, local ones, have limited their web presence to an online brochure. Others have gone beyond this with the development of destination databases that can be used for customer targeting and request fulfilment through an online reservation system (OLRS). These databases can offer full product information, interactive booking capability, and real-time price and availability information. Several destination databases have been developed worldwide, often involving large investment costs, and with varying degrees of success, including the BOSS system in Canada, GULLIVER in Ireland, SWISSLINE in Switzerland and ATLAS in Queensland, Australia.

Destination management systems

Destination management systems take the development of an online destination brand beyond the stages of merely offering an online brochure, or providing an online reservation service. A DMS provides a suite of tools for managing a destination's tourism activities. This includes systems for managing information for all of the constituent tourism organizations' websites as well as sales offices, call centres, literature fulfilment and marketing functions. Also included are systems to manage communications services and OLRS. There are now a number of software companies that offer DMS, usually on a modular basis which allows users to add on facilities, depending on their specific requirements. A typical DMS is illustrated in Figure 8.2.

The modules that make up a DMS are a combination of those that are immediately visible to the public and a range of 'back-office' functions. The following

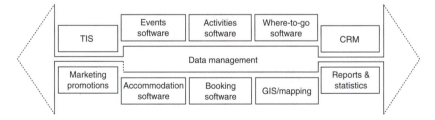

Figure 8.2   Structure of a typical destination management system. TIS: Tourist Information System; CRM: Customer Relationship Management (*Source*: reproduced with permission of BVG Internet)

are typical functions of a DMS (typically a DMS will offer some of these services, but few will offer all of them):

- *website server*: provides templates allowing users of the DMS easily to create and maintain websites for different regions, in specific languages
- *online reservation system*: can be either provided as a self-managed system with its own inventory, or linked to a GDS; the system would be linked to an electronic payment system
- *e-mail management and post office services*: including newsletter subscriber forms, mailing list manager, multiple respondent accounts, automatic responders and online mail administration for POP accounts
- *search facility*: allows users to find information quickly on a subject that may otherwise be difficult to find in a large website
- *personal brochure/personal web*: allows visitors to the system to pick their options and have delivered to them a personal view of the destination that is relevant to their needs
- *programme tracking*: gives an ability to establish and monitor internet pages for integrated marketing promotions and campaigns; from this, the destination can evaluate the effectiveness of a campaign in real time
- *online shopping*: typically for guidebooks
- *promotional services for users*: e.g. e-postcards, visitors journals, guest books, newsgroups, special promotions and screensaver downloads
- *media relations system*: including copies of recently produced press releases
- *calendar*: through which participating organizations can add events and festivals and classify them for multiple listings
- *integrated databases*: can be used to provide tourist information through CD multimedia productions, kiosks, call centres, visitor information bureaux and corporate information systems
- *archives system*: allows partners to add items to a user-searchable archive and to upload files and graphics directly from their browser
- *client profile and survey system*: details of people who have made contact with the DMS (e.g. by e-mail, telephone, personal visit to a Tourist Information Centre or by post) are recorded; profiles can be developed and selected to meet the needs of specific marketing campaigns
- *mobile targeting*: developments in global positioning systems are allowing systems to target customers through mobile phones depending on their location.

It costs a lot of money to develop and maintain a DMS. The World Tourism Organization (2001) has estimated that a major DMS may cost between

$500\,000$ and $\$8\,000\,000$ to develop and typically over $\$250\,000$ annually to operate. Fortunately, destination management organizations do not have to develop these systems and can configure standard systems from suppliers such as AXSES SCI, Travelinx and BVG Internet.

It is not, however, just major tourism centres that develop DMS. There are many examples of successful systems being implemented for much smaller destinations. An example of the application of a DMS in a rural, secondary tourism area is provided in Carmarthenshire, Wales. The local tourism sector comprises around 520 principal tourism businesses and 475 secondary businesses in a diverse range of activities covering accommodation, catering, trekking and golf courses. The Carmarthenshire Tourist Association (CTA) developed a key partnership with the local authority and other agencies in the county and from this developed its first basic website in 1997. In 2001, in conjunction with Carmarthenshire Enterprises, the local enterprise agency, CTA sought to go one stage further with a DMS. The key requirements for a DMS were that it should:

- be sustainable and self-financing
- have a capacity for future growth
- have a proven track record
- be administratively easy to operate
- be automated
- be quickly implemented
- be comprehensible.

For an association that drew support from many non-computer specialists, it was particularly important that the system was quick to use and easily administered, and empowered individual businesses to provide information in a style and form that reflected their own businesses. Developing a style that can span from large, corporate hospitality sites through to one-person trekking businesses can be a challenge. The BVG Internet tourist information system (TIS) met the requirements of the Association and in less than eight weeks from going live over 350 businesses had added their information to the site, many of which claimed that they had never used a computer before. A small team of two staff administered the site on a part-time basis and provided the local networking hub. The site, which can be found at http://www.tourlink.co.uk/indexframenoflash.cfm, is now at the centre of communications within the Carmarthenshire tourism sector.

Destination management systems can be applied at a number of geographical levels, from small town, to regions and whole countries or groups of countries.

Good systems should integrate these levels, in the way that the Visit England site links to regional tourism sites. In some cases, groups of towns or regions that share a common tourism interest have joined together to offer a system that has many of the characteristics of a DMS. One example is BookTownNet, a five-nation, 75-strong small or medium-sized enterprise (SME) consortium of second-hand and antiquarian book dealers located in rural areas of Europe which combined to form an information technology network to attract visitors to book towns (Skogseid and Jansen, 2001).

Management challenges to the development of 'virtual' destination management systems

Recent years have seen growing interest in a form of organization often referred to as the virtual organization. The virtual organization in this context refers to a network of independent companies, suppliers, customers, even one-time rivals linked by information technology to share skills, cost and access to one another's markets and resources. Hale and Whitlam (1997) define as 'virtual' any organization that is continually evolving, redefining and reinventing itself for practical business purposes. The aim of such organizations is to deliver services through structures and processes that are fast, flexible and flat. A characteristic is that they may have no central office or internal hierarchy. Electronic commerce has facilitated the development of virtual organizations.

The virtual organization has great relevance to the marketing of tourism destinations, particularly where they are dominated by small businesses whose limited resources require the outsourcing of many specialist functions. By drawing together essentially freelance individuals, virtual organizations can benefit from an inherent responsiveness to change in the business environment. There are many variants of virtual organization, which capitalize upon the prominence of knowledge and information as key inputs and outputs. Owing to the intangibility of the resources they process, there is no necessity for many virtual organizations to exhibit or support a definite physical architecture or a clear bureaucracy, a tight employment structure or a dedicated resource base, which characterize conventional organizational structures. Here, the term virtual organization can be used to describe the network of independent companies that constitute and market a tourist destination. The outcome of this co-operation is the composite tourism destination product that consumers experience. It should be possible for all businesses within a tourist destination to link their websites so that a visitor to one site would easily be able to find out about related facilities at other companies' websites.

However, despite the potential for creating virtual destinations out of the constituent companies' organizations, the marketing of many tourist destinations appears to remain dominated by the central role of a hierarchical tourist board. For example, in one study of tourism websites in Northern Ireland, the two main sites (provided by The Northern Ireland Tourist Board and Belfast City Council) were found to have a top–down approach for promoting individual tourism businesses (Palmer and McCole, 2000). Visitors could make bookings through these websites. However, no link was provided from the regional site to individual businesses' own websites, despite the latter usually containing a lot more information than was contained in the very basic information given in the regional websites. The rationale may have been to prevent the regional website losing revenue by customers booking directly with the service provider, but it served to highlight the hierarchical nature of the websites. Developing a value chain which incorporates the efforts of destination marketing organizations as well as individual businesses remains a challenge. Some regional sites (and commercial booking agencies) have developed systems where the regional site (or central booking agency) charges a commission for each 'click through' from the site to individual businesses' websites. Nevertheless, many businesses remain suspicious of the auditing of these transactions and resentful of paying a click-through fee, especially when a regional site is financed by government agencies or members' own subscriptions.

Many internet-based destination marketing initiatives have created conflict among members where commissions charged to individual businesses for handling booking requests are perceived as being too high. Of course, such arguments are not new, as commission charged by more conventional co-operative booking initiatives have frequently been challenged. The internet may, however, offer more routes to the final consumer, and so an individual organization's dependency on the destination marketing organization may be lessened by the presence of internet portals. Challenges may arise when individual tourism suppliers attempt to develop their own individual brand identities on a global scale via the internet. Consumers may be faced with multiple tourism suppliers each doing their own thing and promoting to multiple market segments (i.e. lots of channels of distribution/communication), thereby further confusing the consumer. Other challenges for this medium arise from the complexity of information to new users, copyright and legal issues, and security and privacy of information.

The development of application service providers (ASPs) presents further opportunities and challenges for small and medium-sized tourism businesses. Numerous commercial companies now allow a small or medium-sized hotel to operate a sophisticated online booking system, hosted by an ASP. A destination marketing organization's booking service is only one 'route to market' for a small or medium-sized tourism business. While the quality of destination marketing organizations' sites will undoubtedly improve, the alternatives open to individual businesses are also likely to increase.

Leadership of internet-based destination marketing organizations

Although new technology offers exciting challenges and opportunities for destination marketing, we should not lose sight of basic principles that underlie the co-operative efforts which are a prerequisite for success. In particular, it is likely that if the stakeholders in a destination do not trust each other with a conventional marketing programme, then merely adding new technology is in itself unlikely to bring about success. Trust and leadership will remain key issues in electronic destination marketing.

Trust is a major factor in determining the level of activity within groups. The existence of 'hidden agendas' that individual members bring into a group can undermine mutual trust. Unless the motives that underlie these agendas are controlled by mutual agreement, implicit or explicit, there may be little chance of achieving a collaborative spirit within a group and the group's development may become impeded. Successful collaboration depends on the commitment of the group to goals and the degree of trust that is generated within the group. Destination marketing organizations typically involve members being both a competitor and collaborator with fellow group members. A delicate balance exists between the needs of individuals to advance the interests of the business that they represent and the collective needs of the group. Where the balance is seen to favour the individual's own business, a perception of mistrust based on a lack of reciprocity may harm relationships. The development of internet-based co-operation will not change the issue of managing relationships between collaborators, for example in determining the marketing strategy of a destination website or the emphasis that it should assign to different interest groups.

Numerous studies have shown that strong leadership is important for achieving a group's objectives (Mintzberg, 1973; Blake and Mouton, 1978; Adair, 1986), but such leadership may not be sought by individuals who seek essentially social benefits from a co-operative marketing association. Like conventional destination marketing activities, an electronic strategy is unlikely to happen without an effective champion who can lead teams of people in developing and executing an internet strategy. In studies of leadership, it has been noted that being able to follow is an important contributor to good leadership. A common problem with co-operative ventures is the apparent difference in individuals' goals. Co-ordination of co-operative activities can thus prove challenging and necessitate a style of leadership that will accommodate individuals' characteristics. Small business owners who typically comprise the membership of destination marketing organizations may find the transition to followership of one of their peers a difficult challenge. It may be essential for the leader to become part of a social group and occasionally to alienate members by actions that may be sound commercially, but unacceptable socially within a small network of members.

A key task of leadership is to raise finance for an electronic marketing initiative, and to maintain interest in the initiative during the early teething periods. Destination marketing websites have not been immune from cynicism by stakeholders in the destination, who may be quick to seize on high development costs and poor reliability. The issue of paying for access to a destination site has caused tension in many destinations, as noted above, and effective leadership is crucial to reconcile the interests of multiple stakeholders.

Conclusion

The internet offers tremendous opportunities for developing strong destination brands that can deliver real benefits to tourists. The advantages over traditional methods of promoting the destination brand and fulfilling information requests that are specifically aimed at the needs of individual tourists are numerous. However, this chapter has pointed out that having a website in itself is not enough to guarantee continuing success of a tourist destination. In an age when all destinations can develop a website, there must be a coherent strategy to develop, position and promote an electronic presence. Individual tourism operators have never before had so many routes to reach their target markets, and destination marketing organizations are just one means of reaching potential customers.

Of course, even the best electronic strategy will ultimately fail if it is not matched by a consistent delivery of promises. In the early development of the internet, tourism sector businesses have been accused of overpromising on their websites in a way that they might have been more reluctant to do through printed media. Repeat business is only likely to develop if tourists' expectations are met. If they are not met, there are increasing numbers of websites where potential visitors can go to see 'warts and all' accounts of a destination.

References

Adair, J. (1986) *Effective Team Building*. Gower.

Blake, R. and Mouton, J. (1978) *The New Managerial Grid*. Gulf.

Chon, K. S. (1991) Tourism destination image modification process: marketing implications. *Tourism Management* 12: 68–72.

Juliussen, E. and Petska, K. (2002) *Computer Industry Almanac*, see http://www.c-i-a.com/iia_info.htm

Hale, R. and Whitlam, P. (1997) *Towards the Virtual Organization*. McGraw-Hill.

Heath, E. and Wall, G. (1991) *Marketing Tourism Destinations: A Strategic Planning Approach*. Wiley.

Leiper, N. (1996) *Tourism Management*. RMIT Publications.

Mintzberg, H. (1973) *The Nature of Managerial Work*. Harper and Row.

Palmer, A. and Bejou, D. (1995) Tourism destination marketing alliances. *Annals of Tourism Research* 22: 616–629.

Palmer, A. and McCole, P. (2000) The virtual re-intermediation of services: a conceptual framework and empirical investigation. *Journal of Vacation Marketing* 6: 33–47.

Skogseid, I. and Jansen, A. (2001) Booktowns on the Internet: Rural Enterprises Enter the Network Society 385–394 in Veda C. Storey, Sumit Sarkar, Janice I. DeGross (Eds.) Proceedings of the International Conference on Information Systems, ICIS 2001, December 16–19, 2001, New Orleans, Louisiana, USA. Association for Information Systems 2001.

World Tourism Organization (2001) E-Business for tourism: Practical Guidelines for tourism destinations and businesses, available from http://www.world-tourism.org/isroot/wto/pdf/1210-1.pdf, accessed 12 April 2004.

9

The challenge of public relations financial accountability: the case of the USA

Lisa T. Fall and Charles A. Lubbers

Introduction

Financial accountability continues to be a growing concern among communications professionals, including public relations practitioners, who are expected by upper management to quantify the value of their efforts (e.g. Lindenmann, 1993, 1995, 1997; Lubbers, 1995/96; Stephens & Rice, 1998; Noble, 1999; White and Raman, 1999; Cowlett, 2000, 2001; Pratt and Lennon, 2001). Unlike advertising and marketing activities, which are typically bottom-line orientated, many of the outcomes from activities that public relations professionals perform are somewhat intangible and implicitly impact an organization's livelihood in the marketplace (e.g. reputation, image, crisis and relationship management). However, practitioners using this rationale as a defence for not being able to demonstrate the financial impact of their communication strategies and tactics are merely opting to 'cop out'. Although not the easiest of tasks, each assessment technique used needs to be carefully determined so that it can accurately measure the goals and objectives initially intended to be accomplished by the communication programme or campaign.

One of the largest industries in America, the tourism industry, needs to demonstrate fiscal accountability and justify promotion expenditures. Thus, the importance of quantifying the value of a communication programme is no different for the travel, tourism and hospitality (TT&H) industry, which was projected to spend $554.2 million on tourism development and promotions in fiscal year (FY) 2002/03, according the Travel Industry Association of America (TIA, 2003). It is evident from these figures that communication managers should be concerned about justifying the financial returns their promotional efforts earn, given the enormous amount of money they spend.

But the tourism managers' quest to demonstrate the economic impact of their programmes is not merely self-serving. In many instances, a healthy tourism industry equates to a healthy state economy. When consumers travel, they may not realize the financial contribution they are making to the economy by supporting one of the country's most revenue-generating industries. For example, in 2001 the US TT & H industry generated more than $555 billion in total visitation expenditures (including both domestic and international travel). During 2001, spending by US residents and international travellers in the USA averaged $1.5 billion a day, $63 million an hour, translating to $1 million a minute and more than $17 000 a second, according to the American Hotel & Lodging Industry (2003).

Thus, it makes good business sense to demonstrate that if a state allocates a large portion of its budget to the dissemination of messages that encourage prospective travellers to visit a particular destination, then these travellers will indeed travel to that particular state. Visitors will then spend money while there, which generates revenue for the tourism industry at the state level. Hence, revenue generated serves as another factor in the evaluation formula. This concept is known as the 'multiplier effect', and it can negatively or positively affect a bottom line. This multiplier effect is just as critical from a public relations framework. Messages communicated can have both a positive and a negative multiplying effect, depending on what is being said about a given travel destination (Fall, 2000).

Travellers have a plethora of options for spending their discretionary dollars. Thus, tourism managers are very proactive in their approaches to entice would-be visitors. These managers understand that they need to spend money to make money. This industry disburses a tremendous amount of money to promote its products and services by enticing prospective travellers, as well as sustaining those who have previously visited. Since the September 11 terrorist attacks, the travel industry has engaged in tremendous efforts to encourage US residents to continue travelling. Competition continues to heighten among states as tourism promotion managers try to secure a larger share of the growing tourism market. While state tourism officials are 'cautiously optimistic' about the economy, they realize that they must aggressively, strategically and cost-effectively continue to spread their message: visit our destination.

Public relations, tourism and accountability

For more than four decades, James Grunig (e.g. Grunig and Hunt, 1984; Grunig, 1992, 2001, 2002) has conducted research to develop and refine the four models of public relations: press agency, public information, two-way asymmetrical and two-way symmetrical. Both press agency and public information are one-way models that do not encourage feedback and two-way flow of communication between the senders and receivers. According to Grunig (1992), programmes based on the press agency model strive for favourable publicity by means of propaganda-orientated techniques, whereas programmes based on the public information model strive to disseminate persuasive, favourable information to heighten awareness about an organization and its products and services. The two-way asymmetrical model is more strategic in nature and incorporates research; the results are used to develop persuasive messages to influence the behaviour of the target public. The two-way symmetrical mode, which also incorporates research, uses the results to manage conflict and to gain a better understanding of the wants and needs of the target public. Grunig (1992) also points out that organizations grounded in excellence typically practice a mixed-motive model, which combines both symmetrical and asymmetrical models.

At one time, tourism managers predominantly used promotional techniques, which are a function of public relations, to attract travellers. Therefore, in the past they spent more time engaging in Grunig's press agency model. However, the industry, as a whole, has realized that its key public (e.g. travellers to destinations/attractions, guests at hotels, patrons at restaurants, and passengers on aeroplanes and cruise ships) needs to feel 'connected' to the various organizations that they patronize. Travel is a personal activity; an important aspect of a vacation is the overall experience that it provides (Fall, 2000; Amarante, 2002). For that reason, the two-way symmetrical model is increasingly being practised as relationship management continues to become a heightened focus in this industry.

Tourism managers are increasingly implementing ways to communicate with their public on a regular basis and to reward them for their continuing patronage. The TT & H industry is now striving to manage and maintain its relationships (e.g. practising the two-way public relations models) rather than merely to promote its services and enhance awareness (e.g. practising the one-way public relations models). For example, the airline industry has introduced an array of frequent flyer programmes. As a member of these specially designed programmes, a traveller is eligible to participate in a variety of promotions, earn points to be cashed in at co-operating companies, and receive upgrades and numerous other perks. Restaurants, likewise, are following suit. Even attractions such as Disney World, Dollywood and Six Flags have developed methods to reward repeat visitors. In addition, attractions are developing programmes to communicate with travellers year-round, rather than just before peak season arrives.

Two-way interactivity has been heightened by the escalation of the internet. For example, many tourism establishments (hotels and resorts, destinations and attractions) now offer virtual tours so that one can sample the goods ahead of time. Many destination websites offer 'virtual cams' in which cameras are placed in alluring locations so that one can experience anything from the tranquillity of a real-time shot taken from the Mackinac Island Bridge to the excitement of an international balloon festival. In addition to using year-round communication and relationship-building techniques aimed at targeted audiences, tourism managers are becoming more sensitive, and savvy, by providing their public with ways to provide feedback.

However, there is still much room for improvement. When it comes to measuring the effectiveness of these promotional techniques, the industry is not as assertive in its efforts. Tourism managers are concerned with the same kinds of issues that communications managers in other industries face: finding ways to demonstrate financial accountability for their efforts. The Institute for Public Relations Research and Evaluation defines public relations evaluation as: 'Any and all research designed to determine the relative effectiveness of a public relations programme, strategy, or activity, by measuring the outputs and/or outcomes of that programme against a predetermined set of objectives' (Lindenmann, 1997, p. 2). Childers Hon (1997, p. 32) puts the importance of measurement in perspective from a client standpoint: 'Measuring the outcomes of public relations programmes provides data needed to demonstrate that public relations helps organizations and clients meet their performance goals'. Although the definition of evaluation is more or less clear-cut, as is its relevance, the actual tools and measurement techniques are not (e.g. Paine, 1994; Lindenmann, 1995; Childers Hon, 1997; Lindenmann, 1997; Frietag, 1998).

A wide spectrum of research has been conducted within a travel/tourism framework to determine how organizations assess the financial return of their promotional tactics and strategies. For example, Fall (2002) investigated the return on investment (ROI), per-person revenue generated and per-person cost among the top three state tourism promotional spenders. In another study, Fall *et al.* (2002) investigated the message integration and interactivity among state tourism websites in relation to the visitation statistics. Dore and Crouch (2003) studied publicity programmes used by national tourism organizations (NTOs). The authors learned that publicity programmes are becoming critical elements among NTO promotional strategies. They also explain that although promotional programmes are cost effective, they are not cost free. They report that the favoured measurement technique consists of determining publicity value in terms of equivalent paid advertising, but that this method is fraught with problems and inaccuracies.

Perdue and Pitegoff (1995) examined destination marketing organizations and offer guidelines for effective implementation of 'accountability research'. Further, Hawes *et al.* (1991) investigated state tourism offices to determine the scope of marketing and communication-orientated destination goals, strategies, tactics, activities and tasks. Etzel and Wahlers (1985) examined pleasure travellers' use of requested promotional materials, and Pizam (1990) evaluated the effectiveness of travel trade shows and other sales-orientated promotional techniques.

In short, the literature is laden with citations that tout the significance of developing communication evaluation and measurement strategies to demonstrate financial accountability. Further, it emerges that many of the methods used among organizations focus on 'counting outputs'. Lindenmann (1993) explains that counting outputs is one of the lower order methods and does not take into account the measurement of attitude and behavioural change/activity. One method that seems to be overlooked is to measure the relationship between tourism promotion budgets (outputs) and tourism revenue (inputs). Dore and Crouch's (2003) conclusion is echoed throughout this study: tourism managers need to become more adept in developing and implementing public relations programming, and improved methods for measuring promotional effectiveness and impact are greatly needed in this industry.

Hence, this chapter serves three purposes. It seeks to examine the relationship between state tourism budgets and state tourism expenditures (money spent by tourists), to investigate the relationship between state populations and size of promotional budgets, and to determine what states have the best ROI, while controlling for state population. In particular, the chapter investigates the following questions: What is the relationship between state promotion budgets and tourist expenditures in the state? Does the state population determine the size of promotion budgets? Which states have the best ROI when state population is controlled?

The data used in this study were obtained from two sources: the TIA and the United States Census Bureau. All data were collected from the websites of these organizations (http://www.tia.org and http://factfinder.census.gov/). Since the size of the state and the overall state budget may have an impact on promotion budget allocations, US Census Bureau estimates of state populations on 1 July 2000 were obtained from the Population Estimates Program of the Fact Finder section of the US Census website. All data used for calculations and analyses reflect the 2000 fiscal year. Data were analysed using SPSS version 10 for Macintosh. Correlation analysis was used to test the size, direction and significance of relationships between two variables.[1]

Assessing the relationship between state promotion budgets and tourist expenditures in the state

This section presents the comparisons conducted to determine the impact of state expenditures to promote tourism on travel and tourism spending in the state. The results presented in Table 9.1 indicate that there is a moderate and substantial direct relationship between state promotion budget expenditures and tourism expenditures for the states under examination. The Pearson correlation

---

[1] Pearson's r is a superior measure for variables that are continuous and normally distributed and it was used for comparisons involving the measures of state promotion budgets and tourist revenues. Kendall's tau-b and Spearman's rho correlation coefficients can also be tabulated. However, as non-parametric statistics, they are less sensitive for parametric data. In this investigation comparisons involving parametric data sets will provide the full correlation matrix for Pearson's r, but will only report the coefficient values for Kendall's tau-b and Spearman's rho.

Table 9.1   Correlation comparison of the FY 2000 promotion budget and tourist expenditures

		99/00 expenditures	*99/00 actual budget*
99/00 expenditures	Pearson correlation	1.000	0.530**
	Significance (two-tailed)	–	0.000
	n	51	50
99/00 actual budget	Pearson correlation	0.530**	1.000
	Significance (two-tailed)	0.000	–
	n	50	50

** Correlation is significant at the 0.01 level (two-tailed).
Kendall's tau-b and Spearman's rho correlation coefficients for the same comparison were 0.487 and 0.671, respectively.

coefficient of 0.53 is significant at the 0.01 level and, according to Poindexter and McCombs (2000, p. 144), indicates a moderate, positive relationship.

These results, although simplistic in nature, have positive implications for the tourism industry. A significant positive relationship demonstrates that the financial efforts (outputs) that a state puts forth to promote itself to its travellers can be correlated with the revenue (inputs) filtering back to the state in the form of visitor expenditure.

Does the state population determine the size of promotion budgets?

Return on investment can be determined in a number of ways. One of the most basic computations is to compare the state population to the promotion budgets. A (positive) direct correlation in the comparison would indicate that states with the largest populations also have the largest promotions budgets. A negative correlation value would indicate that states with smaller populations were spending more to promote travel and tourism. The results presented in Table 9.2 are not quite as strong for this correlation as for the one presented in Table 9.1. However, there is an indication of a direct relationship. The Pearson correlation coefficient of 0.393 is significant at the 0.01 level and, according to Poindexter and McCombs (2000, p. 144), indicates a borderline low to moderate, positive relationship.

These results also provide insight to tourism officials regarding their pro-motional efforts. Since a significant relationship is apparent, this means that

Table 9.2   Correlation comparison of the FY 2000 promotion budget and state population

		99/00 actual budget	*Census population*
99/00 actual budget	Pearson correlation	1.000	0.393**
	Significance (two-tailed)	–	0.005
	n	50	50
Census population	Pearson correlation	0.393**	1.000
	Significance (two-tailed)	0.005	–
	n	50	51

** Correlation is significant at the 0.01 level (two-tailed).
Kendall's tau-b and Spearman's rho correlation coefficients for the same comparison were slightly stronger at 0.425 and 0.585, respectively.

states with small populations may have to try harder (e.g. spend more) to encourage visitation. Part of the reason for these results may stem from the rationale that in many states, residents frequently travel 'in-state'. Since these residents choose to work and play in their home state, this aspect may equate to less out-of-state travel traffic and diminished tourism-generated revenues.

Which states have the best return on investment when controlling for state population?

Although Table 9.2 indicates that there is a low to moderate relationship between the size of the promotion budget of a state and the state's population, there are yet better ways to measure the return (tourist spending/expenditures) that states receive from their investment (promotion budgets). Another method is to standardize the tourist expenditures and the promotion budgets by converting them to per capita figures. Per capita standardization allows for the ranking of states based on their investments and returns. This formula will also allow the rankings to be used as a method of comparison.

Table 9.3 presents the results of the per capita standardization and ROI ranking comparison. The table presents three types of information for each of the fifty states. First, the per capita spending on tourism and the state's ranking on promotion spending is reported. The rankings are based on the state with the highest per capita spending on promotion being given a rank of 1, the second highest per capita spending a rank of 2, and so on. Second, Table 9.3 presents the per capita tourism revenues and the state's ranking with regard to tourism revenues. The rankings are based on the state with the highest per capita revenue

Table 9.3 Per capita promotion spending and tourism revenues of states

State name	Per capita promotion spending ($)	Rank	Per capita tourism revenues ($)	Rank	Rank difference
Alabama	2.01	32	1147.82	46	−14
Alaska	9.76	3	2401.46	5	−2
Arizona	1.68	36	1837.03	14	+22
Arkansas	4.26	12	1366.32	39	−27
California	0.39	50	2099.09	9	+41
Colorado	1.49	40	2163.70	7	+33
Connecticut	1.61	37	1537.40	30	+7
Delaware	1.59	38	1383.33	38	0
Florida	4.00	14	3474.76	3	+11
Georgia	0.79	46	1766.53	20	+26
Hawaii	49.49	1	11 732.91	1	0
Idaho	3.75	15	1617.62	26	−11
Illinois	4.46	11	1780.90	19	−8
Indiana	0.74	47	994.67	49	−2
Iowa	6.01	8	1424.96	36	−28
Kansas	1.76	35	1267.73	41	−6
Kentucky	1.77	34	1252.03	42	−8
Louisiana	3.64	16	1809.77	16	0
Maine	3.53	18	1623.66	25	−7
Maryland	2.12	31	1514.48	32	−1
Massachusetts	3.60	17	1920.23	11	+6
Michigan	1.58	39	1156.71	45	−6
Minnesota	2.67	27	1403.04	37	−10
Mississippi	4.94	9	1525.92	31	−22
Missouri	2.70	26	1667.90	24	+2
Montana	7.38	5	2108.60	8	−3
Nebraska	1.98	33	1513.45	33	0
Nevada	4.66	10	10 419.56	2	+8
New Hampshire	2.83	22	1892.93	13	+9
New Jersey	0.81	45	1785.89	18	+27
New Mexico	7.21	7	1946.63	10	−3
New York	0.97	43	1912.40	12	+31
North Carolina	1.31	42	1469.33	34	+8
North Dakota	3.31	19	1791.80	17	+2
Ohio	0.55	49	1122.22	47	+2
Oklahoma	2.79	23	1081.45	48	−25
Oregon	0.91	44	1592.32	27	+17
Penn.	2.74	25	1201.97	43	−18
Rhode Island	2.51	28	1357.07	40	−12
South Carolina	2.97	20	1751.32	21	−1
South Dakota	7.34	6	1573.77	29	−23
Tennessee	2.12	30	1710.22	23	+7
Texas	1.36	41	1581.69	28	+13
Utah	2.42	29	1750.67	22	+7
Vermont	10.60	2	2364.90	6	−4
Virginia	2.74	24	1810.69	15	+9
Washington	0.66	48	1438.50	35	+13
West Virginia	4.07	13	908.80	50	−37
Wisconsin	2.87	21	1164.00	44	−23
Wyoming	8.92	4	3029.12	4	0
Column mean	4.13		2199.37		

Washington DC was not included in the table because no information on promotion budgets was available. However, its per capita tourism revenue ranking would have placed it third.

149

from tourism being given a rank of 1, the second highest a rank of 2, and so on. Finally, the difference between the ranking on promotion spending and tourism revenues is reported. This measure offers a determination to see whether promotion expenses for the individuals in a state are in line with the tourist dollars generated. A positive ranking difference indicates that the state's ranking for promotion spending was lower (cost less) than its ranking for tourism revenues (more money from tourists). Negative ranking differences indicate the opposite result; more money is being spent (per capita) for a smaller return of tourist dollars.

The results in Table 9.3 indicate that the mean per capita spending on tourism promotion was $4.13 for FY 2000. However, the per capita expenditures ranged broadly, from California's low rate ($0.39) to Hawaii's number one ranking ($49.49 per person). Both of these states have high rates of tourism, but their expenditures per state resident are vastly different. In fact, Hawaii's per person expenditure is nearly five times that of Vermont, the state with the second highest per capita budget allocations.

The results in Table 9.3 also suggest that state expenditures for tourism offer a lucrative return. Although state promotion budgets clearly do not come close to covering the costs of running the tourism industry, they do represent the state's direct contribution to the effort. The mean return (tourism spending) is just under $2200 per person. However, like the values of state promotion expenditures, the per capita tourism expenditures vary a great deal. West Virginia had the lowest return, ranking 50th with a return of $908.80 per person, despite ranking 13th in per capita promotion spending. In contrast, Hawaii not only is the state spending the most on tourism promotion, but is also making the largest return of $11 732.91 per person.

The third type of analysis represented in Table 9.3 is the indication of the differences in rankings between each state's ranking of promotion budget and financial return via tourism expenditures. As noted in the table, five states have identical rankings, thus indicating a rank difference of zero. These states are Delaware, Hawaii, Louisiana, Nebraska and Wyoming. An additional ten states have a ranking difference of plus or minus five. Thus, more than one-quarter ($n = 15$, 30 per cent) of the states represent promotional spending rankings and tourist expenditure rankings that are very similar. To test the correlation of these two sets of rankings, a correlation analysis was conducted. The results are presented in Table 9.4.

While the coefficients for both Kendall's tau and Spearman's rho are significant at the 0.01 level, they demonstrate a weak, positive relationship. Still, there is some correlation between the amount of money spent and the ROI (as compared using state rankings). However, the weak correlation coefficient suggests

Table 9.4   Correlation comparison of the FY 2000 promotion budget and state population

			Rank of PC PROM	Rank of PC_EXP00
Kendall's tau_b	Rank of PC PROM	Correlation coefficient	1.000	0.259**
		Significance (two-tailed)	–	0.008
		n	50	50
	Rank of PC_EXP00	Correlation coefficient	0.259**	1.000
		Significance (two-tailed)	0.008	–
		n	50	50
Spearman's rho	Rank of PC PROM	Correlation coefficient	1.000	0.372**
		Significance (two-tailed)	–	0.008
		n	50	50
	Rank of PC_EXP00	Correlation coefficient	0.372**	1.000
		Significance (two-tailed)	0.008	–
		n	50	50

** Correlation is significant at the 0.01 level (two-tailed).
The Pearson's r correlation coefficient for the same comparison was 0.372.

that the citizens of some states are getting much more for their promotion dollars than are the citizens of other states. The biggest 'winners' are those states with the largest positive rank difference in Table 9.3: California (+41), Colorado (+33) and New York (+31). The results related to California and New York mirror TIA's 2000 research: California ranked number one as the top US destination state among US residents; New York ranked number five. Since 1995, California and New York have been consistently reported by TIA among the top five states in which domestic and international travellers spend their money.

The biggest 'losers' (those states that are not getting the most return on their investment) are those states with the largest negative rank difference: West Virginia (–37), Iowa (–28) and Arkansas (–27). The states next on the list with largest negative rank differences include Oklahoma (–25), South Dakota (–23) and Wisconsin (–23). Again, supported by TIA travel statistics, none of these three states ranked among the top ten destination states among US residents in 2000. In addition, none of the six states with the largest negative rank difference has a very large population, and these states do not seem to be located in areas that are typically considered tourist destinations, per se. In fact, none of the cities located among these six states is even ranked among the top fifty destination cities as determined from research conducted by *Travel & Leisure Magazine*, in co-operation with Harris Interactive/Yankelovich Partners. Thus, it may be that there is a minimum (threshold) level of promotion necessary to establish a tourism programme. The rationale makes sense: states that do not have large populations, and do not have a high degree of local or regional tourism attractions and/or destinations, will have to exert additional promotion efforts and provide additional revenues to achieve that threshold.

Post-September 11 issues to consider

Results from Yankelovich MONITOR and MONITOR Mindbase, two long-time longitudinal market research studies that track consumer trends and attitudes, reveal data of which communication managers should be aware. According to Walker Smith (2001), consumer priorities have been shifting, and continue to shift, in the aftermath of the terrorist attacks on the USA on 11 September 2001. The 'massive reassessment' of personal priorities among consumers is attributed, in part, to three factors: consumers have grown tired of hype, consumers are thinking 'smarter' when it comes to focusing on themselves, and consumers continue to feel 'overwhelmed' and 'claustrophobic' (Smith, 2001). In short, Smith points out that reprioritization was apparent even before the September 11 terrorist attacks and this self re-evaluation trend continues. From the pre- and post-September 11 data, Walker iterates a six-point refocusing of values, to include more emphasis on family, community, integrity, balance (particularly work/life balance), authenticity and security. These data have serious implications for tourism promotion managers. They need to identify what exactly makes their target travellers 'tick'; for example, what kinds of activities, attractions and culture do they want to engage in? Communication managers should consider engaging in more psychographic-orientated market research when developing consumer profiles. Managers need to identify how the amenities of their state meet the wants and needs of their visitors. Specifically, states need to find ways to showcase opportunities for their visitors to engage in activities that enhance their core values of intimacy, personal balance, family and community orientation, as well as simplicity and security. 'Back to basics' seems to be an overarching implicit theme.

Conclusion

This study provides a platform for further research. As indicated by the meagre representation of public relations programmes being studied among the travel/tourism industry, this area is wide open for examination. Further, the studies conducted are primarily descriptive in nature (e.g. what kinds of communication techniques are used). Research needs to go beyond the 'what' and narrow in on the 'how' and 'why' these communication strategies are effective. Public relations are concerned with influencing behaviour. Once tourism managers can gain a better understanding (prediction) about why various communication strategies are more effective than others are, only then can they start making more logical financial decisions about how they want to spend their communication budgets.

There are a few caveats to this study. First, only aggregate state data were examined. In addition, only one year was studied, therefore providing a 'snapshot' of results. Therefore, a recommendation for future research is to examine longitudinal data so that the results can be used for trend analyses. Further, future studies may include examining data more microscopically, such as at the city level, to determine the ROI. Take the state of Florida, for example. This state has disparate destination 'personalities' that vary by region (e.g. Orlando, Miami, the Keys). Therefore, from a cost-benefit analysis point of view it makes sense to compare where the most tourism revenue is being generated with which regions are spending the most money to bring the spenders to the state, and how they are communicating to get them there.

This study does, however, demonstrate that spending money does, indeed, make money. Hence, managers should weigh their options carefully when it comes to allocating funds towards communication 'outputs'. By incorporating mechanisms for evaluation, they can better determine just which tactics they should continue to use, and which tactics they may want to consider eliminating from their annual communication plan. Results also indicate a weak, yet positive relationship, between a state's census population and the amount of money it spends to promote itself to visitors. Finally, results demonstrate that the majority of states with positive rank differences (e.g. ranking for promotion spending was lower than its ranking for spending by tourists) also boast the most destination-orientated cities. Conversely, those with negative rank differences (e.g. ranking for promotion spending was higher than its ranking for spending by tourists) do not house as many destination-orientated cities. However, just because West Virginia, Iowa and Arkansas are not home to such 'jazzy' cities as Orlando, San Diego and Chicago, this does not dilute the quality of the experience that travellers have when they visit these states. Results do suggest, however, that these states may have to work harder and smarter to develop communication campaigns targeted at niche audiences. Tourism managers need to define skilfully their particular unique selling proposition for travellers, then they must strategically find ways to communicate these messages to travellers who are interested in knowing about such information. They must also ensure that they have implemented mechanisms for measuring the behavioural outcomes of their message dissemination strategies. As this chapter has shown, evaluation plays a beneficial role in this cyclical process.

References

Amarante, K. (2002) Hotel interactive. New CDP study breaks down the travel experience. http://www.hotelinteractive.com (retrieved 9 September 2003).

American Hotel & Lodging Association (2003) Lodging industry profile. http://www.ahla.com/products_info_center_lip.asp (retrieved 4 September 2003).

Childers Hon, L. (1997) Demonstrating effectiveness in public relations: goals, objectives, and evaluation. *Journal of Public Relations Research* 10: 10–136.

Cowlett, M. (2000) How to measure the effectiveness of PR. *Marketing* (14 December): 37–38.

Cowlett, M. (2001) How to gauge the value of publicity. *Marketing* (8 November): 25–26.

Dore, L. and Crouch, G. I. (2003) An exploratory study of publicity programs used by national tourism organizations. *Journal of Vacation Marketing* 9(2): 137–151.

Etzel, M. J. and Wahlers, R. G. (1985) The use of requested promotional material by pleasure travelers. *Journal of Travel Research* 23(4): 2–6.

Fall, L. T. (2000) An exploratory study of the relationship between human values and information sources within a tourism framework. *Journal of Hospitality and Leisure Marketing* 7(1): 1–15.

Fall, L. T. (2002) Examining the economic value of publicity and promotional activities among state tourism communication programs. *Journal of Promotion Management* 8(2): 35–46.

Fall, L. T., Lubbers, C. and White, C. (2002) Message integration and Internet interactivity of state tourism web sites. In Biberman, J. and Alkhafaji, A. (eds) *Business Research Yearbook*, Vol. 9. Saline, MI: McNaughton & Gunn. Pages 60–64.

Freitag, A. (1998) How to measure what we do. *Public Relations Quarterly* 43(2): 42–46.

Grunig, J. E. (1992) *Excellence in Public Relations and Communication Management*. Hillsdale, NJ: Lawrence Erlbaum Associates, pp. 1–30.

Grunig, J. E. (2001) Two-way symmetrical public relations: past, present, and future. In Heath, R. L. (ed.) *Handbook of Public Relations*. Thousand Oaks, CA: Sage, pp. 11–30.

Grunig, J. E. (2002) Qualitative methods for assessing relationships between organizations and publics. Research Paper. Institute for Public Relations Measurement and Evaluation Series.

Grunig, J. E. and Hunt, T. (1984) *Managing Public Relations*. New York: Holt, Rinehart & Winston.

Hawes, D. K., Taylor, D. T. and Hampe, G. D. (1991) Destination marketing by states. *Journal of Travel Research* 30(1): 11–17.

Lindenmann, W. K. (1993) An effectiveness yardstick to measure public relations success. *Public Relations Quarterly* 38(10): 7–9.

Lindenmann, W. K. (1995) *A Guide to Public Relations Research*. Institute for Public Relations Research & Evaluation.

Lindenmann, W. K. (1997) Setting minimum standards for measuring public relations effectiveness. *Public Relations Review* 23(4): 391–408.

Lubbers, C. A. (1995/96) Assessing corporate public relations campaigns: attempting to demonstrate financial accountability. *Journal of Corporate Public Relations*, Volume 6, pages 29–36.

Noble, P. (1999) Towards an inclusive evaluation methodology. *Corporate Communications* 4(1): 14–23.

Paine, K. D. (1994) Move over TQM! Benchmarking is the new tool for the '90s. *Communication World* 11(6): 42–44.

Perdue, R. and Pitegoff, B. E. (1995) Methods of accountability research for destination marketing. *Journal of Travel Research* 28(4): 45–49.

Pizam, A. (1990) Evaluating the effectiveness of trade shows and other tourism sales-promotion techniques. *Journal of Travel Research* 29(1): 3–8.

Poindexter, P. M. and McCombs, M. E. (2000) *Research in Mass Communication: A Practical Guide.* Boston, MA: Bedford/St Martin's.

Pratt, C. B. and Lennon, G. (2001) What's wrong with outcomes evaluation? *Public Relations Quarterly* 46(4): 40–44.

Smith, J. W. (2001) Trying to get back to business as usual during trying times. Yankelovich MONITOR LIVE Teleconference Series (26 September).

Stephens, A. and Rice, A. (1998) What's public relations worth? *Finance Week* (4–10 June): 34–35.

Travel & Leisure Magazine (2003) Top 50 cities in North America. http://www.planet101.com/cities50.htm (retrieved 9 September 2003).

Travel Industry Association of America (2001) *The Economic Review of Travel in America*, 2001 edn (November). Washington, DC: Travel Industry Association of America.

Travel Industry Association of America (2003) State tourism offices budgets down 8% for 2002–2003. Press Release (2 June 2003). http://www.tia.org/press/releases.asp (retrieved 3 September 2003).

White, C. and Raman, N. (1999) The worldwide web as a public relations medium: the use of research, planning, and evaluation in web site development. *Public Relations Review* 25: 405–420.

Part 3

Destination Branding in Practice

10

A challenger brand: Wales, golf as it should be

Roger Pride

Introduction

When it comes to branding, perhaps the most difficult task facing any destination is the quest for true differentiation. Destination managers have been studying their potential customers to find out what exactly they look for from a holiday or short break. Not surprisingly, this research invariably reveals the same or similar information. Although customer needs, wants and motivations will vary from individual to individual and segment to segment, research tends to identify similar customer insights. Having analysed the data, market planners will go on to create groupings of customers with memorable titles. As a result, tourist board marketing departments the world over are targeting various combinations of segments such as 'safe adventurers', 'active explorers', 'culture vultures' and 'fun seekers'. Professional tourist boards will then establish how well their destination delivers against these various motivations and learn more about how these customer segments perceive and rate their product.

All of these data and more are then put into the marketing mixer to arrive at positioning and branding strategies for the destinations concerned. A stroll around the vivid and vibrant exhibition floors of the World Travel Market in London (or any other major travel event) may well lead you to the view that despite all of this expensive research and planning the majority of destinations still struggle to differentiate clearly their offer from the competition.

Hong Kong asks you to 'Live it, love it', while Scotland wants you simply to 'Live it'. Ireland suggests that you 'Live a different life'. Chile is 'A natural inspiration', whereas Karnataka in India is 'A theatre of inspiration'. The Seychelles is 'As pure as it gets', which is presumably meant to be more pure than '100% Pure New Zealand'. Other destinations claim to be the epitome of their particular corner of the globe. Malaysia is 'Truly Asia' and North Cyprus is 'Pure Mediterranean'. Tanzania is 'Authentic Africa'; much the same as Zambia, which is 'Real Africa'. Others seem to have given up on the search for differentiation and fallen into the trap of being all things to all markets: The Caribbean is 'Everything you want it to be' and Namibia is a 'Land of contrasts'. Cyprus is the 'Island for all seasons'. Some destinations achieve differentiation by highlighting a particular unique physical or cultural feature: Arizona is 'the Grand Canyon state', Peru is the 'Land of the Incas' and Hawaii is 'The islands of Aloha'. Occasionally you may come across some places that you feel have achieved standout and originality and have effectively defined their destination proposition. Orlando, 'Destination imagination', and 'Singapore roars' are two good examples.

Wales: a challenger brand

Undoubtedly the marketing and branding strategies of the destinations highlighted above have a great deal more depth than the straplines referred to and the purpose of drawing attention to the above examples is not to criticize the destinations concerned. Indeed, New Zealand is held up by many as an exemplar of good destination branding practice. However, the examples serve to illustrate how, in a very crowded and noisy marketplace, it is very difficult to be original and capture attention.

Imagine, therefore, the challenge facing relatively new or undiscovered destinations. Some with moderate resources have to compete against the established giants and shine a light on their particular offer. Success will not be achieved as a result of imitation and copycat strategies. The marketing strategies pursued must be imaginative, single minded and consistent. Wales is such a destination. It is relatively undiscovered beyond the rest of the UK and, as explained in the first edition of *Destination Branding*, has had a relatively weak and in some cases negative image to overcome. To combat this, those at the Wales Tourist Board, including the author, have always believed in the principles of intelligence, integration and innovation. All of their strategies are based on sound market intelligence. They pursue solutions based on communication ideas that can be integrated throughout all channels and above all seek to innovate and to try out new ideas.

During the selection process for a UK advertising account the ultimately successful agency had recognized these principles exemplified in earlier marketing communications from the Wales Tourist Board, and stated that the board behaved like '… a true challenger brand'. Following this observation I nodded enthusiastically but in truth had never heard of a challenger brand. I took it upon myself to find out more. The rest of this chapter will briefly highlight some of the principles that support challenger branding and goes on to demonstrate how these principles have been used to create a new positioning and branding strategy to help to achieve our aspiration of establishing Wales as a world-class golf destination.

In his book *Eating the Big Fish*, Adam Morgan (1999) persuasively outlines the eight credos of challenger brands and he draws upon examples of challenger brand behaviour from a wide variety of business sectors. The present author recommends it as an essential read for any destination marketer uncomfortable and impatient with being a market follower. Let us briefly examine some of the characteristics of a challenger brand.

- Challenger brands recognize that if they are to make an impact and grow market share from the competition they must think and act differently. They should not assume that past behaviour will point the way to future success. They should look to other business sectors for their inspiration. They need to challenge conventions and assume thought leadership within their own category.
- They must create a strong 'lighthouse identity'. Essentially this means creating a beacon that shines out to consumers that they cannot miss or ignore. Challenger brands do not explain the role they play in the lives of potential consumers; they highlight very clearly what the brand stands for and invite the consumer to navigate by them. A lighthouse identity demands great self-belief.

Morgan illustrates the example of Las Vegas. This destination has been through a variety of positioning statements from 'The American way to play' and 'No one does it better' to 'The entertainment capital of America'. However, Las Vegas now claims that 'Las Vegas is Las Vegas'. A statement of confidence and attitude.

- They must be focused: challenger brands sacrifice activity in certain areas and are brave enough to overcommit in those areas where they believe they will make a real difference. They are prepared to take reasonable risks.
- Perhaps more than anything else challenger brands need to be idea centred, not consumer centred. This does not mean that they lose touch with their customers, but they constantly seek fresh ideas that will help to reinvigorate their relationships with customers. They look beyond conventional advertising and promotional media and are prepared to stimulate discussion and debate to gain recognition. Arguably most of the destination brand propositions illustrated earlier are consumer or in some cases destination (product) centred, but few of them are idea centred.

Wales, Golf as it should be

The challenge of establishing Wales as a world-class golfing destination is a monumental task. Golf is one of the fastest growing sectors of the lucrative holiday market and is the biggest specialist activity holiday sector in the world. Not only is it a big market, but holiday golfers tend to spend a lot more per trip than general leisure visitors, in the case of Wales about four times as much. The potential lucrativeness is unsurprising, as holiday golfers tend to come from the professional and management classes, and as such have high levels of disposable income. Destinations around the globe had identified the income potential of golf long before Wales. The successful ones have become established golf destinations often capitalizing on a strong golfing heritage or massive investment programmes, creating golfing infrastructure specifically catering for the visiting golfer.

Previously in Wales, however, there has never been a serious attempt to penetrate the golf tourism market. Wales does have a long and motivating golfing heritage, which boasts the second oldest golfing union in the world and the invention of the Stapleford scoring system. Wales also has some unpolished golfing Jewels, including superb links courses the kind of which are particularly sought after by American visitors. Despite this, the conventional wisdom in Wales was that these assets were not strong enough to compete seriously with competitor destinations, particularly Scotland and Ireland. With limited promotional budgets it was felt that Wales could compete more strongly for other activity-based markets, notably walking, cycling and other adventure sports.

However, during the late 1990s there were significant enhancements to Wales' golfing product offer. These included the development of the Vale of Glamorgan golf resort and particularly the Celtic Manor golf resort near Newport, the latter being the very costly creation of billionaire Welsh electronics entrepreneur Sir Terry Matthews. This 400-bedroom, five-star resort offers three quality golf courses, vast meeting and conference facilities, and a health and spa complex to rival the best in Europe. Sir Terry's vision was designed to attain a personal goal that most independent observers thought was a pipedream. Sir Terry dreamed of hosting the world's most prestigious golfing event in his native Wales. In 2001 he proved that this was no pipedream when against all the odds Wales won the rights to host the Ryder Cup in 2010. The recently installed Welsh Assembly Government saw this as an opportunity to showcase Wales on the world stage and it became vital to put in place a range of strategies to take full economic advantage of this major event.

Golf tourism would potentially be one of the most visible beneficiaries, and the Wales Tourist Board was tasked with creating a strategy that by 2010 would ensure that Wales would become a world-class golf destination with golf tourism contributing at least £100 million pounds per annum. The achievement of this goal would demand a challenger mentality. Success would demand not only an effective marketing strategy, but also a product investment, development and training plan to ensure that the raw golf assets which predominantly serve a local market will be transformed into a quality golfing experience serving a global audience. This chapter, however, will concentrate on the development and implementation of the brand positioning and communication strategy.

Wales' main competitors are the giants of golf tourism, Scotland and Ireland. A giant cannot be defeated by a single blow; however, a big idea with multiple manifestations might do the job. The first step was to appoint a marketing agency whose mission is to slay Goliath brands. This agency could only be called David. The first step was to undertake an audit of the golf product in Wales and identify assets and advantages from the perspective of the potential markets. Golf in Wales was found to offer the following benefits.

- *Beautiful locations*: the locations of the top courses in Wales are comparable with any in the world. Many are located in national parks or officially designated areas of outstanding beauty. In particular, many of the links courses are scenically stunning.

- *Easy access*: in Wales it is generally still possible, even at the magnet courses, to secure tee-off spots at times to suit visiting golfers. In comparison with those of the major competitors the Welsh courses are easily accessible from major markets in the rest of the UK or from major gateway airports.
- *Excellent value*: in Wales visitors will not need to take out a mortgage to pay for a round of golf. Again this is true even at the trophy courses. The cost of a decent round of golf in the competitor destinations has escalated dramatically in recent years.
- *Unhurried golf*: in Wales you can generally play golf at your own pace. Visitors will not be squeezed into unsuitable tee times.
- *Unstuffy golf*: at the majority of Welsh courses visitors are genuinely welcome. The clubs often have a less formal atmosphere than those of the main competitors. Visitors will not feel small or embarrassed at Welsh clubs.

Of course, the Wales Tourist Board studied its competitors and found out more about the dynamics of the golf tourism market, but a challenger mentality demands an awareness of emerging trends and that the established myths be discounted. Golfer demographics are changing, with significant growth in the younger 29–49 age bracket. In addition, over 50 per cent of new golfers are women. Golf suppliers are reacting to the younger, less male demographics and bringing out new publications such as *Putt* and *Bogey*. Lyle & Scott and Pringle are putting golf fashion on the street, while Burberry is putting fashion on the golf course. In the professional ranks there is clear evidence of bright young things coming through and challenging conventions in terms of dress and behaviour. This was summed up in an article in the English daily newspaper, the *Guardian*, in summer 2003, which examined the changing golf scene and exemplified this by comparing rising star Ian Poulter, with his spiked hair dyed red and his footballer good looks, with the rather more staid Colin Montgomery, who epitomizes establishment golf with his V-neck sweaters. Research showed that the majority of golf destinations cater for establishment golf. There also appeared to be a great deal of conformity in the way that golf destinations promoted themselves.

Wales would not achieve its goals by becoming part of this conformity or by being a pale imitation of its successful golfing competitors. The agency believed that inroads would only be made by positioning Wales as the antidote to the golfing scene in the competitor countries. As the agency stated in their initial presentation: 'We need to attract the younger more dynamic element of the golfing world ... this will be done by setting out our store as the antidote to what exists – leave the colonel bufton-tuftons to Scotland and England – we want the younger, moneyed, spontaneous community who will come to Wales again and again because they can … .'

The next step was to turn these findings into a positioning and strategy that had a challenger mentality at its heart. The positioning needed to be more than a strapline. It needed to be idea centred. It had not only to motivate the markets but also to inspire the golf sector in Wales. It had to be capable of being communicated across all channels. It needed to be a lighthouse identity, and challenge consumers' understanding and perception of golf in Wales. It needed to break the conventions of previous golf tourism marketing.

The idea recommended by David was 'Come to Wales and experience golf as it should be'. The idea represents the antidote to the clear positioning of Wales' competitors: the seriousness of Scotland, the corporateness of England, the booziness of Ireland. It truly is a challenger idea as it rewrites the rules, represents thought leadership, and provokes re-evaluation of Wales and of what a golf holiday should be. The strapline would be 'Wales, golf as it should be'.

The launch of the campaign followed the principles of sacrifice and over-commit. It was vital to make a big initial impact and quickly establish the proposition, and this was achieved through high-impact media and placement, including the use of television. The highest circulation golf media in the UK were selected, but we were not content with single- or even double-page spreads. We opted for front covers and six-page foldout spreads. We wanted Wales to be talked about. The look and feel of the print advertisements were also very different. For example, 'Stuffy golf' contrasted the caricature image of the golf club bore in his garish golfing garb with a young, stylish couple experiencing 'Golf as it should be' on the beautiful links course of Pennard on the Gower Peninsula. The copy reads 'There's stuffy golf … and there's golf in Wales' (Figures 10.1–10.4).

A range of ideas was developed to communicate the core proposition further. A range of golf merchandise was created which, as well as displaying the strapline, features a smiley golf ball. In order to reinforce the brand when golfers actually come to play at the courses, items such as 'Golf as it should be messages' are placed at the bottom of golf holes: when better to communicate with golfers than when they actually pick their golf balls out of the hole? There are plans to produce items such as clocks to be displayed in golf club houses with the line on the face and the numbers appearing as 1ish, 2ish, and so on. This type of activity not only reinforces the message to golfers, but also binds the golf clubs into the idea, and is an excellent form of internal marketing.

Figure 10.1   Wales, golf as it should be: stuffy golf

Figure 10.2   Wales, golf as it should be: bunker

Figure 10.3   Wales, golf as it should be: flag

Figure 10.4   Wales, golf as it should be: putter

Media communication is also a vital part of the marketing plan. Naturally, specialist golf travel writers will be introduced to Wales to experience the product, but it is anticipated that the 'Golf as it should be' idea will generate debate and discussion about golf in general and golf holidays in particular. In true challenger style, we will be doing our bit to prompt that discussion by sponsoring 'Golf as it should be' letter pages in golfing media and infiltrating press conferences to place appropriate questions.

Conclusion

All of this activity is already generating recognition and results. The world's golf travel writers have already voted Wales 'Undiscovered golf destination of the year' for 2003. Golf clubs in Wales are reporting heightened interest and visits. From here, the initiative will expand to cover the key international markets of the USA and Ireland. Like all challenger brands, in order to attain such big ambitions, there is a need to think and behave differently from the competitors: to be bold and take reasonable risks, and to be confident and innovative. Golf tourists and the golf establishment may not always agree with us, but they won't be able to ignore us. When 2010 comes around we hope that golfers around the globe will be saying 'now that was a Ryder Cup, as it should be'.

Reference

Morgan, A. (1999) *Eating the Big Fish: How challenger Brands can Compete Against Leader Brands*. Chichester: Wiley.

11

Brand Shanghai: harnessing the inner force of people and place

Fiona Gilmore

Introduction

Shanghai is a city with the potential, once again, to sit alongside New York and London if it can overcome the obstacles in its path. In 1982, the green light was given to rebuild the city and reignite people's passions for the place. The vision was exciting and ambitious. The challenge was much greater than simply to restore the grandeur and magnificence of the colonial architecture, but to create a model city and environment for the rest of the world to admire and seek to emulate. The strategy was to market the dream at the outset.

How a city is perceived, the image it creates of its physical and environmental desirability, affects not only the levels of investment by property developers and companies, but also the decisions of employers and employees to live and work there. Intuitive marketers recognize the importance of creating the vista at the earliest opportunity. Shanghai was a symbol of modernity in the 1930s and 1940s and further to its reopening in 1990, it has been seen by the rest of China and the world as a place of immense opportunity, both cultural and economic. Yet despite appearances, the city has thus far failed to live up to expectations. Central to its problems are the lack of political autonomy and problems in the quality of life for citizens. But there is another issue at stake.

In the information age the challenge for cities is to nourish the imagination of its citizens, the inner force. Economic prosperity and competitiveness depend not only upon a city's links with the outside world through information technology and the transport infrastructure, but also on its capacity to build new business and exploit innovation. A city's schools and universities play a central role because they generate intellectual capital, invigorate culture and feed ideas into the business community. At the same time, the arts and cultural scene of a city must be nurtured for it stimulates the imagination, and creates for the city an image and a reputation that will help to attract investment and talented individuals: great minds naturally gravitate towards environments that are vibrant and creative.

In twenty years of development since reform, Shanghai has moved away from the postindustrial era to the information era and is beginning to acknowledge that its greatest assets are its citizens and their creativity. It is this inner force that must now be harnessed if the city is to achieve its aspirations. There is work to be done, but the city's recent win to host the 2010 World Expo, with its focus on revitalizing cities, will provide Shanghai with the impetus to take the next big step as well as create a rich source of ideas for the city and its revitalization. There is evidence that, as its post-World Tourism Organization (WTO) aspirations play out, China is becoming a less dominant force: this will remove the final obstacle in turning the city's dream into reality.

A blueprint for modernity

Shanghai was founded in the eleventh century as a tiny fishing settlement situated on the rich alluvial soils of the Yangzi River delta on the west bank of the Huangpu River, and so it remained for several centuries. By the sixteenth century, the town had grown into a small sea port with a booming cotton industry. In 1842, the town was invaded by the British in the First Opium War. In defeat, Shanghai was named one of the five treaty ports open to foreign occupation under the terms of the Nanking Treaty. The main portions of the city were divided into the British-dominated International Settlement and the French Concession, and new inhabitants were granted special privileges, namely extraterritoriality, which meant they were free from prosecution under Chinese law. Shanghai emerged from the shadow of greed and defeat, to become the richest, most sophisticated and powerful city in all Asia, on a par with the cities of Paris, New York and London.

As the only port in the world that did not require entry visas or passports, the city became a magnet for tens of thousands of foreigners, from Jews and missionaries to businessmen and traders. Nowhere else did a population chase pleasure and decadence with such abandoned zeal as in Shanghai and nowhere else in the world afforded greater opportunity for the free-spirited entrepreneur. Neither a colony nor wholly owned by China, inhabited by citizens of every nation in the world, but ruled by none, Shanghai was an anomaly amongst cities. By the 1930s and 1940s, the city had spread its stardust around the world. The image it evoked was one of mystery and adventure, a mixture of great wealth and adversity, and licence of every kind: it was a place where musicians and intellectuals rubbed shoulders with gangsters and drug barons in the night clubs, gambling dens and back alleys. No cruise itinerary was complete without a stop at the 'Paris of the Orient', the 'whore of the East'.

While war and revolution raged across the rest of China, Shanghai seemed to belong to a different time and place. But its foreign domination of Chinese soil met growing resistance, manifest in the formation of the Chinese Communist Party which held its first National Congress in a secret location in the city in 1921. By 1927 the Nationalists and Communists had joined forces to take over the city. By 1937 the city was occupied by the Japanese, and when Japan was finally defeated in 1945, the Western powers agreed to dismantle the International Settlement and hand administrative power over to the Nationalist Chinese Government. In 1949, Communism finally turned on the metropolis and its liberal past, and a door was slammed shut.

For several decades, Shanghai and the rest of China were under Communist control. Opium dens were closed and the worst of the slums cleared away. The foreigners left the factories and businesses were slowly nationalized. Orthodox Communism began to loosen its grip after Mao's death in 1976. Two years later, Deng Xiaoping returned to power and he set the country on its gradual process of reform and opening up to the world. Initially, the focus for development was the cities in the south, Shenzhen and Guangdong. While Shanghai was to provide the funding for these experimental reforms, the city itself was more or less neglected. Then in the early 1990s, Deng Xiaoping decided that it was time to unshackle Shanghai. Pudong was established as the centre of finance and the city's economy began to grow at more than 20 per cent per annum.

The city set itself a momentous task: to create a new image that would signify prosperity and a return to modernity through the creation of symbols and icons. Its blueprint for the vision was a reinterpretation and redefinition of its former self, that pre-Communist colonial wonder. A massive programme of redevelopment got underway, fuelled by a hunger to prove to both China and the world that it could become world class once again. The process of urban regeneration changed the face of central areas that until 1990 were almost exactly as they had been in the 1940s. Today the city can boast the world's tallest hotel, the biggest container port and the longest steel-arch bridge. It has plans to build the biggest Ferris wheel by 2005, is in the process of building the world's first high-speed magnetic levitation (maglev) train and in 2006 a Universal Studios Theme Park is set to open.

Colonial Shanghai symbolized China's 'first quest for modernity through industrialization and urbanization' (Tianshu, 2001). That period is now a rich source of inspiration for the transformation of the city as it embraces global capitalism. Zhu Rongji, the former mayor of Shanghai and China's Premier, drew on Shanghai's colonial achievements in commerce and finance to attract potential investors. In Zhu's view, what makes a Shanghai citizen a worthy business partner is 'his or her notion of legality and willingness to bear the burden of a contract' (Tianshu, 2001). A sense of pride is worn on the sleeve of the people in Shanghai, fuelled by the wellspring of past glories and a collective understanding of the city's future aspirations.

Old buildings have been restored and renovated. Cafes, restaurants, theatres and movie houses ossified under communism are open for business with their Western name back up above the door. Shanghai's famous Red Mansion Coffee House is Chez Louis once more. The Old Man Jazz Band now performs all year around in the Peace Hotel. But perhaps the most impressive transformation of all is the skyline. Expressions of Shanghai's aspiration shot up across the sky at an astonishing pace and in just fifteen years of economic boom time, Shanghai has achieved a skyline that took fifty years to create in New York and thirty in Hong Kong. The city has more than 4500 towers, and has now begun construction on what it claims will be the world's tallest building, a 492-metre, 101-storey tower with a gaping hole or 'moon gate' cut out of the middle (York, 2003).

The imperative to build tall

From the pyramids and Stonehenge to the great medieval cathedrals, humans have expressed a desire to push stone and brick to their limits. The expressive potential for building vertically was articulated by Louis Sullivan in his 1896 essay entitled 'The tall office building artistically considered', published shortly after William Le Baron Jenny's eight-storey tall Leitner Building. Sullivan identifies 'loftiness' as the conceit of tall buildings both in a literal sense and as a metaphor for its symbolic intent. Civilizations have always used buildings to impress. The Romans and Greeks overawed those they conquered with great constructions, forcing the people dwelling in the shadows below to bow down in defeat. Religious orders erected churches and temples to inspire reverence and piety, and leaders through history have used monuments to symbolize might and generate allegiance, as well as to convey an image of financial wealth and material success.

Skyscrapers occupy a central place in the 'iconography of modernity' (Pumphrey, 1987). They sing of grand accomplishment and fierce competition, and help those looking in to differentiate one city from the next. They are the iconography of the city, the city brand identity. The London Eye is testament to the rich equity in the skyscape. Its glass pods rotate slowly to allow the language of the skyline to be apprehended in person, where previously consumption of such an offering would have to be via a picture or postcard.

With a ravenous hunger for modernity and an aspiration loftier than most, Shanghai propelled itself into the skies in an act of image building on a grand scale. Its strategy went something like 'the bigger, the better', and planners admit that there was actually very little planning ahead of construction, that the planning bureau may well have been a man with a measuring stick (York, 2003). So unique communities were bulldozed to make way for the glitzy towers and 1.5 million citizens were forced out of the city centre. Now some of the towers stand empty, testament to the overzealous construction industry saturating the property market.

Yet there is undeniable pride in the people for the city and its achievements. Oozing from every inch of every tower and record-breaking icon is a self-belief, which defies other great cities to match it, even beat it. How can we not symbolize the future, it screams, when we have the tallest, the largest and the longest? The taste of past success is not easy to forget. 'Everybody in Shanghai believes the city will become the world's greatest in the next few decades, some even sooner', said Liu, a Shanghai taxi driver. But there is pressing inner work to be done.

The story from the inside

Shanghai's population rose from a ballpark reckoning of between 250 000 and 500 000 in 1843, to one million by 1880, to almost four million by 1935 (MacPherson, 2002). Today Shanghai boasts a population of around 17 million, of whom 8 million live in the city proper. But, of those 8 million, 3 million residents still live in very crowded conditions with inadequate access to drinking water and sanitation, and the water in Shanghai's main supply, the Huangpu River, is heavily polluted. Other concerns include the lack of available green space, the quality of education and opportunities for the tertiary educated.

Xu Anqi, a research fellow with the Shanghai Academy of Social Sciences, spent a year interviewing Shanghai residents to find out their own feelings on life in Shanghai, exploring issues including marriage, the family unit, health, gender, social policies and lifestyles (Xu Anqi, 2000). The result was a comprehensive dossier on the quality of life of the Shanghainese, which has since been incorporated into the 2003 Blue Paper on Cultural Development in Shanghai. In her investigation, Xu found that despite increases in earnings and disposable income, the material life of the ordinary Shanghai person was far from satisfactory. Most people gave a very low rating for the indices of income and housing. Education was also a problem area. Following industrial restructuring and employment reform many middle-aged workers were forced into early retirement because of a lack of formal skills and adequate schooling.

In her research Xu also discovered that, despite the frustrations of the people of Shanghai with their quality of life, they enjoyed a warm, closely knit and supportive community. For example, those without jobs were offered help by their neighbours or made to feel valued by taking part in voluntary activities. The problems of the individual were shared among the community and a sort of collective healing was at work. Poverty was not imbued with a sense of shame and the hint that it was a byproduct of something not done, as is sometimes the case in Western societies. For the individual, being worse off in the material sense had no cause to weaken the spirit. Civic pride was shown to reflect a moral obligation to each other as much as to the city's structural feats. Now that is one thing that some of the world's great cities do not have: social connectivity and a commitment to the welfare of neighbours.

Fire for the imagination

Pinning down what makes a city great is no easy undertaking, says Deyan Sudjic, author of *The Hundred Mile City*. One thing all great cities appear to have in common is that they 'belong to a self-selected group that organize their futures' (Sudjic, 1993). Mayors with political leadership such as Giuliani in New York, and perhaps now London, which has for the first time elected a mayor for Greater London, can make all the difference. Barcelona has been fortunate to have a string of visionary mayors. Even more effective, argues Sudjic, are the national leaders who concentrate their efforts on capital cities: Mahathir in Kuala Lumpar, Mitterand in Paris. A lack of independence from a central controlling force whose concerns are spread too thinly across a nation will weaken a city's vitality and unique spirit.

The British have never really accepted that 'cities are at the heart of their economy and civilization' (Hutton, 2002). The real Britain lurks in the suburbs, the rosy cottages and stately homes in pristine parkland. London, with all its manifest problems, is an exception. It is a true world city buzzing with ideas and new industries, a beacon for the rest of Britain, and increasingly the rest of the world. But for cities outside London, it is a different story. The task to revitalize is usually handed to an external force: Whitehall or a well-meaning quango, but some areas are breaking free. In 2000 the British cities of Sheffield, Manchester, Bristol, Birmingham, Leeds, Liverpool and Newcastle, later to be joined by Nottingham, formed the 'core cities group'. The group is self-governing, driven by the ethos that vibrant cities are the solution not the cause of economic and social problems, but that vibrancy is not something that can be trucked in from elsewhere. Rather, it emerges when a city's citizens and civic leaders are given a voice in decisions about their futures. They are the people with the real passion for the city and it is their vitality that should be harnessed (Hutton, 2002). That, says the group, can only happen when a city is given political autonomy. Given Britain's long history of a highly centralized government, the move is a radical one.

Eyeing the skyline of Birmingham, one is faced with an anomaly of monstrous proportions. A gigantic, curved hump clad in winking metal discs has taken root between the steeples of the city. Is it a spaceship, a giant Christmas bauble or a sea creature from the future cloaked in drawing-pin armoury? The intruder is, in fact, the new Selfridges retail store, part of Birmingham's Bullring. In choosing the design of architects Future Systems and Vittorio Radice, Selfridges did away with the first law of retail: that nothing, ever, should detract from the business of buying and selling. Their objective was to create 'an energy that inspires its customers' so the building has been deliberately left without a shop sign, so as to compound the mystery, and stir up the imagination. Like a magnet, tugging at the senses, the high-tech store is an expression of a renewed vitality as the city stakes a claim in its future. It is an unleashing of the creative spirit of Birmingham, urging its people to imagine their own future: to 'go create'.

In all the major developed cities of the world, core growth is based on the knowledge industries. The metropolis has been replaced by 'ideopolis' (Judis and Teixeira, 2002), in which economic prosperity and competitiveness depend not on the ability to make things, but on generating ideas that can be sold to the world. In this age of intellectual capital both insight and innovation are more highly prized than physical wealth or infrastructure. According to The Right Hon. Chris Smith, the imagination of its people is a nation's 'greatest resource, nourishing invention, economic advantage, scientific discovery, technological advance, better administration, jobs, communities and a more secure society' (Smith, 1998).

For ideas to prosper, people need an environment that supports and inspires the creative process, such as an open and vibrant arts and cultural scene that is empowered not repressed, and an education system that encourages individuals to assimilate what is around them to come up with something new and useful. This is the challenge for the modern-day city: to set in place the conditions that will fire the imagination of its citizens to create their own future.

Shanghai's education system, although greatly improved, is still dogged by rote learning. As Professor Hanmin Zhou, Deputy Chief Commissioner of the Pudong People's Government, explains:

We need an education system where teachers no longer restrict creativity in our young people. The teachers themselves have to start thinking and teaching differently. Let me give you an analogy of what I mean. The people of Shanghai are all stuck at the neck of the bottle. There is so much potential there that is waiting to be released. What we have to do is to break the neck of this bottle that is holding us back. The first and foremost step is a mental preparation. So the importance of education is crucial (Zhou, 2003).

The outcome of the bottleneck is a city with an industry that is great at imitation and copying, making Shanghai and its surrounds the manufacturing capital of the world, but devoid of its own nationally and internationally competitive brand names. Only three local brand names of clothes, Kaikai, Hailuo and Shanshan, survive in the harsh competition. A Shanghai origin was once a major selling point for brands in China, promising quality and style in its products until the 1980s. Although the government injected financial and other support into the industry, the effort proved more or less useless, owing to the stifling of innovation by a heavy-handed government that used to vote in favour of the SOEs at the expense of privately owned enterprises (Yatsko, 2000).

What about Shanghai's arts scene, the training ground for the imagination? In Shanghai there is an art scene that borders on a more generalized underground, but it is still muzzled by bureaucracy and censorship. At its centre is writer and club promoter Mian Mian, also known as Kika. Her frank, semi-autobiographical collection of short stories, *La, La, La*, tells of sex, drugs and rock'n'roll, and has made her a cult hero among China's generation Y, but the volume was banned shortly after publication when Jiang Zemin was reported to have singled her out in a Politburo meeting as a 'decadent influence' on Chinese youth. Together with the notorious DJ Coco Zhao, one of China's few publicly gay figures, Mian Mian promotes club nights in the city showcasing the best of new Chinese artists and music (Mian, 1997).

Artists occasionally organize unofficial shows, although much less often than in Beijing. In 1999, the avant garde 'Art for sale' received much attention, ingeniously using shops on the busy Huaihai Road as the venues for exhibitions, but the exhibition was shut down after only three days because the artists had 'failed to apply for the necessary permissions' (Napack, 2000). The Shanghart Gallery is another focal point for artists and the only one in Shanghai devoted to avant-garde art. It represents most of the local artists, from abstractionists like Ding Yi to neo-conceptualists Shi Yong and Zhou Tiehai. However, the gallery director, Lorenz Helbling, is Swiss and the clientele mostly foreign.

The lack of a substantial arts culture is not because Shanghai people do not like art. In the 1920s and 1930s, Shanghai was the artistic centre of China, favoured by intellectuals and creatives from every discipline for its freedom of expression, and opportunities to connect with Western and Japanese styles. However, that rich mix of influences has left a legacy that is disabling Shanghai culture, for the city's residents would now rather assimilate international culture than anything quirky or local. A cosmopolitan city needs world-class cultural centres and Mayor Xu Kuangdi has poured millions into venues such as the Shanghai Museum, with its fabulous galleries of Chinese antiquities, the new Shanghai Opera and now the Shanghai Art Museum with its collection of unreconstructed Socialist–Realist kitsch, with the occasional painting by a relatively 'safe' contemporary artist (Napack, 2000).

The free spirit of old Shanghai has left its mark on its citizens, and the city remains a beacon for entrepreneurs and thinkers both inside and outside China.

The head offices of the major media and advertising services around the globe have planted their China offices in the city centre, and it has become the testing ground for new products. As Professor Zhou says, 'once you make it in Shanghai, you are a brand forever' (Zhou, 2003). But the lack of absolute freedom in the city, a general low awareness of the importance of developing local tradition and problems in the quality of life – problems affecting all China – are hampering the flow of that spirit.

Shanghai is not without its own passionate leaders who have transformed the city through 'sheer force of will' (Sudjic, 1993). In the 1980s, as China began reform, Shanghai was more or less neglected, its wealth used to fund experiments elsewhere in China. When Beijing finally opened the lid on Shanghai, its redevelopment took on a momentum that would not have been possible without former mayors Jiang Zemin, now China's President, and Zhu Rongji, now Premier. They fought hard against the red tape to market the aspiration for international status. Then in 2001 grassroots democracy expanded from rural parts of China to urban areas, a move described by sociologists as a breakthrough in the country's political system. Thousands of residents in several cities, such as Shanghai, Nanjing and Hangzhou, elected their community councils and leading council officials for the first time on the Chinese mainland. The election reflects a new respect for the aspirations of residents and an understanding of the critical role of self-regulation in creating great cities.

Rediscovering its soul

Now, with growing freedom, civic leaders are demanding for their citizens the preservation of historical buildings, the creation of more green space and the construction of dwellings that do not dwarf the man and woman in the street and block out their daylight. In the process, the city is revealing to the world its softer, more humane core, a core not so hell-bent on ostentation and achieving some stereotype of modernity but rather, the quest to establish a sustainable city.

The new approach is a holistic one responding to the emotional and spiritual needs of citizens, with their quality of life at its heart. It finds expression in the new goal that the city has defined for itself: to 'create a harmonious ecological environment for human beings, to establish a 21st Century metropolis' (Shanghai Urban Planning Exhibition Hall, 2003). Shanghai has already begun work on its plans to triple green space per inhabitant, from 3.6 square metres today, to 10 square metres by 2020. There are rules to lower the height of new buildings, as well as reduce neighbourhood density, and greater emphasis is now placed on the preservation and rejuvenation of historical buildings. The urbanization of the city is coming down to earth, to street level.

The archetypal symbol for the new Shanghai is perhaps Xin Tian Di, or 'new heaven and earth', a cluster of restaurants and boutique shops that sits behind the restored facades of 1920s Shanghai courtyard houses. The inscription on the nameplate says 'where the Shanghai of yesterday meets the Shanghai of tomorrow, today'. For a city hooked on modernity, the shift towards sustainable urban regeneration is critical to its aims. The modern world is no longer rocked by superlatives. Now good environmental conditions are not only crucial to quality of life, they are fundamental to global economic competitiveness (The World Bank Group, 2001). As Shanghai shifts focus, its vision becomes deeper, more fundamental, more long term.

Its crack at sustainability has not gone unnoticed. In December 2002, fireworks criss-crossed the night sky in Shanghai as the Bureau of International Exhibitions in Paris voted in favour of the city hosting the World Exposition in 2010. Knocking out Poland's Wroclaw, Mexico's Queretaro, Moscow and finally Yeoso in South Korea, the event will rewrite history books. Since it began in 1851, it has never before been held in a developing country. The bid win was a culmination of a hard-driven marketing campaign, in which China won support from multinational corporations across the world, and has been hailed as one of the city's greatest achievements. China is a country that surely had exhausted its quota for hosting world events after Beijing won the right to stage the 2008 Olympics. The city also beat rival Moscow, a contender in dire need of world attention; and its triumph came in the wake of economic downturn and gloomy forecasts.

A melting pot of ideas

The World Expo, described as 'the Olympic Games of economics, science and technology and culture' (Anon, 2002) is a non-commercial event that attracts visitors from around the world. Its aims are to promote co-operation and exchange between countries and further world development, giving participating countries the chance to become involved in world issues, while they witness the talents of their neighbours and showcase their own achievements. It is estimated that 70 million visitors will attend the half-year event, with direct investment exceeding 3 billion US dollars. This will create huge business opportunities for Shanghai; although a non-commercial event, businesses in the city will flourish. It will also spur the city's urban renewal.

With a history of over 150 years, the Expo has become a major source of new ideas, concepts and technologies, and has also played a role in ensuring their practical application. Many history-making inventions such as Bell's telephone and the Wright Brothers' plane made their first appearance at World Expos. The Eiffel Tower became the symbol of Paris throughout the world at the Paris World Expo in 1889, pushing boundaries in the disciplines of architectural design and construction. A number of concepts that we take for granted today, such as department stores, holiday villages and amusement parks, also owe their inspiration to the World Expo.

In addition, the World Expo fosters discussion of many problems critical to the development of society, such as environmental protection and population control. Shanghai has chosen to promote the theme 'Better city, better life', which fits with the city's development plans to improve the quality of life of its residents as well as rapid economic expansion. The ultimate objective of urbanization is to allow people to enjoy better lives, and key to that is environmental improvement. 'We want to have an ecological city based on human needs', says Professor Zhu Linchu, deputy director-general of the Shanghai Government's development research centre (quoted in Anon, 2003). Come the Expo, Shanghai will be host to the world's most innovative and progressive thinking on the subject.

Shanghai has been involved in World Expos on and off since the First Expo held in London in 1851, when Shanghai merchant Xu Rongcun brought along twelve packets of homespun 'Huzhuo Silk'. He won both the gold and the silver prizes. The event is documented in Xu's family annals published in 1884 and in the official Expo report published by the Royal Society of London in 1852. Both documents now can be found in the Shanghai Library. For the 1904 St Louis Expo, now famous for the Wright Brothers' plane, China's Qing government constructed the 'Chinese village' and 'China Exhibition Hall'. At the 1915 Panama Expo, Maotai, China's infamous liquor, took gold while Shen Shou's embroidery won silver.

The 2010 bid proposals reveal a pledge by the mayor to invest around $3 billion in transport and infrastructure development ahead of the event, with up to ten times more expected to be spent on related infrastructure projects. Many projects had been in the pipeline long before the final vote. The venues for the event will be constructed along the Huangpu River, a tributary of the Yangtze that runs through the city. Docks and warehouses along its banks will be transformed into modern exhibition halls, with construction of the new being combined with the restoration of old city districts. 'We want to make it like an

Asian version of the River Seine in Paris', says Shanghai Bidding Office Vice Chairman Huang Yaocheng. For around 25 000 citizens, venue construction will force them to move elsewhere, but the majority see the relocation as an opportunity to improve their living conditions and quality of life.

Tang Zhiping, a local official in charge of city planning, says: 'We are going to dig a canal and build a green corridor in the area. After the exposition, the canal and corridor will remain, and the venues will become shopping malls, and recreation and cultural centres. There will be museums in the present dock and warehouse districts' (CRI, 2002). Central to the plans is the cleaning up of the city and the introduction of green space. Factories will be moved to the outskirts of the city and landscapers are planting 800 hectares of trees and grass each year. By 2020, green land will comprise 35 per cent of the city's total area.

In anticipation of increased traffic arising from the World Expo, construction of another three runways at Pudong Airport was completed last year, increasing passenger capacity from 20 million passengers each year to 80 million. Before long, visitors will be able to travel from the airport to the main Pudong area in the rocket-like maglev train in eight minutes. The government also has plans to invest $6 billion to develop a 3600 kilometre network of new roads, increasing traffic capacity in the city by 60 per cent and reducing congestion across the bridges and tunnels that cross the Huangpu River. This will help to reduce pollution in the river. The city's efforts in respect of the World Expo 2010 leave its 17 million residents with a substantial legacy, allowing them to enjoy a better quality of life, improved housing, more open space, an expanded green belt and a greatly rejuvenated riverside. But for the city to really flourish, to sit alongside London and New York, the innate creativity of the people must now be released.

Conclusion: every city needs its Soho

'Everyone in Shanghai understands that we need to think freely in order to become successful', says Professor Zhou, but he adds: 'the way in which Shanghai has developed from an obscure fishing village 700 years ago into an international metropolis where businesses from around the world gather, forms an intrinsic part of the city, and nurtures a belief that our success depends on an ability to readily absorb foreign advancements, no matter where they come from' (Zhou, 2003). The result of this unquestioning permeability is a great cosmopolitan city, but one that lacks a truly authentic core. In other words, the city's own indigenous culture has been allowed to sink under the influences from abroad.

The impact of a vibrant cultural scene within the knowledge economy cannot be underestimated. Arts and culture are major embodiments of the human imagination and they breathe life into a city. They enhance the environment, stimulate thinking and build an image that brings in investment and talent from outside. A rich arts and cultural scene creates a buzz towards which the greatest minds gravitate. It is the groundswell of city life and the richest resource for its people. Every city needs its Soho, its eccentrics, its poets and painters, its citizens who choose to follow a different path, as well as its high life and glitz. Shanghai must remember what it once knew in the 1920s and 1930s, when it could boast Aldous Huxley, Noel Coward and W. H. Auden among its visitors. It is time for the city to encourage its own arts and cultural scene to flourish.

I believe it is the task of the business community as well as the government to inspire in the people a desire to preserve and develop their own unique arts culture. Business and civic leaders should set aside and hand over to the people the old theatres and municipal buildings, dance halls and casinos. These will then be the focal point for the city's burgeoning arts scene, the Soho or Hoxton of Shanghai, providing a central hub, a rattle bag for the city's poetry festivals, art shows, operas, open mike sessions, plays, stand-up comedians, dance and music festivals, and so on, for expressions of the spirit of creativity that resides in the people.

It is understandable that the new emerging middle class in Shanghai set their sights on their offspring becoming lawyers, doctors or accountants, but it is important that the children themselves feel that they can follow the less conventional routes taken by the great writers, artists and poets who preceded them. By overaspiring, society may well be underachieving in the creative disciplines, and it is in those disciplines that Shanghai needs its stars.

Shanghai has spent the past fifteen years creating a shimmering outer force. It is now acknowledging that cities are living things and makeovers need to make allowances for the human factor. The final challenge is to substantiate the outer force with an even stronger, more vital inner core. In recent times, it has been the lack of political autonomy that inhibited the development of a unique culture and subculture. But things are changing post-WTO. The city that was once bound up in aspiration must now attempt to imbue its inside, its people, with the same shining confidence that fills its skyline. It must grant the licence to unleash the creative spirit, to give to the artists, inventors, poets, and musicians the physical and symbolic space to create.

References

Anon (2002) Shanghai Mayor confident of successful World Expo. *People's Daily* (18 September). http://english.peopledaily.com.cn/200209/18/ eng20020918_ 103444.shtml

Anon (2003) What will city gain from expo? *International Herald Tribune* (6 February). http://www.iht.com/articles/85840.html

CRI (2002) Construction of venues for World Exposition beautify Shanghai. *CRI Online.* http://francais.cri.com.cn/english/2002/Nov/80051.htm

Hutton, W. (2002) Put the cities in charge. *The Observer* (7 July).

Judis, J. B. and Teixeira, R. (2002) Majority rules. *New Republic* (5 August).

MacPherson, K. L. (2002) Shanghai's history: back to the future. *Harvard Asia Pacific Review.* http://web.mit.edu/lipoff/www/hapr/spring02_wto/ shanghai.pdf

Mian, M. (1997) *La, La, La.* Hong Kong.

Napack, J. (2000) Letter from Shanghai. New York: ArtNet Worldwide Corporation (13 July). http://www.artnet.com/magazine/reviews/napack/ napack7-13-00.asp

Pumphrey, M. (1987) The flapper, the housewife and the making of modernity. *Cultural Studies* 1(2): 179–194.

Shanghai Urban Planning Exhibition Hall (2003) 50 Renmin Da Dao, Shanghai 2003, PR China.

Smith, C. (1998) *Creative Britain.* London: Faber and Faber.

Sudjic, D. (1993) *The 100 Mile City.* Flamingo.

Sullivan, L. H. (1896) The tall office building artistically considered. *Lippincott's Magazine.*

The World Bank Group (2001) Making the environment a priority in urban development. The World Bank Group (9 July). http://web.worldbank.org/ WBSITE/EXTERNAL/NEWS/0,contentMDK:20018630~menuPK:3445 9~pagePK:34370~piPK:34424~theSitePK:4607,00.html

Tianshu, P. (2001) Shanghai nostalgia: historical memory, community-building, and place-making in a late socialist city. Harvard. http://mumford.cas. albany.edu/chinanet/conferences/Tianshu.doc

Xu Anqi (2000) Quality of life in Shanghai surveyed. *China Daily* (17 February). http://www.china.org.cn/english/China/56008.htm

Yatsko, P. (2000) *New Shanghai: The Rocky Rebirth of China's Legendary City.* Singapore: Wiley.

York, G. (2003) Shanghai's skyscrapers fall from public favour. *Globe and Mail* (15 February). http://www.globeandmail.com/servlet/ArticleNews/ TPStory/LAC/20030215/USHANEC/International/Idx

Zhou, H. (2003) Spectacular Shanghai. In Gilmore, F. and Dumont, S. (eds) *Brand Warriors China*. London: Profile Books, pp. 51–62.

12

Western Australia: building a state brand

Shane R. Crockett and Leiza J. Wood

Introduction

In today's cut-throat marketplace, only those destinations that have a clear market position and appealing attractions will remain at the top of consumer minds when they book their holidays. Although travel agents continue to provide booking and support services, the choice of destination clearly lies with the consumer. In the highly competitive and dynamic global tourism environment, there is a need to develop a clear identity, or 'brand' based on reality, while also reflecting the core strengths and 'personality' of its product. In this crowded marketplace, building and maintaining brand value is the key to business success and, as a result, brand management is quickly shifting from a peripheral marketing concern to the core business strategy. More often than not, it is the brand strategy that will determine who is successful in today's competitive business environment.

This is certainly true of destinations and, according to the World Tourism Organization (Jones, 1998) there is a clear contemporary trend towards highly branded destinations. As Ahmed (1991) states, 'Holiday makers of the 21st century will be looking for places with a trendy image. A strong and clear state image can increase consumer confidence in its attractions and consumer predisposition to purchase them.'

This chapter outlines the approach of the Western Australian Tourism Commission (WATC) to destination branding during 1996–2000. Based on intensive consumer research, Brand Western Australia (Brand WA) resulted in an entire organizational shift and repositioned Western Australia as a premier nature-based tourism destination in the global market. The cornerstone of the strategy was a partnership between government and industry, and this philosophy formed the platform for all policy direction. To ensure delivery of the marketing promise, infrastructure development and partnerships with other key government agencies were a fundamental part of the Brand WA strategy, creating a statewide rather than merely a tourism brand.

Essentially, Brand WA was a co-operative marketing strategy that aimed to differentiate Western Australia in the global marketplace. It was developed for the state of Western Australia so that any person or organization promoting Western Australia's destination attributes, products, services, investment, and so on, could market Western Australia in a unified and consistent manner. Brand WA was built on a solid research foundation undertaken in 1996 that resulted in a set of descriptors for the personality and values of Western Australia, and an 'essence' that captured the underlying spirit of the state. Therefore, Brand WA captured the distinctive character of Western Australian people, the state's unique natural beauty, wide open spaces and pristine environment, the colours of the landscape and the free-spirited nature of the Western Australian lifestyle. The WATC adopted a totally integrated and inclusive approach to destination branding that encompassed marketing and development strategies, and in the process crafted a unique identity for Western Australia.

Largely based on the chapter included in the original edition of this book, this chapter will describe the brand development and extension strategies adopted by Western Australia during 1996–2000 and locate them in the context of fundamental brand-building principles. It initially outlines the macro-tourism environment of Western Australia during this period, analyses the repositioning challenge at that time and then summarizes the development of Brand WA. Finally, it discusses and evaluates the fully integrated destination marketing, development and partnership strategies pursed by the state during

1996–2000. Although the direction of the brand has since shifted, this case study stands as an excellent example of the value of partnerships and co-operation in destination branding.

Positioning the brand

Differentiating Western Australia

Western Australia, home to 1.8 million people and offering a high standard of living, constitutes one-third of the Australian continent (with a landmass of 2.5 million square kilometres). Bounded by more than 12 000 kilometres of pristine coastline and characterized by extremes of climate ranging from tropical to desert, with warm Mediterranean and cool temperatures, Western Australia offers a range of tourism experiences. Indeed, the tourism industry provides significant economic and development opportunities for Western Australia, particularly in the regional centres, which are home to many of the state's unique natural attractions. In 2000 tourism in Western Australia was an Aus\$4.1 billion industry, attracting more than 1.46 million annual international and national visitors to the state as its fourth largest export industry (WATC, 2000a). It employed some 78 000 Western Australians or 9 per cent of the state workforce, and represented approximately 4 per cent of the gross state product (WATC, 2000b). Western Australia attracted 13 per cent of Australia's international and 8 per cent of its domestic tourism market (Bureau of Tourism Research, 1999) (Figure 12.1).

In order to foster Western Australia's tourism industry, WATC was given the role to accelerate the sustainable growth of the tourism industry for the

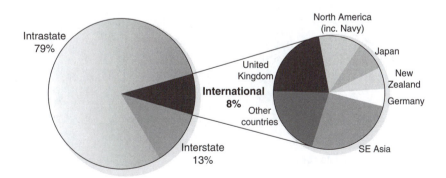

Figure 12.1   Visitors to Western Australia by origin market 1999

long-term social and economic benefit of the state. The WATC is a state government statutory authority and by virtue of enabling legislation is charged with two core objectives:

- to promote Western Australia as an attractive tourist, event and convention destination within Australia and overseas
- to promote, foster and facilitate investment in and the development of new tourist infrastructure, services, product and the improvement of existing tourist facilities and services in Western Australia.

As can be seen from Figure 12.1, three clearly defined markets were apparent: Western Australians travelling within their own state, visitors from other parts of Australia, and overseas visitors. In assessing the success of tourism, the WATC recognized that visitor expenditure or 'export income' is a critical measure of success (Figure 12.2) and that visitor numbers do not always demonstrate the real shifts in export earnings for tourism (Figure 12.1). Hence, there is always a balance of marketing priorities between interstate and international markets and the WATC encouraged its contracted regional tourism associations to undertake the majority of regional marketing.

In respect to its product, Western Australia offers among the finest nature-based experiences and tourist attractions in Australia. However, research undertaken in 1994 (303 Advertising, 1994) revealed that at that time Western Australia and its capital Perth lacked a meaningful identity in the global marketplace. There was a need for Western Australia to develop a strong identity that encapsulated the state's unique attributes and personality that could be marketed to those markets representing the best potential for return on investment.

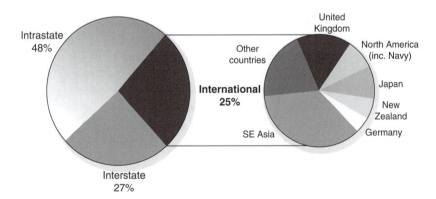

Figure 12.2 Total visitor expenditure in Western Australia by origin market 1999

The vision was to produce a clear identity encompassing identified brand values. This brand would drive all marketing and development strategies. It would pervade all forms of communication and stimulate the core of the travel consumer's behaviour and decision-making process to position the state of Western Australia competitively in the global marketplace. As a result, in November 1996, the WATC launched Brand WA.

The essence of branding

Kotler *et al.* (1996) suggest that the positioning task consists of three steps: identifying a set of possible competitive advantages upon which to build a position, selecting the right competitive advantages, and effectively communicating and delivering the chosen position to a carefully selected target market. Aaker's (1996) expanded model suggests that a brand encompasses many variables which all influence the brand's value proposition, credibility, brand–customer relationships and ultimately the brand's positioning. These include the brand as:

- a product (place) (e.g. attributes, place of origin, quality/value)
- an organization (place) (e.g. attributes, innovation, local versus global)
- a person (e.g. personality, brand–customer relationships)
- a symbol (e.g. visual imagery and metaphors, brand heritage).

Any analysis of successful brands worldwide reveals one overwhelming element: they all have a clearly defined core personality or purpose. A brand personality can be defined as the set of human characteristics associated with a given brand (Aaker, J., 1995); like a human personality, it is both distinctive and enduring (Aaker, D., 1996). Aaker (1996) defines the core identity as being 'the central, timeless essence of the brand' which remains constant even as the brand travels to new markets and products. Depending on the target market, advertising strategies, communication tones, positioning statements and, in some cases, even the logos can all be changed, but what remains constant is the core personality or purpose. For example, in the world of sports and fashion, Nike has crafted a unique and instantly recognized identity synonymous with innovation, excitement, and the pursuit of excellence in health and fitness. McDonald's, with its golden arches, conjures up images of convenience, value and consistency of product range, and extends to associations involving children, families and fun. Another example is found in Singapore Airlines, which instantly communicates to the public that it offers a unique, professional and somewhat exotic service. Female flight attendants (Singapore Girl) and their batik Sarong Kebaya uniforms have become an image and a standard that are instantly recognized and appreciated by passengers, and competitive airlines would find it difficult to achieve significant market share using a similar approach (Kotler, 1996). This concept of branding also extends to tourist destinations, and the most successful destinations have achieved this to an extent where the mention of their name evokes mental images and perceived experiences. Thus, for example, The Seychelles promotes an exotic island experience, while the UK is clearly one of the world's most sought-after cultural and historical destinations.

To be a famous destination brand, Western Australia needed to be more than the sum of its products, however beautifully presented, just as Nikes are more than sport shoes. The destination needed to find the unique piece of information that positioned its experience in potential visitors' minds differently from everywhere else in the world. The brand mission, therefore, needed to capture the very essence of the Western Australian experience and its effect on the visitor/consumer. To deliver this, Brand WA was an ambitious plan to unite the tourism industry and other business sectors to present a consistent image of Western Australia to interstate and overseas markets. It was more than just a tourism marketing campaign, and encompassed destination awareness, product awareness, consumer desire, tourism product, infrastructure and industry professional development. In addition, it was recognized that in order to be successful in 'branding', infrastructure development, promotional co-ordination, produce enhancement and protection against environmental degradation were essential to the success of the state as a tourist destination. To this end, the WATC established its 'tourism development strategy', which included the 'nature-based tourism strategy', to ensure that Western Australia's holiday product and infrastructure would preserve its natural product and deliver its marketing promise. Underpinning the WATC's core philosophies were its partnerships with industry that ensured that the WATC's destination marketing and management was complementary to the development and promotional activities of individual tourist providers and other stakeholders.

In turn, Brand WA and the tourism development strategy provided the catalyst for an entire organizational restructuring within the WATC, encompassing a new corporate culture, new direction, increased accountability, performance measurement and partnerships with industry, together with a clear customer focus. Developing a strong and distinctive image calls for creativity and brilliant execution, and no organization can implant an image in the public's mind overnight. To differentiate Western Australia in the marketplace and to create a strong destination image, Brand WA also needed to be an innovative long-term strategy based on the fundamental principles of brand management. This chapter, therefore, will now outline the creative and integrated approach under-taken by the WATC since its launch of Brand WA in 1996 until 2000.

Brand Western Australia development

The process

The development of Brand WA was led by the WATC and involved an exten-sive consultative process with the possible end-users of Brand WA. A Brand Strategy Group, representing Western Australia's broader community, met regu-larly to co-ordinate the overall process. The composition of this group included the Premier of Western Australia, the City of Perth's Lord Mayor, the Department of Commerce and Trade, Western Australian business leaders in banking and export, and representatives from the inbound tourism industry (including the Perth Convention Bureau). The group's task was to test and endorse the foundation research and creative concepts throughout the develop-ment of Western Australia's brand. This endorsement was essential, as it was to be a 'state brand' that tourism could then market.

In the development of Brand WA, it was also decided to maximize the link-age between it and the Australian Tourist Commission's (ATC) Brand Australia strategy. In many of Western Australia's target markets, Brand Australia has a very large promotional presence and, in many market segments, travellers first decide to come to Australia then, within that holiday experience, choose which particular location within Australia. Western Australia would add depth to and be a core brand of Brand Australia, reflecting the 'big nature' aspect of Brand Australia's core personality. At the same time, Brand WA would benefit from the promotional strength attained through synergy with Brand Australia. To this end, ATC representatives were intimately involved in the development of Brand WA.

Underpinning the Brand WA strategy was the commitment to a partnership philosophy with industry and other key stakeholders. This was reflected in the establishment of advisory councils comprising industry representatives who provided advice and recommendations on all major marketing and industry development activities undertaken by the WATC. In addition, ten regional tourism associations (RTAs) representing tourism regions throughout the state were formed to develop a flexible framework to produce and implement indi-vidual marketing and development plans while reflecting the broader focus of Western Australia's tourism initiatives. Destination branding is difficult since tourism (and its related industries) is a composite product consisting of many components, including accommodation, transport, catering establishments, tourist attractions, arts, entertainment and the natural environment. Through a multiagency and cross-industry approach, Brand WA ensured that each stakeholder took ownership and assumed responsibility for enhancing favourable brand images.

The foundation research

In developing Brand WA, it was vital for the core personality of the destination to be clearly defined and reflected in all marketing strategies. Marketing intelligence (derived from a comprehensive qualitative research programme) was used to shape all aspects of the strategy and, to establish credible and representative brand attributes, research was conducted among overseas visitors and Western Australians. There were three main components of the research programme:

- consultation with the possible end-users of Brand WA
- a comprehensive market research programme in key national and international markets
- a target market selection process.

This extensive consultative process included: businesses likely to export, businesses in origin international markets likely to consider investing in Western Australia, the arts, the Western Australia tourism industry, Western Australian residents, heads of government agencies, the tourist industry in source markets and visitors to the state. Further, the WATC undertook an intensive qualitative research programme conducted by Donovan Research (1996) in Western Australia's key national and international tourism markets. This research analysed global tourism trends, consumer behaviour and the decision-making processes of travel consumers, and aligned these against visitor perceptions of Western Australia, its services and attractions. The perceptual issues probed included:

- the attributes that tourists ranked as high motivators for their travel
- consumer perceptions of Western Australia and Perth as a holiday destination
- what travellers imagined when they thought of Western Australia and of Perth
- consumer perceptions of the state's major strengths and weaknesses as a holiday destination.

The research revealed that Western Australia offered most of the attributes that tourists rank as high motivators of travel, such as the ability to relax and recharge, a fresh, clean environment, and unspoilt natural scenery. People believed, however, that Perth (the state capital) was quiet and lacked activity. In essence, Western Australia was felt to be strong on nature-based imagery and attractions, but lacking a meaningful identity. A major reassessment of where and how the state was marketed as a destination was required.

To compete effectively in the global tourism market, any destination must be selective about which target markets represent the best return on investment. Previously, Western Australia's work in this area had been predominantly subjective with very little objective data analysis. As described earlier, in reassessing its marketing strategy, the WATC aligned visitor numbers with visitor expenditure to assist in evaluating the optimal yield return. The target market selection process was divided into two parts; first, the selection of the highest potential countries in which to market, and second, if appropriate, which target segments should be marketed to in those countries. Given that, at that time, Australia as a market delivered 92 per cent of all visitors to Western Australia and 75 per cent of visitor expenditure, this was immediately included as a target country. The market segment results are described in the Brand WA media campaigns (see Table 12.1).

The selection of the other potential international markets was a far more complex task. An overriding philosophy was that, as a state, Western Australia had limited marketing resources and, as such, acknowledged that the state could not be in all markets at once. The Donovan research was used to determine the target markets in each location and to select the best ways, in terms of both the messages used and the media, to reach those target markets. In addition, the WATC and the International Advisory Council simultaneously developed an objective selection model named the market potential assessment formula (MPAF), a dynamic selection mechanism that assesses the value and potential of international markets using the criteria of:

- *access*: access/airline capacity; visa rejection rate
- *growth*: growth rate of outbound travel population; index size of outbound population; growth rate of visitation to Australia
- *value*: market share of visitors to Australia
- *synergy*: ATC's activity in the market; airline 'online' in market.

The MPAF enabled the commission to set priorities and allocate resources to work the market effectively. Of the twenty markets analysed, the MPAF identified the UK, Germany, Japan, Singapore and Malaysia as core markets for Western Australia that could be pursued on the budget allocation. This did not mean that other markets would be totally ignored. Rather, they would be continually monitored to see whether their potential improved, at which time resources could be applied. To this end, Italy, China, Hong Kong and South Africa were also identified as showing a strong possibility of becoming a priority market in the short to medium term.

Once the objectives and target market have been defined, the marketing communicator must decide what response is sought (Kotler *et al.*, 1996). In the case of Western Australia, top-of-mind awareness was the initial primary indicator of success. Postcampaign research conducted in each market measured its success on two essential factors, these being 'perceived knowledge' of Perth/Western Australia as a holiday destination and 'propensity to consider' Perth/Western Australia for a holiday. Further, visitor nights and visitor expenditure targets were set and measured yearly, although it is important to note that these targets were intended to guide the industry, rather than being definitive measures of the WATC's success. Research on perceptions, marketing strategies, positioning, and strengths, weaknesses, opportunities, threats and constraints (SWOTC) analyses were also ongoing and were used to provide a methodical, consistent and evolving branding approach.

The result

The result of the overall research was a clear brand position. Brand WA emerged as a clear, focused strategy with a defined purpose and personality. Western Australia's pristine environment made it well suited to marketing a fresh, new, nature-based tourism destination with friendly, spirited people and the freedom and space to travel. As described above, the strength of a brand lay in its capacity to remain true to its core personality or purpose, irrespective of its target audiences or mode of communication. Hence, in the development and research foundation of Brand WA, it was considered vital that the core personality of the destination was clearly defined and that all marketing strategies were true to the personality. The core personality elements of Brand WA were found to be:

- fresh
- natural
- free
- spirited.

These were the constants of Western Australia's proposition as a destination. Based on these core personality traits, an integrated visual language was prepared by the design team Cato Partners with internationally acclaimed designer

Ken Cato, to ensure that all visual communications reflected the core personality. The designer's challenge was to create a distinctive style and graphic theme to present the complex, diverse and unique personality of the destination. The visual identity programme created a distinctive 'broader visual language' featuring the elements of a warm yellow sun, vast canopy of blue sky and wide horizon under which the unique attributes of the state could be featured (Figure 12.3). To reflect the diversity of Western Australia and communicate beyond the traditional tourist market, a unique colour pallet and series of graphic icons were developed to reflect the arts, business, technology, events and thematic aspects of individual regions. These integrated visual components increased the personality of Brand WA's identity. They could also be marketed to strategic partners to promote their individual objectives, thereby creating sub-brands under the overall umbrella of Brand WA. The visual language was not just a logo, in fact it was deliberately not a logo, but rather a set of design briefs which ensured that the visual elements of Western Australia's marketing always reflected the core personality, adding to the strength of the brand. Although a logo was developed in the visual language, it was developed as only one of the many visual tools that could be used to impart the personality of Brand WA.

On the basis of the foundation research, the Brand WA strategy was developed as a five-year holistic package with a number of marketing and development strategies aimed at maximizing Western Australia's market exposure, servicing its core tourism sectors, facilitating effective industry partnerships, and developing industry product and infrastructure, all of which would deliver on the marketing promise. These strategies shaped the initial development of Brand WA and were further reviewed after additional research and consultation. The tourism industry plan for 2000–2005, Partnership 21, extended the Brand

Figure 12.3　Brand Western Australia visual identity system

WA strategy for the tourism industry. Partnership 21 researched and identified the latest emerging trends of the travel consumer towards experiential travel, revitalization and freedom. As travellers become more experienced, they are seeking more personalized and interactive experiences. As Pritchard and Morgan (1998, pp. 216–217) have said: 'When consumers make brand choice about products – including tourism services and destinations – they are making lifestyle statements since they are trying to buy not only into an image, but also into an emotional relationship.' Through Partnership 21, Western Australia sought to continue with Brand WA's strong nature-based positioning, further enhancing it with an environmentally positive addition to the brand personality. The new dimension was the emotional connection of being 'touched by nature', providing opportunities for people to learn more about the destination and its products through interaction rather than through a passive viewing approach.

Brand WA marketing strategies

The following section discusses the advertising and marketing strategies developed for tourism to capitalize on the brand. Strategies to establish Brand WA are discussed along with the later strategies determined under Partnership 21. The overall marketing and promotional mix was determined as follows.

- *Price/value*: Western Australia has previously been positioned in its core markets as a value-for-money destination, and therefore the marketing promotions were not principally price led, but rather reflected a value-added component.
- *Product*: the product was principally centred around nature-based product and experiences, with a heavy focus on regional attractions.
- *Place*: marketing and promotional activities were primarily delivered through broadcast consumer media such as advertising and publicity. The tourism product is delivered through traditional and electronic distribution channels utilizing wholesale packages, retail travel agents and other travel retailers such as airlines and booking companies. The consumer website, www.westernaustralia.net, was seen as central to assisting visitors to conduct their information search, and its e-booking platform essential in providing conversion via a gateway to the tourism industry. A virtual industry structure was developed, integrating visitor servicing, retail sales and access to product knowledge through a virtual call centre, a statewide visitor centre network, a comprehensive statewide database of tourism product and a single entry point for all of Western Australia's tourism operators.

- *Promotion*: the Brand WA strategy relied heavily on consumer advertising, utilizing celebrity endorsement television commercials that were supported by a co-ordinated publicity campaign encouraging the publication of positive tourism stories on Western Australia. The WATC also participated in selected consumer and trade shows throughout the region and core markets.

Mass marketing and clever marketing

Although word-of-mouth advertising plays an important part in the promotion of any holiday destination, it is consumer awareness created through marketing and communication campaigns, supported by appropriate collateral, that is the key to increasing awareness levels of a destination in its core markets. As the fresh and natural aspects of Western Australia were clearly seen as the state's major competitive advantage in all key markets, the core position underpinning Brand WA was the notion that Western Australia offered a holiday experience that is fresh, natural, free and spirited, and refreshingly different from other holiday destinations. The overriding objective was to develop a long-term campaign designed to build awareness of Western Australia as a holiday destination, in a highly competitive, dynamic and expensive global marketplace.

Celebrity endorsement was seen as an effective means of providing a point of differentiation between Western Australia and other destinations. Kotler *et al.* (1996) suggest that celebrities are likely to be effective when they personify a key product attribute. The WATC secured the services of international supermodel and actress Elle Macpherson. Ms Macpherson, an Australian, was seen to embody the 'personality' of the state and had the ability to take this message to the world in a way that no paid advertising could. This endorsement provided Western Australia's tourism advertising with high levels of recall and enquiry, as well as millions of dollars in free publicity. Once the initial brand campaigns has been undertaken in all core markets, the next step was to convert awareness into purchase. Each of the twelve Brand WA television commercials was tagged with packaged tourism product or point-to-point airfare that related to the destination being advertised. Direct-response press and radio in some cases were also used. All international campaigns included a value-added component within the product offer marketed, for example offers and bonuses at local tourist attractions.

Brand WA was launched in November 1996 and involved annual campaigns in most core national and international tourism markets. Promising postcampaign international research conducted by Donovan Research revealed positive changes in attitude and belief measures in all markets, and increased awareness across the board. Although primarily intended to increase awareness, the initial six-week UK campaign in September 1997 directly resulted in 5886 visitors generating Aus$7.3 million of expenditure within Western Australia, a 500 per cent return on the advertising outlay. Following the success of the initial Brand WA commercials, Elle Macpherson was contracted for an additional four commercials which were produced in October 1998 and broadcast in some core markets. The combined UK campaigns generated in excess of Aus$25 million in direct visitor expenditure, and according to the World Tourism and Travel Council formula, this should be multiplied by three to estimate the total flow of benefits.

During 1998–2001 Western Australia recorded an 11.8 per cent jump in total visitation, while interstate visitation was up 15.7 per cent on 1998, against a national average of only 0.4 per cent. In the process Perth climbed from obscurity to become the UK's third most favoured city worldwide (Guardian Observer, 2000). In 2000 the local Western Australia market generated some 5.35 million visitors (Bureau of Tourism Research, 2000) and represented around 45 per cent of total visitor expenditure. Like all segments, this market needed to be actively encouraged to visit Western Australia rather than vacationing in other states or overseas. The campaign reminded Western Australians of their state's great features and included:

- a positioning campaign to reposition the state in 'top-of-mind awareness' of local Western Australians as a destination with a wealth of nature-based attractions and experiences
- a campaign to build on this repositioning by encouraging specific travel within Western Australia
- travel and lifestyle programmes broadcast by three Perth metropolitan commercial television stations and a commercial radio station promoting Perth and Western Australia regional destinations
- tactical initiatives to stimulate travel during low and shoulder periods (e.g. winter breaks).

This integrated approach achieved significant success. For example, the 'winter breaks' tactical initiative in 1999 boasted high consumer awareness of 42.6 per cent (Roy Morgan Research, 1999) and returned 57 787 bed-nights, representing a 29 per cent increase over the previous year and an accumulated increase of 59 per cent since the 1996 initiative. Mass-media campaigns were conducted in co-operation with industry and reflected and reinforced the established brand image. Mass media was also used to promote the tourism website www.westernaustralia.net in combination with brand awareness campaigns.

Television commercials of fifteen seconds' duration were chosen for the national market, forty seconds for Singapore and Malaysia, and twenty-second commercials for the UK market, for a number of reasons. Commercials of this length enable each to tell a unique story with a single focus and viewer expectation is heightened through the desire to 'stay tuned for the next chapter', all of which maximizes impact. By using a shorter commercial time, the advertisements can be repeated more frequently and cost-effectively, thus improving the reach and frequency amongst the target audience. It also provided the opportunity to include tactical tags of product and calls to action. In the national market, a reach and frequency of 97 per cent was achieved. The strategy for longer TV commercials in the South-East Asian market emphasized the myriad of activities and experiences available in a holiday to remember (Table 12.1).

Although television is the most powerful brand-building medium, in some market categories it is not necessary or is cost-prohibitive. To this end, the WATC also effectively used media and trade familiarizations to generate extensive publicity to promote destination brand awareness. One example was the leveraging of the ATC's Visiting Journalists Program (VJP), which during 1998–2001 resulted in excess of Aus$120 million in free publicity for the state. Mass marketing will always have its place. However, in the era of one-to-one marketing, a successful marketing strategy must integrate mass marketing and one-to-one activities. In this case, the successful consumer website www.westernaustralia.net and its advanced product and consumer database also facilitated customized marketing opportunities.

Niche marketing

Niche marketing to selected groups such as adventure, trekking, diving, wildflowers and wine tourism, and the use of electronic marketing for advertising, communicating and developing databases, maximize destination marketing opportunities. Special interest tourism is growing on a global scale and Western Australia is well positioned to meet the demands of this broad-based market opportunity. During 1999–2001, the WATC and industry partners increased marketing activities and developed tourism products in a range of special interest tourism strategies, including nature-based, wine, diving and cultural tourism. In addition, WATC also targeted business tourists through its Conventions and Incentives Travel Strategy – Operation Welcome Mat. Based on research that highlighted the importance of making South-East Asian visitors 'feel welcome' in a destination, the WATC, in partnership with the Perth Convention Bureau, embarked on a cohesive strategy to attract the top 100 meetings, incentive, corporate and exhibitions (MICE) decision makers from

Table 12.1 Brand Western Australia media campaign summary

Core market	Market segment	Proposition	Strategy
National: Sydney/ Melbourne	• Longer stay holiday-makers • 30–59-year-olds • Higher income earners	Only Perth and Western Australia's natural environment offers an adventurous escape to the unspoilt Australia	Brand and retail: mix of 15- and 30-second TV commercials and press Timing: April 1997, October 1997, September 1999, September 2000
International: Singapore	• Short-break holiday-makers • 18–35-year-olds • Higher household income • Extended family	Only Perth and Western Australia's natural harmony offers the opportunity to participate in Australian country and city activities	Brand: 1 × 40-second TV commercial in English and Mandarin Retail: 1 × 20-second TV commercial in English and Mandarin Quarter-page mono-press Timing: July 1997, March 1999 Chinese New Year campaign: November 1998 In 1999 and 2000 the Singapore campaign consisted of 1 × 20-second brand commercial with a 10-second tactical tag. Press was used as the primary tactical medium
Indonesia	• Short-break holiday-makers • 25–45-year-olds • Upper socioeconomic grouping	Only Perth's natural harmony offers the opportunity to see Australia's natural beauty from the comfort of a city environment	Brand: 1 × 45-second TV commercial in Bahasa Indonesian Retail: 1 × 15-second TV commercial in Bahasa Indonesian Quarter-page mono-press Timing: July 1997 Withdrew from market in 1998, determined by MPAF
Malaysia	• Upper middle class 18–29-year-olds Ethnic Chinese and Malays • Young families with children under 12 years	Only Perth's natural harmony offers the freedom to see Australian country and city activities	Brand: half-page colour press Retail: 30-second radio advertisement in English Half-page mono-press Timing: April/May 1997, March 1999 Press remains the major focus in this market owing to broadcast restrictions
UK	• Long-haul holiday-makers • 30–59-year-olds • Upper income levels	Western Australia's natural harmony offers an adventurous escape to the true nature of unspoilt Australia	Brand: 3 × 20-second TV commercials Retail: 1 × 10-second TV commercial Timing: September 1997, March 1998, March 1999 The 2000 campaign consisted of a 20-second compilation of Elle/destination images with a 10-second tag. Press once again was the primary tactical medium

around the world to Perth. Operation Welcome Mat hosted over 120 buyers from all over the world on site inspections to Western Australia and the value of incentive business secured for Western Australia from these markets during 1998–2001 totalled just under Aus$6 million.

Addressing any negatives

To counter the negative perceptions of Western Australia being a little slow and lacking activity, a programme of special events was initiated. Launched in 1997, this programme, known as the 'Best on Earth in Perth', featured twelve major international sporting and cultural events over twelve months, including seven world championships, and worked to create a sense of activity and excitement. Further programmes were developed in later years, featuring a combination of regular events and events that were new to Perth and that provided a global focus on Western Australia. This multidimensional campaign also gained extensive international media exposure through the broadcast of fifteen-second 'picture postcards' showcasing regional Western Australia, en route to commercial breaks in telecasting. The market penetration of these postcards was far greater than any advertising could achieve, particularly when they were shown in countries such as the UK or Japan. The 'Best on Earth in Perth' in 1999–2000 featured fourteen international sporting and cultural events. The events supported by EventsCorp in the calendar generated Aus$66 million in economic impact for the state.

Development strategies

Delivering on the promise

In establishing a brand, it is important that structures are in place to deliver on the brand's promise. In the case of Western Australia, this was primarily achieved by establishing a brand based on reality. For example, Brand WA had as one of its core personality traits the 'natural' characteristic. Western Australia offers a great array of spectacular nature and could deliver on that promise. To ensure the sustainability of this characteristic and tourism growth in Western Australia, the WATC developed a nature-based tourism strategy. In addition, commencing in 1997–1998, Aus$6 million was allocated to develop tourism infrastructure projects throughout Western Australia over a four-year period. This commitment to infrastructure and product development was essential to maintain and improve quality experiences for visitors to Western Australia.

Some of Brand WA's personality traits were also seen to be dependent upon community attitudes, such as the quality of service delivered by the tourism product and the general 'friendly and welcoming' appeal of the state. To ensure this strength was not eroded, the WATC worked in association with the state's tourism industry body, Tourism Council Australia (TCA) and implemented a quality assurance programme aimed at improving the quality of service delivered by Western Australia tourism operators. This model was subsequently adopted nationally and renamed the National Tourism Accreditation Program. As tourists become more sophisticated, so do their expectations. Delivering on expectation is very much dependent upon the quality of the service, product or experience provided. Quality delivery is only part of the answer to exceeding tourists' expectations and many people outside the direct tourism industry, such as service station proprietors, customs officers, restaurant owners and shopkeepers also affect visitors' experiences. Therefore, in 1996–1997 the WATC introduced a Western Australian community-based campaign, 'Keep up the good work'. The campaign message was 'All Western Australians affect a visitor's satisfaction with our state and, as such, we all need to keep up the good work for our visitors, if we are to reap the rewards of tourism'. This was seen as a long-term campaign involving mass media, community presentations and workshops. All of this reinforcement becomes a vital element in creating the positive word-of-mouth promotion necessary for any destination brand to be successful. In order for the WATC and its industry to be effective an integrated partnership was developed. Partnership 21 formalized these relationships into a partnership model by defining and assigning the various tourism roles and responsibilities. Visitor servicing was also enhanced through the development of a statewide visitor servicing network. This Western Australia Tourism Network integrated visitor servicing, retail sales and access to product knowledge through a virtual call centre, a statewide visitor centre network, a comprehensive statewide database of tourism product and a single entry point for all of Western Australia's tourism operators. Assimilated at the national level, the virtual structure was seen to facilitate efficient and effective collection, distribution and promotion of tourism information and services.

Brand extension

Just as Brand WA reflected a part of 'Brand Australia's big nature – big city', Western Australian regional brands reflected specific regional branding under the overall umbrella of Brand WA. This was based on the premise that, as consumers become more familiar with the brand, they seek more detailed knowledge, and as Brand WA developed a presence and position in its target markets, it would need continually to extend itself to build on its core personality.

Consequently, it needed to become more complex and multilayered to maintain its consumer appeal. In the case of Western Australia, the extension was achieved through a number of sub-brands, an important part of which were regional brands. Ten regional brands were developed in conjunction with the state's ten RTAs, along with over twenty locality brands, ensuring that the personality of the destination and sound marketing intelligence were employed, and were consistent with the umbrella brand. Each had its own positioning, image, target markets, competitive strengths, marketing mix, product development and tourism strategies. As Brand WA evolved, regional and locality brands became more inclusive with community partnerships adding further value. The benefits to regions and localities included the:

- highlighting of the product (e.g. tourism: attractions, facilities, infrastructure; agriculture; export)
- creation of economic opportunity
- creation of local support for local products
- promotion of a clear and consistent brand image and message
- fostering of strong community effort
- breeding of public and private sector partnerships
- creation of a marketing focus on the consumer/target market
- promotion of destinational positioning for destinational marketing purposes by broad stakeholder groups
- demonstration that product differentiation on regional brand marketing techniques works.

Destination ownership

Destination branding extends to combining all things associated with the 'place' (i.e. its products and services from various industries such as agriculture, tourism, sports, arts, investment, technology and education) under one brand. Its aim is to capture the essence of the destination in a unified manner that can be consumed simultaneously at a symbolic and experiential level. Tourism is an industry that impacts on many aspects of the Western Australian business sector, economy and lifestyle. The Brand WA philosophy, its promise and its visual imagery needed to have the support of other government agencies, businesses and communities to be successful in creating a unified identity for Western Australia. For the brand to be successful in the long term, it needed to reflect the entire state's culture or personality, and residents should have ownership of the brand. It was necessary to incorporate all the elements, including individual businesses and organizations which are inextricably linked to the 'total overall product', that make up the state and its personality. A co-operative approach was essential to achieve a positive long-term image of Western Australia.

Poon (1993) originally proposed the diagonal integration concept within the ambit of tourism to include the collaborative branding and marketing of products and services that rely on tourism to survive and fringe tourism industries. Brand WA extended diagonal integration to include all Western Australian brand associations (e.g. tourism and fringe-tourism products, activities and associations such as taxis, leisurewear, education, investment attraction, product place of origin, and regions and localities) under a single brand image (i.e. Western Australia: 'fresh, natural, free and spirited', with consistent but flexible visual branding). The WATC worked closely with all key government agencies to market and manage Brand WA's image and philosophy to its audiences. Brand WA was thus integrated into projects with a broad community focus, including Brand WA vehicle number plates, vehicle registration stickers, driver's licences and welcome signage throughout the state and at regional gateways. A Brand WA merchandise range incorporating clothing and souvenirs was produced and distributed throughout retail stores and on the internet. A particularly successful aspect of this extension was the introduction of the Brand WA livery on taxis, often the first contact for visitors on arrival in the state.

A brand ownership campaign was also initiated, where approved licensees were able to use the visual elements of Brand WA in their own marketing and promotional efforts, thus supporting the Brand identity. Brand WA thus became a platform on which other sub-brands could be superimposed to create uniquely Western Australian identities while still retaining a degree of individuality. The integrity of Brand WA was maintained by a clever juxtaposition of the brand with the organization's core identity. The local industry welcomed the introduction in 1996 of the distinctive Brand WA and fully supported the fresh, natural, free and spirited image it portrayed. More than 300 organizations were approved to use Brand WA as part of their promotional activities, including advertising, promotion, stationery and corporate livery. The synergy, created by industry working with and reinforcing Brand WA's visual elements and philosophies, generated greater impact from overall marketing expenditure.

Commercial television stations also broadcast weekly travel and lifestyle programmes throughout the year reflecting brand attributes and imagery, contributing to heightened destination ownership. These programmes attracted extensive viewing, often ranking in the top ten of weekly viewing statistics. At the core of any successful branding is a unified and consistent approach that adds value to the brand. Consistency in the messages and design, within a flexible framework, avoids proliferation of the brand, and ensures maximum leverage against a brand that has had significant investment based on fundamental brand-building techniques. This value adding resulted in an extremely strong brand and tangible competitive advantages for the state of Western Australia. All of these activities represented creative ways to strengthen fundamental brand-building activities and enhanced the image of Western Australia within the state, as well as nationally and internationally.

Conclusion

This chapter has presented the WATC's methodical approach to positioning Western Australia as a premier nature-based tourism destination in a worldwide market in the late 1990s and early 2000s. It presents a summary of the complex processes that went into the establishment of a brand for Western Australia and the complementary strategies that partnered the brand. Brand WA was seen to be a very broad strategy incorporating trade, consumer and events marketing, visual branding, convention activities, product and infrastructure development, regional marketing, place of origin product marketing, and even the way in which WATC and its stakeholders interacted and communicated. Brand WA was launched in 1996 and proved successful in its core markets; in 2000, the Brand WA strategy won the Australian and state Public Sector Marketing Leadership Awards bestowed by the Australian Marketing Institute.

Partnership with industry and its stakeholders was at the core of the WATC's philosophies. The WATC developed a comprehensive approach to mould a unique image for Western Australia in true partnership with industry, and the success of Brand WA and its associated strategies was outstanding. Over the period 1995/96 to 1999/2000, international visitors to Western Australia increased by 24.47 per cent to 590 000, interstate visitors to Western Australia jumped by 64.48 per cent to 977 000 and Western Australia intrastate visitors increased by 4.96 per cent to 5 541 000 visitors (Bureau of Tourism Research, 2000). Meanwhile, the WATC attracted revenue of Aus$10 703 755 in 1999/2000, representing a massive 80.24 per cent increase from 1994/95. The state government contributed funding of Aus$33 812 000 in 1999/2000, an increase of 47.14 per cent over 1995/96, thereby demonstrating the government's heightened value of the tourism industry. The holistic Brand WA strategy produced strong operational efficiency gains at the WATC and overheads were reduced by 32 per cent from Aus$10 650 000 in 1992/93 to Aus$7 242 000 in 1999/2000.

Although Western Australia has since shifted its brand emphasis, this chapter's review of its activities during 1996–2000 clearly demonstrates the value of collective marketing between government agencies and industry. Brand WA was an innovative and totally integrated approach to destination branding and levered opportunities for the tourism industry and other organizations involved in marketing Western Australia to maximize their marketing activities. Of the many lessons learnt by its developers, perhaps the key ones were that branding requires time, flexibility, co-operation, capital and truth in brand values.

Note

This chapter, originally written by Shane Crockett and Leiza Wood, has been updated for this edition by the book's editors.

References

Aaker, D. A. (1996) *Building Strong Brands*. Sydney: Free Press.

Aaker, J. L. (1995) Conceptualizing and measuring brand personality: a brand personality scale. Working Paper, Stanford University.

303 Advertising (1994) Developing a marketing strategy for Western Australia. Commissioned by the Western Australian Tourism Commission, Eventscorp Division.

Ahmed, Z. U. (1991) The influence of the components of a state's tourist image on product positioning strategy. *Tourism Management* (December): 334–340.

Bureau of Tourism Research (1999) Canberra: BTR.

Bureau of Tourism Research (2000) *National Visitor Survey*. Canberra: BTR.

Donovan Research (1996) *Partnership Western Australia: Developing Brand Western Australia*.

Guardian Observer (2000) *Guardian Travel Awards*. UK.

Jones, C. B. (1998) *The New Tourism and Leisure Environment*. World Tourism Organization. www.econres.com/papers

Kotler, P., Bowen, J. and Makens, J. (1996) *Marketing for Hospitality & Tourism*. New Jersey: Prentice Hall.

Poon, A. (1993) *Tourism, Technology and Competitive Strategies*. Wallingford: CAB International, p. 215.

Pritchard, A. and Morgan, N. (1998) Mood marketing – the new destination branding strategy: a case study of Wales. *Journal of Vacation Marketing* 4: 215–229.

Roy Morgan Research (1999) Holiday tracking survey. Roy Morgan Research.

WATC (1996) *Brand WA Strategy*. Western Australian Tourism Commission.

WATC (2000a) *Annual Report*. Western Australian Tourism Commission.

WATC (2000b) *Partnership 21 2000–2005*. Tourism industry plan, working strategy reviewed annually. Western Australian Tourism Commission.

13

New Zealand and *The Lord of the Rings*: leveraging public and media relations

Rachel Piggott, Nigel Morgan and Annette Pritchard

Introduction

There is a growing body of research on destination branding, yet a key area of activity – public and media relations – remains very much underrepresented in the academic literature. This chapter spotlights the value of targeted and integrated public relations (PR) activities in destination brand building and co-ordination, focusing particularly on those activities aimed at harnessing the power of the international media. It begins by briefly reviewing the role of PR in destination brand co-ordination, noting that PR can prove a highly cost-effective and credible alternative to conventional advertising in today's world of escalating media costs. The chapter then explores how the Tourism New Zealand (TNZ) brand managers are using PR to promote this destination, which faces a major marketing challenge. The current initiatives of TNZ represent the first ever global branding strategy for the destination and the chapter examines how PR is being used to support New Zealand's overall branding strategy by tapping into the power of the international media to showcase its landscapes, peoples, cultures and tourism activities. It concludes that PR, linked to the opportunities presented by special events and movies (such as *The Lord of the Rings*) and the world wide web, can be a cost-effective tool in the drive to create strong destination brand relationships.

Destination branding and the power of public relations

A considerable amount of research has discussed the management and formation of place image and many authors have attempted to conceptualize the components of destination image (Um and Crompton, 1990; Echtner and Brent-Ritchie, 1991; Gartner, 1996; Walmsley and Young, 1998). In addition, many researchers have investigated the image formation process, beginning with Gunn's (1988) work on induced and organic images. In particular, they have examined the three main influences on destination image formation, namely promotional material, secondary experiences (e.g. the opinions of others) and the media (Gartner, 1993, 1996; Ross, 1994; Font, 1996). Of particular interest here is work that has discussed the role of movies in shaping place image (Butler, 1990; Riley *et al.*, 1998; Busby and Klug, 2001). The assumption of much of this destination image-formation literature is that these three key influences combine with personal or individual factors (Ashworth and Voogd, 1990) to produce a destination image (Font, 1996; Baloglu and McClearly, 1999). The relative significance and credibility of the media in shaping such images are of central importance to the role of PR in destination promotional strategies, a point to which we will return below.

Destination marketing occurs through a variety of spheres, most obviously in advertising, through direct marketing, personal selling, on websites and in brochures, but also through PR and place marketers' co-operation with tourist trails, event organizers, travel journalists and cinema commissioning agencies. The challenge for most destination marketers is to get their destination onto the potential consumer's mental shopping list of possible vacation venues. However, most destination marketing organizations (DMOs) have very small budgets with which to create global brands, and yet they are competing for consumer mindshare not just with other destinations, but also with every other global brand. For example, in the case of the DMO discussed in this chapter, TNZ had an annual media budget of NZ$12 million in 2001/02 (TNZ, 2000a). It is thus clearly a niche player in the global marketplace and tight DMO budgets and rising media costs both contribute to a highly competitive promotion environment for such a small country.

In this context, it is clear that niche players have to out-think rather than out-spend the competition, and in this battle traditional marketing techniques cannot effectively address the share of voice problem. The answer lies in creating innovative, attention-grabbing communications on a tight budget and maximizing the media spend. In today's era of relationship marketing, the opportunities presented by PR, particularly 'wired' and lifestyle-orientated PR, offer a cost-efficient and effective alternative to simple mass media 'sloganeering' for such DMOs. This is especially true in a world where tourists are increasingly seeking lifestyle fulfilment and experience as opposed to seeing differentiation in the more tangible elements of the destination product such as accommodation and attractions.

Whereas publicity involves merely 'information from an outside source used by the news media based on its news value' (Cutlip *et al.*, 1994, p. 8), PR is a much more holistic concept involving the proactive development of good relationships with a range of stakeholders and publics and the co-ordinated handling of negative events and media stories. It is undoubtedly true that much of a destination's publicity is unplanned and unconnected with tourism, which is not to say that this might directly impact on a destination's tourism fortunes, both positively and negatively. Events, celebrities and movies associated with places can all enhance (e.g. Catherine Zeta Jones, Swansea/Wales, and *Crocodile Dundee*, Australia) or damage reputations (e.g. severe acute respiratory syndrome (SARS), south-east Asia and Canada). In such cases, tourism organizations have sought to shape, influence or deflect media interest that may help or hinder the promotion and development of their particular destinations (Nielsen, 2001; Frisby, 2002). In other cases, the PR activities of DMOs are planned and integrated into the wider promotional strategy for the destination. Here, place marketers actively promote their destinations as locations for movies (e.g. providing tax incentives for movie-makers to shoot movies in Ireland) or events (e.g. the 2010 golf Ryder Cup in Wales) and produce press kits and host visits for travel writers and journalists (Dore and Crouch, 2003).

The potential PR value of events as a means of raising tourists' awareness of a destination is a common justification for places to host events (Boyle, 1997). In fact, as Brown *et al.* (2002, p. 167) pointed out in the first edition of this book, 'the economic value of an event to the host city or region is often predicted on the media attention that the event obtains'. In many cases, the most significant impact on a destination's brand image is achieved if consumers recognize a 'fit' between the event's image and that of the place (Gwinner and Eaton, 1999). Thus, featuring event images alongside those of the destination's product mix that reinforce aspects of its brand proposition, significantly enhances the overall impact (Washburn *et al.*, 2000). For example, as a result of the operational success of the Sydney Olympic Games and the synergistic PR work of the Australian Tourist Commission (ATC), its managing director claimed that the 2000 Games changed forever the way the world sees Australia, advancing its brand by a decade (Morse, 2001). The key to this advance, however, was the ATC's success in broadening and deepening perceptions of the destination, adding culture, sophistication and a cosmopolitan appeal to the existing youth, sun and beach brand values of Brand Australia (Morgan and Pritchard, 1999). Key to the ATC's four-year, US$6.7 million Olympic strategy was promoting Australia through a media relations programme and the ATC worked hard to target the international media to try to ensure that the images broadcast by the world's media were consistent with Brand Australia's core values of a friendly, vibrant, free-spirited place offering a sophisticated lifestyle. In the five years leading up to the Games, the ATC hosted approximately 5000 media personnel, generating US$2.1 billion in media coverage during 1997–2000, and enhanced the country's reputation (Brown *et al.*, 2002).

Such strategies aimed at influencing the travel media are also exemplified by the Wales Tourist Board's (WTB) PR activities surrounding the American Association of Travel Writers' Annual Convention, which moved outside the USA for the first time when Wales hosted the event in 2000. This PR coup provided a unique opportunity to showcase Wales' tourism products and generated extensive editorial coverage for Wales in the USA, creating an additional platform to synergize with other advertising and PR activities in the USA, such as the initiative in 1999/2000 that capitalized on the Welsh diaspora's emotional connections to the home country in the millennium year (Morgan *et al.*, 2002b). Closer to home, the WTB have also used innovative PR in the domestic market. This has included driving dirty, grimy vans through the cities of London and Birmingham with the line 'Clean air is 2 hours away – Wales/Cymru, two hours and a million miles away' finger-written on their rear windows. WTB also distributed air fresheners to London taxi drivers emblazoned with the line 'Real fresh air is only 2 hours away – Wales/Cymru, two hours and a million miles away' and sponsored workmen on London's orbital motorway (the M25) to wear raingear bearing the same strapline (Pride, 2002). Such PR activities attracted considerable press coverage and synergized with the creative applications developed for each domestic target segment, all linked by a very distinctive creative style and supported by the strapline 'Wales, two hours and a million miles away'. The WTB campaigns achieved significant standout from other destination campaigns and despite very challenging marketing conditions, achieved encouraging results. Wales' share of trips and spend grew and recent monitoring research reveals increases in the awareness and ranking of Wales as a short-break destination (Pride, 2002).

Yet, despite the increasingly central role of integrated PR in destination marketing, PR is construed by academics as less important than the other elements of the promotional mix. It is less likely than advertising to be the focus of published research, it is less often linked to tangible objectives and, as a result, its success is much harder to evaluate. As Dore and Crouch (2003) note in one of the few published studies, research on the PR programmes of DMOs tends to be exploratory and is largely concerned with providing future research platforms. With one or two exceptions (e.g. Fall, 2002; and Fall and Lubbers in this collection), there are few empirical studies of the role or effectiveness of such activities. Dore and Crouch (2003) suggest that despite this lack of academic interest, DMOs attach a very high significance to publicity and PR activities, valuing them as major contributors to their marketing strategies. They argue that DMOs 'have found that carefully designed and managed publicity programmes present an opportunity to gain extensive promotion of the destination at a relatively low cost' (Dore and Crouch, 2003, p. 148). In terms of expenditure, these programmes may rate behind advertising and personal selling, but in terms of promotional importance, they are of primary significance because of their greater cost-effectiveness. Indeed, more PR is being orientated towards the market than ever before in tourism destination marketing, a particularly significant development given DMOs' need to engage the tourist interactively and create long-term customer relationships.

The promotional challenge for New Zealand

A destination that is currently using PR as a key tool in developing its interactive brand relationship, based around its natural environment, is New Zealand (Morgan and Pritchard, in press; Morgan *et al.*, 2002a, 2003), a geographically small country with more sheep than people (New Zealand has a population of just over 4 million). However, despite the small numbers of tourists – New Zealand attracts 1.7 million annual overseas visitors – tourism is extremely important to its economy (TNZ, 2000a). Although agriculture is responsible for 50 per cent of all New Zealand's exports, tourism is its biggest industry and largest employer, earning NZ$4.2 billion in foreign exchange earnings (TNZ, 2000a). Yet the New Zealand tourism industry has a very small share of voice in the global marketplace. Share of voice is driven by a number of factors, including integration across all marketing activities, consistent brand positioning, and the influencing of partners' and other organizations' promotional activities in the marketplace.

New Zealand's competitor set includes Australia (owing to its close proximity), Canada, South Africa and Ireland (as a result of their similar landscape and features) and Vietnam, Cuba and the South Pacific (undiscovered 'new' destinations). Of these, its primary competitors (Canada, South Africa, Ireland and Australia) have at least doubled their promotional spend over the past five years. The main rival, Australia, not only has a major DMO (the ATC), but also has six individual states with their own promotional budgets – some, individually, as much as New Zealand's total budget. In addition, both Hong Kong and Singapore are strong competitors with proactive, targeted DMOs supported by the strong marketing presence of their key stakeholder partners of Cathay Pacific and Singapore Airlines (Piggott, 2001). For New Zealand, therefore, its global branding campaign needs not only to position the country, but also to address the share of voice disadvantage by extending promotional funds and activity. Co-operative promotion and PR are thus key to achieving its ambitious campaign goals of creating a strong, global brand, doubling tourism receipts to NZ$3 billion by 2005 (Warren and Thompson, 2000) and recovering ground lost to Australia (TNZ, 2000b).

Tourism New Zealand's revised positioning is that of 'Being at one' and its essence is that of 'connection', be it either reconnecting with oneself or one's family, or connecting with the landscape of New Zealand. The values behind 'Being at one' are intended to reflect the contemporary consumer who seeks authenticity of experience and integration with local cultures, and who wants to wander off the beaten track. This positioning builds on and refines the previous 'New Pacific freedom' positioning, which conveyed adventure, spirit and freedom, emotive expressions which combined against the backdrop of New Zealand's landscape. The long-term brand essence and positioning should not be confused with the less permanent campaign tagline, '100% Pure New Zealand'. This is the principal campaign line, although a number of derivatives and extensions have also been used, such as '100% Pure romance', '100% Pure spirit' and 'In five days you'll feel 100%'. The 100% logo incorporates an image of the country's two islands (North and South) while the strapline '100% Pure New Zealand' seeks to qualify a number of experiences and scenes as being 'authentically' or '100%' 'Pure New Zealand'. The theme of 100 per cent and purity is echoed in all the visuals and the copy of the material, with the scenery, its wines and foods, its people and its experiences being seen as being authentic: untainted, unadulterated, unaffected and undiluted (Morgan *et al.*, 2002a, 2003).

The role of public relations in the brand relationships

Tourism New Zealand began the global campaign in 1999 by phasing a new corporate identity into its activity internationally and launching a campaign with the simple message '100% Pure New Zealand' (TNZ, 2000a). The brand was launched market by market between July 1999 and February 2000 to coincide with seasonal promotional opportunities and has since been refreshed during 2003 to align with the new 'Being at one' positioning. From the outset advertising centred on above-the-line activity; mainly television and print (magazines) and the executions showcased New Zealand's diverse landscapes, peoples, cultures and adventure (Figures 13.1–13.4). The key markets for media activity are currently the USA, the UK, Australia and Japan. The largest numbers of visitors to New Zealand are generated from these regions and visitors from Japan are among the highest spenders, bringing much needed foreign exchange earnings into the economy.

Figure 13.1   'Spa', New Zealand's 100% campaign (courtesy of Tourism New Zealand)

Figure 13.2 'Mountain biker', New Zealand's 100% campaign (courtesy of Tourism New Zealand)

Figure 13.3 'Skinny dipping', New Zealand's 100% campaign (courtesy of Tourism New Zealand)

Figure 13.4 'Moeraki boulder', New Zealand's 100% campaign (courtesy of Tourism New Zealand)

Successful branding is not realized by advertising alone and when niche destination players have small budgets this is particularly apparent. As we have seen above, for all destinations, publicity and PR, harnessed to interactive media, direct marketing and events capitalization will do more to raise a country's profile than traditional advertising ever can. The prime targets of the New Zealand brand are 'interactive travellers', people young in body or heart who love travel, seek new experiences and enjoy the challenge of new destinations. Tourism New Zealand wants to build a strong, interactive destination brand relationship with these highly influential opinion formers who could exert significant influence and help to make New Zealand a fashionable and famous destination. Such consumers are often very webwise and significantly, the world wide web is integral to the New Zealand brand, complementing other advertising and PR activities.

New Zealand's attempt to build this consumer-based relationship is closely aligned with the hosting of the America's Cup over 2001–2003 and *The Lord of the Rings* (LOTR) movie trilogy, released over 2001–2003. During 2001–2002 the America's Cup generated an estimated NZ$62 million additional expenditure for the New Zealand economy and sustained over 1100 full-time equivalent jobs (Market Economics, 2002). Recognizing the economic and marketing value of the event, TNZ organized a considerable raft of PR activities in all its key global markets before the 2003 defence of the America's Cup. For example, in co-operation with the official America's Cup travel agent, various articles featuring both the event and the destination appeared in publications with high-earning audience profiles in both Germany and Switzerland. The latter is a significant territory as New Zealand remains a fashionable destination among the Swiss youth and language segment (attracted by New Zealand's 'new' qualities as an experience and adventure destination), despite the difficult marketing conditions that currently reflect the economic downturn in Germany (TNZ, 2002). In the UK, the market for New Zealand also remains buoyant and PR activity is particularly focused towards publications that appeal to those highly sought after upscale opinion-formers who are attracted by challenge and lifestyle experiences. Thus, special features and articles on New Zealand appeared in *The Financial Times*, *The Sunday Times* (walking), *Food & Travel* (Auckland's restaurants) and *Tatler* (America's Cup).

While the America's Cup has been a key platform for the destination, the international media coverage of the LOTR has been (and continues to be) huge. Filmed solely in New Zealand, the LOTR trilogy has associated the country with adventure and breathtaking, otherworldly scenery over a three-year period. Tourism New Zealand's International Media Programme team worked hard to bring over media throughout 2001 in the build-up to the release of *The Fellowship of the Ring* (the first instalment in the trilogy) in December of that year. The LOTR coverage has been heavily focused on the USA and the UK and TNZ's priority was to ensure that wherever possible, an element of destinational coverage of New Zealand was included in the newspaper and magazine supplements and features devoted to the films. In the UK major editorial features on the LOTR (run with TNZ images) have appeared in *The Independent*, *The Sunday Times*, *The Telegraph* (and *The Telegraph on Sunday*), *The Mirror*, *The Guardian*, *The Observer* and *The London Evening Standard*. In the USA, New Zealand has achieved a similarly strong print presence with one of the most important features appearing in the upscale *Conde Nast Traveler*. This feature foregrounded the LOTR Middle-earth story and highlighted the links between New Zealand, the films and the stunning locations (TNZ, 2002).

A major coup was TNZ's negotiations with American television channels to incorporate special footage into the US-based Fox television morning shows in major US cities and to use New Zealand tourism footage in three *Making of Middle-earth* documentaries. Shown on channels including *National Geographic* and *Sci Fi*, these focused on the making of the first movie and related key locations in the film to tourism activities in the areas. Further PR opportunities have been offered by the LOTR's nominations at the Academy Awards® (winning four in 2001 and picking up six nominations in 2002 and 11 in 2003). To capitalize on the media interest in this global event, TNZ placed advertisements in *The Los Angeles Times* in March 2002, March 2003 and March 2004 to cement the connection between the movie and New Zealand as a destination. The advertisements promoted New Zealand as the film set by featuring a clapperboard with a scenic shot of New Zealand in the background. To underline further the continuing association with the three films, the 2003 advertisement ran with the words 'Best supporting country in a motion picture. Again', as did the 2004 advertisement (Figures 13.5 and 13.6).

Television, magazine and newspaper travel features comprise only one element in TNZ's consumer-orientated PR strategy. This activity is complemented by a strong interactive web presence. The destination cyberscene is highly competitive and the current challenge is for destinations to convert e-browsers into e-buyers and, above all, to match and where possible exceed other e-tailer

Figure 13.5   Best supporting country in a motion picture (courtesy of Tourism New Zealand)

Figure 13.6 Best supporting country in a motion picture. Again (courtesy of Tourism New Zealand)

experiences (Morgan *et al.*, 2001). Destinations have to convey a sense of place or brand experience (through webcams, weather updates, music clips, oral histories, collection highlights, virtual tours, etc.) rather than merely delivering a site encounter. Although destinations are well placed to deliver interactive web experiences, many sites fail to offer such engaging virtual experiences of place. The award-winning TNZ website (www.newzealand.com) has, however, successfully achieved this, following its extensive redesigns in 2001 and again in 2003.

The 2001 redesign more closely reflected the visual values associated with the 'New Pacific freedom' positioning. Then, in March 2003 the New Zealand government purchased the URL newzealand.com on behalf of Trade New Zealand and TNZ. As a result of the 2003 redesign, the web consumer is now directed through this address to a generic 'splash' about New Zealand which highlights different aspects of the country, from its landscapes to its cuisine and wines. Browsers can then choose to click through to business opportunities or to travel – via www.travel.newzealand.com. The website reflects the 'Being at one' positioning in a creative and operational sense and an intuitive navigation system disseminates the vast amount of site information. The site enables visitors easily to explore pages about specific topics and regions and there are 4500 operators linked to the site, driving www.travel.newzealand.com higher up search engine rankings. The visually attractive website is user friendly and navigable, and above all stimulates interest and provokes reactions, encouraging the average visitor to the website to stay for longer and to visit more pages. Such interactive appeals help to explain why the website was attracting more than 65 000 unique visitors each month by 2002 (Morgan *et al.*, 2002a). Web visitors can also click through to 'souvenirs' and download and send copies of the New Zealand adverts and photographs of natural environments as e-postcards (Figure 13.7). This all adds to New Zealand's conversational appeal, celebrity and anticipation value and, as the website text says, it means: 'You'll have a slice of New Zealand with you always!'

A central attraction in respect to celebrity, of course, is the website's high-profile promotion of the country as 'New Zealand, Home of Middle-earth'. Visitors to the website's homepage can click onto a link which takes them to 'New Zealand, Home of Middle-earth'. The text on this page comments:

> *Here's your opportunity to take a closer look at the country behind* The Lord of the Rings *film trilogy. New Zealand's diverse and sometimes extreme landscapes made it the one place in the world that could bring Tolkien's epic masterpiece to life. Discover the amazing real-life locations behind the films, and learn about the unique experiences of the cast and crew.* (http://www.newzealand.com/homeofmiddleearth)

Figure 13.7   e-postcards can be completed and sent from the website
(www.newzealand.com)

Central to the site is a navigable, interactive map of New Zealand featuring hot buttons directing visitors to interviews, details of memorable locations used in the films and tourism attractions endorsed by the film crew. The map is accompanied by an introduction by one of the films' actors, Karl Urban, who says, 'Of course, we New Zealanders are lucky enough to live in Middle-earth all of the time' and invites visitors to 'understand why the overseas cast members were reluctant to leave'. Having explored the interactive map, browsers can follow a link to:

> *Take your own road trip through the spectacular landscape of Middle-earth with these driving routes. Whether you're interested in visiting the locations where* The Lord of the Rings *was filmed or planning your own New Zealand adventure, you'll find an excursion to fit your needs.* (http://www.newzealand.com/homeofmiddleearth/)

The most regularly followed link from this page, however, allows web browsers to 'Experience Middle-earth' in a 'behind the scenes feature packed with stunning photographs and interviews with the cast and crew who helped to bring Tolkien's *The Lord of the Rings* to life'. This six-part feature opens with an introduction which tells us that this 'enormous epic set in vast fictional worlds … could not have been made anywhere else' (http://www.newzealand.com/homeofmiddleearth).

In a synergistic move to support this PR work of the DMO, one of its major partner organizations, Air New Zealand (ANZ) has positioned itself as the official 'Airline to Middle-earth', further emphasizing the links between New Zealand and the LOTR. To celebrate this connection, ANZ has emblazoned two of its planes with imagery from the movies, aircraft that will literally transport travellers to the spectacular film locations. Internet browsers on ANZ's home page are invited to 'Fly with Air New Zealand to Middle-earth', a journey that can begin by a simple click of the appropriate hot button (http://erequestairnz. co. nz/lotr_auhtm). Film fans and travellers alike can enjoy a bird's eye view of most of Middle-earth's locations when travelling ANZ domestic routes. On the 'Middle-earth Express' (ANZ's most popular tourist flight from Auckland to Queenstown) travellers are told that they can experience twelve top LOTR locations, including Weathertop, Mordor and Ithilien Woodlands. Approaching Queenstown, travellers can also view (amongst other sites) the Pillars of the Argonath, South of Rivendell and Dimrell Dale. In a complementary move, ANZ have also appointed author Ian Brodie as their LOTR ambassador. Brodie is author of *Locations Guidebook to the LOTR* (currently in its third reprint), which gives global positioning system satellite references for fans who want to walk in the footsteps of director Peter Jackson (ANZ, 2002).

Such web-based activity has produced TNZ and ANZ websites that are highly engaging. LOTR has also provided a welcome additional stimulus to the development of the New Zealand brand values, highlighting the new, adventurous, other-worldly qualities integral to the destination. These are complemented and further enhanced by the adventurous and challenging attributes of the America's Cup. Undoubtedly, the role of PR in creating this powerful, attractive and emotionally appealing brand identity cannot be underestimated as New Zealand strives to create strong relationships with potential visitors and the highly influential media, which can do so much to enhance (or damage) a destination's attempts to create interactive brand relationships.

Conclusion

The PR-led branding strategy of New Zealand has been an obvious success, enabling the destination to surpass Australia in its campaign delivery during 2003. It is an excellent example of how niche destinations with a small share of voice need to work with partners on a collaborative and integrative basis outside traditional advertising. Such destinations must be alive to alternatives to advertising and focus on the branding opportunities offered by sports, cultural and political events. PR opportunities are particularly effective in enhancing lifestyle appeals, experiences and fulfilment. As we have seen here, the filming of LOTR in New Zealand has provided worldwide interest and a platform for lifestyle-based PR appeals and promotional campaigns. Arguably, LOTR presented a unique opportunity that was the envy of other destination marketers. While not every destination has such an opportunity, too few effectively capitalize on those opportunities that do present themselves, perhaps because of a lack of flexibility in their strategic planning, a lack of resources or poor direction from senior managers.

In this chapter we have argued that PR remains an ill-defined, undervalued and underresearched aspect of destination marketing and brand building. This marginalization continues despite its potential to provide a highly cost-effective and credible partner to support and enhance advertising strategies: a vital tool in a world where DMO brands compete for consumer mindshare with a plethora of lifestyle brands. As we have seen, effective PR is particularly critical to the branding initiatives of small countries like New Zealand which are seeking to become travel brands with emotional appeal. In a world where a handful of major countries attracts almost three-quarters of international tourist arrivals (Piggott, 2001), the smaller destinations have to squeeze maximum value from their smaller budgets, out-thinking rather than outsmarting the competition. As the experience of New Zealand demonstrates, this may well be a difficult but by no means an impossible task, particularly if the power of industry partners and tools such as PR and the world wide web can be harnessed.

In New Zealand's case, it has used PR and the web to create strong brand relationships, not only interactively engaging visitors pre-trip, but also providing direct marketing opportunities for relationship building, which can be resurrected and sustained post-trip. That the potential of such marketing activities deserves much more attention from both academics and practitioners cannot be denied – as is the case with joint destination marketing partnerships. It is undoubtedly true that in our increasingly competitive and precarious tourism marketplace, the ability to harness and manage PR effectively will continue to increase in significance. This focus on PR will also need to be integrated into destination brand development strategies aimed at building and enhancing interactive relationships with the tourism consumer which are key to producing desirable and emotionally appealing destinations. There is little argument that PR is a valuable tool in communicating with today's leisure consumers, many of whom demand highly involving experiences from their vacations. However, it is most effective when it is integrated with the overall brand strategy and PR 'happenings' and activities are synergized to reinforce the brand values. While there are clearly opportunities for DMOs to communicate with a receptive audience using a variety of media, a more sophisticated approach takes advantage of and actively creates opportunities consciously to integrate mutually compatible elements of the destination brand with events and activities. This requires the proactive selection of suitable partners, the identification of markets that will respond favourably to the mix of brand values and a determination to set clearly focused PR outputs and targets.

References

ANZ (2002) Air New Zealand press release (16 December). http://www.scoop.co.nz/mason/stories

Ashworth, G. J. and Voogd, H. (1990) *Selling the City*. London: Belhaven.

Baloglu, S. and McClearly, K. W. (1999) A model of destination image formation. *Annals of Tourism Research* 26: 868–897.

Butler, R. W. (1990) The influence of the media in shaping international tourist patterns. *Tourism Recreation Research* 15(2): 46–53.

Busby, G. and Klug, J. (2001) Movie-induced tourism: the challenge of measurement and other issues. *Journal of Vacation Marketing* 7: 316–332.

Boyle, M. (1997) Civic boosterism in the politics of local economic development: 'institutional positions' and 'strategic orientations' in the consumption of hallmark events. *Environment and Planning A* 29: 1975–1997.

Brown, G., Chalip, L., Jago, L. and Mules, T. (2002) The Sydney Olympics and brand Australia. In Morgan, N. J., Pritchard, A. and Pride, R. (eds) *Destination Branding: Creating the Unique Destination Proposition*. Oxford: Butterworth-Heinemann, pp. 163–185.

Cutlip, S. M., Center, A. H. and Broom, G. M. (1994) *Effective Public Relations*, 8th edn. Englewood Cliffs, NJ: Prentice Hall.

Dore, L. and Crouch, G. I., (2003) Promoting destinations: an exploratory study of publicity programmes used by national tourism organisations. *Journal of Vacation Marketing* 9: 137–151.

Echtner, C. M. and Brent-Ritchie, J. R. (1991) The meaning and measurement of tourism destination image. *Journal of Tourism Studies* 2(2): 2–12.

Fall, L. T. (2002) Examining the economic value of publicity and promotional activities among state tourism communication programs. *Journal of Promotional Management* 8(2): 35–47.

Font, X. (1996) Managing the tourist destination image, *Journal of Vacation Marketing* 3: 123–131.

Frisby, E. (2002) Communicating in a crisis: the British Tourist Authority's responses to the foot-and-mouth outbreak and 11th September 2001. *Journal of Vacation Marketing* 9: 89–100.

Gartner, W. (1993) Image formation process. *Journal of Travel Research* 28(2): 16–20.

Gartner, W. (1996) *Tourism Development: Principles, Processes and Policies*. New York: Van Nostrand Reinhold.

Gunn, C. (1988) *Tourism Planning*. New York: Taylor and Francis.

Gwinner, K. P. and Eaton, J. (1999) Building brand image through event sponsorship: the role of image transfer, *Journal of Advertising* 28(4): 47–57.

http://erequestairnz.co.nz/lotr_auhtm, accessed 26 June 2003.

Market Economics (2002) *The America's Cup Build-up to the 2003 Defence. Economic Impact Assessment*. Prepared for the New Zealand Ministry of Tourism.

Morgan, N. J. and Pritchard, A. (1999) Building destination brands. The cases of Wales and Australia. *Journal of Brand Management* 7: 102–119.

Morgan, N. J. and Pritchard, A. (in press) (PR)omoting place: the role of PR in building New Zealand's brand relationships. *Journal of Promotion Management*.

Morgan, N. J., Pritchard, A. and Abbot, S. (2001) Consumers, travel and technology: a bright future for the Web or television shopping? *Journal of Vacation Marketing* 7: 110–124.

Morgan, N. J., Pritchard, A. and Piggott, R. (2002a) New Zealand, 100% Pure. The creation of a powerful niche destination brand. *Journal of Brand Management* 9: 335–354.

Morgan, N. J., Pritchard, A. and Pride, R. (2002b) Marketing to the Welsh diaspora: the appeal to hiraeth and homecoming. *Journal of Vacation Marketing* 9: 69–80.

Morgan, N. J., Pritchard, A. and Piggott, R. (2003) Destination branding and the role of the stakeholders: the case of New Zealand. *Journal of Vacation Marketing* 9: 285–299.

Morse, J. (2001) The Sydney 2000 Olympic Games: how the Australian Tourist Commission leveraged the games for tourism. *Journal of Vacation Marketing* 7: 101–109.

Nielsen, C. (2001) *Tourism and the Media*. Melbourne: Hospitality Press.

Piggott, R. (2001) Building a brand for a country. Can commercial marketing practices achieve this in a government-funded environment? Unpublished MBA dissertation, University of Hull.

Pride, R. (2002) Brand Wales: 'natural revival'. In Morgan, N. J., Pritchard, A. and Pride, R. (eds) *Destination Branding: Creating the unique destination proposition*. Oxford: Butterworth-Heinemann, pp. 109–123.

Riley, R., Baker, D. and Van Doren, C. S. (1998) Movie induced tourism. *Annals of Tourism Research* 25: 919–935.

Ross, G. F. (1994) *The Psychology of Tourism*. Melbourne: Hospitality Press.

TNZ (2000a) *Annual Report 1999–2000*. Auckland: Tourism New Zealand.

TNZ (2000b) *Growing New Zealand's Share of the UK Travel Market*. Auckland: Tourism New Zealand.

TNZ (2002) Regionalrap (24 October). http://www.tourisminfo.govt.nz/documents

Um, S. and Crompton, J. L. (1990) Attitude determinants in tourism destination choice. *Annals of Tourism Research* 17: 432–448.

Walmsley, D. J. and Young, M. (1998) Evaluative images and tourism: the use of personal constructs to describe the structure of destination images. *Journal of Travel Research* 36(3): 65–69.

Warren, S. and Thompson, W. (2000) New Zealand: 100% Pure. *Locum Destination Review* 1: 22–26.

Washburn, J. H., Till, B. D. and Priluck, R. (2000) Co-branding: brand equity and trial effects. *Journal of Consumer Marketing* 17: 591–604.

www.newzealand.com (accessed 14 November 2003).

14

Brand Louisiana: capitalizing on music and cuisine

Jan Slater

Introduction

Branding evolved out of the Industrial Revolution as a means for a manufacturer to identify itself as the maker of a certain product. The brand then became the identifier for the consumer, promising consistency and quality. The basic textbook description of a brand defines it as 'a distinguishing name and/or symbol' that provides some identity to the goods or service, while providing some differentiation from the competitors (Aaker, 1991). This branding differentiation helps consumers to make choices in a cluttered environment. Today, brands are not just goods or services. They have permeated every level of society. Politics, governments, charities, sports teams, utilities, media, individuals and even cities, states and countries have endorsed branding as a means of setting themselves apart amidst the clutter of competitors. In today's international marketplace, there's little doubt that 'everything and everyone is capable of becoming a brand' (Clifton and Maughan, 2000).

One industry that has embraced the branding craze is tourism bureaux and destination marketers. Once known for advertising that was considered 'wall-paper' (the same pretty scenery), the tourism industry is using branding as a means of emphasizing the feel of the place, developing a personality of the location. This differentiates the destination from the typical travelogue attraction because the branded destination is an experience, not just a place to go (Anon, 1999b). This branding mentality has been observed in recent campaigns for Australia ('Come and say G'day'), New Zealand's '100% Pure New Zealand', Montana's 'Big sky country' campaign and 'It's a whole other country' for Texas. In fact, it is estimated that state governments in the USA will spend US$554.2 million in 2002–2003 to promote tourism in the fifty states (Travel Industry Association of America, 2003).

Building a brand in today's marketplace is difficult and presents many bar-riers and challenges (Aaker, 1996). The key to successful brand building is iden-tifying what the brand stands for and effectively delivering that message. This brand identity is central to the direction, purpose and meaning for the brand. Aaker (1996, p. 68) posits that the brand identity 'should help establish a rela-tionship between the brand and the customer by generating a value proposition involving functional, emotional or self-expressive benefits'. While this is difficult, it is not impossible. This chapter will describe the brand-building success story of Louisiana, a powerful travel destination brand.

Background: Louisiana's history

Certainly, the tourist's attraction to Louisiana is due in part to the varied and colourful history the state has endured. Its past has created a very eclectic pre-sent state of mind. In particular, its combined Spanish, French, Native American and African–American heritage offers a unique cultural and leisure experience that is expressed in its landscape, its architecture, its food, its music, its land-marks, its waterways and its people. Louisiana was named for Louis XIV, who was the reigning monarch of France in 1682 when the French explorer, Sieur de LaSalle, took possession of the rich, bountiful country at the mouth of the Mississippi River. The area grew and developed as a French colony, building the town of New Orleans in 1718. However, the Louisiana country remained unprofitable for France and the government ceded the territories to Spain. The province was firmly under Spanish control in 1769 when Spanish Governor

Alejandro O'Reilly divided the territory into twelve administrative districts called posts, and twenty-two ecclesiastical parishes. Although the system of posts was later abolished, the parishes remain intact today as the primary county-level units under state government. By 1800 Spain had returned the province to France, concerned about ongoing deficits and the possibility of fighting the Americans to retain control. On 20 April 1803, Napoleon Bonaparte sold the territory of Louisiana to the USA for $15 million. Over 900 000 square miles were included in the Louisiana Purchase. Eventually, thirteen states or parts of states would be carved out of the territory. Only one would retain the name and the influences of its founders and developers: Louisiana.

Admitted to the Union as the eighteenth state in 1812, Louisiana was to suffer great losses during the Civil War. Seceding from the Union in 1861 to join the Confederacy, Louisiana was undisturbed for a year after the war broke out. But by 1862, New Orleans had been captured for its access to the Mississippi River. By May 1865, many of the Louisiana Confederate units had disbanded. The losses were great in terms of money, livestock, land and lives. But the South did rise again, and so did Louisiana. Today, tourists can visit the battlefields of the Civil War, watch the steamboats along the mighty Mississippi, tour the great plantations, pay tribute to Native American ceremonial mounds, skin an alligator, eat crawfish, celebrate Mardi Gras, and enjoy some of the best jazz, blues, bluegrass, zydeco or gospel music in the world. What best summarizes this most unique blend of history and culture has become the unofficial state motto: 'joie de vivre', the joy of living. In addition, that unofficial slogan translates into a successful brand identity that has positioned Louisiana as one of the fastest growing tourism destinations in the USA.

Building the Louisiana brand

Tourism in the USA is big business. According to Dr Suzanne Cook, senior vice president for the Travel Industry Association of America, more than 1 billion people made domestic trips in the USA during 2002 (http://www.tia.org/Travel/tvt.asp). In addition, more than 48.5 million international visitors made trips to the USA. This US$554.2 million investment every year allows state governments to promote various attractions within their borders to lure the adventurers, fun-seekers, sun-worshipers, beachcombers, mountain climbers, snow bunnies, sailors or just the traditional family to spend time and money in the state. No matter the budget size, the challenge still remains for the state to depict the territory as a unique place, creating some point of differentiation that provides the tourist with more than just a destination spot. It provides an experience unlike any other. It is simply an issue of branding the state by creating an identity, an image, a feeling about the place and what it has to offer. The state of Louisiana did just that in developing a branding strategy.

As is typical in the USA, state governments manage the state tourism funds and development. Louisiana is no different. The Department of Culture, Recreation and Tourism (DCRT) is a cabinet agency, which is governed by the lieutenant governor of the state, an elected official. The lieutenant governor appoints the secretary to run the agency. In Louisiana, the Lt Governor is Kathleen Babineaux Blanco, and she appointed Phillip J. Jones as cabinet secretary to the DCRT. It was their combined mission to 'create a greater awareness of Louisiana's culture, history, and natural resources' to visitors as well as locals that provided the foundation for building the Louisiana brand (http://www.crt.state.la.us/crt/tourism.htm). They were helped by a New Orleans advertising agency, Peter A. Mayer Advertising. The relationship between the agency and the government tourism office would become as strong as the brand itself.

Finding a brand specialist

The DCRT has always used an advertising agency. Because tourism is a government agency, Louisiana law requires the account be reviewed every three years. The Mayer agency had pitched for the account twice, both times unsuccessfully. The agency was invited to compete for the business again in 1993, when a new lieutenant governor put the account up for review a year early. This time Peter A. Mayer Advertising would come to the bargaining table with a powerful proposition. According to Mayer president, Mark Mayer, the agency created a consortium with three other communications firms in the state. A separate entity, named Peter A. Mayer Advertising and Partners, was born out of the co-operative that includes Williams Creative Group, a public relations firm in Shreveport; G.Mc & Co., a multicultural agency in New Orleans; and the Graham Group, an advertising agency based in Lafayette.

The development of the co-operative was not because Mayer was not large enough to handle the business. The Mayer agency is the largest in the state, billing US$60 million annually. Mark Mayer asserts that 'we felt the geographic diversity would help in our understanding' of how to sell the state to tourists. The partnership provided a 'better sense of the different elements of the state in terms of regional, political and cultural differences', Mayer continues. In fact, for those very reasons the partnership turned out to be a tremendous advantage, and the co-operative won the Louisiana tourism business in 1993 and remains the agency of record today.

Creating the brand identity

During the initial presentation to the state, Mayer and Partners proposed an entirely new approach to marketing Louisiana. Previously, the focus of tourism had been solely on food. There is no doubt Louisiana is known for food. It has a long history of a variety of rare cuisines that range from jambalaya, gumbo, beignets and meat pies to boiled crawfish and shrimp etouffee. Even the telephone number to gain tourist information had a food flavour: 1-800-99-GUMBO. But just like the famous gumbo, Louisiana had a lot of everything in it. Mayer and Partners thought the food focus too limiting for branding the state.

Good branding stems from good research, so the partners began by analysing existing research. While much research had been conducted regarding state tourism, it had not been used extensively. Mark Mayer asked to read the research in hopes of 'uncovering some unique element that motivated the visitor to choose Louisiana'. He was right; the answers were in the data. The research showed that Louisiana offered several unique destination elements to travellers in addition to the food attraction. A syndicated research study that uses a large consumer panel and scores individual states against national norms indicated that tourists were drawn to Louisiana because its attractions were distinctive. In addition to the food, visitors identified the state's scenery, architecture, history, culture and music among its greatest strengths. With this information, the partners did what any smart branding company would do: used this competitive differentiation to develop a strong brand position and identity.

The next step was to develop a creative strategy that incorporated the positioning with the various attractions in creative executions for a specific target group. Initially, the target audience was identified as frequent domestic out-of-state travellers, between the ages of 25 and 54 with incomes of US$30 000 plus. Six different campaigns were created and tested in focus groups against the positioning statement. Then the field was narrowed to three campaigns that were considered to be the most motivational. Those rough executions were tested against a large panel of potential visitors to determine the best campaign. The first advertisement to run was titled 'The words', with what would become the signature of Louisiana: the red lipstick logo and the 1-800-99-GUMBO response mechanism. According to Mark Mayer, 'we've run various versions of that campaign, but it hasn't really changed one bit. The focus is still food, culture, music, scenery, architecture, and history.' In fact, little has changed from the initial campaign developed in 1993, except that a slogan was added to the campaign in 1997. Following the appointment of Phillip J. Jones as secretary of the DCRT in 1996, more research was conducted to test the advertising and the images generated by the campaign. The research reinforced that Louisiana was unique, different from anything else. Mayer states, 'We had a monopoly. What made Louisiana different you couldn't get anywhere else'.

Jones had served as Director of Legislative and Intergovernmental Affairs for the Travel and Tourism Administration within the US Department of Commerce. In addition, he had been a spokesperson for the first ever White House Conference on Travel and Tourism, which developed a national tourism strategy under the Clinton Administration. Being a Louisiana native, it was a homecoming of sorts when Jones was appointed to oversee the state tourism activities. He felt that a slogan would be beneficial to the tourism campaign to leverage Louisiana even further. The research showed Louisiana was different and basically provided 'the road map' for a slogan, as Jones recalls. Out of the research conducted in 1996, the slogan 'Louisiana. Come as You Are. *Leave Different®*' was developed and used in all materials as the 1997 tourism campaign was launched (Peter A. Mayer Advertising and Partners, 1997).

As with any strong brand, every point of consumer contact must reinforce the brand image. While the brand strategy remains the same, the flexibility of the positioning allows the agency to adopt various themes: food, music, culture, history, and so on. Within the current campaign, there was a special emphasis on music to take advantage of Ken Burns' documentary on *Jazz*, and the Satchmo

Figure 14.1 The advertisements for both domestic and international markets are similar in style and tone, reinforcing the brand

231

Figure 14.2 The consumer television advertisements for Louisiana use similar visuals as in the print advertisements that highlight the state. The spots are tagged with the logo and the 1-800 telephone number

Summer Fest, a celebration of Louis Armstrong's 100th birthday. However, the brand image remains dominant in all the tourism communication tools. The slogan, the lipstick logo and the overall design features provide strong continuity of the image in every advertisement or promotional piece. Domestic and international advertising conveys similar design qualities (Figure 14.1). The official tour guide incorporates the same photography and use of the logo and slogan throughout the 300-plus-page book. The television commercials showcase the photography as well, and highlight a picture of the tour guide, the logo and the telephone number (Figure 14.2). The website and newspaper advertisements splash the signature Louisiana logo across the pages, interspersed with distinctive Louisiana photography. Trade publications targeted to travel agents, visitors bureaux and tour operators use similar graphics and design. Peter A. Mayer

Advertising and Partners have created a strong visual and strategically positioned brand for the state of Louisiana. Furthermore, they have been able to deliver the brand message to the right people at the right time.

The power behind the brand

Strong creative concepts, a memorable slogan and beautiful advertisements that speak to the target group are only one-third of the brand battle. The creative element has to be supported by efficient and effective media exposure, and the budget has to be strong enough to support the advertising exposure as well as other tactical communication efforts such as publicity and promotion. The power behind the Louisiana brand has been a substantial advertising budget, well-targeted media placements and an effective integrated campaign that allows the image advertising to be the cornerstone, while other methods of communicating the brand's uniqueness stretch from that base.

Budget

In most US states, tourism is funded from a portion of the state sales tax on goods and services collected by the state government. Louisiana is no different. Nevertheless, while the money may be earmarked for tourism, the secretary of DCRT must still submit and defend its budgetary requests to the governor each year. In 1996, the year Jones took his cabinet position, the Louisiana tourism budget was US$13 million. The budget for 2002 was US$17 million. The budget has not grown as planned owing to the industry decline following the events of 11 September 2001. Nevertheless, this is an increase of 30 per cent in just six years. The state has been ranked among the top ten state travel budgets in recent years (Anon, 1999a). Jones states the fact of the matter, 'The more money we spend, the more visitors we get'. Furthermore, Jones spends his budget wisely. Administration is kept low, at 5 per cent of the budget. Ten per cent goes to fulfilment, sending out consumer information based on enquiries. Another 10 per cent is spent on staffing and maintaining ten welcome centres throughout the state, and the remaining 75 per cent of the budget is spent on marketing and advertising efforts. With the consistent increases in the budget and the effective management of their resources, DCRT and its agency have managed to provide the power to expose a strong creative strategy and execution.

Media

Delivering the brand message is more challenging today than ever before. While the choices for media delivery have increased, the audiences for many media vehicles have become more fragmented. Intercepting the consumer in the right place at the right time means that planning the media delivery requires understanding a well-defined target and using some creativity in reaching them. The current primary target audience for the Louisiana brand is families, adults aged 25 and 54, with children still at home and household incomes of US$40 000 plus per year (Louisiana DCRT, 2000a). In addition, secondary targets comprise the following: seniors, adults aged 55 plus, no children at home with a household income of US$40 000 plus per year; and African–Americans and Hispanic–Americans, aged 25 and 54 with household income of US$30 000 plus. According to Mayer, these audiences are reached through a combination of print, television and some radio advertising. Print is the primary media choice, which receives approximately 60 per cent of the advertising dollars, with 40 per cent being allocated to spot television and radio in various regions.

Strong branding requires strong research throughout. The media plan for Louisiana tourism uses brand development indexing (BDI) to rank and index all US markets to 'determine their propensity to generate visitors to Louisiana' (Louisiana DCRT, 2001a, p. 17). The top twenty major markets are then analysed and the key markets are identified for spot television and radio flights for the yearly campaign. The current BDI rankings are provided in Table 14.1. 'An index of 100 indicates that consumers living in a particular market are likely to visit

Table 14.1   The thirteen markets for Louisiana's media campaign

Market	BDI
Beaumont/Pt. Arthur, Texas	1328
Biloxi/Gulfport, Mississippi	1254
Jackson, Mississippi	1146
Tyler-Longview, Texas	1015
Laurel/Hattiesburg, Mississippi	962
Houston, Texas	781
Mobile, Alabama/Pensacola, Florida	562
Dallas, Texas	434
Greenwood/Greenville, Mississippi	417
Little Rock, Arkansas	354
Montgomery/Selma, Alabama	277
Waco/Temple, Texas	245
Corpus Christi, Texas	228
Greenville/Spartanburg, Mississippi	221
Austin, Texas	194
Memphis, Tennessee	190
Oklahoma City, Oklahoma	149
San Antonio, Texas	136
Birmingham, Alabama	135
Huntsville/Florence, Alabama	126

Louisiana at the same rate as the national average. This means that an index of 200 would indicate that the market is twice as productive in generating visitors to Louisiana as the national average' (Louisiana DCRT, 2001, p. 17).

For example, during the 2000/01 campaign, thirteen markets were chosen for spot television and radio flights. These included Albuquerque, New Mexico; Atlanta, Georgia; Austin, Texas; Dallas, Texas; Houston, Texas; Jackson, Mississippi; Jacksonville, Florida; Little Rock, Arkansas; Memphis, Tennessee; Mobile, Alabama; Pensacola, Florida; Springfield, Illinois; Tucson, Arizona and Tyler, Texas (Figure 14.3). In addition to television and radio, consumer magazines (both regional and national), trade publications, newspapers and travel directories are used as part of the media mix. Some of the publications include: *AAA Tourbook, Better Homes & Gardens, Black Enterprise, Bon Appetit, Family Circle, Gourmet, Harpers, Modern Maturity, National Geographic Traveler, New Yorker, Parade, Texas Monthly, USA Today* and *Walking*. In total, more than 50 publications have been used in exposing the campaign (Louisiana DCRT, 2001). All advertisements in these publications include the 1-800-99-GUMBO number for ordering the *Louisiana Tour Guide*. Travel directories run with a bound-in business reply card and a reader service listing. Each advertisement is coded so that enquiries can be tracked accordingly.

In addition to traditional media, the website LouisianaTravel.com provides additional image support as well as serving as an efficient and effective means of generating enquiries. The website hosts special features on current events,

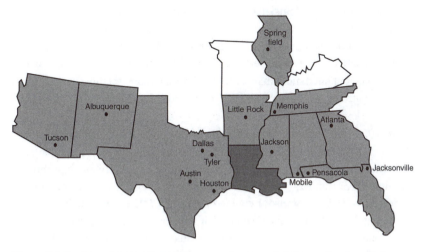

Figure 14.3   The 2000/01 Louisiana campaign targeted the regional markets determined to have the best potential

235

special sections for travel agents, an opportunity to view all the various regions of the state, and a place to make online reservations at hotels and restaurants throughout the state. Furthermore, international visitors to the site can download printable versions of the international brochures in country-specific languages. According to Phillip Jones, 'we embraced the web early and have seen some huge results'. Huge indeed. Seventy per cent of all enquiries come from the website, which totals more than 1.7 million enquiries. According to the research, 37 per cent of those enquiries were converted into actual visitors to the state (Louisiana DCRT, 2001).

Promotions and public relations

To capitalize on the advertising investment in the Louisiana brand, the promotions and public relations activities are planned in conjunction with the advertising campaign exposure. The promotions and public relations work in tandem as the promotions attract the media and public relations efforts leverage the coverage. For example, Louisiana is a promotional partner with the Montreal International Jazz Festival in Quebec. During the ten-day festival, Louisiana sponsors a daily Mardi Gras parade, the 'Gumbo Louisiane' stage, which hosts Louisiana musicians, and several food kiosks for sampling Louisiana fare. The promotion is a natural tie-in with the state's jazz heritage and the state attracts many visitors from Quebec. But the awareness and press coverage that it generates provide a solid return on the investment in the promotion. In 1999, the state received an US$8 million return on an investment of US$250 000. This included more than 200 newspaper articles, 200 minutes of television reports and radio coverage (Louisiana DCRT, 1999a). The 2000 promotion garnered US$3.4 million in television and radio exposure and US$2 million in newspaper coverage of Louisiana's participation in this international event (Louisiana DCRT, 2000b). Francofete, which celebrated the 300 years of French influence in Louisiana, generated more than US$14 million in public relations coverage and helped to attract 20.7 million tourists to the state (Louisiana DCRT, 1999b).

In 2003, the state celebrated the bicentennial of the Louisiana Purchase. This year-long event was the focus of the entire Louisiana Tourism campaign for the year, with 600 events scheduled, US$1 million in advertising exposure and multiple opportunities for public relations coverage. The celebration was expected to increase tourism by 19 per cent over 2002 figures, with an expectation that 25 million tourists would visit the state for the Louisiana Purchase bicentennial. Each parish (county) participated in the celebration, allowing for statewide involvement and coverage of events such as international art exhibits, historic exhibits, historical re-enactments, lectures, musical productions and festivals. In addition, to kick off the campaign the bicentennial bus launched the year-long campaign on 20 December 2002 (the American flag was raised over New Orleans on 20 December 1803). The bicentennial bus toured nine cities and seven states. Mayer and Partners created the campaign supported by thirty-second television spots airing on various cable networks, and print advertisements in travel and regional magazines. The reach for the campaign extended beyond the traditional target of people within a 300-mile driving distance of the state. The campaign reached the states that were influenced by the Louisiana Purchase, including Texas, Arkansas, Oklahoma, Iowa, Missouri and Tennessee (Stingley, 2003). The theme and style of the bicentennial campaign were similar to the foundational 'Come as you are' campaign, but naturally focused more on the historical aspects of the state. Dee Smith, vice president and creative director for Peter A. Mayer Advertising, said the creative team attempted to show that history was not boring. According to Smith, 'we wanted people to see when we celebrate history, we celebrate it the way we celebrate everything – with a party' (Charski, 2003).

In addition to special promotions as described above, the state has formed promotional alliances with various entities in order to showcase Louisiana. Filmmaker Ken Burns debuted his *Jazz* documentary in 2001 and with Louisiana prominently featured as the birthplace of jazz, the state arranged for cards to request that Louisiana tourism information be included in each videotape, DVD and CD sold. Tabasco®, a local manufacturer of hot sauce, agreed to promote the state with a special tourism offer on its packaging and the 1-800-99-GUMBO telephone number. Record label Putumayo agreed to focus on Louisiana music and ran special promotions in selected Barnes & Noble bookstores showcasing events that included zydeco musicians and Cajun chefs. A special arrangement with American Express allows the tourism department to send more than 200 000 mailers to cardholders who visited a competitive travel state. Every tactic (whether promotion, advertising or public relations) conveys the same brand message: what Louisiana has, you cannot get anywhere else.

Evaluation

The final step in a strong brand strategy is to determine whether the campaign has been successful in meeting its objectives. This is necessary in order to improve the campaign or to provide guidance for change. Those behind the efforts in developing and maintaining the Louisiana brand understand that research is important at the front end and the back end of the campaign. Therefore, extensive research is conducted to evaluate the effectiveness of the advertising and promotional campaigns. Conversion studies are used annually and conducted by the University of New Orleans to measure the percentages of enquiries converted to visitors. In addition, research is done by the university to determine the cost of attracting a visitor and the return on the advertising investment. The Marketing Workshop, Inc., a research firm in Atlanta, Georgia, works with the Office of Tourism to measure awareness generated from the advertising. The survey measures advertisement recall, image awareness and intentions to travel to Louisiana and other selected states (Louisiana DCRT, 2001, p. 14). In addition to the primary research just discussed, the state also purchases an annual syndicated study from the US Travel Data Center that measures the economic impact of travel on Louisiana. The study predominantly measures how much a traveller spends in the state, and the economic effect that tourism has on employment and tax receipts by counties. It also provides a means to track the state's tourism market share.

Conclusion

When Lt Governor Blanco unveiled the 'Louisiana: Come as you are. *Leave Different*' campaign on 15 January 1997, she was quoted as saying, 'We are hopeful this campaign... will help us continue our growth in the tourism industry' (Louisiana DCRT, 1997). At that time, the 23 million visitors to the state created a US$6.6 billion economic impact on the state's economy. By 1999, 25 million tourists were visiting the state and spending on average US$120 per day per person. Tourism had grown to US$8.2 billion, the second largest industry in the state, with 118 000 jobs directly attributed to tourism. The economic impact of tourism has grown by 40 per cent in just seven years, showing no signs of slowing down. By 2000, the figure had grown to US$8.7 billion and it was expected to top US$9 billion in 2003 with the Louisiana Purchase celebration (Louisiana DCRT, 2001; Anon, 2003). Furthermore, the number of visitor enquiries (any request for information on Louisiana as a travel destination) surpassed 2.5 million, showing an increase of 150 per cent since 1996, and a 344 per cent increase since 1993. However, the cost of generating those enquiries had been reduced by more than 50 per cent in the same period. The campaign is not only successful, it is efficient as well.

The Travel Industry Association of America claims that Louisiana's tourism growth rate for the past five years has climbed 17.6 per cent compared with national increase of less than 7.5 per cent and a regional increase of only 2.9 per cent (Salomon, 2000; Louisiana DCRT, 2000a). Furthermore, a study released by Plog Research on visitor satisfaction revealed that the state delivers on its brand promise. Louisiana was one of two states in the southern region of the

Table 14.2   The top twelve US states for traveller satisfaction

1.	Hawaii	7.	Maine
2.	Florida	8.	Arizona
3.	California	9.	New York
4.	Nevada	10.	Washington
5.	Alaska	11.	Montana
6.	Colorado	12.	Louisiana

USA named in the top twelve national destinations for traveller satisfaction. The previous study had ranked Louisiana twenty-first. Other states making the list are included with rankings (Louisiana DCRT, 2001) in Table 14.2.

As any good brand manager knows, building a brand is only part of the battle. Maintaining the brand is just as formidable. The lieutenant governor, the secretary of DCRT, and Peter Mayer Advertising and Partners are just as cognizant of the task that lies ahead of them. While enjoying successes in developing the Louisiana brand, no one is resting on their laurels. Growth is still the major tourism objective and there is the understanding that a long-term strategy is required to keep that goal in mind as well as to keep Louisiana in the minds of travellers.

In planning for future growth, the lieutenant governor assembled specialists from the US travel industry to discuss the changes and challenges that the state may face in the coming years. The Louisiana Tourism Collegium 2010 was held in Baton Rouge in November 2000. In addressing concerns regarding sustaining Louisiana's travel growth, the forum drafted a long-term action plan. The plan outlines six key areas in which recommendations were made. The areas include: technology, infrastructure, marketing, education, training and quality of life. Lieutenant Governor Blanco was quoted as saying, 'To accomplish our goals, we need the full participation of every community in Louisiana. As we enhance our technology and train our hospitality professionals, we also need to strengthen the quality of life across the state through an increased sense of pride in our culture, our heritage and the unique experience Louisiana offers …' (Richard, 2000). The brand position is evidenced even in the lieutenant governor's remarks: what Louisiana offers is not available anywhere else.

The stewards of the Louisiana brand have invested heavily in the equity of the brand. According to branding expert David Aaker (1996), the Louisiana brand involves all the factors identified with a strong brand. They are as follows:

- A strong brand identity with a competitive advantage has been developed. The brand identity drives the brand association that Louisiana is a unique, historical, cultural, musical, culinary experience.
- The brand has achieved awareness via extensive and strategic exposure to its strong, consistent message.
- The brand has perceived quality in the fact that visitors believe what they read, see and hear about the state, and those expectations are fulfilled once the visit has been made. The brand delivers on its promise in providing something that is unavailable elsewhere.
- There is brand loyalty in that there are repeat visitors and the state does an excellent job in providing visitors with a reason to return, e.g. the Louisiana Purchase celebration and the Satchmo Summer Fest.

All of these brand assets add value to the brand, in turn providing brand equity. Strong brand equity generates growth and profits. In the case of Louisiana, the brand has been successful in generating both more visitors to the state and a strong economic return on the investment. As stated in the early paragraphs of this chapter, 'everything and everyone is capable of becoming a brand'. This study of the Louisiana brand is a textbook case as to the importance of brand development and maintenance. It further underscores that branding is not just about identity; it is about differentiation from the competitors. By nature, Louisiana has that differentiation. It took a branding campaign to make the world aware of it.

Acknowledgements

The author would like to thank Mr Mark Mayer, President of Peter A. Mayer Advertising, and Mr Phillip J. Jones, secretary of the Louisiana Department of Culture, Recreation & Tourism, for their assistance with this chapter. Both were interviewed for this piece. As of November 2003, Mr Jones is no longer with the Louisiana DCRT, but is the president and CEO of the Dallas, Texas Convention and Visitors Bureau. On 15 November 2003, Kathleen Babineauex Blanco was elected Governor of the State of Louisiana.

References

Aaker, D. A. (1991) *Managing Brand Equity*. Free Press.
Aaker, D. A. (1996) *Building Strong Brands*. Free Press.

Anon. (1999a) Illinois tops state tourist spending. *Hotel and Motel Management* (17 August): 14.

Anon. (1999b) Taking the less traveled road. *Brandweek* (4 October).

Anon. (2003) Louisiana tourism almost 19 percent up over last year. *Associated Press Wire Service* (17 October).

Charski, M. (2003) Mayer enlivens Louisiana history. *Adweek* (20 January).

Clifton, R. and Maughan, E. (2000) *The Future of Brands*. New York University Press.

Louisiana DCRT (1997) Blanco unveils new advertising campaign. Press release (14 January).

Louisiana DCRT (1999a) Tourism benefits from promotional partnership. Press release (27 August).

Louisiana DCRT (1999b) Louisiana Office of Tourism recognized for public relations efforts. Press release (19 October).

Louisiana DCRT (2000a) State's visitors spent over US$8 billion in 1999. Press release (2 June).

Louisiana DCRT (2000b) Louisiana entertains record crowds at Montreal Jazz Festival. Press release (22 August).

Louisiana DCRT (2001) *Louisiana Marketing Report 2000–2001*. Louisiana Department of Culture, Recreation and Tourism.

Louisiana website. http://www.crt.state.la.us/crt/tourism.htm

Peter, A. Mayer Advertising and Partners (1997) Lt. Governor Blanco introduces new tourism advertising campaign at 1997 Travel and Tourism Summit. Press Release (15 January).

Richard, J. (2000) Ten-year action plan formed at tourism forum. Louisiana Department of Culture, Recreation and Tourism. Press Release (29 November).

Salomon, A. (2000) The marketing 100, *Advertising Age* (26 June): s 30.

Stingley, A. (2003) Bus trip takes Louisiana Purchase Bicentennial message on tour. *The Times* (10 January): 1B.

Travel Industry Association of America. website http://www.tia.org/Travel/tvt.asp

Travel Industry Association of America (2003) State tourism office budgets down 8% for 2002–2003. Press release (2 June).

15

Brand Singapore: the hub of 'New Asia'

Can Seng Ooi

Introduction

Singapore is a tropical island city-state in South-East Asia. It has no natural resources, and a physical size of only about 680 square kilometres. Its population is made up of three official ethnic groups: Chinese, Malay and Indian. Singapore is also the most economically developed country in South-East Asia. As a former British colony, English is one of its four official languages, and is frequently used as the nation's *lingua franca*. Since its independence in 1965, Singapore has been offering its oriental and multicultural society for tourist consumption. With a population of 4 million, this tropical city has managed to attract more than 7 million visitors in 2002. Tourism is one of the island state's largest foreign exchange earners. The Singapore Tourism Board (STB) estimates that the direct contribution to the Singapore economy is 5 per cent, with 130 000 people employed in the industry (STB, 2002a, p. 17).

However, the growth in the Singapore tourism industry is uneven and faces frequent threats. Many of such threats stem from the fierce competition in South-East Asia. Bangkok, Kuala Lumpur, Jakarta and Manila are all lively neighbouring cities that are also vying for tourists. In the mid-1990s, with increased competition from the region, Singapore saw its growth in number of visitors slowing down and the average length of stay and per capita visitor spending figures fall. The 11 September 2001 attacks in the USA, the 12 October 2002 Bali bombing, the war on Iraq and the outbreak of severe acute respiratory syndrome (SARS) in early 2003 also played a part in bringing the tourism industry to its knees. However, seeing through these crises is a general tourism strategy, which is encapsulated in the brand 'New Asia – Singapore'. The brand provides a vision for the Singapore tourism industry that extends beyond the city-state.

'New Asia – Singapore' was launched in 1996. It is part of a master plan to meet competition, restructure local tourism businesses and create new products for the Singapore tourism industry. In the blueprint, the STB does not limit its tourism promotion activities to the island city-state; it sees Singapore as the tourism hub of the Far East and Australasia, a region running from China to New Zealand. The STB also visualizes Singapore as the tourism capital of South-East Asia. As the capital, tourists should visit or pass through Singapore when they are in the region. The 'New Asia – Singapore' brand embraces this regional vision and strategy. The brand also provides a focused marketing direction for the country as a stand-alone destination. It wants the world to perceive Singapore in a particular way, experience Singapore as New Asia, and make Singapore New Asian. Many parties and agencies are involved in realizing the 'New Asia – Singapore' brand, and this brand identity is constantly relaunched through supplementary campaigns to create constant global awareness of Singapore as a tourism destination.

This chapter will examine the branding of Singapore in a dynamic and holistic manner. The branding process is an evolving one, as the strategies change under new circumstances. A discussion on the Singapore brand story will be presented in the following section. However, this branding process must be understood within the broader tourism strategy of Singapore; as mentioned already, Singapore wants to be the tourism capital of South-East Asia, and it wants to offer convenient access to destinations in Asia and Australasia. The third section will discuss the regional plans in the context of branding

Singapore. The fourth section deals with a number of challenges that the STB faces in the branding of Singapore. The concluding section will summarize the earlier discussions.

New Asia, the soul of Singapore

In 1995, four National Tourism Plan Committees (NTPC) were formed in Singapore. They released their *Tourism 21: Vision of a Tourism Capital* report in 1996. That report is Singapore's tourism master plan. In the plan, the national tourism authority is given more responsibilities, the tourism business is redefined and Singapore as a tourist destination is repositioned. Subsequently, the tourism authority, Singapore Tourist Promotion Board (STPB) was renamed Singapore Tourism Board (STB) in November 1997.

The new destination brand identity, 'New Asia – Singapore', was launched in January 1996. The STPB proclaimed that the positioning 'better captures the essence of today's Singapore' (STPB, 1996). The former eleven-year-old 'Surprising Singapore' position was stated to be no longer adequate in communicating 'the breadth of the mature Singapore tourism product, or the vision of Singapore tourism' (STPB, 1996). 'New Asia – Singapore' was also selected after it was tested through a survey of 1300 departing tourists from Singapore. Respondents were asked what impressions of Singapore they found endearing, and their preference for alternative brands. The respondents took to 'New Asia – Singapore' (STPB, 1996). Through that process, 'New Asia – Singapore' provides a clear vision on how to repackage and reinvent the destination. It aims to generate new interests, new products and new possibilities for the Singapore tourism industry.

'New Asia – Singapore' is regularly promoted through special campaigns. For instance, when it was first launched, 'New Asia – Singapore' was promoted with the tagline 'So easy to enjoy. So hard to forget'. At the turn of the millennium, the promotion campaign was 'Millennia mania', as the city-state celebrated and welcomed the new era. After the 11 September 2001 attacks in the USA, which led to the slowdown in the global tourism market, STB initiated the 'Live it up!' campaign, and immediately after the World Health Organization removed Singapore from its SARS blacklist at the end of May 2003, STB launched 'Singapore roars!' Such campaigns are tactical, during which specific markets are targeted, special events are organized and certain attractions are highlighted. In these campaigns, colourful images of 'New Asia – Singapore' are promoted aggressively throughout the world. Advertisements are found in international newsmagazines, on global television networks and on the internet.

Singapore has changed its tourism positioning only three times since 1964. In the 1960s and 1970s, Singapore was 'Instant Asia', where one could find an array of Asian cultures, peoples, festivals and cuisine conveniently exhibited in a single destination (Chang, 1997, pp. 548–553). In the 1980s, 'Surprising Singapore' positioned Singapore by placing contrasting images of modernity and Asian exoticism together. The coexistence of East and West, old and new was highlighted (Chang, 1997, pp. 553–555; Leong, 1997). Since the 1990s, Singapore has promoted itself as 'New Asia – Singapore'. There is a subtle shift in focus from 'Surprising Singapore' to 'New Asia – Singapore'. 'Surprising Singapore' promised pockets of unexpected diverse and distinct ethnic cultures in a modern city, 'New Asia – Singapore' offers ethnic cultures fused into modern development. Metaphorically, 'Surprising Singapore' describes a smorgasbord of various ethnic cultures in a modern environment, whereas 'New Asia – Singapore' presents Singapore as a melting pot of Eastern and Western cultures.

'New Asia – Singapore' is a response to the overwhelming presence of modernity and development in the city-state (Figure 15.1). The rapid modernization and economic development of Singapore have led to tourists lamenting that Singapore is too modern. The repositioning from 'Surprising Singapore' to 'New Asia – Singapore' is not one of introducing modern development into the Singapore cultural mix; instead, it is to maintain a sense of oriental exoticism in its brand imagery. Many Asian aspects of Singapore society are increasingly difficult to observe and experience by tourists. 'New Asia – Singapore' accentuates oriental aspects of the city to tourists. For example, in an explanatory brief, the STPB Destination Marketing Division (11 September 1997a) stated that 'New Asia' can be found in Singaporean lifestyle, food, music and various attractions. It explains that although Singaporeans live in a modern environment, their lifestyles reflect some traditional ways of life. Practices such as hanging clothes to dry on bamboo poles in high-rise buildings, dishes such as *roti prata* filled with cheese (an Indian pancake normally filled with egg or just plain, eaten with spicy curry), cultural institutions such as the Asian Civilizations Museum and the Esplanade – Theatres on the Bay (offering traditional and modern Asian art and cultures with ultramodern technologies), and places such as Suntec City, with its modern buildings organized according to the ancient Chinese belief of geomancy, are examples of New Asia. 'New Asia – Singapore' aims to remind people of the Asian soul behind the modern façade.

By melting modernity and exotic Asia together, STB paints an indigenous Singapore. It asserts that Singapore has progressed and developed in an Asian

Figure 15.1 Where is Asia in Singapore? The Merlion, Singapore's tourism icon, in the midst of the city's modern environment

manner, and its oriental traditions have also been changed and modernized. These metamorphosed aspects of culture are considered truly Singaporean. The brand formulation also alludes to the point that Asia is heading in the same direction, although Singapore is ahead in South-East Asia. Subsequently, 'New Asia – Singapore' hopes to offer products that are both complementary and different from competitors in the region. As will be discussed in the next section, Singapore does not want to draw tourists away from its regional competitors; instead, the STB wants the brand to complement other regional destination images, and implicitly communicate South-East Asia as a single destination, so that more tourists will visit various destinations in the region and at the same time use Singapore as the base and hub for their journeys.

Within Singapore, the STB has also developed a number of 'New Asia – Singapore' tourism products since 1996. For instance, STB launched the Tourism Development Assistance Scheme (TDAS) in 1998. The scheme allocated US$50 million to be used over ten years. More money will be offered if necessary (*The Straits Times*, 1998b). Among other things, proposed products consistent with the 'New Asia – Singapore' theme would be developed with the use of these funds. Through TDAS, for instance, the STB and the Agri-Food and Veterinary Authority of Singapore assisted five urban farms within the Singapore's Agrotechnology Parks to enhance and develop visitor-friendly programmes. In the name of agritourism, the parks would showcase a brand of intensive modern city farming technologies, in rare and rustic Singapore settings. These farms would offer exotic and endangered plants, environmentally friendly and pesticide-free vegetables, ornamental fish and tropical orchids (STB, 2000a). Also through TDAS, tourists can now ride on a wider and sturdier version of the trishaw, with better-trained trishaw riders. The improved vehicle has a battery-operated motor, a lightweight fibreglass side-carriage and reinforced, stainless steel wheels. But 'the original design of the trishaw is retained for authenticity' (STB press release, 27 September 2002c). That also means that a trishaw can now carry two passengers easily, instead of usually only one in the original narrower and non-motorized vehicles.

Making Singapore 'New Asia'

'New Asia – Singapore' attempts to describe and capture the 'essence' of Singapore. This point is reflected in the STPB Destination Marketing Division brief, 'New Asia – Singapore': the concept' (STPB, 1997, emphasis in original):

'New Asia – Singapore' *is not a product one consciously creates. It is* the sum total of the way we live, work and think. *The products are an expression of all that.*

The STPB Destination Marketing Division brief also states:

In short, 'New Asia – Singapore' expresses the essence of today's Singapore: a vibrant, multicultural, sophisticated city-state where tradition and modernity, East and West meet in harmony; a place where one can see and feel the energy that makes New Asia – Singapore the exemplar of the dynamism of the South-East Asia region.

However, 'New Asia – Singapore' is also a vision. It generates new tourism products (e.g. through TDAS) and forms perceptions and images for visitors by focusing the attention of tourists on selected delightful things in Singapore. The STB also works with other state agencies to enhance Singaporean street and cultural life. For example, STB is actively rejuvenating Chinatown together with the Urban Redevelopment Authority, Land Transport Authority, National Heritage Board and National Parks Board by, among other things, reintroducing street markets, putting up Chinese road signs, setting up a heritage centre, and sprucing and linking up pockets of greens in the area as part of the 'Chinatown Experience Guide Plan' (STB, 2002b). Another example of the STB actively working to reinvigorate the local environment is that at the height of the SARS crisis, the board launched a 'Step out!' campaign asking 'Singaporeans to step out of their homes and have fun in a socially responsible manner' (STB, 2003c). The 'Step out!' programme aimed at stimulating the tourism industry, and STB believes that 'the return to normalcy and vibrancy in the local scene is a precondition for the return of leisure travellers to Singapore' (STB, 2003c). In yet another programme, the STB is a significant driver behind the revitalization of the art and cultural scene in Singapore. For instance, in 1995, the STB proposed the founding of the Singapore Art Museum, the Asian Civilizations Museum and the Singapore History Museum, as well as the Esplanade – Theatres by the Bay. These are now central cultural institutions and are also prominent tourism attractions of the city-state. These are parts of STB's plans to make Singapore New Asian, a regional cultural centre and a 'Global city for the arts' (STPB and MITA, 1995). 'New Asia – Singapore' is thus not only promoted globally, but it is being enacted and subsequently introduced to the local population. It is also a vision to rejuvenate and liven up the island state.

New Asia, future of the region

At the same time when 'New Asia – Singapore' was introduced, there was a major shift in thinking about Singapore as a destination. As the term 'New Asia' suggests, the STB wants to highlight Singapore as part of Asia, and a continent that is changing and progressing. The first mission of the STB is (http://www.stb.com.sg/corporate):

> *Our purpose is to establish Singapore as a leading force in global tourism and a unique and attractive destination, offering an integrated tourism experience linked to regional development.*

While 'New Asia – Singapore' aims to make Singapore into a unique and attractive destination, that must also be understood within the country's broader tourism regionalization plans. Instead of trying to draw tourists away from neighbouring destinations, STB wants tourists to visit these destinations and also Singapore. As an urban setting with limited physical resources, Singapore wants to redefine its competitive situation (NTPC, 1996, pp. 24–25). STB seeks regional co-operation by expanding Singapore's tourism activities beyond the city-state. To a large extent, 'New Asia – Singapore' brand images complement the exotic images of neighbouring countries; the brand informs on Singapore's modern infrastructure and shows the future face of Asia. Implicitly, Singapore asserts itself as the centre and capital of the region, in particular South-East Asia, and it considers itself a unique and central piece of mosaic in this region. As part of the regionalization plans, STB (1997, p. 7) states:

The aim is to combine Singapore's unique big-city appeal with the complementary natural, historical and cultural attractiveness of neighbouring destinations to create a stronger, collective tourism product that benefits all parties. This strategy will increase visitor traffic significantly and enhance the long-term competitiveness of the overall tourism industry.

In fact, Singapore has been relatively successful in seeking regional co-operation from the Association of South-East Asian Nations (ASEAN). ASEAN consists of Brunei, Burma (Myanmar), Cambodia, Indonesia, Laos, Malaysia, the Philippines, Singapore, Thailand and Vietnam, and has been politically defined as South-East Asia (Figure 15.2). ASEAN co-operation in tourism was first formalized in 1976 following the formation of the Subcommittee on Tourism under the ASEAN Committee on Trade and Tourism. But nothing much happened until January 1998, when the level of co-operation was given a boost after the first formal meeting of ASEAN Tourism Ministers in Cebu City, Philippines (ASEAN, 1998a). The annual meetings of tourism ministers from ASEAN aim to demonstrate the 'common resolve to give ASEAN cooperation in tourism top-level direction, guidance, impetus and strength' (ASEAN, 1998a, point 2). During the 1998 meeting, ASEAN governments adopted a 'Plan of Action on ASEAN Cooperation in Tourism' (ASEAN, 1998b). This plan has five strategic themes. They are:

1. Marketing the ASEAN region as a single tourism destination
2. Encouraging tourism investments
3. Tourism personnel and development
4. Environmentally sustainable tourism
5. Facilitation of intra-ASEAN travel.

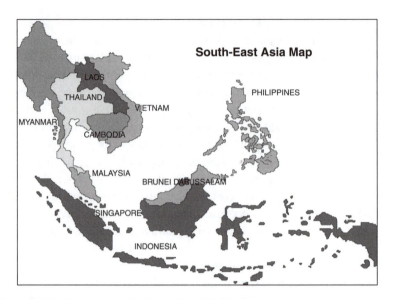

Figure 15.2   Singapore is in the middle of South-East Asia, and the Singapore Tourism Board wants visitors to the region to use Singapore as a base and hub

Since 2001, ASEAN has had a Visit ASEAN Campaign; however, this regional campaign remains limited compared with the individual efforts by individual countries. Regardless, through its regionalization strategy, Singapore intends to become a central component in regional travel packages (NTPC, 1996, p. 49). For instance, Singapore Airlines offers and promotes flights to regional tourism places via Singapore, and Singapore airports offer airlines incentives to use it as an air transport base. Under fierce competition from other South-East Asian cities and to make Singapore a well-connected city, the government presented a US$124 million Air Hub Development Fund to retain and attract more airlines to use Singapore (*Straits Times*, 2002). With the aim of making Singapore the starting and ending point of visitors' sojourn into the region, Singapore embarked on a strategy of 'gateway tourism' (Low and Toh, 1997). 'New Asia – Singapore', with its promoted modern and Asian image, is also meant to reflect the country as a transport hub in Asia, which conveniently connects to neighbouring destinations.

Besides offering accessibility to the region, a second strategy to make Singapore into a tourism capital is for the city-state to act as a representative of the region (as if it is the capital), especially in the field of art and culture. As discussed earlier, the 'New Asia – Singapore' vision aims to make Singapore into a 'Global city for the arts' (Chang, 2000; STPB and MITA, 1995). For instance, the Asia Civilization Museum (ACM) and the Singapore Art Museum

(SAM) import Asian art and heritage to Singapore; the ACM showcases ancient Asian heritages from the Middle East to China, while SAM displays contemporary visual art from South-East Asia (Ooi, 2002b, pp. 208–214). Besides that, Singapore aims to cultivate the art business by inviting famous artists to perform, holding crowd-pulling exhibitions and providing good infrastructure for artistic expression (Chang, 2000). Grand and spectacular cultural events will attract tourists from within and outside the region. However, to be a comprehensive and credible city for the arts, Singapore also wants to promote businesses in auctioneering, museum ownership and management, professional services (e.g. art consultancy) and support services (e.g. insurance and restoration) (STPB and MITA, 1995, p. 11). Singapore aims to demonstrate a New Asian confidence, and build an Asian Renaissance City; it wants to be an Eastern counterpart to Western art cities such as London and New York. The plan will make New Asian Singapore into a destination that tourists have to visit because it is the cultural capital of the region.

A third strategy to make Singapore into the tourism capital of the region is to extend Singaporean help to other destinations. Singaporean tourism-related companies are developing tourism infrastructure and help to manage tourism attractions around the region, arguably within the ASEAN framework. For instance, in 2001, STB and the Tourism Authority of Thailand organized an investment seminar to boost tourism investment into Thailand (STB, 2001). By promoting outward tourism investments, Singaporean tourism-related companies – hotels, attraction operators, transport services, and so on – tap into the region's tourism resources and draw attractive investment returns back into Singapore. Such investments will develop and improve regional tourism attractions and infrastructure, and establish close links between these destinations and Singapore. For example, Prime Minister Goh Chok Toh has asked the Trade and Industry Ministry and the STB to draw up a masterplan to promote tourism in Cambodia. When he was in Siem Reap, the gateway to the Angkor temples, he said, 'Nobody can replicate Angkor Wat'. The prime minister also observed during his trip that 'If you have a stomach-ache, then what? There's not a single toilet in the whole area' (*Straits Times Weekly Edition*, 2001a, p. 3). He saw the tourism potential in Siem Reap, but the area was limited by the lack of amenities. It was reported that SilkAir, a subsidiary of Singapore Airlines, is interested in obtaining the right to fly passengers directly from Siem Reap to Phnom Penh, a right reserved for Cambodian airlines (*Straits Times Weekly Edition*, 2001b, p. 3).

The 'New Asia – Singapore' brand is thus not just about promoting and making the island state into an attractive destination; rather, it is embedded in a wider tourism strategy to make Singapore central in regional tourism. Singapore

Airlines aims to transport tourists to the region via Singapore. Singaporean companies are developing tourism infrastructure, including hotels and attractions, to upgrade regional attractions and profit from tourists visiting the sites. The Renaissance City programme enhances 'New Asia – Singapore', and it communicates the idea that Singapore is part of the region and it is the capital, implying that it is the most important and interesting place to visit, and a convenient place for tourists to base themselves during their travels. The brand offers a vision and plays the complementary role of presenting Singapore as a society developed in an Asian way, in contrast to many of the other diverse and exotic places in the neighbourhood.

Challenges to branding Singapore

The branding process involves more than producing a slogan or a visual. The 'New Asia – Singapore' brand fits into the ambitious tourism strategy of Singapore. However, the branding process is neither even nor plain sailing. There are at least four goals behind the branding of a destination, and the STB has to face challenges in attaining these goals. The first challenge is in the use of the brand to shape the world's image of Singapore. The second is in using the brand to package Singapore into a tourism destination. The third challenge lies in the search for Singapore's uniqueness. The fourth is in using the brand story to craft tourism experiences.

Superficial perceptions and shaping imaginations

A destination brand aims to shape public perceptions. A branding campaign is part of the 'image modification process' (Andersen and Prentice, 1997, p. 463). Many people rely heavily on their own perceptions when they decide where to go for a holiday (Baloglu and McCleary, 1999; Nickerson and Moisey, 1999). People form their own images of a place based on their own experiences and what they have learned from different sources, such as news stories, travel programmes, films, geography lessons, and travel tales from friends and relatives. While perception is not everything, brand power is 'essentially the power of customer-perceived quality' (Pagano, 1994, p. 67).

The destination brand is competing in the image economy. The presented 'New Asia – Singapore' images are competing and supplementing other sources of images of Singapore. STB has been resilient and careful in managing its image. It ignores certain images in the branding of Singapore; for example, Singapore is perceived as a soft authoritarian state, with strict imposition of rules; it is commonly dubbed 'fine city' because of the penalties meted out on people who, for instance, jaywalk, vandalize or do not flush public toilets after use (Ooi, 2002b, p. 151–153). STB ignores this perception and continues to promote the country with the 'New Asia – Singapore' messages.

However, this strategy is not used when certain unattractive images are very salient. For instance, Singapore was in the news almost yearly because of the smog that engulfs the city-state from forest fires in Indonesia and Malaysia (Quah and Johnston, 2001). The SARS outbreak in 2003 also gave bad publicity to the city-state. STB could not ignore those global images that were flashed across the world. It responded by offering regular information updates on the SARS situation during the crisis, and the air quality during the smog-filled periods on the internet. Such reassurances do not necessarily attract tourists, although these steps help to increase transparency and increase the world's confidence in Singapore. Such information will also not perpetuate the negative images that potential tourists may have of Singapore if they have checked STB's websites (www.stb.com.sg; www.visitsingapore.com).

The unrest in South-East Asia, especially during the 1997/98 Asian financial crisis (e.g. riots in Indonesia, demonstrations in Malaysia, kidnappings in the Philippines) and also the Bali bombing in October 2003 have led to the STB proceeding more slowly with its promotion of Singapore as the centre of a regional destination. STB has not been as aggressive as it would like to be in promoting 'New Asia – Singapore' as part of the region. Nevertheless, it continues efforts to establish itself as the regional tourism capital. Singapore still aims to be the tourism hub, and the government encourages long-term tourism investments in the region.

The process of modifying the world's perception of the country destination is not a simple one, but one that is negotiated. In many instances, there is very little that Singapore can do when less attractive strong images from the region are projected around the world. Consequently, the original brand story of wanting to sell 'New Asia – Singapore' as the centre of South-East Asia is being watered down.

Packaging and inventing cultures

Destination branding selectively and aesthetically packages the place (McCleary and Whitney, 1994; B. Richards, 1992). The previous discussion alludes to the point that the brand packages the place into a set of images. These images help the world to imagine the country. However, inevitably, the brand also packages the sights and attractions because there are many sights, activities

and places in a country destination, and not everything is attractive or interesting for tourists. In 'New Asia – Singapore', many sights, events and happenings
are accentuated while other aspects of society are marginalized and ignored
(e.g. Singapore's red-light districts, uninspiring industrial areas and unchallenging
political discussions). Branding inadvertently frames and packages the destination into a relatively well-defined product, which focuses on attractions and
activities that are considered significant and alluring.

New tourism products are also created and invented by STB. Not only does
STB highlight bits of New Asia to tourists, it also uses its political and financial resources to allow tourism operators to create new products. In addition,
it co-operates with other state agencies to create a modern and yet oriental
Singapore. While Singaporeans are generally tolerant towards the deliberate
touristification of their society by the STB, the organization has now also established responsibilities towards Singaporean social and cultural environments
(Ooi, 2002a). For instance, the STB came under fire by shopkeepers in
Chinatown when their businesses were slow. Many residents in Chinatown criti-
cized the STB because some areas, redrawn through its revitalization plans,
were poorly designed (*Straits Times*, 2003). Effectively, the STB has been
accepted as yet another state social engineering agency, and that entails responsibilities beyond tourism.

The social engineering of Singapore strategy cannot be repeated in the shaping of South-East Asia. Singapore could not do much to end the political and
social troubles of other sovereign states in South-East Asia. Furthermore, the
ambition of wanting Singapore to be the capital of the region is challenged by
other countries, as neighbouring countries also want to be considered regional
centres. Co-operation may not be forthcoming. For instance, the ACM finds it
difficult to acquire artefacts for its exhibitions, as countries of origin, such as
China, India and Cambodia, are officially unwilling to part with their priceless
cultural properties. Subsequently, the ACM has to build its collections from the
open market, and parts of their collections come from unclear sources. This
does not reflect well in the making of Singapore into a renaissance city.

In recent years, Singapore's regional strategies have become more selective
and less evenly communicated, in spite of the ASEAN framework (ASEAN,
1998b, 2003). For instance, instead of using an ASEAN strategy, over the past
few years, Singapore teamed up with the Hong Kong Tourism Board and the
Tourism Authority of Thailand to participate at the World Travel Mart under the
theme 'Together in Asia' (STB, 2002, p. 13). These destinations host trade guests

together, while featuring their own destinations. Hong Kong and Thailand are also relatively stable, compared with Indonesia and Burma, for instance.

Unique self and significant others

The branding of a destination is to stand out in the global tourism market, in order to compete with other destinations. Inherently, the brand asserts the place's uniqueness. This is part of the competition between destinations as they attempt to attract more tourists to their own countries. The assertion of uniqueness has become an institutionalized global practice for celebrating destination identity. This uniqueness often emphasizes the historical, social and cultural values of the host society (Boniface and Fowler, 1993; Hall, 1999; Lanfant, 1995; Oakes, 1993; Richards, 1996).

'New Asia – Singapore' indicates that the search for uniqueness is both an internal reflection and an externally directed negotiation. There are at least two layers of uniqueness in the Singapore brand. The first layer is that Singapore is a multicultural blend of old and new, East and West. This identity is supposedly distinct from other more exotic and pristine countries in the neighbourhood. The second layer of uniqueness presentation taps into a different framework, which makes Singapore the centre. Singapore is asserting itself as the premier art centre and tourism capital of Asia. Singapore sees itself leading in economic and cultural development, while complementing the other places in the region.

In the first layer of uniqueness, the STB is storying many cultural products in Singapore as New Asian. However, many of these products are not unique in themselves except for their being situated in Singapore and their product stories having a Singaporean flavour. Stories can also be copied. So, for instance, cities from Cairo to Copenhagen offer a mixture of old and new buildings, many places in the world also offer people the opportunity to shop comfortably in old historical buildings, and fusion dishes are commonly found around the globe, although their blend may differ. While the New Asia stories are uniquely Singapore, many tourists seem less impressed with the pedantic details when they are engaged in leisure tourism. Furthermore, Singapore is facing competition from other destinations, including Malaysia's 'Truly Asia', which offers similar products but with a wider variety. Although the tourism authorities may be convinced that they have unique products, many tourists may be less convinced, as they find the distinctions sophistic and not really enriching their tourism experiences. This point will be discussed again in the next section.

In the second layer of uniqueness, the 'New Asia – Singapore' brand and its regionalization ambitions originally targeted the long-haul markets. In

January 2003, STB announced that markets from South-East Asia, China and India made up nearly half of total arrivals to Singapore in recent years. The 'New Asia' idea is less interesting for these relatively near markets. Instead, Singapore, as a modern, technologically advanced and shopper-friendly country, is offering cheap bargains, superior healthcare and well-recognized education services to visitors from the region. As a result, STB reorganized itself, so as better to serve these tourists and new circumstances (STB, 2003b). The 'New Asia' brand has to be reconsidered regularly. The tourism industry in Singapore has led to constant reflections on how different the destination is from its core markets. The spread of tourism in the world economy leads to extraversion and internationalization of the society. The process of extraversion and internationalization is directed towards significant markets. The Singapore experience has shown that the saliency of the unique selling proposition, as encapsulated in the brand, has to be constantly re-evaluated.

Tourist gazes and brand experiences

A destination brand can direct tourists' attention and shape tourism experiences. The STB wants tourists to interpret Singapore as 'New Asia', meaning that Singapore is an exciting place with the cultural blending of East and West, old and new. The brand can help to bring about this experience because it is used as gaze lenses by tourists to interpret the place (Ooi, 2002b). As discussed earlier, a destination brand packages the place-product in terms of images and attractions. A branding promotion campaign would also provide a framework for tourists to view the destination before they visit the destination. This prearrival framework will shape their eventual tourism experiences. Studies have shown that tourists approach a tourism site with their own interpretations, and this process enriches their tourism experiences (McIntosh and Prentice, 1999; Moscardo, 1996; Andersen and Prentice, 2003; Waller and Lea, 1999). Preconceived ideas and previsit images will not only form the bases for tourists to understand the destination, but also form the bases for a more engaged and experiential consumption of tourism products when they are visiting. Tourists who cognize the 'New Asia – Singapore' brand story will interpret the destination in like manner (Ooi 2002b, pp. 151–156). Basically, the brand offers a story around which tourists can build their experiences. The brand helps tourists to develop a consistent and meaningful sense of place, and offers a 'brand experience' (Olins, 2000, p. 56).

The creation of the 'New Asia – Singapore' experience faces two problems. First, researchers have noted that a brand as a universal, consistent message may not appeal to everyone. So, the brand story needs to be adapted to cater for different groups of tourists; as STB is realizing now, with the increasing importance of near-market tourists, the brand story has to be reconfigured. The technologically advanced and shopper-friendly image of Singapore is a big draw for many Asian tourists.

Second, as mentioned earlier, the marketing campaigns such as 'Millennium mania' and 'Singapore roars!' have supplemented, or even overshadowed, the New Asia brand. The New Asia brand story offers focus to the packaging and invention of cultural tourism products, but the message, as discussed earlier, is rather academic. The STB realizes that many tourists are not interested in such a relatively high-brow story; it is also rather difficult to capture that New Asian experience by tourists themselves, and the New Asian experience is not particularly overwhelming. Subsequently, to capture the imagination of tourists and to promise exciting experiences, STB has presented simpler and more exciting-sounding campaigns to sell Singapore, while still offering New Asian products and images, spiced with emotionally pleasant and attention-grabbing details.

Conclusion

'New Asia – Singapore' and its story are not invented out of nothing. The story makes use of many aspects of Singaporean cultures in formulating the identity, but the identity is also enhanced through new tourism and cultural products. The STB, by collaborating with other state agencies, enhances local cultures. The STB introduces changes, which are being assimilated into local society. The Singapore destination brand identity is asserted, and the crystallized public image is introduced to the local population for it to recognize itself. However, the acceptance and appropriation of tourism-driven cultures into Singaporean society reflect the general social cultural attitude of the people. Singapore has evolved into a pragmatic society under a soft authoritarian regime (Chua, 1995, pp. 68–70; Ooi, 2002a). Singapore embraces foreign influences, adopts new technologies, seizes international business opportunities and appropriates foreign cultures. While the state attempts to control 'undesirable' foreign influences, this city-state constantly embraces the world economically. Its open trade policies often entail accepting many influences from the world. Tourism is one of them.

With a long-term perspective, Singapore has also tried to make itself relevant within the regional tourism market. It wants to be the tourism capital and transport hub. 'New Asia – Singapore' communicates that idea. Singaporean companies are also developing tourism attractions and infrastructure in other countries to realize that vision. In the short term, the STB highlights Singapore as being in the middle of an exciting and exotic region, and at the same time, is careful not to associate the country with images of instability streaming out from the region. In sum, the 'New Asia – Singapore' brand is constantly being negotiated and managed by the STB. What it highlights changes over time, as the message is simplified for tourists, so as to promise and offer more spontaneous and exciting experiences. The branding process is constantly evolving.

References

Andersen, V. and Prentice, R. (2003) Festival as creative destination. *Annals of Tourism Research* 30: 7–30.

ASEAN (1998a) *Joint Press Statement: First Meeting of ASEAN Tourism Ministers*. Association of South-East Asian Nations.

ASEAN (1998b) *Ministerial Understanding on ASEAN Cooperation in Tourism*. Association of South-East Asian Nations.

ASEAN (2003) *Joint Press Statement: Sixth Meeting of ASEAN Tourism Ministers*. Association of South-East Asian Nations.

Baloglu, S. and McCleary, K. (1999) U.S. international pleasure travelers' images of four Mediterranean destinations: a comparison of visitors and nonvisitors. *Journal of Travel Research* 38: 144–153.

Boniface, P. and Fowler, P. J. (1993) *Heritage and Tourism in 'the Global Village'*. Routledge.

Chang, T. C. (1997) From 'Instant Asia' to multi-faceted jewel': urban imaging strategies and tourism development in Singapore. *Urban Geography* 18: 542–562.

Chang, T. C. (2000) Renaissance Revisited: Singapore as a 'Global City for the Arts'. *International Journal of Urban and Regional Research* 24: 818–831.

Chua, B. H. (1995) *Communitarian Ideology and Democracy in Singapore*. Routledge.

Hall, D. (1999) Destination building, niche marketing and national image projection in Central and Eastern Europe. *Journal of Vacation Marketing* 5: 227–237.

Lanfant, M. F. (1995) Introduction. In Lanfant, M. F., Allcock, J. B. and Bruner, E. M. (eds) *International Tourism: Identity and Change*. Sage, pp. 1–23.

Leong, W. T. (1997) Commodifying ethnicity: state and ethnic tourism in Singapore. In Picard, M. and Wood, R. E. (eds) *Tourism, Ethnicity, and the State in Asian and Pacific Societies*. University of Hawaii Press, pp. 71–98.

Low, L. and Toh, M. H. (1997) Singapore: development of gateway tourism. In Go, F. M. and Jenkins, C. L. (eds) *Tourism and Economic Development in Asia and Australasia*. Cassell, pp. 237–254.

McCleary, K. W. and Whitney, D. L. (1994) Projecting Western consumer attitudes toward travel to six Eastern European countries. In Uysal, M. (ed.) *Global Tourist Behavior.* International Business Press, pp. 239–256.

McIntosh, A. J. and Prentice, R. C. (1999) Affirming authenticity: consuming cultural heritage. *Annals of Tourism Research* 26: 589–612.

Moscardo, G. (1996) Mindful visitors: heritage and tourism. *Annals of Tourism Research* 23: 376–397.

Nickerson, N. P. and Moisey, R. N. (1999) Branding a state from features to positioning: making it simple? *Journal of Vacation Marketing* 5: 217–226.

NTPC (1996) *Tourism 21: Vision of a Tourism Capital.* National Tourism Plan Committees. Singapore Tourism Promotion Board.

Oakes, T. S. (1993) The cultural space of modernity: ethnic tourism and place identity in China. *Society and Space* 11: 47–66.

Olins, W. (2000) How brands are taking over the corporation. In Schultz, M., Hatch, M. J. and Larsen, M. H. (eds) *The Expressive Organization.* Oxford University Press pp. 51–65.

Ooi, C. S. (2002a) *Cultural Tourism & Tourism Cultures: The Business of Mediating Experiences in Copenhagen and Singapore.* Copenhagen: Copenhagen Business School Press.

Ooi, C. S. (2002b) *Cultural Tourism & Tourism Cultures: The Business of Mediating Experiences in Copenhagen and Singapore.* Copenhagen: Copenhagen Business School Press.

Ooi, C. S. (2002c) Contrasting strategies – Tourism in Denmark and Singapore. *Annals of Tourism Research,* 29: 689–706.

Pagano, C. (1994) The management of global brands. In Stobart, P. (ed.) *Brand Power.* Macmillan, pp. 53–64.

Quah, E. and Johnston, D. M. (2001) Fires and haze: Singapore's costs and responsibilities. In L. Low and D. M. Johnston (eds), *Singapore Inc. Public Policy Options in the Third Millennium* (pp. 157–177). Singapore: Asia Pacific Press.

Richards, B. (1992) *How to Market Tourist Attractions, Festivals, and Special Events.* Longman.

Richards, G. (1996) Production and consumption of European cultural tourism. *Annals of Tourism Research* 23: 261–283.

STB (1997) Singapore Tourism Board regional tourism.

STB (2000) Singapore Tourism Board press release (19 May). Agri-tourism: nature trails in New Asia – Singapore.

STB (2001) Singapore Tourism Board press release (18 May). STB and Tourism Authority of Thailand join hands to create investment opportunities in Thailand.

STB (2002a) Singapore Tourism Board annual report 2001/2002.

STB (2002b) Singapore Tourism Board press release (22 June). The greening of Chinatown.

STB (2002c) Singapore Tourism Board press release (27 September). New-generation trishaws for a safer, smoother ride.

STB (2003b) Singapore Tourism Board press release (27 January). Major change at STB to drive growth for Singapore's tourism industry.

STB (2003c) Singapore Tourism Board press release (8 July). A big thank you to the estimated 1.4 million people who took part in Step Out! Singapore.

STPB (1996) Singapore Tourist Promotion Board press release (4 January). STPB launches new branding and destination marketing tagline for Singapore.

STPB (1997) *Destination Marketing Brief.* Singapore Tourist Promotion Board.

STPB and MITA (1995) *Singapore: Global City for the Arts.* Singapore Tourist Promotion Board and Ministry of Information and the Arts.

Straits Times (1998b) (4 May). New $80m (US$50m) assistance scheme for tourist firms.

Straits Times (2002) (26 November). $210m boost for air hub status.

Straits Times (2003) (7 March). Tourism Board to track Chinatown's revival closely.

Straits Times Weekly Edition (2001a) (12 May). Singapore to help draw tourists.

Straits Times Weekly Edition (2001b) (12 May). Two nations likely to boost links.

Waller, J. and Lea, S. E. A. (1999) Seeking the real Spain? Authenticity in motivation. *Annals of Tourism Research* 26: 110–129.

16

Brand Philadelphia: the power of spotlight events

Michael F. Smith

Introduction

Destination brand images typically are promoted through a combination of controlled and uncontrolled media. Inherent to the success of any promotional campaign is the selection of the proper 'media mix', that combination of channels through which branding messages are delivered (Gartner, 1993). A great deal of scholarly attention has been paid to the so-called controlled media, such as advertising and websites (Day *et al.*, 2002; Morgan *et al.*, 2002).

While media relations efforts are considered part of the destination branding campaign's media mix, news media placements are often uncontrolled. The news media have to be induced to cover a destination in the first place. Even when a destination receives media coverage, that coverage typically is relegated to the travel section or, perhaps, the business pages of a news outlet. While such placement certainly targets travellers actively seeking information about destinations, it does not always create the sort of top-of-mind penetration that is essential for brand awareness and consumer decision making. Furthermore, the place marketers exercise little control over the content of the coverage. Thus, important new aspects of the destination's brand may not receive adequate coverage. When destinations do receive coverage in the main sections of news outlets, it is usually because something has gone wrong. The incidents of tourist shootings in Florida in the early 1990s are an example of this.

An increasing number of destinations have looked to major events to lure large numbers of visitors, attract investment and tourist spending, and generate media coverage. Some examples include the Summer and Winter Olympic Games, major entertainment events or festivals and significant political meetings. Some scholars have labelled these efforts 'mega events' because of their scale and scope (Deccio and Baloglu, 2002). However, from a branding perspective, it is more appropriate to label these 'spotlight events', because of the opportunities they afford destination brand managers.

Between 31 July and 3 August 2000, approximately 50 000 visitors came to Philadelphia, Pennsylvania. Nearly 15 000 were media representatives from around the world. They all came to the 'city of brotherly love' to watch George W. Bush officially become the Republican nominee for the 2000 US presidential election. This was the fifth time the Republicans had come to Philadelphia for their convention and the party's first visit since 1948 (Cross and Levinson, 2000).

Managing this event was Philadelphia 2000, a non-partisan, non-profit organization responsible for all details of the event, from logistics to lodging. One of Philadelphia 2000's subcommittees was 'Marketing Philadelphia to the Media', a group of about 150 public relations (PR) professionals. If Philadelphia 2000 was responsible for security, transportation, hospitality, co-ordinating city services and volunteer recruiting, then the Media Committee was responsible for explaining these efforts to the media and the public.

The 2000 Republican National Convention (RNC) offers an interesting case study of how places can use spotlight events as an opportunity to garner valuable media exposure, lure potential corporate and association decision makers, and reinvigorate community development efforts, if they are managed well and have a little luck. Using a combination of participant observation, analysis of official documents and a review of media coverage, this chapter will analyse some of Philadelphia's efforts to take advantage of these opportunities. Specifically, Philadelphia used this national event to reinforce and extend the city's branding messages for both national and regional audiences. In order to explore this, this chapter will (1) develop a framework for understanding spotlight events and media relations in creating a brand identity, (2) describe the method used in this study, (3) analyse the key themes in the city's branding messages, and (4) offer some conclusions about spotlight events and place promotion.

Spotlight events and branding efforts

In order to understand the role that hosting the RNC played in branding Philadelphia, it is necessary to understand the PR opportunities and challenges inherent in hosting a major event. The following section will first explore the role of events in destination promotion, the place of media relations in creating a brand image, and the branding opportunities inherent in spotlight events.

For a number of years, communities have relied on special events as a staple of their promotional campaigns. Events have several benefits for those attempting to influence public perception and behaviour. First, they bring people into a place, especially people who may make decisions about long-term investments in a place. Susan Schwenderman, Director of International Marketing for the Philadelphia Convention and Visitor's Bureau, claims that the best way to sell a place to association convention planners is to bring them to the city and let them experience it themselves (Schwenderman, 2002). Second, if the event is of sufficient importance, it can generate media coverage, both in the general news media and among tourism writers. Third, events generate revenue for the city, from hotel rooms sold to facilities rental to the sales of cheesesteaks from the corner restaurant. Finally, after an event is over, it can leave the city with other tangible and intangible byproducts. These include infrastructure improvements, such as new facilities; enhanced reputation for future campaigns or events; and a sense of community pride and involvement. Most places host a number of events annually, ranging from community holiday celebrations to major association conventions. Many events go largely unnoticed, except by the people directly involved.

Some events, however, stand out because they offer rare opportunities for destinations to 'perform' on a national or international stage; these spotlight events feature several characteristics that make them tempting as branding devices and interesting for scholars. First, the participants in spotlight events are either numerous or important, or both. For example, the Olympics attract not only world-class athletes, but also thousands of fans. Second, spotlight events appeal to national and, perhaps, international audiences. The 2002 World Cup soccer tournament, for example, had people on the US East Coast getting up at 6 a.m. for the start of their favourite teams' matches in Asia. Third, spotlight events attract a tremendous amount of media coverage, typically because of the first two characteristics.

Perhaps most interesting is that spotlight events truly put places in the spotlight, usually emanating from the lights of television cameras – with the potential for either great success or abject failure. Perhaps 'microscope' might be a better term for the scrutiny that places undergo during a spotlight event. Media relations are a common tool for PR practitioners because it is commonly believed that reaching audiences through news media is less expensive than purchasing advertising. As concerns rise over the cost of branding efforts in light of reduced budgets (Morgan *et al.*, 2002), media relations have become more attractive to place promoters. The caveat is that developing a major event can be costly. Fortunately, such events also generally attract funding from a greater variety of sources.

The presence of national and international media often amplifies the relationship between a place's image and its issues (Smith, 1993). Place promoters can use spotlight events to define a place and its primary attributes and to influence public perceptions of a place – its image – by influencing media coverage. Boulding (1956) defined an image as 'what I believe to be true', and argued that an image is composed of everything a public knows about a place, a person or an idea. He suggested that an image is 'built up as a result of all past experience of the possessor of the image' (Boulding, 1956, p. 8). By engaging in media relations, PR practitioners hope to influence what the public knows about a place. Positive media coverage helps promoters; negative media coverage does not (but still adds to the knowledge a public has about a place). A beneficial image influences the choices of tourists seeking a place to visit (Tapachai and Waryszak, 2000).

Most contemporary PR research argues that one cannot 'create' an image; rather, places must use what exists or can exist in the community and communicate about that 'truth' (Day, 1980). Spotlight events allow place promoters the opportunity to influence a great number of media representatives and, by extension, members of the public. An image is greatly influenced by a place's issues. Crable and Vibbert (1983) defined an issue as a problem or situation to which people have attached significance and made arguments about. Cheney and Vibbert (1987) argued that the terms 'issue' and 'image' are reflexive, and suggested that the issues that an organization faces influence its image. By extension, the issues that a community faces, and the evaluative judgement of those issues by the relevant public, influence the image of the community held by that public.

Two types of issue surround spotlight events. The first are issues related to the event itself. Do things run smoothly? Do the visitors have a good, safe, productive time? Often these issues arise around things such as accommodation, transportation, security and whether or not the event lives up to its promise. These issues affect not just visitors, but also an area's residents, who are affected by the logistics of the event. The second type of issue relates to the challenges and opportunities that a community faces daily. These include things such as economic development, education, urban blight and suburban sprawl. The influence of these issues is intertwined: a well-run event can boost a destination's ability to deal with issues, and an attractive destination improves the potential for a successful event. In the summer of 2000, Philadelphia faced several of these issues, which will be discussed later in the chapter.

As spotlight events, presidential nominating conventions feature several unique characteristics. First, the conventions are increasingly being viewed as tightly scripted showcases for candidates, devoid of any suspense and, thus, real news. When the Republicans met in San Diego in 1996, networks limited convention coverage to an hour each evening, and Ted Koppel's *Nightline* television programme left the city early because there was nothing to report (Zoglin, 1996). When there is little news in the convention hall, reporters hit the streets in search of local stories. Second, the media often use the host city as an exemplar of the issues facing voters in the general election. Often, the media seek a wide range of stories, some of which do not reflect well on the city. Finally, presidential conventions are not very popular with most regional residents, mainly because of the potential for tremendous inconvenience. An analysis of local news coverage of the San Diego convention revealed that most of the local stories had to do with traffic problems, the cost of the convention to the city and the displacement of local residents who lived near the convention centre (Smith, 2000). In 2000, the fact that Philadelphia is a heavily Democratic town, which had sought and won the host bid under the leadership of a Democratic mayor, only exacerbated the potential for tension between the city and its Republican visitors.

Thus, in the summer of 2000, Philadelphia was poised to host a spotlight event that held both great potential and great danger for the city's image. With an understanding of the notion of spotlight events, we may now discuss the methods through which the case study described in this chapter was developed. It is based on a combination of participant observation, analysis of official documents developed during the convention, reports published by the local host committee, Philadelphia 2000, and an analysis of media coverage.

The principal method of investigation was participant observation. From February to September 2000, the author served as a volunteer member of Philadelphia 2000's 'Marketing Philadelphia to the Media Committee'. His primary responsibility was working with the Local and Regional Media Relations Subcommittee; however, he also attended meetings of several other working groups. At each meeting, he took extensive notes, which were transcribed soon afterwards. The Local and Regional Media Relations Committee members were responsible for pitching stories to media in Philadelphia and the five surrounding suburban counties. In addition, the author helped to co-ordinate and staff two of the three press rooms that were established for the event. Upon volunteering, the author informed the committee organizers that, in addition to refreshing his PR skills, he was planning to collect information to be used in future research. (Note: the author is neither a Republican nor a native Philadelphian.)

The second method used in this study was an analysis of many of the documents produced by the Media Committee. These included press releases, fact sheets, backgrounders, position papers, the official Delegate and Media Guide, and miscellaneous documents such as meeting agendas. For example, of the 330 press releases generated for the convention, one-quarter of them came from the Media Committee (Philadelphia 2000, 2000b). These documents (seemingly mundane PR 'deliverables') were part of the discourse of the city's efforts to promote itself. As such, they conveyed strategies aimed at influencing a variety of audiences. As several interpretative scholars have argued (Leong, 1989), the commonplace documents of an organization – and, one could argue, a place – help to form the reality of a place for an audience.

The third source of data for this project was a report produced by Philadelphia 2000 in developing an entry for various Public Relations Society of America awards. The report summarizes the host committee's analysis of the success of its promotional efforts, offers data on the quantity and placement of media stories about Philadelphia and the convention, and presents some qualitative evaluation of the event.

Finally, media accounts of the convention and Philadelphia were used. A Lexis-Nexis search of media articles from December 1999 to October 2000 revealed more than 743 national newspaper stories, fifty national magazine stories and 400 regional newspaper and wire service stories. The period chosen represents the point between the formation of the Philadelphia 2000 media relations structure and the immediate aftermath of the convention, before stories about the host city were subsumed by accounts of the election campaign. For each article found, its placement, general theme, and the qualitative evaluation of the city and its promotional efforts were noted.

Branding themes in media relations messages

In analysing Philadelphia 2000's messages and activities, three major themes emerged. These themes established the 'Philadelphia story' that the city wanted to promote. These have been labelled thus: 'Philadelphia is more than the Liberty Bell', 'Don't leave town when the Republicans visit' and 'Philadelphia isn't as bad as Philadelphians say it is'. These messages were meant to influence Philadelphia's brand image in the minds of distinct market segments.

Philadelphia is more than the Liberty Bell

An ongoing challenge for those promoting Philadelphia is to define the city as a place that offers visitors more than a few buildings that set the stage for the political drama that led to the signing of the Declaration of Independence. In many people's minds, Philadelphia's attractions extended no further than Independence Mall or the Liberty Bell. Several years before the RNC, the Greater Philadelphia Tourism and Marketing Committee (GPTMC) ran 'The place that loves you back' campaign, the aim of which was to improve the city's desirability as a tourist destination for those within driving distance of Philadelphia (Smith, 1998). The $12 million campaign ran for three years, raised the travelling public's awareness of the city and region, and helped to spur the development of the major hotel projects that prompted the Republican National Committee to choose Philadelphia to host its convention. During the RNC, the city tried to communicate that both Philadelphia and the entire region were stories worth covering. Furthermore, city business leaders attempted to move reporters (and corporate leaders) into considering Philadelphia as a place to live and work. To achieve these ends, Philadelphia 2000 created press materials and tours that highlighted a number of 'beyond history' themes and conducted a 'mini campaign' to promote business opportunities.

The 'beyond history' theme was framed in the Official Delegate and Media Guide, which was assembled by a Media Committee task group. The guide began with articles about some of the familiar historical themes, including the city's history with the RNC. The guide then moved into articles about Philadelphia's neighbourhoods and surrounding counties, New Jersey and

Delaware's attractions, and then highlights of the region's strengths, including good restaurants, shopping, sports, culture, business and medicine. The guides were mailed to all the journalists and delegates several weeks before the convention, along with a short videotape highlighting Philadelphia's features.

Philadelphia 2000 hosted a variety of media tours and events designed to highlight both the city and the region. Media tours allow PR professionals to provide specific information about a place's features and to develop in-depth story angles for reporters. Philadelphia 2000 began the media tours two weeks before the convention started in order to give the media time to develop story angles. Kotler *et al.* (1994, p. 17) suggest that planners need to 'identify ... a place's characteristics [that] represent degrees of strength or weakness in terms of what the buyers are seeking'. In this case, the media tours were arranged to capitalize on the familiar aspect of Philadelphia's image – history – then move into less familiar aspects.

Four guided tours were planned to highlight the historical features of the city. The four were the 'Best of' Philadelphia tour, which highlighted primary landmarks, locations for television stand-up reports and 'vantage points of America's birthplace'; 'Ethnic markets: the world between two rivers', which focused on the city's diverse culture and cuisine; 'Filmed in Philadelphia', which highlighted parts of the city featured in movies, such as *Rocky* and *The Sixth Sense*; and 'City of homes: Philadelphia neighborhoods', which took the media around the various neighbourhoods that make up the city (Philadelphia 2000, 2000a). These four tours helped to reinforce some of the common themes in Philadelphia's identity: history, diversity and neighbourhoods.

From these tours, regional tourism boards co-operated with the Media Committee to offer up to thirty tours around the region. These tours were built around themes that went beyond the historical (and beyond the city). Themes included 'Literature and mass media in Philadelphia', 'Science and technology in Franklin's wake' and 'Vanguard of the arts: opera to hip hop and academy to gallery' (Butler *et al.*, 2000). Other tours led the media to Wilmington, Delaware, New Hope, Pennsylvania, and Haddonfield, New Jersey.

In both the media guide and the tours, the storylines about the region developed in a sort of concentric pattern, beginning with Philadelphia's history and moving into the neighbourhoods and cultural centres and on into the suburbs and neighbouring states. In each case, the media received information that helped to inform perspectives on Philadelphia, reaffirming its image as a historical centre, but also affirming the idea that there is more to the region than just the Liberty Bell.

In addition to the tours, Philadelphia used at least one mini-campaign to appeal to audiences other than tourists. The Greater Philadelphia Chamber of Commerce and Greater Philadelphia First, two business associations, used the convention to promote Philadelphia as a place to do business. Using the tagline 'May we have the pleasure of your company?', the campaign focused on the region's assets as a place to locate a business. In addition to signage around most of the major public gathering points for the convention, the groups held media briefings on the Philadelphia business climate and produced a brochure that was distributed to delegates. The brochure claimed that 'Philadelphia means business', and highlighted some of the region's attributes, including a skilled workforce, one of the highest concentration of universities and colleges in America, and bustling transportation hubs (Greater Philadelphia Chamber of Commerce/Greater Philadelphia First, 2000). Like the interpersonal strategies of taking the media on tour, the business leaders offered personal tours, briefings or meals with 'business ambassadors'.

Don't leave town when the Republicans visit

Morgan *et al.* (2002) suggested that one area in need of further research is the impact of branding efforts on local residents. In this case, not everyone was excited about having the Republicans visit Philadelphia. As noted earlier, every place faces significant issues when hosting a spotlight event, including transportation, overcrowding and the inconvenience caused by new construction or renovations made to accommodate the event.

The presidential nominating convention brought additional considerations. First, the event was not open to the public, but only to the approximately 5000 delegates and party officials. So, in return for all the disruptions, Philadelphians would have little opportunity to participate in the convention. Despite this, regional residents were calling Philadelphia 2000 asking how they could attend the convention. Second, protesters were expected to disrupt the convention. The First Union Center had a wide security perimeter surrounding it, but the delegates were staying in hotels in Center City, nearly 2 miles from the convention site. Thus, protests were expected to disrupt Center City. Previous globalization protests in Seattle and Washington DC had resulted in significant damage to property. Finally, Philadelphia is a Democratic stronghold surrounded by a region populated largely by Republicans. Given that the convention was being held near the beginning of the traditional summer holiday season, there appeared to be widespread feeling that many in the city would head out of the city to enjoy their vacations while the Republicans were there. Thus, a major challenge for Philadelphia 2000 was to convince Philadelphians that the convention was also for them. Two major strategies were used to convince regional residents to stay in the city and become involved in the convention: volunteer recruiting and PoliticalFest.

Philadelphia 2000 sought to recruit volunteers to assist with a variety of activities through the 'Make the convention connection' campaign (Philadelphia 2000, 2000c). Volunteers were recruited to provide transportation between hotels and the convention site, to ferry delegates and the media around the sprawling First Union complex, to greet delegates at the airport, to show people around the city and to assist with some media activities. The campaign targeted employee groups through the 'Corporate team' programme and recruited a select group of volunteers assigned to be 'Philadelphia Friends', who would liaise full-time with the 55 state delegations for the entire week of the convention. The campaign was led by Pat Croce, one of the city's most enthusiastic promoters and president of the Philadelphia 76ers basketball team.

The campaign was successful, with over 10 000 volunteers recruited in just eight weeks, and over 15 000 in total, 5000 over the target goal. The volunteers went through training to acquaint them with their duties and convention information. In order to improve their 'people skills', volunteers worked with Dale Carnegie trainers.

The byproduct of the volunteer recruitment campaign was that several thousand Philadelphia residents gained 'official' positions with the convention and helped to promote their region. Most of the volunteers relied on regional public transportation to move into their jobs, and in the evening, commuter trains were filled with volunteers enthusiastically discussing their experiences. In sum, the volunteer recruiting effort resulted in residents 'connecting' with the convention.

From a media relations standpoint, the thirty-five training sessions, held across the region, afforded local and regional media an opportunity to cover their local volunteers as they experienced the convention, thus suggesting that residents from a variety of different locales were connected to a major political event that most people do not have the opportunity to witness. Therefore, the connection was not only with volunteers, but also, by extension, with their communities.

The second major initiative was 'PoliticalFest ... where the party begins', an event that was touted as the first-of-its kind 'world's fair' of American politics (Schwenderman, 2000b). The event's goal was stated by Karen Dougherty Buchholz, president of Philadelphia 2000: 'PoliticalFest offers everyone a chance to participate in the convention. We wanted to demonstrate our civic pride through a special exhibit that everyone could enjoy, and also mark the greater Philadelphia region's amazingly rich history in government and politics' (Schwenderman, 2000b). PoliticalFest began several days before the convention, and thus had the attention of the media and residents all to itself before media attention turned to the Republicans.

PolticalFest reflected a trend in spotlight events, where the main event is complemented by another major event designed for those unable to participate in the spotlight event. For example, sports all-star games, such as those hosted by the National Basketball Association and Major League Baseball, feature 'fan fests' that allow those unable to get tickets to the games to come close to the venue to experience some of the excitement generated by the main event.

PoliticalFest featured a variety of interactive exhibits designed to inform visitors about the White House, the presidency and the process of campaigning. One local television station sponsored an exhibit in which people could put on a correspondent's blazer and do a stand-up report from a mock convention floor. People could climb aboard President Nixon's Air Force One, sit behind the desk in the Oval Office, design their own campaign posters and watch the actual convention from a giant screen in an area set up like the First Union Center. The exhibits included material from seven Presidential libraries and the Smithsonian Institution. One of the more unusual exhibits was a Parade of Bells, where over 30 states created 'Liberty Bells' that reflected their state's character. Indiana, for example, used a basketball hoop and ball, while Michigan's bell was made from car parts. Louisiana created a papier mâché bell festooned with beads. Many of the exhibits, especially the Parade of Bells, generated national media coverage.

To promote the event throughout the region, PoliticalFest planners embarked on twelve whistle-stop tours to regional malls in Pennsylvania and New Jersey (Schwenderman, 2000a). The tours were designed to give people a taste of what they might experience at the actual event and also to promote local media coverage promoting PoliticalFest. It featured a mock caboose. Media relations volunteers encouraged families to make their own campaign posters and hats, then have their picture taken on the back of the caboose. The whistle-stop tour garnered extensive media attention from regional publications, several of which put the local stop on the front page with photographs.

More than 80 000 paid admissions were recorded for PolticalFest. Since the media and official delegates were given free admission to the event, this meant that nearly 60 000 Philadelphia area residents travelled into Center City at a time when many of their neighbours claimed that they should stay away.

Philadelphia isn't as bad as Philadelphians say it is

The phrase was chosen to characterize this theme was coined in the 1960s by area advertising executive Elliot Curson (Armstrong, 1998). This saying captured an essential truth about the character of the city: the citizenry seems to suffer from a perpetual case of self-loathing. In this case, however, it also referred to perceptions of visitors and residents alike that Philadelphia's issues may undermine its attempts at managing its image. Philadelphia 2000 co-chair David Cohen said, 'People didn't have low expectations of Philadelphia; they had no expectations ... They thought of Philadelphia: old city, falling apart, dirty, unsafe' (Clines, 2000).

As noted earlier, Philadelphia faced several issues leading up to the convention. City workers threatened to go on strike unless a contract agreement was reached. The Philadelphia school district faced a state takeover because of poor performance. Several row homes in the city had collapsed during the summer, triggering concern about the issue of urban blight. In the most notable incident, a carjacking suspect was arrested by a group of approximately a dozen police officers, who pulled him from the vehicle and wrestled him to the ground. Although not as brutal, a local television station's film of the arrest conjured up images of the infamous Rodney King beating in Los Angeles several years before. The arrest raised questions about how the police might respond to protesters engaged in civil disobedience at the RNC. All of these challenges were laid upon the desk of the recently elected mayor of Philadelphia, John Street, who had the unenviable task of following in the footsteps of Ed Rendell, his immensely popular predecessor who was nicknamed 'America's mayor' after pulling Philadelphia from near bankruptcy and luring the Republican convention to Philadelphia (Brown, 2000).

These issues had been widely reported by both local and national media in the weeks leading up to the convention. It would not have been too surprising for the delegates to believe that they were entering a destination rife with problems. To counter this perception, Philadelphia 2000 and other community groups set out to address some of the problems. Although some of the solutions were short term, others are likely to have long-lasting effects. The specific strategies that supported this theme involved projects that subverted the city's image as a dangerous, unclean place.

One example of these projects was undertaken by the Center City District, a private-sector organization that took responsibility for making Philadelphia's downtown area a better place to do business. The Center City District announced a programme designed to make the area 'Clean ... Safe ... and Attractive' for the convention (Shannon, not dated). Among the projects outlined were additional pavement sweeping and the installation of banners. More substantially, the Center City District helped the city to co-ordinate a 'multi-million dollar streetscape improvement program' which included '... new pedestrian lights, furnishings, trees, and landscaping'. Furthermore, there were plans to increase the number of Community Service Representatives, whose function was to serve as 'additional "eyes and ears" for the police and as goodwill ambassadors to welcome the delegates and other visitors to the city'.

The value of these representatives, as well as a similar group established by the Philadelphia Police Department, became evident during the first day of the convention. A group of local protesters wanted to march down Broad Street from Center City to the First Union Center. At first, there was a tense standoff. However, the representatives mediated the dispute between the protesters and police, and the march was allowed to proceed. Given the controversy surrounding the police and the carjacking suspect, this was a welcome easing of tensions between the police and the public. Police did have a major confrontation with protestors during the second day of the convention, which resulted in over 300 arrests, but generally received good reviews for diffusing the protests non-violently ('The kind blue line', 2000).

The Center City District news release emphasized the fact that the improvement projects were designed as an 'ongoing public space improvement effort' (Shannon, not dated), thus suggesting that the projects being completed for the convention would benefit the region after the Republicans went home. Other projects were undertaken by the city and surrounding communities. New Jersey officials cleaned up a notorious section of bars and strip joints along Admiral Wilson Boulevard leading toward one of the bridges into Philadelphia. Philadelphia 2000 co-ordinated the 'Clean and Green' committee to co-ordinate a variety of city departments and transportation agencies to 'create physical and permanent improvements to the greater Philadelphia region' (Besa, 2000). A variety of projects was announced that involved cleaning up and improving public spaces, transportation centres and community facilities (Office of the City Representative, 2000a, b; Syrnick, 2000). The city hosted a clean-up day about two weeks before the convention, during which the highly regarded Mural Arts project created murals at city pools and recreation centres in some of the most economically challenged neighbourhoods.

The overall message communicated was that Philadelphia was a welcoming, clean, safe city. According to at least one volunteer, that was the message received: 'I was proud to be part of the history being made and happy that Philadelphia showed how hospitable and accommodating the city could be. I was told by all whom I met that it was the most helpful, friendly, secured convention that they had attended. We lived up to our saying, "City of Brotherly Love"' (quoted in Philadelphia 2000, 2000b).

Conclusion

The RNC generated nearly $345 million for the region's economy (Von Bergen, 2000). More valuable, however, may have been the media coverage generated by the event. According to a Philadelphia 2000 report, nearly 20 000 stories were generated in the print media, including 6672 stories during the convention week itself. In the Philadelphia region, the *Philadelphia Inquirer* alone ran 531 stories. In addition, broadcast media generated more than 5500 stories during the three-week period from 28 July to 18 August (Philadelphia 2000, 2000b).

More importantly, the coverage was largely favourable to the city. Many of the national media carried positive stories about the city's rebirth, while travel magazines such as US Airway's *Attaché* and American Airline's *American Way* featured Philadelphia as a desirable tourist destination. National news anchor Dan Rather said, 'Philadelphia has done a tremendous job in emanating a sense of kindness and gentleness to everybody. It's the talk of the press corps here. A really impressive job' (Philadelphia 2000, 2000b).

For Philadelphia's branding efforts, the news was especially good. The media coverage generally reflected the branding themes. In addition to stories emanating from the historical sites, reporters covered new restaurants, trendy night spots, and upscale shopping locations and accommodation offered by the city (Frumkin, 2000; Williams, 2000). In addition, several news outlets framed Philadelphia as a city on the rebound, with promising developments in business and industry (Rubin, 2000).

As noted earlier, a place's issues mix with the image both communicated to and perceived by the media. The view of Philadelphia offered by Philadelphia 2000 was not an uncontested view. Local community activists organized an Independent Media Center and offered to take the media on a tour of the 'real' Philadelphia, through neighbourhoods still affected by blight and crime (Gonzalez, 2000). Other media events did not go as planned. For example, the

Media Committee cancelled several tours to outlying areas because of low levels of interest. Overall, however, the convention went off as planned and Philadelphia benefited from its time in the spotlight.

What can be learned from examining Philadelphia's experience of hosting a spotlight event? First, spotlight events require a tremendous amount of organization and co-ordination to be successful. Nearly 20 000 volunteers, area businesses, state, local and federal government agencies, and 150 PR professionals had to work together to co-ordinate the event. The volunteers came from state and local tourism bureaux; major local tourist attractions, ranging from Independence Hall to the King of Prussia Mall; sites associated with the convention, such as the Pennsylvania Convention Center, site of PoliticalFest, and the First Union Center, site of the convention; and various PR agencies. Morgan *et al.* (2002) suggested that one challenge in managing major branding campaigns is the competition among multiple agencies representing various destinations. In this case, the anticipated benefits to all the constituencies of hosting the RNC helped to reduce the level of conflict that such a large, diverse group might have experienced. Local reporter Clark DeLeon noted that 'It was a show of technology, resolve, preparation, passion, pageantry, protest, and hospitality that was years in the making. And it showed' (Philadelphia 2000, 2000b, p. 12).

Second, the event demonstrated that places can use spotlight events as a means to reinforce and extend other branding messages. Philadelphia is more than just historical buildings, it is also a good place to live, work and visit. Hosting the convention gave Philadelphia a chance to tell the story that tourism and business officials had been telling in various campaigns for several years before 2000. Since the convention, the storylines have been amplified into several other campaigns. The impact of these efforts remain to be seen, but as the vice president of the city's Convention and Visitor's Bureau noted, 'We showed them that we can deliver a safe, clean, and exciting environment … that exposure was priceless. Now it makes it easier for our customers to go to their own boards and say they want to come to Philadelphia. The sell job is done' (Philadelphia 2000, 2000b, p. 15).

Acknowledgement

The author wishes to thank Susan Schwenderman of the Philadelphia Convention and Visitor's Bureau for her assistance.

References

Armstrong, J. M. (1998) What's a motto you? *Philadelphia Daily News* (14 February): 5.

Besa, K. (2000) Philadelphia 2000 coordinates Clean and Green committee to beautify Philadelphia for the GOP convention. Press release (July): 2 pp.

Boulding, K. (1956) *The Image*. Ann Arbor: University of Michigan Press.

Brown, J. (2000) Philly cheerleaders still smiling despite onslaught of unflattering news. *Associated Press Wire Service* (20 July).

Butler, P., Schneider, C. and Schwenderman, S. (2000) Media tours for 2000 Republican National Convention: designed to provide story content, regional angles, and good vantage point. Press release (July).

Cheney, G. and Vibbert, S. L. (1987) Corporate discourse: public relations and issue management. In Jablin, F. M., Putnam, L. L., Roberts, K. H., and Porter, L. W. (eds) *Handbook of Organizational Communication*. Newbury Park: Sage, pp. 165–194.

Clines, F. X. (2000) Even Democrats are part of Philadelphia's welcome wagon for Republicans. *New York Times* (3 May): A6.

Crable, R. E. and Vibbert, S. L. (1983) Managing issues and influencing public policy. *Public Relations Review* 11: 3–16.

Cross, R. and Levinson, D. (2000) Following the convention trail. *Philadelphia: Official Delegate and Media Guide for the 2000 Republican National Convention*, pp. 36–38

Day, C. R. (1980) Do companies have personalities? *Industry Week* 72, 75–76, 78.

Day, J., Skidmore, S. and Koller, T. (2002) Image selection in destination positioning: a new approach. *Journal of Vacation Marketing* 8: 177–186.

Deccio, D. and Baloglu, S. (2002) Nonhost community resident reaction to the 2002 winter Olympics: the spillover impacts. *Journal of Travel Research* 41 (August): 46–56.

Frumkin, P. (2000) They'd rather be in Philadelphia. *Nation's Restaurant News* (14 August): 1.

Gartner, W. (1993) Image formation process. *Journal of Travel and Tourism* 2: 191–215.

Gonzalez, J. (2000) Light touch of color: minority outreach doesn't impress locals. *New York Daily News* (4 August): 32.

Greater Philadelphia Chamber of Commerce/Greater Philadelphia First (2000) May we have the pleasure of your company. Brochure. Earle Palmer Brown advertising.

Kotler, P., Haider, D. and Rein, I. (1994) There's no place like our place. *Public Management* 17 (February).

Leong, W. (1989) Culture and the state: manufacturing traditions for tourism. *Critical Studies in Mass Communication* 6: 355–375.

Morgan, N. J., Pritchard, A. and Piggott, R. (2002) Destination branding and the role of the stakeholders: the case of New Zealand. Paper presented to the Annual Meeting of the National Communication Association, New Orleans, Louisiana.

Office of the City Representative (2000a) Philadelphia International Airport debuts a 200 foot long mural painted by local school children. Press release (17 July).

Office of the City Representative (2000b) Philadelphia International Airport's landscaping program in full bloom. Press release.

Philadelphia 2000 (2000a) Fact sheet: media tours.

Philadelphia 2000 (2000b) Image impact: Philadelphia and the 2000 Republican National Convention. Philadelphia PRSA Pepperpot Award Competition entry. 3.

Philadelphia 2000 (2000c) Make the convention connection fact sheet.

Rubin, D. (2000) Remaking history in Philadelphia. *Engineering News Record* (7 August): 36.

Schwenderman, S. (2000a) All aboard for a political road trip: Philadelphia 2000's PolticalFest Whistle Stop Tours Roll Out in Greater Philadelphia (16 June).

Schwenderman, S. (2000b) A Festival of American Politics in Philadelphia: PoliticalFest at the Pennsylvania Convention Center, July 26–August 3, 2000. Press release (23 May).

Schwenderman, S. (2002) Personal interview.

Shannon, M. (not dated) Center City District gears up for the Republican National Convention. Press release: 1.

Smith, M. (1993) Place images and place issues: conceptual and practical considerations in place marketing. Paper presented to the Place Images Seminar, Speech Communication Association, Miami, FL.

Smith, M. (1998) Coming to terms with the place that loves you back: Philadelphia's Tourism Marketing Campaign. Paper presented to the National Communication Association, New York City.

Smith, M. (2000) Local and regional media study, 1996 Republican National Convention, San Diego. Unpublished research report prepared for Philadelphia 2000.

Syrnick, J. R. (2000) Streets Department status on projects affecting the 2000 Republican National Convention. Fact sheet.

Tapachai, N. and Waryszak, R. (2000) An examination of the role of beneficial image in tourist destination selection. *Journal of Travel Research* 39 (August): 37–44.

The kind blue line; Philadelphia police deftly control GOP protests (2000) *Pittsburgh Post Gazette* (11 August): A24.

Von Bergen, J. M. (2000) Report says Republican convention yields many benefits to Philadelphia. *Philadelphia Inquirer* (8 December): C1.

Williams, J. (2000) 'The Greatest' joins Fox at fundraiser. *USA Today* (3 August): 10A.

Zoglin, R. (1996) The last TV show. *Time* (26 August): 22.

17

Developing Brand Australia: examining the role of events

Graham Brown, Laurence Chalip, Leo Jago and
Trevor Mules

Introduction

According to Janiskee (1996, p. 100), 'this is the age of special events'. It is certainly difficult to visit a major city without being confronted by an impressive list of sport and cultural events that compete to capture the attention of tourists. The events add to the city's range of tourist attractions and they often actively seek media coverage as a promotional strategy, hoping that more people will be encouraged to visit the city in the future. Thus, the relationship between events and tourism has become intrinsically linked. One significant element of this relationship is the way in which images associated with an event may be transferred to the destination. In this way the destination brand may be strengthened, enhanced or changed.

The aim of this chapter is to consider the relationship between events and destination branding from a number of perspectives. After discussing the growing importance of event tourism, the nature of destination image is examined in the context of conceptual and applied frameworks. An attempt is then made to determine the status of the relationship between event management and tourism by reporting recent insight gained in Australia. The findings from a research project that focused exclusively on the role of events in destination branding are discussed before considering the implications of the Sydney Olympic Games on Brand Australia.

The section on the Sydney Olympics provides an opportunity to assess the extent to which it is possible to manage outcomes associated with an event of this size and complexity. It serves as a valuable case study because the 2000 Olympics are widely regarded as a particularly successful event and tourism objectives were accorded a more important role in Sydney than at any previous Olympic Games. 'No other host country has taken the opportunity to use the Games to promote the whole country's tourism image as well as the host city's. No other country has worked so closely with the Olympic partners to develop mutual benefits from linking the tourism brand with their products and services' (Australian Tourist Commission (ATC), 2001b, p. 5).

The emergence of event tourism

Observation and anecdotal evidence suggests that the number of special events has increased substantially over time (Getz, 1991; Getz and Wicks, 1994; Janiskee, 1994). However, they are not a recent phenomenon. The first Olympic Games were held in 776 BC and religious events and festivals have been held throughout the ages. What is new is the scale of event tourism, with many cities seeking to specialize in the creation and hosting of special events because of the economic benefits that they bring (Lynch and Veal, 1996). Event management is now regarded as a distinct field of study (Getz, 2000b) but it is still at a formative stage and no definitional consensus has emerged in the literature (e.g. Ritchie, 1984; Burns *et al.*, 1986; Getz, 1989, 1991; Hall, 1992; Jago and Shaw, 1994, 1998; Arcodia and Robb, 2000). Jago and Shaw (1998, p. 29) have proposed that a special event is:

A one-time or infrequently occurring event of limited duration that provides the consumer with a leisure and social opportunity beyond everyday experience. Such events, which attract, or have the potential to attract, tourists, are often held to raise the profile, image, or awareness of a region.

The term 'event tourism', which formalized the link between events and tourism, was coined in the 1980s (Getz, 1997) and has been defined as 'the systematic planning, development and marketing of festivals and special events as tourist attractions, catalysts, and image builders' (Getz and Wicks, 1993, p. 2). Much of the attention that has been accorded to special events has been tourism based, as places have come to recognize the power of special events to attract visitors from outside the region. The Formula One Grand Prix held in Melbourne in 2000 attracted 14 per cent of its visitors from overseas, and 19 per cent from out of state (National Institute of Economic and Industry Research, 2000), while the 1998 Gold Coast Wintersun Festival attracted 2 per cent of its visitors from overseas and 61 per cent from interstate (Fredline *et al.*, 1999). It is important to recognize the role played by local communities in special events as they often depend heavily on the patronage of the local market for their success (Getz, 1997; Crompton and McKay, 1997). Despite this, tourist attendance at special events continues to be seen as a major objective, partly because event tourists have a higher-than-average daily expenditure, although the expenditure profile varies with the type of event (Getz, 1994a).

The success of special events in capturing market appeal has been attributed to the fact that they match important changes in the demand for leisure activities; namely, they are 'short-term, easily accessible, with a flexible time commitment, and offer options for all ages' (Robinson and Noel, 1991, p. 79). Some of the reasons for the dramatic increase in the popularity of special events also relate to demographic and psychographic changes that have occurred, such as:

- increasing levels of average disposable income
- a move to more frequent short-term holiday breaks
- increasing interest in experiential travel
- increasing interest in authenticity
- increasing interest in culture.

Special events have been used to supplement natural and existing built attractions (Burns *et al.*, 1986) as, in many cases, little additional infrastructure is required. They can be held in most locations and, in principle, can be scheduled at times and in places to reduce the impacts of seasonality or to reduce crowding and damage in more sensitive areas (Getz, 1991). People who travel to special events have been classed as high-quality tourists (Getz, 1994c), as they are often concerned about the social and environmental impacts of their behaviour, making them well suited to sustainable development (Uysal and Gitelson, 1994). Hughes (1993a), however, cautioned that it is still not clear that special event tourists are in fact more beneficial than other categories of tourist.

Special events can be an important motivator for travel behaviour, both day trip and overnight. As Getz (1989, p. 125) observed, 'Although the majority of events have probably arisen for non-tourist reasons ... there is clearly a trend to exploit them for tourism and to create new events deliberately as tourist attractions'. Pleasure travel as a result of attendance at special events accounts for about 3 per cent of the total pleasure travel in the USA, but it is one of the fastest growing segments of the tourism industry (Backman *et al.*, 1995). A study conducted by Wicks and Fesenmaier (1995) that involved a survey of 2100 randomly selected households found that 57 per cent of all pleasure trips in the previous year had included a special event. Of these, 55 per cent indicated that attendance at a special event resulted in an overnight stay, which demonstrated the importance of the field of special events to the tourism industry.

Governments have become interested in special events largely because of their ability to attract visitors, and hence visitor spending, as well as their ability to raise the awareness of the host region for future tourism (Mules and Faulkner, 1996). The importance of special events for Australia's tourism industry was recognized in the National Tourism Strategy (Commonwealth Department of Tourism, 1992), and most state tourism strategies, produced since 1992, have acknowledged special events as an important tourism development option (e.g. Tourism Victoria, 1993, 1997). As a consequence of these strategies, special event divisions have been established in most of Australia's State and Territory Tourism Organizations (Jago and Shaw, 1998). The special event divisions that have been established by many of Australia's cities also generally fall within tourism departments.

The growing importance of special events is such that they 'are starting to dominate natural or physical features in the identification of cities' (Burns *et al.*, 1986, p. 5). They can have very wide-ranging impacts and a given event can be staged for a large number of reasons, as indicated in the following literature:

- increased visitation to a region (Ritchie, 1984; Getz, 1989, 1991; Tourism South Australia, 1990; Hall, 1992; Kang and Perdue, 1994; Light, 1996)
- positive economic impact (Ritchie, 1984, 1996; Burns *et al.*, 1986; Goeldner and Long, 1987; Witt, 1988; Hall, 1990, 1992; Getz, 1991; Murphy and Carmichael, 1991; McCann and Thompson, 1992; Faulkner, 1993; Kang and Perdue, 1994; Light, 1996; Mules and Faulkner, 1996)
- increased employment (Ritchie, 1984; Hall, 1992)
- improvement in a destination's image or awareness (Ritchie, 1984; Burns *et al.*, 1986; Kaspar, 1987; Travis and Croize, 1987; Witt, 1988a–c; Hall, 1990, 1992, 1996; Ritchie and Smith, 1991; Roche, 1994; Wells, 1994; Backman *et al.*, 1995)

- enhanced tourism development (Hall, 1987; Ritchie and Yangzhou, 1987; Pyo *et al.*, 1988; Getz, 1989; Chacko and Schaffer, 1993; Faulkner, 1993; Spilling, 1996)
- ability to act as a catalyst for development (Kaspar, 1987; Hall, 1990, 1992; Getz, 1991, 1997; Hughes, 1993b; Law, 1993; Mihalik, 1994; Roche, 1994; Evans, 1995; Hodges and Hall, 1996; Light, 1996; Spilling, 1996)
- reduction in seasonal fluctuations or extension of the tourism season (Ritchie and Beliveau, 1974; Goeldner and Long, 1987; Kaspar, 1987; Getz, 1989, 1991, 1997)
- animation of static attractions (Getz, 1991)
- enhanced community pride (Ritchie, 1984; Getz, 1989; Hall, 1992; Roche, 1994; Williams *et al.*, 1995; Light, 1996)
- advancement of political objectives (Hall, 1992; Getz, 1994b).

Since many events require government assistance in order to be staged, a justification is usually required in economic terms (Burgan and Mules, 2000). This helps to explain the focus on economic impact of much of the research that has been conducted to date. This, however, represents a preoccupation with the short-term implications of staging events. There is substantial scope to explore further the role that events can play as catalysts for development and in helping to build an image for a region that will attract longer term visitation.

Events and branding: a conceptual framework

Despite the growth of event tourism, little attention has been given to the psychological processes that undergird the ways that events can impact a destination's brand. In essence, the linking of a destination's brand to one or more events is a co-operative branding activity. The event's brand image is linked to that of the destination. The use of co-operative branding enjoyed a 40 per cent growth in the latter years of the twentieth century (Spethmann and Benezra, 1994), suggesting that marketers have found it to be a useful tactic for building brand equity. One result of that growth has been a parallel growth in the literature on brand alliance effects (e.g. Rao and Ruekert, 1994; Simonin and Ruth, 1998; Till and Shimp, 1998; Gwinner and Eaton, 1999). This section of the chapter considers implications of that literature for the use of events in destination branding.

Brands are typically linked in order to increase brand awareness and/or to enhance or change brand image. The use of events as a means to enhance consumers' awareness of a destination is a common reason that destinations seek to host events (Whitson and Macintosh, 1996; Boyle, 1997). Indeed, the economic value of an event to the host city or region is often predicated on the media attention that the event obtains (Mules and Faulkner, 1996). However, the use of events as a means to enhance or change a destination's image is less well understood. For an event to have an impact on a destination's image there must be some spillover from the event's image onto the destination's image. Although the effects of an event's image on a destination's image have not been well demonstrated, evidence from the sponsorship literature suggests that the strongest benefits to brand image from an event will accrue when consumers perceive a meaningful match between the image of the event and that of the destination (Gwinner and Eaton, 1999; McDaniel, 1999; Speed and Thompson, 2000). However, from the standpoint of both theory and practice, this conclusion suffers two deficiencies. First, it fails to specify what factors render an appropriate match. Second, by mandating a strong match-up at the outset, the focus is placed on the enhancement of image, rather than on a change of image. In many instances, destinations seek to use events to change their image (Bramwell, 1997; van den Berg et al., 2000). In such instances, there will, at the outset, be some degree of mismatch between the event's image and that of the destination. What is being sought is a transfer of image such that the initial mismatch is resolved by shifting desired aspects of the event's image to the destination.

To address both brand image enhancement and brand image change, any prescription must be able to specify what engenders a match-up and what renders some potential for image change. In other words, what constitutes an appropriate basis for selecting and using events to obtain a desired effect on the destination's image? To address that question, it is useful to consider the psychological basis of brand equity. Cognitive psychologists have for some time held that knowledge is represented as associative networks (e.g. Collins and Loftus, 1975; Anderson, 1983; Halford et al., 1998). Accordingly, knowledge consists of a set of nodes that are connected through a network of associations. The nodes and their relations form an 'association set'. Association sets have been found to be useful descriptors of brand image (Keller, 1993; Henderson et al., 1998). When two brands are paired, the image of one brand can be strengthened when its association set shares common elements with the association set of the brand with which it is paired (Gwinner and Eaton, 1999). Further, a transfer of brand image from one brand to another occurs when consumers assimilate a node from one brand's association set into the association set for the brand with which it is paired (Till and Shimp, 1998).

By way of illustration, consider the hypothetical set of relationships depicted in Figure 17.1. The figure represents a fictitious market segment's

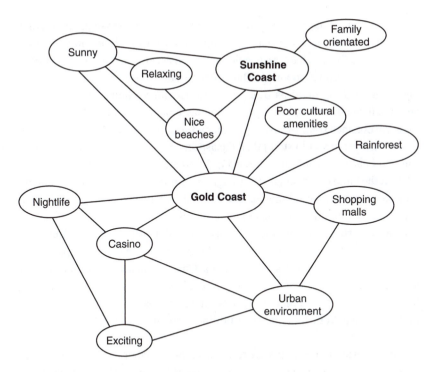

Figure 17.1 Hypothetical association set for vacations in south-eastern Queensland, Australia

association set for holiday destinations in south-eastern Queensland, Australia. For this segment, two destinations are represented as nodes: the Gold Coast (located to the south of Brisbane) and the Sunshine Coast (located to the north of Brisbane). In this example, the Gold Coast enjoys a more complex set of associations than does the Sunshine Coast. The key point of differentiation is that the Gold Coast is seen to be more urbanized and, consequently, more exciting. The destination is also seen to offer rainforest settings, but that aspect is unelaborated in this particular association set. The Sunshine Coast is seen to be more family orientated than the Gold Coast. Nevertheless, in this example, the two destinations are linked in memory, both directly and through the shared features of beach and sun, as well as the shared disadvantage that this market segment perceives the cultural amenities to be poor.

The strategic use of events

Now, let us consider how each destination represented in Figure 17.1 might consider its choice of events in order to enhance or change its image among the market segment. Let us further consider how either destination might use events to enhance its strategic position relative to that market segment. If either destination wishes to use events to strengthen its existing brand image, it will choose events for which the association set is consistent with one or more aspects of the current destination image. Thus, either destination could benefit by choosing events that highlight its beaches and/or its sunny climate; for example, a beach volleyball tournament, a surfing competition or a triathlon. Assuming that the event obtained some exposure to the target segment through media (via stories or advertising), it would strengthen the aspects of brand image associated with sun and beach. It would not, however, differentiate one destination from the other. If the Gold Coast sought to strengthen its point of differentiation from the Sunshine Coast, it would include events on its calendar that accentuate urban excitement or nightlife. For example, motorcycle or auto racing along a city course could showcase the destination as an exciting urban locale. A music festival with night-time concerts could highlight the destination as a place with exciting nightlife. In contrast, the Sunshine Coast could accentuate its competitive advantage over the Gold Coast by adding events with a strong family theme. For example, events requiring siblings or a parent and child to participate jointly would further that aspect of the destination's image.

Either destination might seek to enhance or to elaborate its image further through events that it includes on its calendar. For example, the Gold Coast might seek to enhance the saliency of the rainforest node by elaborating that node through events. Orienteering competitions through the rainforest might be used to feature the distinctive plant life and landscapes of the rainforest. A bird-watching competition or festival might contribute nodes associated with distinctive wildlife of the rainforest. Similarly, either destination might seek to change its image by using events to alter a negative aspect of its brand image. For example, to counter the image of poor cultural amenities, events designed to showcase cultural performances or activities could be added. These might include a performing arts festival or an art contest. Finally, either destination could seek to introduce an entirely new node into its association set. For example, the Sunshine Coast might seek to counter the nightlife elements of the Gold Coast's image by building a node for fine dining. In that instance, an event featuring competitions among leading chefs or a festival of fine wines might prove useful.

The example elaborated above illustrates the requisite logic for linking events to destination branding. Four key conclusions emerge from the example:

- In order to build events into destination branding, destination managers should seek to develop a portfolio of events. Different events may be used to strengthen, enhance or change particular aspects of the destination's brand image in particular market segments.

■ Before destination managers can determine which events will meet their destination's branding needs, they must determine how the destination is perceived in the marketplace. They need to map (through market research) the relevant association set of target market segments (Henderson *et al.*, 1998).

■ To determine what kinds of events to consider, destination managers must decide which aspects of their destination's brand image they wish to strengthen, enhance or change.

■ To select and use an event appropriately, the destination manager needs to identify the association set by which target markets are likely to encode and interpret the event.

It is not being suggested here that events are sufficient in and of themselves to build a destination's brand. In fact, a recent study, which used an experimental design, found some forms of event media to have a negative effect on destination image (Chalip *et al.*, 2003). However, events can represent a component of the destination's product mix that can be used for tactical leverage. The key insight is that destination managers can be strategic in their choice of events and in the ways that they build events into the destination's marketing communications campaign. This latter point is worth exploring further. It is unlikely that all nodes of a destination's association set will be valued by a market segment. Each market segment will value particular aspects more than others. Returning to the example in Figure 17.1, the market segment being illustrated might place a high value on outdoor settings, but might not value shopping, nightlife or gambling. If so, then marketing communications to that market segment should feature visuals or mentions of events that play up the beach or rainforest nodes, and should not feature visuals or mentions of events that play up urban excitement or nightlife. In other words, the marketing communications campaign should focus on those aspects of a destination's brand that are attractive to the target market.

This facet of marketing communications illustrates an important aspect of events. Each event can be used beyond the time in which it takes place. The event's role in destination branding need not be limited to whatever media or visitor experiences are obtained while the event is happening. Visuals about the event and/or mentions of the event can be incorporated into marketing communications (advertisements, brochures, video postcards, media releases) throughout the year to support the destination's desired brand image. By placing event images or mentions alongside images or mentions of other elements of the destination's product mix that highlight comparable aspects of brand image, the overall impact should be enhanced (MacKay and Fesenmaier, 1997; Baloglu and McCleary, 1999; Washburn *et al.*, 2000).

Events and destination branding: exploring the relationship in Australia

The Australian Co-operative Research Centre for Sustainable Tourism (CRC Tourism) is a partnership between the federal government, the tourism industry and university tourism researchers. It was formed in 1997 to facilitate strategic tourism research. The mission of CRC Tourism is 'developing and managing intellectual property to deliver innovation to business, community and government to enhance the environmental, economic and social sustainability of tourism' (www.crctourism.com.au). Research in the CRC Tourism programme is project based, and in 2000 funding was made available to examine the role of events in destination branding. The project sought to answer questions about:

- how, and to what degree, destination marketers incorporate events into their marketing strategies
- how events have an impact on the image or 'brand' of the destination
- whether events could be used more effectively to build a destination's brand image.

It was decided to conduct an initial scoping study to understand better the current situation by consulting widely with tourism and event management professionals throughout Australia. It represented an attempt to gain an industry perspective and to determine the type of research that was considered necessary to assist future decision making. The ultimate objective was to provide information for destination marketing managers and event organizers that would allow them to use events more strategically in creating an image for their destination, and thereby to support their marketing of the destination. It should be noted that the project complemented other CRC Tourism projects that investigated the impact of the 2000 Sydney Olympic Games on awareness of, and interest in Australia.

Destination marketing, and the promotion and marketing of events, is predominantly a function of the second and third tiers of government in Australia. Most state governments have established special entities to bid for and manage events. These include the Queensland Events Corporation and the Australian

Major Events Company (which is an agency of the South Australian State Government, despite the national-sounding name). Local governments also provide financial support for events that they feel may help to induce tourism into their region. Because of the predominant role of state government in the bidding, funding and managing of events, it was decided to use state-based organizations as primary sources of information on current knowledge and practices in the industry. Consultation with senior staff in these organizations, and in organizations involved in general marketing of the tourism destination, was achieved by holding workshops in capital cities throughout Australia.

Efficiency of the process was achieved by gathering information in one sitting. The cost of having a number of stakeholders in one room at one time was that they may not venture opinions or thoughts in an open forum that they would offer in private. A consistent approach to consultation was achieved by running each workshop using a standard protocol for group decision making and problem solving (Chalip, 2001). This protocol consisted of five phases.

1. *Introduction*: a brief explanation of the project was followed by the participants being asked to write down on provided notepads three events/destinations where the event has enhanced the imaging of the destination, three events/destinations where this enhancement has not occurred, and reasons in each case.
2. *Mixed breakout session*: participants were divided into two groups, with a mixture of destination marketers and event organizers in each group. The purpose of breaking into smaller groups was to allow discussion to occur based on the events/destinations on each person's list, and on the reasons that had been written down. Each group nominated one of their number to be a group leader and spokesperson. Each group session was attended by someone from the research team who recorded the discussion points.
3. *Feedback and discussion*: each spokesperson presented to the reassembled group a summary of the discussion of their respective breakout group. This phase was intended to explore commonalities of events and reasons why some events work and some do not in branding the destination.
4. *Specialist breakout session*: destination marketers were formed into one group and event organizers into another. Each appointed a spokesperson. Discussion focused on the nature of professional relationships between the two groups, how each views the activities of the other from 'over the fence', and how the use of events in destination branding could be better organized and managed.
5. *Conclusion*: the group reassembled, with each group's spokesperson summarizing the issues.

Throughout the process, members of the research team took notes and/or recorded the discussion on audiotape for future transcription. After a number of such sessions, many common themes were observed regarding how events help to brand the destination. There was also discussion by more than one group over whether tourism destinations had single or multiple brand images, and whether destinations should strive for a strong single brand or whether they should be flexible and support all markets.

The general findings from the process have been that events can be successful in branding a destination and enhancing its image, particularly those that possess the following characteristics.

Longevity

The passage of time was needed to allow the event to become associated with the destination in the minds of potential visitors. The Melbourne Cup was mentioned favourably in this regard by most workshops, both in Melbourne and elsewhere. Although an almost organic process seemed to be described in the case of some events which seemed to grow into the local environment over time, it needs to be recognized that single events can have a major impact on the image of a destination, especially if leveraged appropriately.

Community support

Events that had strong support in their host communities were more successful as image makers. Host communities tended to celebrate such events, to join in the festivities, and to decorate streets and buildings, thereby raising the awareness of others about the destination, especially the awareness of media. Psychologically, an event may have an impact on self-identity. This will be a positive outcome if people enjoy being associated with an event that has an image that matches the way they wish to be seen. It was also said that long-running, home-grown events were more likely to receive strong community support than events that were foisted on the community by outsiders. However, this was recognized as being the case only for recurring events. Once again, one-off events such as the Sydney Olympics could also generate strong community support if correctly organized.

Professionalism of organization

Where an event had a reputation for professional management, this professionalism was seen to rub off onto the image of the destination. However, if the event was not compatible with the destination, this advantage was lost. Some motorsport events were seen as having this characteristic in that the management and organization were seen as world class, thereby enhancing the image. The same events were often thrust upon their host destinations without regard for the nature of the tourism product of the host. Successful events that grow in size and complexity may require specialist expertise to be brought into the area. This may be accompanied by concerns about a loss of 'local' control in terms of the way that the event is organized and promoted and the way that images about the host environment are projected.

Compatibility with the destination

An event needed to fit with the destination in order to be successful in imaging. Thus, outdoor, water-sport events seemed to fit well with Queensland, which already had an image as a 'sun, sea and sand' destination, whereas theatre, opera and cultural events seemed to fit well with Adelaide, which hosts Australia's longest running arts festival.

Ongoing tourism benefits accrue if an event serves to stimulate visitation throughout the year. For example, this will occur if skiers are attracted to a particular resort because it hosted a ski event. Retail outlets and other industrial sectors in the resort can take advantage of the consistency between the market appeal of the event and the activities supported by the location where it occurs. However, the scope to attract a number of target markets may be compromised by an approach that focuses exclusively on a single type of event.

Media coverage

It was universally agreed that media coverage was essential for an event to play a role in destination branding. To achieve international coverage, the event needed to be large and have unique characteristics. Brisbane's Goodwill Games was given as one example. The need for media management will be discussed in more detail in the context of the Sydney Olympics.

Research

The industry representatives expressed a desire to learn more about information flows and information processing. There was concern about whether information was communicated adequately between the different tourism and event stake-holders and a recognition that little understanding exists about the way in which potential tourists are influenced by the images that they receive about an event.

In the discussion of the interaction between destination marketers and event managers, it was noted that in each city there were good channels of communication between the two. However, there was an expressed need for wider communication with the tourism industry and the community. The latter was seen as important where events were receiving public funding. There was also a suggestion that there needed to be a network of event managers and organizers so that there could be more sharing of skills and knowledge.

In addition to the workshops conducted in the capital cities, one workshop was conducted in a regional centre. Many of the same issues emerged. However, it was suggested that association with a location that has a clearly defined image is a particularly critical factor if events are to be successful in smaller communities. This was illustrated by explaining that the East Coast Blues and Roots Festival has become known as the Byron Blues Festival, and the Northern Rivers Writers Festival is referred to as the Byron Writers Festival. In both cases, these events have come to be seen as intrinsically linked with Byron Bay, which has an iconic status as a tourist destination and as a community with a unique lifestyle.

In conclusion, it should be noted that many workshop participants struggled to separate the success of the event per se from its success as an image builder. This may have been because the concept of using events as destination image builders was new to them. The tendency in Australia to emphasize the economic impact of events (Mules and Faulkner, 1996) may have blinded the tourism industry to more subtle ways of benefiting from events. A more complete review of the study described in this section is provided by Jago et al. (2003).

A case that examines some of the subtle opportunities presented by an event and the considerable work required to exploit these opportunities will now be described. It is, in some ways, exceptional owing the scale of the event and the length of time spent in its planning and preparation. However, the Sydney Olympic Games showed how destination branding can be achieved as an outcome of communications associated with an event. It provides insight of relevance to other locations and lessons that are applicable to other events.

The Sydney Olympics and Brand Australia

At the closing ceremony of the 2000 Olympics, the Sydney Games were declared 'the best ever' by the President of the International Olympic Committee (IOC), Juan Antonio Samaranch, and Australia's Olympic tourism strategy had been described as a role model for future host cities. The IOC's director of marketing suggested that 'Australia is the first Olympic host nation to take full advantage of the Games to vigorously pursue tourism for the benefit of the whole country. It's something we've never seen take place to this level before, and it's a model that we would like to see carried forward to future Olympic Games in Athens and beyond' (Payne, 1998). The managing director of the ATC claimed that the Games changed forever the way the world sees Australia and that Australia's international tourism brand had been advanced by ten years (Morse, 2001a). It is undeniable that television coverage raised the profile of Australia, with an estimated 3.7 billion people watching events, set against backdrops such as the Opera House, Sydney Harbour and Bondi Beach. Although this coverage was a destination marketer's dream, these images conformed to the existing stereotypes held about Australia and may have done little to broaden understanding about the country. This is significant as broadening understanding about Australia in international markets was one of the main objectives of the ATC's Brand Australia campaign.

Brand Australia was launched by the ATC in 1995, two years after Sydney had been awarded the right to host the 2000 Games. It was the culmination of two years of research that had identified the need to broaden Australia's image

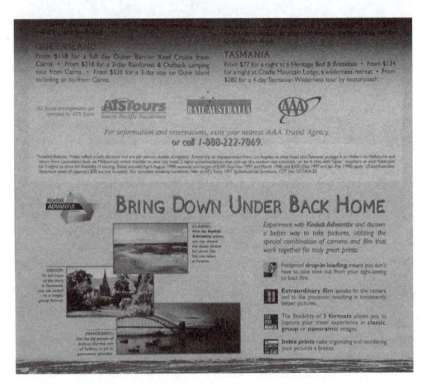

Figure 17.2 'Bring down under back home'

and promote the holiday experience rather than specific cities and regions. It was also to be used to oversee strategies attempting to capitalize on the 2000 Olympics (ATC, 1996). A logo, featuring a kangaroo, as the country's most recognizable symbol, set against a red sun and blue waves, was used as a unifying link to help to cement the brand image. The relationship between the brand and the Olympics was acknowledged explicitly at the launch of a three-year brand advertising campaign in 1998: 'With this campaign we have the opportunity to use the extraordinary interest in Australia surrounding the 2000 Olympic Games to build awareness and add depth and dimension to the country's image' (Morse, 1998).

The ATC's US$6.7 million, four-year Olympic strategy focused on promoting Australia through a media relations programme and the development of alliances with Olympic organizations and partners such as broadcast rights holders and sponsors (Figures 17.2 and 17.3). Underpinning the strategy was a desire to add new dimensions by promoting more than the typical images and

Figure 17.3 'Taste of Australia': Visa advertising

themes. This was achieved by bringing together Brand Australia, the Olympic brand and the brands of Olympic partners. This process was predicated on the establishment of an effective relationship between the ATC and the Sydney Organising Committee for the Olympic Games. It was this latter committee and the IOC that referred sponsors, broadcast rights holders, National Olympic Committees and the media to the ATC, providing opportunities for the ATC to give advice about marketing and brand imagery. The ATC sought to convince members of The Olympic Program (sponsors) of the benefits of linking their Olympic promotions with Brand Australia. The resulting projects included collaborations on competitions, hospitality packages and advertising campaigns. These activities generated US$170 million in additional exposure for Australia (ATC, 2001b).

The most significant relationship for the ATC with a single sponsor was with Visa. This resulted in television commercials that were screened around the world, supplements in magazines, travel offers distributed to cardholders worldwide and billboard advertising featuring Australian images that dominated the waterfront area of Shanghai for a year. All carried the slogan 'Australia prefers Visa'. This designation was the product of an alliance signed in 1997 between Visa and tourism organizations in Australia, including the ATC. American Express voiced concern that it implied government endorsement (Washington, 1997b), but from Visa's perspective it was a perfect fit. Sydney's 'aspirational value' as a destination had been the central and integrative theme of the long-term marketing strategy conducted by Visa in conjunction with its member banks (Smythe, 1999).

The managing director of the ATC countered arguments against the exclusive nature of the arrangement with Visa by claiming that funds from Olympic sponsors enhanced the ATC's ability to promote Australia overseas (McMahon, 1998). It was supported in the press as 'an example of the innovative "partnering" sponsors are using to enhance the value of their Olympic sponsorship. The tourism industry appears to be a major winner from the "partnering" trend' (Washington, 1997a). From Visa's perspective the partnership was also regarded as a success. It helped to produce an increase of 23 per cent in card usage by overseas visitors to Australia in 1999 and, during the Games, transaction levels at official Olympic sites surpassed those recorded by Visa at the Atlanta Games. At Olympic Park, Aus$20 million was spent on Visa cards at point-of-sale transactions and more than Aus$5 million was withdrawn from Visa ATMs.

By working with the world's broadcasters, the ATC had aimed to make the Olympics a two-week documentary on all aspects of Australian life. Heightened interest in Australia in the lead-up to the Games was also exploited wherever possible. For instance, the UK's leading travel show, *The Holiday Programme*, focused its tenth anniversary programme on Australia, in January 1999. It was watched by 8.2 million viewers and featured Sydney, as the Olympic city, but also showed other destinations around the country. In 1996, when the television rights were under negotiation, NBC agreed to provide US$6 million in free commercial airtime to promote Australia as host country of the Olympics. The ATC assisted the American broadcaster in the production of a highly effective advertisement that linked the Olympic brand with Brand Australia. This was an attempt by NBC to build interest in the forthcoming Games in the US market and it was achieved by linking colours of the Australian landscape with the colours of the Olympic rings. It was considered by the ATC to be critical that the images projected by NBC and the other broadcasters were consistent with the values of the brand, and this required presenting Australia as a vibrant, friendly, colourful, free-spirited place that offers a sophisticated lifestyle. The tactics used to ensure that this was achieved took many forms, but included the preparation of a detailed Film Locations Guide and the provision of story ideas and profiles of colourful characters and places to direct interest to a variety of regions throughout Australia.

In the five years leading up to the Games, the ATC hosted around 5000 media participants, with many invited as part of the Visiting Journalist Program. This programme generated US$2.1 billion in coverage in the period 1997–2000 in magazines, newspapers, radio and television coverage around the world (ATC, 2001b). It is claimed that trends in media coverage have increasingly shown Australia's contemporary urban culture, food and wine, arts and cultural themes, as well as a strong interest in the lifestyle of Australian people (ATC, 2001a). Media initiatives by the ATC, during the Games, included assisting in the design of the Main Press Centre at Olympic Park by incorporating images reflective of Brand Australia. The ATC was also one of five public-sector agencies (with the Department of Foreign Affairs and Trade, Tourism New South Wales, the Sydney Harbour Foreshore Authority, and the New South Wales Department of State and Regional Development) that developed a media centre in the city for non-accredited media. It was considered to be particularly important to provide facilities and information to support the activities of journalists who would not have access to Olympic venues and events. It was thought that their focus would inevitably be more on the city, its people and broader issues about the impact of the Games in Australia.

It would seem that the relationship between a national brand and a major event, such as the Olympic Games, is influenced by a heightened level of interest in the host country. This can be translated into additional opportunities for the tourism industry to communicate with a receptive audience using a variety of media. However, a more sophisticated approach is one that takes advantage of opportunities consciously to integrate mutually compatible elements of a number of brands, including the destination brand. This requires the selection of suitable partners, the identification of markets that will respond favourably to the mix of brand values, and a desire among the different parties to think creatively in an environment that is subject to many rules and a very focused temporal horizon. Brown (2000) has advocated the need for research to understand better the outcomes of complementary brand development with sponsors of major events.

The final, critical issue concerns the impact of the visitor experience. Many people who attend an event will return to their homes to give first-hand accounts of their experience. The destination brand is inevitably implicated by the success of the event and the level of satisfaction experienced by people who, in the case of the Olympics, attended the event as spectators, corporate guests, athletes, officials and the media. All will hold values associated with the destination brand that will affect their desire to return as tourists and the type of word-of-mouth promotion that becomes a product of the stories they tell about their Games experiences.

Brand Australia in the post-Olympic era

In the period immediately following the Sydney Olympics, there was every indication that Australia was set to benefit from the exposure that had been created by the Games. Records were set for the number of international visitor arrivals in the month of December and forward bookings were strong, with the level of demand attributed, by overseas operators, to the impact of the Games (Brown, 2001). A view expressed by the managing director of the ATC, that '2001 is the year when the Australian tourism industry will begin to cash in on the world wide publicity generated by the Games' (Morse, 2001b), seemed to be vindicated when international visitor arrivals rose by a further 7.6 per cent in the first quarter of 2001. However, by mid-year, changing global economic conditions and lower consumer confidence made growth forecasts seem unrealistic, causing the new managing director of the ATC to caution that 'the immediate impact of the Games has now subsided' (Boundy, 2001). Any residual Games effect was destroyed by the collapse of Ansett airlines in Australia and the terrorist attacks in the USA, which both occurred in September 2001. Subsequent crises, including the outbreak of severe acute respiratory syndrome (SARS) and the war in Iraq, meant that, by early 2003, inbound arrivals to

Australia had declined for two consecutive years. This was the first time that this had happened for over twenty years.

The prospects for tourism were dramatically different in 2003 than they had been in 2000, yet some legacies of the Olympic era remain. The Rugby World Cup offered an opportunity to repeat much of the ATC's Olympic strategy with, once again, considerable emphasis placed on attempts to work with the world's media. Visa signed to be a major sponsor of the World Cup and chose to revive the successful relationship with tourism organizations, from which it had benefited as an Olympic sponsor. Jacobs Creek added to an impressive list of sport event sponsorships by becoming a sponsor of the Rugby World Cup. Significantly, the wine maker was also the major sponsor of the World Food Media Awards that were held in conjunction with Tasting Australia. As an event that is held every two years in South Australia, Tasting Australia would seem to be an excellent example of the contemporary relationship between events and destination branding in Australia. The format of the event and the market it attracts are consistent with the ATC's current emphasis on the development of market segments, with attention focused on areas of special opportunity such as food and wine. It also attracts considerable interest among specialist, international media, while retaining strong patronage from local residents. Thus, even during an extended period of crisis for the tourism industry, there has been further evidence that events, the media, sponsors and the host community remain important elements of destination branding strategies.

Conclusion

Despite the significant role that events have come to play in tourism, there has been little research that addresses the use of events in destination branding. Nevertheless, as the Olympic example shows, even a one-off event can have a significant impact on a destination's brand. Further, workshops with destination marketers and event organizers have demonstrated that both groups seek a deeper understanding of the ways that events can assist the development of a destination's brand. The conceptual frameworks from which to start construction of relevant models and methods have been formulated in the work on co-operative branding.

The experience, research and theory described in this chapter suggest the value of further work on the role that events have in strengthening, elaborating or changing a destination's brand. More work is needed that examines the ways in which to use event visuals and mentions most effectively in a destination's marketing communications, before, during, and after the event. Further work is needed to develop appropriate measures of event impacts on brand image. The use of added partners in co-operative branding activities, particularly event sponsors, needs to be explored. The best means to leverage one-off versus recurring events need to be identified. The relevant considerations when building an event portfolio for a destination need to be determined. Events have a distinctive capacity to excite residents and to appeal to target markets. They become the basis for images, stories and emotions. The challenge to destination marketers is to find the best ways to use event images, stories and emotions to capture the consumer's attention and build the destination's brand.

References

Anderson, J. R. (1983) *The Architecture of Cognition*. Cambridge, MA: Harvard University Press.

Arcodia, C. and Robb, A. (2000) A taxonomy of event management terms. In Allen, J., Harris, R., Jago, L. and Veal, A. (eds) *Events Beyond 2000: Setting the Agenda*. Proceedings of Conference on Event Evaluation, Research and Education, UTS, Sydney, pp. 154–160.

ATC (1996) *Annual Report 1995/96*. Australian Tourist Commission.

ATC (2001a) *Australia's Olympics. Special Post Games Tourism Report*. Australian Tourist Commission.

ATC (2001b) *Olympic Games Strategy. Overview* (March). Australian Tourist Commission.

Backman, K., Backman, S., Uysal, M. and Mohr Sunshine, K. (1995) Event tourism: an examination of motivations and activities. *Festival Management and Event Tourism* 3(1): 15–24.

Baloglu, S. and McCleary, K. W. (1999) A model of destination image formation. *Annals of Tourism Research* 26: 868–897.

Boundy, K. (2001) International visitors up by 5 per cent in the first six months. Australian Tourist Commission. Press Release (19 July).

Boyle, M. (1997) Civic boosterism in the politics of local economic development – 'institutional positions' and 'strategic orientations' in the consumption of hallmark events. *Environment and Planning A* 29: 1975–1997.

Bramwell, B. (1997) Strategic planning before and after a mega-event. *Tourism Management* 18: 167–176.

Brown, G. (2000) Emerging issues in Olympic sponsorship. *Sport Management Review* 3(1): 71–92.

Brown, G. (2001) An invitation to the world. *Olympic Review* 37: 15–20.

Burgan, B. and Mules, T. (2000) Event analysis – understanding the divide between cost benefit and economic impact assessment. In Allen, J., Harris, R.,

Jago, L. and Veal, A. (eds) *Events Beyond 2000: Setting the Agenda.* Proceedings of Conference on Event Evaluation, Research and Education, UTS, Sydney, pp. 46–51.

Burns, J., Hatch, J. and Mules, T. (eds) (1986) *The Adelaide Grand Prix: The Impact of a Special Event.* Adelaide: Centre for South Australian Economic Studies.

Chacko, H. and Schaffer, J. (1993) The evolution of a festival: Creole Christmas in New Orleans. *Tourism Management* 14: 475–482.

Chalip, L. (2001) Group decision making and problem solving. In Parkhouse, B. L. (ed.) *The Management of Sport: Its Foundation and Application*, 3rd edn. Boston, MA: McGraw-Hill, pp. 93–110

Chalip, L., Green, B. C. and Hill, B. (2003) Effects of sport event media on destination image and intention to visit. *Journal of Sport Management* 17: 214–234.

Collins, A. M. and Loftus, E. F. (1975) Theory of semantic processing. *Psychological Review* 82: 407–428.

Commonwealth Department of Tourism (1992) *Tourism, Australia's Passport to Growth: A National Tourism Strategy.* Canberra: Australian Government Publishing Service.

Crompton, J. and McKay, S. (1997) Motives of visitors attending festival events. *Annals of Tourism Research* 24: 425–439.

Evans, G. (1995) The role of the festival in urban regeneration: planning for the British Millennium Festival. Paper presented at International Festivals Association Second European Research Symposium, Edinburgh (17 August).

Faulkner, B. (1993) *Evaluating the Tourism Impact of Hallmark Events.* Occasional Paper No. 16. Canberra: Bureau of Tourism Research.

Fredline, E., Mules, T., Raybould, M. and Tomljenovic, R. (1999) Sweet little rock and roller: the economic impact of the 1998 Wintersun Festival. *Proceedings of the Ninth Australian Tourism and Hospitality Research Conference.* Canberra: Bureau of Tourism Research.

Getz, D. (1989) Special events: defining the product. *Tourism Management* 10(2): 125–137.

Getz, D. (1991) *Festivals, Special Events and Tourism.* New York: Van Nostrand Reinhold.

Getz, D. (1994a) Event tourism: evaluating the impacts. In Ritchie, J. and Goeldner, C. (eds) *Travel, Tourism and Hospitality Research.* New York: Wiley, pp. 437–450.

Getz, D. (1994b) Event tourism and the authenticity dilemma. In Theobald, W. (ed.) *Global Tourism; The Next Decade.* Oxford: Butterworth-Heinemann, pp. 313–329.

Getz, D. (1994c) In pursuit of the quality tourist. Paper presented at Tourism Down-under Conference, Massey University, Palmerston North (December).

Getz, D. (1997) *Event Management and Event Tourism*. New York: Cognizant Communications Corporation.

Getz, D. (2000b) Developing a research agenda for the event management field. In Allen, J., Harris, R., Jago, L. and Veal, A. (eds) *Events Beyond 2000: Setting the Agenda*. Proceedings of Conference on Event Evaluation, Research and Education, UTS, Sydney, pp. 10–21.

Getz, D. and Wicks, B. (1993) Editorial. *Festival Management and Event Tourism* 1(1): 1–3.

Getz, D. and Wicks, B. (1994) Professionalism and certification for festival and event practitioners: trends and issues, *Festival Management and Event Tourism* 2(2): 103–109.

Goeldner, C. and Long, P. (1987) The role and impact of mega-events and attractions on tourism development in North America. *Proceedings of the 37th Congress of AIEST*, Calgary, 28: 119–131.

Gwinner, K. P. and Eaton, J. (1999) Building brand image through event sponsorship: the role of image transfer. *Journal of Advertising* 28(4): 47–57.

Halford, G. S., Bain, J. D., Maybery, M. T. and Andrews, G. (1998) Induction of relational schemas: common processes in reasoning and complex learning. *Cognitive Psychology* 35: 201–245.

Hall, C. (1987) The effects of hallmark events on cities. *Journal of Travel Research* 26(2): 44–45.

Hall, C. (1990) The impacts of hallmark tourist events. Workshop Paper at *Metropolis 90*, 3rd International Congress of the World Association of the Major Metropolises, Recreation and Tourism Development Branch of the City of Melbourne, Melbourne.

Hall, C. (1992) *Hallmark Tourist Events: Impacts, Management and Planning*. London: Belhaven Press.

Hall, C. (1996) Hallmark events and urban reimaging strategies. In Harrison, L. and Husbands, W. (eds) *Practising Responsible Tourism; International Case Studies in Tourism Planning, Policy and Development*. Toronto: Wiley, pp. 366–379.

Henderson, G. R., Iacobucci, D. and Calder, B. J. (1998) Brand diagnostics: mapping branding effects using consumer associative networks. *European Journal of Operational Research* 111: 306–327.

Hodges, J. and Hall, C. (1996) The housing and social impacts of mega-events: lessons for the Sydney 2000 Olympics. In Kearsley, G. (ed.) *Tourism Down Under II; Towards a More Sustainable Tourism*. Dunedin: Centre for Tourism, University of Otago, pp. 152–166.

Hughes, H. (1993a) Olympic tourism and urban regeneration. *Festival Management and Event Tourism* 1(4): 157–162.

Hughes, H. (1993b) The role of hallmark event tourism in urban regeneration. Paper presented at The First International Conference on Investments and Financing in the Tourism Industry, Jerusalem.

Jago, L. and Shaw, R. (1994) Categorisation of special events: a market perspective. In Conference Proceedings, *Tourism Down Under: Perceptions, Problems and Proposals*. Palmerston North: Massey University, pp. 682–708.

Jago, L. and Shaw, R. (1998) Special events: a conceptual and differential framework. *Festival Management and Event Tourism* 5(1/2): 21–32.

Jago, L., Chalip, L., Brown, G., Mules, T. and Ali, S. (2003) Building events into destination branding: insights from experts. *Event Management* 8(1): 3–14.

Janiskee, R. (1994) Some macroscale growth trends in America's community festival industry. *Festival Management and Event Tourism* 2(1): 10–14.

Janiskee, R. (1996) Historic houses and special events. *Annals of Tourism Research* 23: 398–414.

Kang, Y. and Perdue, R. (1994) Long-term impact of a mega-event on international tourism to the host country: a conceptual model and the case of the 1988 Seoul Olympics. In Uysal, M. (ed.) *Global Tourist Behaviour*. New York: International Business Press, pp. 205–225.

Kaspar, C. (1987) The role and impact of mega-events and attractions on national and regional tourism development. Introduction into the General Topic of the 37th AIEST Congress. *Proceedings of the 37th Congress of AIEST*, Calgary, 28: 11–12.

Keller, K. L. (1993) Conceptualizing, measuring, and managing customer-based brand equity. *Journal of Marketing* 57: 1–22.

Law, C. (1993) *Urban Tourism; Attracting Visitors to Large Cities*. London: Mansell.

Light, D. (1996) Characteristics of the audience for 'events' at a heritage site. *Tourism Management* 17(3): 183–190.

Lynch, R. and Veal, A. (1996) *Australian Leisure*. South Melbourne: Addison Wesley Longman Australia.

McCann, C. and Thompson, G. (1992) An economic analysis of the first Western Australian State Masters Games. *Journal of Tourism Studies* 3(1): 28–34.

McDaniel, S. R. (1999) An investigation of match-up effects in event sponsorship advertising: the implications of consumer advertising schemas. *Psychology and Marketing* 16: 163–184.

MacKay, K. J. and Fesenmaier, D. R. (1997) Pictorial element of destination image formation. *Annals of Tourism Research* 24: 537–565.

McMahon, I. (1998) AmEx, QH clash with ATC over marketing. *Travel Week* (28 October): 3.

Mihalik, B. (1994) Mega-event legacies of the 1996 Atlanta Olympics. In Murphy, P. (ed.) *Quality Management in Urban Tourism: Balancing Business and Environment*. Proceedings, University of Victoria, Victoria, Canada, pp. 151–161.

Morse, J. (1998) $150 million campaign set to boost tourism arrivals and export earnings. *Brand Australia. A New Image for a New Millennium*. Australian Tourist Commission.

Morse, J. (2001a) The Olympic Games and Australian Tourism. Presentation made at the Sport Tourism Conference, Barcelona, Spain (23 February).

Morse, J. (2001b) Tourism expectations high for 2001. Australian Tourist Commission. Press Release (6 February).

Mules, T. and Faulkner, B. (1996) An economic perspective on special events. *Tourism Economics* 2(2): 107–117.

Murphy, P. and Carmichael, B. (1991) Assessing the tourism benefits of an open access sports tournament: the 1989 B.C. Winter Games. *Journal of Travel Research* 29(3): 32–36.

National Institute of Economic and Industry Research (2000) *The 2000 Qantas Australian Grand Prix*. Melbourne: Victorian Department of State and Regional Development.

Payne, M. (1998) Presenatation at the Regent Hotel, Sydney (14 October).

Pyo, S., Cook, R. and Howell, R. (1988) Summer Olympic tourism market; learning from the past. *Tourism Management* 9(2): 137–144.

Rao, A. R. and Ruekert, R. W. (1994) Brand alliances as signals of product quality. *Sloan Management Review* 36(1): 87–97.

Ritchie, J. (1984) Assessing the impact of hallmark events: conceptual and research issues. *Journal of Travel Research* 23(1): 2–11.

Ritchie, B. (1996) How special are special events? An impact study of the National Mutual New Zealand Masters Games on Dunedin's economy. In Kearsley, G. (ed.) *Tourism Down Under II; Towards a More Sustainable Tourism*. Dunedin: Centre for Tourism, University of Otago, pp. 73–79.

Ritchie, J. and Beliveau, D. (1974) Hallmark events: an evaluation of a strategic response to seasonality in the travel market. *Journal of Travel Research* 13(2): 14–20.

Ritchie, J. and Smith, B. (1991) The impact of a mega-event on host region awareness: a longitudinal study. *Journal of Travel Research* 30(1): 3–10.

Ritchie, J. and Yangzhou, J. (1987) The role and impact of mega-events and attractions on national and regional tourism: a conceptual and methodological overview. *Proceedings of the 37th Congress of AIEST*, Calgary, 28: 17–58.

Robinson, A. and Noel, J. (1991) Research needs for festivals: a management perspective. *Journal of Applied Recreation Research* 16(1): 78–88.

Roche, M. (1994) Mega-events and urban policy. *Annals of Tourism Research* 21(1): 1–19.

Simonin, B. L. and Ruth, J. A. (1998) Is a company known by the company it keeps? Assessing the spillover effects of brand alliances on brand attitudes. *Journal of Marketing Research* 35: 30–42.

Smythe, S. (1999) Personal communication with the vice president, Sponsorship and Event Marketing, Visa.

Speed, R. and Thompson, P. (2000) Determinants of sports sponsorship response. *Journal of the Academy of Marketing Science* 28: 226–238.

Spethmann, B. and Benezra, K. (1994) Co-brand or be damned. *Brandweek* 35(45): 20–25.

Spilling, O. (1996) Mega-event as a strategy for regional development: the case of the 1994 Lillehammer Olympic Games. *Proceedings of Institute of Tourism and Service Economics*. International Conference, International Centre for Research and Education in Tourism, Innsbruck, pp. 128–154.

Till, B. D. and Shimp, T. A. (1998) Endorsers in advertising: the case of negative celebrity information. *Journal of Advertising* 27(1): 67–82.

Tourism South Australia (1990) *Planning of Festivals and Special Events*. Tourism South Australia, Adelaide.

Tourism Victoria (1993) *Strategic Business Plan 1997–2001; Building Partnerships*. Melbourne: Tourism Victoria.

Tourism Victoria (1997) *Strategic Business Plan 1997–2001; Building Partnerships*. Melbourne: Tourism Victoria.

Travis, A. and Croize, J. (1987) The role and impact of mega-events and attractions on tourism development in Europe: a micro perspective. *Proceedings of the 37th Congress of AIEST*, Calgary, 28: 59–78.

Uysal, M. and Gitelson, R. (1994) Assessment of economic impacts: festivals and special events. *Festival Management and Event Tourism* 2(1): 3–9.

van den Berg, L., Braun, E. and Otgaar, A. H. J. (2000) *Sports and City Marketing in European Cities*. Rotterdam: euricur.

Washburn, J. H., Till, B. D. and Priluck, R. (2000) Co-branding: brand equity and trial effects. *Journal of Consumer Marketing* 17: 591–604.

Washington, S. (1997a) Visa opens fire in card games. *Australian Financial Review* (17 November): 5.

Washington, S. (1997b) Visa deal sparks major card row. *Australian Financial Review* (18 November): 4.

Wells, J. (1994) Floriade: a study in re-imaging Australia's capital through event tourism. Working Paper, Tourism Down-Under Conference, Massey University, Palmerston North.

Whitson, D. and Macintosh, D. (1996) The global circus: international sport, tourism, and the marketing of cities. *Journal of Sport and Social Issues* 20: 278–297.

Wicks, B. and Fesenmaier, D. (1995) Market potential for special events: a Midwestern case study. *Festival Management and Event Tourism* 3(1): 25–31.

Williams, P., Hainsworth, D. and Dossa, K. (1995) Community development and special event tourism: the men's World Cup of skiing at Whistler, British Columbia. *Journal of Tourism Studies* 6(2): 11–20.

Witt, S. (1988) Mega-events and mega-attractions. *Tourism Management* 9(1): 76–77.

Index